Asian Iconography Series - I

Five Hundred Buddhist Deities

Musashi Tachikawa
Masahide Mori
Shinobu yamaguchi

Adroit Publishers
Delhi - 110 053

Asian Iconography Series - I

Five Hundred Buddhist Deities

ISBN No.81 - 87392- 11 - 0

Originally published as five Hundred Buddhist Deities, Senri Ethnological Reports 2, National Museum of Ethnology, Osaka, Japan, 1995.

Published by
ADROIT PUBLISHERS
C-8/2, Yamuna Vihar,
Delhi-110053

Printed by
P.K.Jain & Co. New Delhi
Tel: 011-320 1593, 320 1594

Preface

From the fall of 1979 up to the fall of 1980 I had the chance to conduct a research at the Indian Institute, the University of Hamburg, where I found a set of wooden prints of line-drawings of Tibetan Buddhist deities. The set consists about one hundred seventy folios, each of which is divided into three squares. In each square (6.2 - 6.4 x 6.2 - 6.4 cm in size) one or a few Buddhist deities are depicted with soft and fine lines. At first glance, I was fascinated with the fine techniques of wood engraving. With the permission of the Indian Institute, the University of Hamburg, I made a xylographic copy of the iconographical set of Tibetan Buddhist deities.

A short time later I learned that the set of the line-drawings was the so-called *Five Hundred Gods of Narthang*. In 1964 Lokesh Chandra published handwritten pictures of the *Five Hundred Gods of Narthang* (*A New Tibeto-Mongol Pantheon*, Part 9), a xylographic copy of which Raghu Vira was given by a Tibetan priest in Ulanbator.

The set preserved at Hamburg, however, lacks eight percent of the complete set. After I came back to Japan, I fortunately obtained the missing folios of the *Five Hundred Gods of Narthang* through the kindness of the Library of Tibetan Works and Archives, Dharmshala.

Recently interest in Buddhist iconography has been increasing remarkably. The wooden prints of the *Five Hundred Gods of Narthang* furnish high quality of materials for the study of Buddhist iconography. This volume is a result of a research project of the National Museum of Ethnology entitled "Studies of religious iconography in South Asia" (headed by M. Tachikawa, 1992-1994).

Here I would like to express my deepest gratitude for giving us the permission to reprint the copy of the *Five Hundred Gods of Narthang* to the Indian Institute, the University of Hamburg, and the Library of Tibetan Works and Archives, Dharmshala. I also would like to thank Mr. rGya mtsho rtse rin, Director, the Library of Tibetan Works and Archives, Dharmshala for sending the films of the *Five Hundred Gods of Narthang*. Last but not least, I would like to thank Mr. Taiji Oya, President, Mandala World Cooperation, who took great pain to help me obtain the films from Dharmshala.

Musashi Tachikawa

Contents

Introduction

In the fifteenth regnal year of the Manchu emperor Chia ch'ing, i.e., in 1810, the Imperial Treasurer bLo bzang dkon mchog, Chin wang Phung tshog rdo rje together with his son and ministers, and No yon sprul sku Ratnadhvaja requested the Fourth Pan chen bLa ma bsTan pa'i nyi ma phyogs las rnam rgyal to initiate them into the great Mandala of the First Buddha *(dang po'i sangs rgyas dkyil 'khor chen po)* by giving the four kinds of tantric consecration rites: the preliminary *abhiṣeka ('jug pa'i dbang)*, the higher and still higher *abhiṣekas (gong ma gong chen gyi dbang),* and the *mahāvajrācārya abhiṣeka (rdo rje slob dpon chen po'i dbang).* At their request, the Fourth Pan chen bLa ma gave the four kinds of consecration rites to hundreds of laymen and monks.[1]

On this occasion the Pan chen bLa ma used as the basic text for those rites the *Yi dam rgya mtsho'i sgrub thabs rin chen 'byung gnas kyi lhan thabs rin 'byung don gsal (Rin lhan),*[2] which he compiled on the basis of Tāranātha's *Yi dam rgya mtsho'i sgrub thabs rin chen 'byung gnas.*[3] He was further requested to publish the wooden prints of the images of the deities described in his text. Chos rje mkhas grub and dGe slong Tshe ring worked as the supervisors of the project, and bLo bzang sbyin pa, bLo bzang bkra shis, Ngag dbang shes rab, bLo bzang chos dar and bLo bzang tshe dpag drew the original line-drawings of the hundreds of deities appearing in the text. The collection of the printed line-drawings of those deities accompanied with their *mantras* is named the *Rin 'byung rnar thang brgya rtsa rdor 'phreng bcas nas gsungs pa'i bris sku mthong ba don ldan* (176 folios), which is usually called the *Five Hundred Gods of Narthang.* It is divided into three parts, which are respectively given the following marginal subtitles:

(1) Rin 'byung (ff.1-143),
(2) rNar thang (ff. 1-13), and
(3) rDor 'phreng (ff. 1-20).

The first part, i.e., Rin 'byung, is based upon the *Rin lhan*, the second, rNar thang, is an appendix to the *Rin lhan,* and the third, rDor 'phreng, is based upon Abhayākaragupta's *Vajrāvalī* and lCang skya Nga dbang blo bzang chos ldan's *rDzogs 'phreng dang rdor 'phreng gnyis kyi cho ga phyags len gyi rim pa lag tu blangs bde bar dgod pa.* Each folio contains three squares, and in each square a deity is depicted. The reverse side of each square has the *mantra* of the deity. The following two pages show the folio 33 of the Rin 'byung of the original size (cf. pp. 131-133).

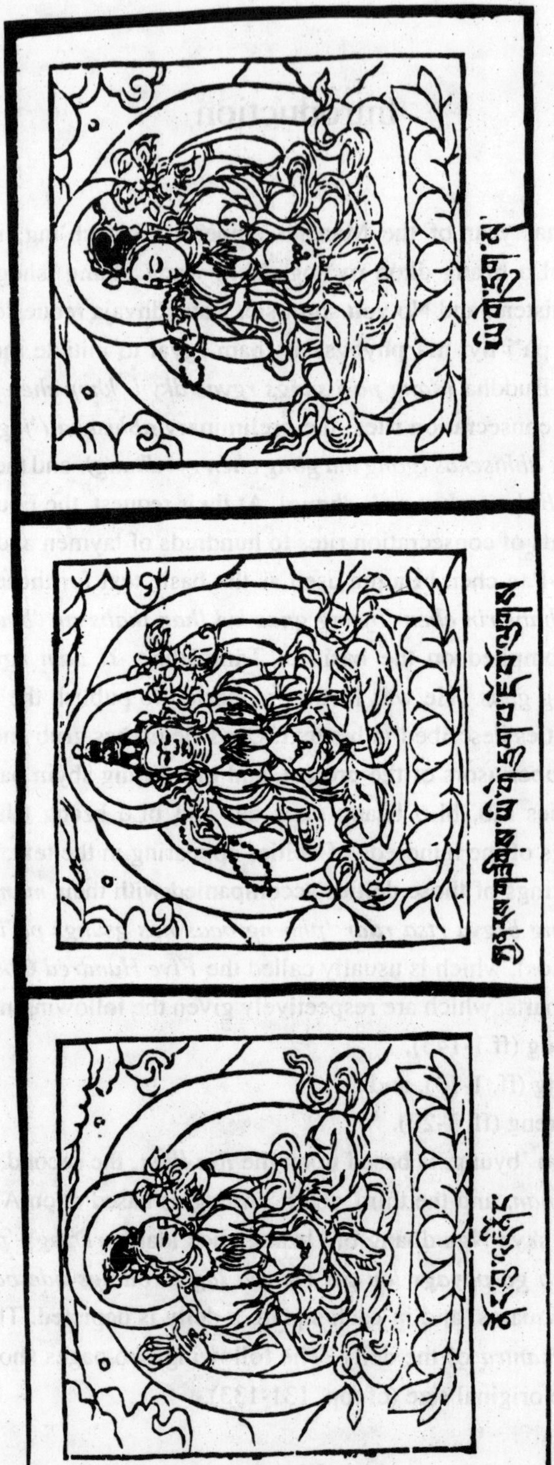

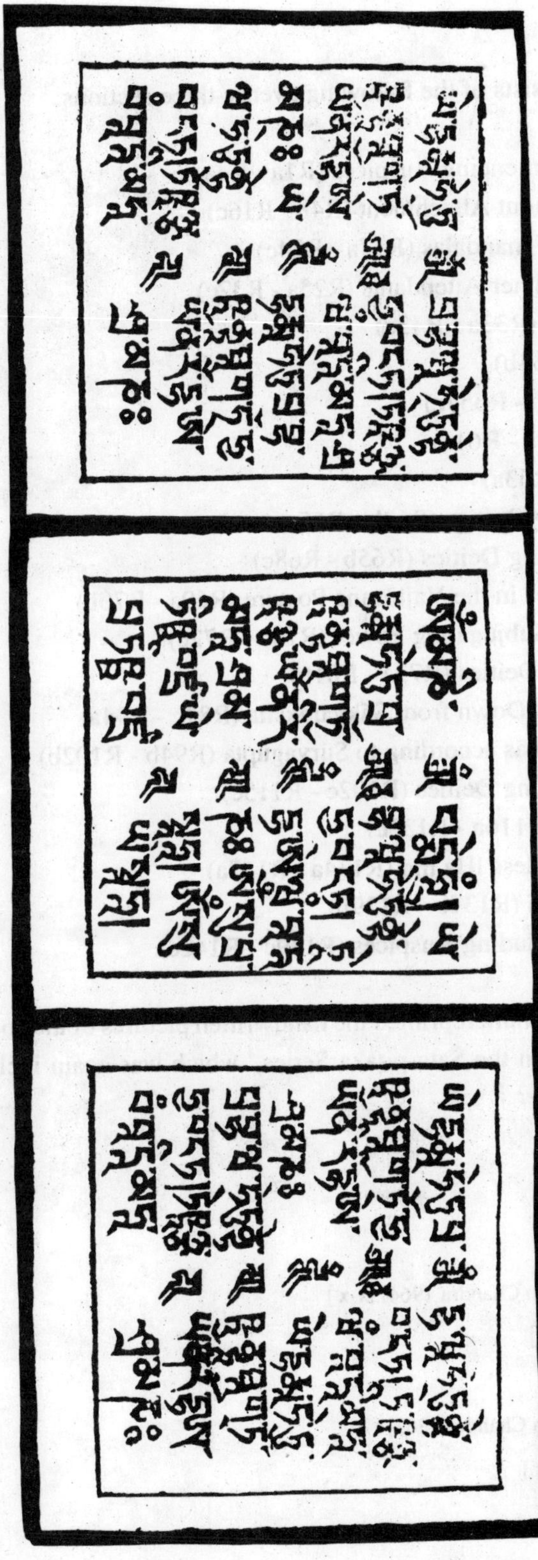

The *Rin lhan* consists of the following twenty-three sections:

1. Deities of Commencing Auspices (R1a - R4a)
2. Tathāgatas without Attachment (R4b - R16c)
3. Main Deities of maṇḍalas (R17a - R24c)
4. Vajravārāhī and her Attendants (R25a - R32c)
5. Avalokiteśvara (R33a - R43c)
6. Tārā (R44a - R54b)
7. Vajrapāṇi (R54c - R557c)
8. Hayagrīva (R58a - R61a)
9. Acala (R61b - R63a)
10. Life-bestowing Deities (R63b - R65a)
11. Prajñā-bestowing Deities (R65b - R68c)
12. Tutelary Deities in the Vajrāsana Posture (R69a - R70b)
13. Goddesses of Subjugating Power (R70c - R72c)
14. Miscellaneous Deities (R73a - R81b)
15. Deities Handed Down from Śākyaraksita (R81c - R94a)
16. Twenty-one Tārās according to Sūryagupta (R94b - R102b)
17. Wealth-bestowing Deities (R102c - R115c)
18-20. Mahākāla (R116a - R133c)
21. Terrifying Goddess lHa mo (R134a - R137a)
22. Yama and Yamī (R137b - R139b)
23. Deities of Concluding Auspices (R139c - R142c)

In 1964 Lokesh Chandra reprinted the handwritten pictures of the so-called *Five Hundred Gods of Narthang* in the Śata-piṭaka Series,[4] which was again included in his *Buddhist Iconography of Tibet*.[5]

Notes

[1] [Raghu Vira & Lokesh Chandra 1964: ix-x]

[2] [Lokesh Candra 1974]

[3] [Tāranātha 1976]

[4] [Raghu Vira & Lokesh Chandra 1963]

[5] [Lokesh Chandra 1986]

List of the Deities

The following is the list of the deities appearing in the Rin 'byung, the sNar thang, and the rDor 'phreng. The asterisk following a number indicates that the line-drawing of the deity bearing the number was missing from the collection of the Indian Institute, the University of Hamburg, and has been complemented by the collection of the Library of Tibetan Works and Archives, Dharmshala. In preparing this reprint edition, we have principally adopted the line-drawings of the Hamburg edition, which is usually clearer than the Dharmshala edition.

R: Rin 'byung
N: rNar thang
D: rDor 'phreng
L: the deity-number used in [Lokesh Chandra 1986: 205-378]

No.	L	Tib.	Skt. etc.
		Rin 'byung	
1*(R0a)	511	rGyal tshab rje	
2*(R0b)	512	rJe rin po che	
3*(R0c)	513	mKhas grub rje	
4(R1a)	514	Jo lugs sgrol dkar	Sita Tārā of Atiśa school
5(R1b)	515	sGrol dkar ba ri'i lugs	Sita Tārā of Ba ri school
6(R1c)	516	gNyan lugs sgrol dkar	Sita Tārā of gNyan school
7(R2a)	517	Nags rin lugs kyi sgrol dkar	Sita Tārā of Nags rin school
8(R2b)	518	dByangs can ma dkar mo	Sita Sarasvatī
9(R2c)	519	gNyan sgrol yan lag drug pa	Ṣadaṅgatārā of gNyan
10(R3a)	520	Ku ru ku lle	Kurukullā
11(R3b)	521	'Dod rgyal dmar po	Rakta Kāmarāja
12(R3c)	522	Tshogs bdag dmar chen	Mahāraktagaṇapati
13(R4a)	523	rDo rje sems dpa' ser po	Pīta Vajrasattva
14(R4b)	524	Thub pa rdo rje gdan pa gtso 'khor gsum	Vajrāsanamuni with two disciples
15(R4c)	525	Thub pa dam tshig gsum bkod	Trisamayavyūhamuni with four deities
16(R5a)	526	Thub dbang	Munīndra
17(R5b)	527	Yan lag 'byung	Aṅgaja
18(R5c)	528	Ma pham pa	Ajita

No.	L	Tib.	Skt. etc.
19(R6a)	529	Nags na gnas	Vanavāsin
20(R6b)	530	Dus ldan	Kālika
21(R6c)	531	rDo rje mo'i bu	Vajrīputra
22(R7a)	532	bZang po	Bhadra
23(R7b)	533	gSer be'u	Kanakavatsa
24(R7c)	534	Bha ra dhva dza gser can	Kanakabharadvāja
25(R8a)	535	Ba ku la	Bakula
26(R8b)	536	sGra gcan 'dzin	Rāhula
27(R8c)	537	Lam phran bstan	Cūḍapanthaka
28(R9a)	538	Bha ra dhva dza bsod snyoms len	Piṇḍolabharadvāja
29(R9b)	539	Lam bstan	Panthaka
30(R9c)	540	Klu'i sde	Nāgasena
31(R10a)	541	sBed byed	Gopaka
32(R10b)	542	Mi phyed	Abheda
33(R10c)	543	dGe bsnyen dharma	Upāsaka Dharma
34(R11a)	544	Hwa shang	
35(R11b)	545	Yul 'khor bsrung	Dhṛtarāṣṭra
36(R11c)	546	'Phags skyes po	Virūḍhaka
37(R12a)	547	Mig mi bzàng	Virūpākṣa
38(R12b)	548	rNam thos sras	Vaiśravaṇa
39(R12c)	549	bKa' gdams lha bzhi'i nang gi shākya thub pa	Śākyamuni among the four bKa' gdams deities
40(R13a)	550	Zla ltar snang byed	Candravairocana
41(R13b)	551	sMan bla	Bhaiṣajyaguru
42(R13c)	552	Nyi ltar snang byed	Sūryavairocana
43(R14a)	553	Chos bsgrags rgya mtsho	Dharmakīrtisāgara
44(R14b)	554	mNgon mkhyen rgyal po	Abhijñarāja
45(R14c)	555	Mya ngan med mchog	Aśokottama
46(R15a)	556	Rin chen zla ba	Ratnacandra
47(R15b)	557	gSer bzang dri med	Suvarṇabhadravimala
48(R15c)	558	mTshan legs	Sunāman
49(R16a)	559	'Khor Byams pa, sGrib sel	Attendant Maitreya and Nīvaraṇaviṣkambhin
50(R16b)	560	Klu dbang rgyal po	Nāgeśvararāja
51(R16c)	561	'Khor 'Jam dpal, sPyan ras gzigs	Attendants Mañjuśrī and Avalokiteśvara
52(R17a)	562	gSang 'dus 'jam rdor	Guhyasamāja Mañjuvajra
53(R17b)	563	gSang 'dus lhan skyes	Sahaja Guhyasamāja
54(R17c)	564	Ma hā ma ya	Mahāmāyā
55*(R18a)	565	bDe mchog lhan skyes	Sahaja Saṃvara
56*(R18b)	566	Go cha'i rdo rje sems dpa'	Kavaca Vajrasattva

No.	L	Tib.	Skt. etc.
57*(R18c)	567	Go cha'i rnam snang	Kavaca Vairocana
58(R19a)	568	Go cha'i padma gar dbang	Kavaca Padmanarteśvara
59(R19b)	569	Go cha'i he ru ka nag po	Kavaca Kṛṣṇa Heruka
60(R19c)	570	Go cha'i rdo rje nyi ma	Kavaca Vajrasūrya
61(R20a)	571	Go cha'i rta mchog	Kavaca Paramāśva
62(R20b)	572	Go cha'i rdo rje phag mo	Kavaca Vajravārāhī
63(R20c)	573	Go cha'i gshin rje ma	Kavaca Yāminī
64(R21a)	574	Go cha'i rmongs byed ma	Kavaca Mohinī
65(R21b)	575	Go cha'i skrag byed ma	Kavaca Santrāsinī
66(R21c)	576	Go cha'i bskyed byed ma	Kavaca Sañcālinī
67(R22a)	577	Go cha'i tsaṇḍi ka	Kavaca Caṇḍikā
68(R22b)	578	bDe mchog dkar po	Sita Saṃvara
69(R22c)	579	bDe mchog dkar po tshe sgrub	Āyuḥsādhana Sita Saṃvara
70*(R23a)	580	'Jig rten dbang phyug yi ge bdun pa	Saptākṣara Lokeśvara
71*(R23b)	581	Kyai rdor lhan skyes	Sahaja Hevajra
72*(R23c)	582	Dus 'khor lhan skyes	Sahaja Kālacakra
73*(R24a)	583	rDo rje shugs	Vajravega
74*(R24b)	584	gShed dmar	Rakta Yamāri
75*(R24c)	585	'Jigs byed bsdus pa	Saṃkṣiptabhairava
76*(R25a)	586	dPyal lugs rdo rje phag mo	Vajravārāhī of dPyal school
77*(R25b)	587	Nā ro mkha' spyod	Nāroḍākinī
78*(R25c)	588	Mai tri mkha' spyod	Maitriḍākinī
79(R26a)	589	Indra mkha' spyod	Indraḍākinī
80(R26b)	590	Phag mo don grub	Arthasādhanavārāhī
81(R26c)	591	dBu bcad ma	Chinnamuṇḍā
82(R27a)	592	rDo rje rab sngags ma	Vajrapraṇavā
83(R27b)	593	rNam snang ma	Vairocanī
84(R27c)	594	Phag mo gnam zhabs ma	Ūrdhvapādī Vārāhī
85(R28a)	595	Phag mo kurma pā dī	Kūrmapādī Vārāhī
86(R28b)	596	Bram ze dPal 'dzin lugs kyi rdo rje phag mo	Varjavārāhī of Brāhmaṇa Śrīdhara school
87(R28c)	597	Nā ro mkha' spyod (*'di lhag*)	Nāḍīḍākinī
88(R29a)	598	Go bzlog lhan skyes	Sahaja Go bzlog
89(R29b)	599	Phag mo khros nag	Kālī Kruddha Vārāhī
90(R29c)	600	rDo rje mkha' 'gro ma	Vajraḍākinī
91(R30a)	601	lHo Rin chen mkha' 'gro ma	Ratnaḍākinī in the south
92(R30b)	602	Nub Padma mkha' 'gro ma	Padmaḍākinī in the west
93(R30c)	603	Byang Las kyi mkha' 'gro ma	Karmaḍākinī in the north
94(R31a)	604	Dam tshig mkha' 'gro	Samayaḍākinī
95(R31b)	605	sNa tshogs mkha' 'gro	Viśvaḍākinī

No.	L	Tib.	Skt. etc.
96(R31c)	606	Thams cad mkha' 'gro	Sarvaḍākinī
97(R32a)	607	'Jig rten mkha' 'gro	Lokaḍākinī
98(R32b)	608	Phag dkar shes rab gsal byed	Prajñālokakṛtya Sita Vārāhī
99(R32c)	609	Phag dkar shes rab gsal byed	Prajñālokakṛtya Sita Vārāhī
100(R33a)	610	Nor bu 'dzin pa	Maṇidhārin
101(R33b)	611	sPyan ras gzigs yi ge drug pa jo bo lugs	Ṣaḍakṣarāvalokiteśvara of Atīśa school
102(R33c)	612	Yi ge drug ma	Ṣaḍakṣarī
103(R34a)	613	bKa' gdams lha bzhi'i nang gi spyan ras gzigs	Avalokiteśvara among the four bKa' gdams deities
104(R34b)	614	sPyan ras gzigs bcu gcig zhal dpal mo'i lugs	Eleven-faced Avalokiteśvara of Lakṣmī school
105(R34c)	615	Don zhags lha lnga Ba ri lugs	5-deity Amoghapāśa of Ba ri school
106(R35a)	616	'Khor Don zhags dmar po, rTa mgrin	Attendant Rakta Amoghapāśa and Hayagrīva
107(R35b)	617	Don zhags ser po	Pīta Amoghapāśa
108(R35c)	618	'Khor Khro gnyer can ma, Ral gcig ma	Attendant Bhṛkuṭī and Ekajaṭā
109(R36a)	619	'Khor sGrol ma, Nor bzang gzhon nu	Attendant Tārā and Sudhanakumāra
110(R36b)	620	Don zhags kha che paṇ chen lugs	Amoghapāśa of Kāśmīra-mahāpaṇḍita school
111(R36c)	621	'Khor rTa mgrin, Khro gnyer can ma	Attendant Hayagrīva and Bhṛkuṭī
112(R37a)	622	'Khor Nor bzang, sGrol ma	Attendant Sudhana and Tārā
113(R37b)	623	sPyan ras gzigs kha sarpa ṇi	Khasarpaṇa Avalokiteśvara
114(R37c)	624	'Khor Khro gnyer can ma, rTa mgrin	Attendant Bhṛkuṭī and Hayagrīva
115(R38a)	625	sPyan ras gzigs sems nyid ngal gso (*'di lhag*)	Cittaviśrāmaṇa Avalokiteśvara
116(R38b)	626	sPyan ras gzigs yid bzhin nor bu lha lnga	5-deity Cintāmaṇi Avalokiteśvara
117(R38c)	627	sPyan ras gzigs sems nyid ngal gso	Cittaviśrāmaṇa Avalokiteśvara
118(R39a)	628	'Jig rten dbang phyug gsang sgrub	Guhyasādhana Lokeśvara
119(R39b)	629	sPyan ras gzigs nam mkha' rgyal po	Gaganarāja Avalokiteśvara
120(R39c)	630	sPyan ras gzigs yid bzhin 'khor lo	Cintāmanicakra Avalokiteśvara
121(R40a)	631	bCu gcig zhal 'jigs pa brgyad skyobs	Eleven-faced Aṣṭābhayatrāṇa
122(R40b)	632	Me'i 'jigs skyobs	Agnibhayatrāṇa

No.	L	Tib.	Skt. etc.
123(R40c)	633	Chu'i 'jigs skyobs	Jalabhayatrāṇa
124(R41a)	634	Seng ge'i 'jigs skyobs	Siṃhabhayatrāṇa
125(R41b)	635	Glang po'i 'jigs skyobs	Hastibhayatrāṇa
126(R41c)	636	Chad pa'i 'jigs skyobs	Daṇḍabhayatrāṇa
127(R42a)	636(*sic*)	Klu'i 'jigs skyobs	Nāgabhayatrāṇa
128(R42b)	637	mKha' 'gro'i 'jigs skyobs	Ḍākinībhayatrāṇa
129(R42c)	638	Mi rgod 'jigs skyobs	Corabhayatrāṇa
130(R43a)	639	sPyan ras gzigs rdo rje snying po	Vajragarbha Avalokiteśvara
131(R43b)	640	Seng ge sgra	Siṃhanāda
132(R43c)	641	sPyan ras gzigs rgyal ba rgya mtsho	Jinasāgara Avalokiteśvara
133(R44a)	642	bKa' gdams lha bzhi'i nang gi sgrol ma	Tārā among the four bKa' gdams deities
134(R44b)	643	sGrol ljang kha che paṇ chen lugs	Śyāma Tārā of Kāśmīra-mahāpaṇḍita school
135(R44c)	644	sGrol dkar kha che paṇ chen lugs	Sita Tārā of Kāśmīramahā-paṇḍita school
136(R45a)	645	sGrol ma nying zhi mtshan khro	Divāśāntarātrikruddha Tārā
137(R45b)	646	O rgyan sgrol ma gnas kyi dbang phyug ma	Pīṭhīśvarī Uḍḍiyāna Tārā
138(R45c)	647	sGrol ma yid bzhin nor bu	Cintāmaṇi Tārā
139(R46-48a)	648	sGrol ma dmar mo sa lugs	Rakta Tārā of Sa skya school
140(R46-48b)	649	sGrol ma nor sbyin ma	Dhanada Tārā
141(R46-48c)	650	sGrol ma ser mo	Pīta Tārā
141*a**(R47a)		Rin chen grol ma	Ratnatārā
141*b**(R47b)		Padma grol ma	Padmatārā
141*c**(R47c)		Sangs rgyas grol ma	Buddhatārā
141*d**(R48a)		Me tog grol ma	Puṣpatārā
141*e**(R48b)		bDug pa grol ma	Dhūpatārā
141*f**(R48c)		Mar me grol ma	Dīpatārā
142(R49, 50a)	651	Dzambha la ser po	Pīta Jambhala
143(R49, 50b)	652	rNam thos sras	Vaiśravaṇa
144(R49, 50c)	653	rMi lam ston pa'i sgrol ma	Svapnadeśaka Tārā
144*a**(R49a)		Dri'i grol ma	Gandhatārā
144*b**(R49b)		rDo rje lcags kyu ma	Vajrāṅkuśī
144*c**(R49c)		rDo rje zhags pa ma	Vajrapāśī
144*d**(R50a)		lCags sgrog ma	Sphoṭā
144*e**(R50b)		Dril bu ma	Ghaṇṭā
144*f**(R50c)		rDo rje sgrol ma	Vajratārā
145(R51, 52a)	654	sGrol ma	Tārā
146(R51, 52b)	655	So sor 'brang ma	Pratisarā

No.	L	Tib.	Skt. etc.
147(R51, 52c)	656	'Od zer can ma	Mārīcī
148(R53a)	657	'Khor Phag mo	Attendant Vārāhī
149(R53b)	658	'Khor Ral gcig ma	Attendant Ekajaṭā
150(R53c)	659	Phyag brgyad sgrol ma	Eight-armed Tārā
151(R54a)	660	rJe btsun ma kā pa li tā ra	Bhaṭṭārikā Kapāla Tārā
152(R54b)	661	'Phags ma tsunda tā ra	Ārya Cundā Tārā
153(R54c)	662	Phyag rdor u tsa rya	Ucārya Vajrapāṇi
154(R55a)	663	Phyag rdor gos sngon can	Nīlāmbaradhara Vajrapāṇi
155(R55b)	664	Phyag rdor sa lugs	Vajrapāṇi of Sa skya school
156(R55c)	665	Phyag rdor gtum chen bsrung ba'i mkhar ras chung lugs	Caṇḍamahāroṣaṇa Vajrapāṇi of Ras chung school
157(R56a)	666	Phyag rdor gtum po khra thogs	Khra thogs Caṇḍa Vajrapāṇi
158(R56b)	667	Phyag rdor gtum chung dmar po	Rakta Alpacaṇḍa Vajrapāṇi
159(R56c)	668	Phyag rdor gos sngon can 'gro bzang lugs	Nīlāmbaradhara Vajrapāṇi of 'Gro bzang school
160(R57a)	669	Phyag rdor khang brtsegs	Kūṭāgāra Vajrapāṇi
161(R57b)	670	Phyag rdor 'byung po 'dul byed	Bhūtaḍāmara Vajrapāṇi
162(R57c)	671	Phyag rdor 'byung po 'dul byed gsar ma	Nava Bhūtaḍāmara Vajrapāṇi
163(R58a)	672	rTa mgrin dpa' gcig lhan skyes jo bo'i lugs	Sahaja Ekavīra Hayagrīva of Atīśa school
164(R58b)	673	rTa mgrin khyung gshog can jo bo'i lugs	Garuḍapakṣavat Hayagrīva of Atīśa school
165(R58c)	674	rTa mgrin shwa na bzhi skor jo bo lugs	Caturḍākinīparivāra Hayagrīva of Atīśa school
166(R59a)	675	'Khor rDo rje las byed ma	Attendant Vajrakarmakarī
167(R59b)	676	'Khor gShin rje las byed ma	Attendant Yamakarmakarī
168(R59c)	677	'Khor Klu mo las byed ma	Attendant Nāgīkarmakarī
169(R60a)	678	'Khor gNod sbyin las byed ma	Attendant Yakṣakarmakarī
170(R60b)	679	rTa mgrin kha che paṇ chen lugs	Hayagrīva of Kāśmīra-mahāpaṇḍita school
171(R60c)	680	rTa mgrin skyer sgang lugs	Hayagrīva of Skyer sgang school
172(R61a)	681	rTa mgrin lcags ral can	Lohakhaḍga Hayagrīva
173(R61b)	682	Mi g'yo sngon po pus btsugs ma	Avaninihitajānu Nīla Acala
174(R61c)	683	Mi g'yo ba sngon po bka' gdams lugs	Nīla Acala of bKa' dgams school
175(R62a)	684	Mi g'yo ba dkar po	Sita Acala
176(R62b)	685	Mi g'yo ba phyag bzhi pa	Four-armed Acala
177(R62c)	686	Mi g'yo ba zhabs bzhi pa	Catuṣpada Acala

No.	L	Tib.	Skt. etc.
178(R63a)	687	Mi g'yo ba spre'u brgyad ma	Aṣṭakapi Acala
179(R63b)	688	Tshe dpag med sprul sku	Nirmāṇakāya Amitāyus
180(R63c)	689	Tshe dpag med ba ri lugs	Amitāyus of Ba ri school
181*(R64a)	690	Tshe dpag med dkar po	Sita Amitāyus
182*(R64b)	691	Tshe dpag med dkar po mi tra'i lugs	Sita Amitāyus of Mitra school
183*(R64c)	692	gTsug tor rnam rgyal ma	Uṣṇīṣavijayā
184(R65a)	693	'Chi med rdo rje lha mo	Amaravajradevī
185(R65b)	694	'Jam dbyangs dkar po kha che paṇ chen lugs	Sita Mañjughoṣa of Kāśmīramahāpaṇḍita school
186(R65c)	695	'Jam dbyangs a ra pa tsa na dmar ser sa lugs	Raktapīta Arapacana Mañjughoṣa of Sa skya school
187(R66a)	696	'Jam dbyangs gang blo ma'i bstod sgrub mar grags pa	Pūrṇamatistotrasādhanakīrtita Mañjughoṣa
188(R66b)	697	'Jam dbyangs smra ba'i seng ge	Vādisiṃha Mañjughoṣa
189(R66c)	698	'Jam dkar shes rab 'khor lo	Prajñācakra Sita Mañjughoṣa
190(R67a)	699	Sher phyin ma dkar mo	Sita Prajñāpāramitā
191(R67b)	700	Sher phyin ser mo	Pīta Prajñāpāramitā
192(R67c)	701	Byams pa	Maitreya
193(R68a)	702	dByangs can ma dkar mo phyag bzhi pa	Four-armed Sita Sarasvatī
194(R68b)	703	dByangs can ma dmar mo	Rakta Sarasvatī
195(R68c)	704	'Od zer can ma khab skud can	Sūcīsūtradharā Mārīcī
196(R69a)	705	gZungs las byung ba'i 'od zer can ma	Dhāraṇīvinirgatā Mārīcī
197(R69b)	706	Thub pa me ru shi ṣa	Meruśikhara Muni
198(R69c)	707	sPyan ras gzigs yi ge phyed dang bzhi pa	Ardhacaturthākṣara Avalokiteśvara
199(R70a)	708	Sangs rgyas spyan ma	Buddhalocanā
200(R70b)	709	Thub pa dam tshig gsum bkod	Trisamayavyūha Muni
201(R70c)	710	Ku ru kulle gsang sgrub	Guhyasādhana Kurukullā
202(R70'a)	711	'Khor rDo rje mkha' 'gro ma	Attendant Vajraḍākinī
203(R70'b)	712	'Khor Rin chen mkha' 'gro ma	Attendant Ratnaḍākinī
204(R70'c)	713	'Khor Padma mkha' 'gro ma	Attendant Padmaḍākinī
205(R71a)	714	'Khor Las kyi mkha' 'gro ma	Attendant Karmaḍākinī
206(R71b)	715	dPal mo snying gi gser thig can	Garbhasuvarṇasūtra Śrī
207(R71c)	716	Nor rgyun ma dmar mo	Rakta Vasudhārā
208(R72a)	717	lHa mo ti nu	Ti nu Devī
209(R72b)	718	rJe btsun ma Thod pa rgyan	Bhaṭṭārikā Kapālinī
210(R72c)	719	gSang ba ye shes	Guhyajñāna
211(R73a)	720	rDo rje rnam 'joms dkar po	Sita Vajravidāraṇa
212(R73b)	721	rDo rje rnam 'joms mthing kha	Nīla Vajravidāraṇa

No.	L	Tib.	Skt. etc.
213(R73c)	722	rDo rje rnam 'joms ljang sngon	Śyāmanīla Vajravidāraṇa
214(R74a)	723	Khro bo bgegs mthar byed	Krodha Vighnāntaka
215(R74b)	724	sNa tshogs yum dkar mo	Sita Viśvamātṛ
216(R74c)	725	rDo rje gur nas gsungs pa'i so sor 'brang ma	Vajrapañjarabhāṣitā Pratisarā
217(R75a)	726	gTsug tor gdugs dkar	Uṣṇīṣasitātapatrā
218(R75b)	727	Ri khrod lo ma gyon ma ser mo	Pīta Parṇaśabarī
219(R75c)	728	Ri khrod lo ma gyon ma dmar mo	Rakta Parṇaśabarī
220(R76a)	729	Ri khrod lo ma gyon ma sngon po	Nīla Parṇaśabarī
221(R76b)	730	Ri khrod lo ma gyon ma nag mo	Kṛṣṇa Parṇaśabarī
222(R76c)	731	Ri khrod lo ma gyon ma ljang gu	Śyāma Parṇaśabarī
223(R77a)	732	gZa' yum rig pa'i rgyal mo	Vidyārājñī Grahamātṛkā
224(R77b)	733	Khro bo sme brtsegs dud kha	Dhūmavarṇa Krodha Bhurkumkūṭa
225(R77c)	734	Khro bo sme brtsegs ljang khu	Śyāma Krodha Bhurkumkūṭa
226*(R78a)	735	Khro mo sme brtsegs	Krodha Bhurkumkūṭī
227*(R78b)	736	bDe mchog khro bo rig tshig	Bhayanāśana Krodha Saṃvara
228*(R78c)	737	bDe mchog rdo rje mkha' lding	Vajragaruḍa Saṃvara
229(R79a)	738	Dus 'khor khyung khra rgyud lugs	Tantrakrama śabala Kālacakra Garuḍa
230(R79b)	739	Khyung khra man ngag lugs	Upadeśakrama Śabala Garuḍa
231(R79c)	740	Khyung ser bka' gdams lugs	Pīta Garuḍa of bKa' gdams school
232(R80a)	741	'Jam dbyangs nag po	Kṛṣṇa Mañjughoṣa
233(R80b)	742	lHa mo shra ma ṇa	Śramaṇā Devī
234(R80c)	743	Seng gdong ma sngon mo	Nīla Siṃhavaktrā
235(R81a)	744	Seng gdong ma dmar mo	Rakta Siṃhavaktrā
236(R81b)	745	'Jam dpal nāga rakṣa	Nāgarakṣa Mañjuśrī
237(R81c)	746	rGyal ba shākya thub pa	Jina Sākyamuni
238(R82a)	747	Sangs rgyas rnam gzigs	Vaiśyin Buddha
239(R82b)	748	Sangs rgyas gtsug tor can	Śikhin Buddha
240(R82c)	749	Sangs rgyas thams cad skyob	Viśvabhū Buddha
241(R83a)	750	Sangs rgyas 'khor ba 'jig	Krakucchanda Buddha
242(R83b)	751	Sangs rgyas gser thub	Kanakamuni Buddha
243(R83c)	752	Sangs rgyas 'od srung	Kāśyapa Buddha
244(R84a)	753	Khro bo chen po	Mahākrodha
245(R84b)	754	Phyag na rdo rje zhi ba	Śānta Vajrapāṇi
246(R84c)	755	'Od dpag med	Amitābha
247(R85a)	756	Byams pa	Maitreya

No.	L	Tib.	Skt. etc.
248(R85b)	757	Kun tu bzang po	Samantabhadra
249(R85c)	758	Nam mkha'i snying po	Ākāśagarbha
250(R86a)	759	Sa'i snying po	Kṣitigarbha
251(R86b)	760	sGrib pa rnam sel	Nīvaraṇaviṣkambhin
252(R86c)	761	sPyan ras gzigs 'jigs pa brgyad skyob	Aṣṭabhayatrāṇa Avalokiteśvara
253(R87a)	762	sPyan ras gzigs sna tshogs dbang po	Viśveśa Avalokiteśvara
254(R87b)	763	sPyan ras gzigs padma'i phyag	Padmapāṇi Avalokiteśvara
255(R87c)	764	sPyan ras gzigs su kha va ti	Sukhāvatī Avalokiteśvara
256(R88a)	765	sPyan ras gzigs don yod lcags kyu	Amoghāṅkuśa Avalokiteśvara
257(R88b)	766	sPyan ras gzigs don yod mchod pa'i nor bu	Amoghapūjāmaṇi Avalokiteśvara
258(R88c)	767	gSang bdag lhan skyes zhi ba	Śānta Sahaja Guhyapati
259(R89a)	768	gSang ba'i bdag po khro bo	Krodha Guhyapati
260(R89b)	769	lHa mo mā ma ki	Māmakī Devī
261(R89c)	770	lHa mo gos dkar mo	Pāṇḍaravāsinī Devī
262(R90a)	771	gTsug tor rnam rgyal phyag gnyis ma	Two-armed Uṣṇīṣavijayā
263(R90b)	772	lHa mo tsunda dkar mo	Sita Cundā Devī
264(R90c)	773	Khro bo gzhan gyis mi thub pa	Krodha Aparājita
265*(R91a)	774	rTa mgrin dkar po	Sita Hayagrīva
266*(R91b)	775	Mi g'yo ba dmar po	Rakta Acala
267*(R91c)	776	'Od zer can ma rta ljang can	Śyāmāśva Mārīcī
268(R92a)	777	rGyal mtshan rtse mo'i dpung rgyan	Dhvajāgrakeyūrā
269(R92b)	778	lHa mo ro langs ma	Vetālī Devī
270(R92c)	779	gNod sbyin no 'brog ma	Hārītī Yakṣiṇī
271(R93a)	780	Tshogs bdag ser po	Pīta Gaṇapati
272(R93b)	781	'Phags pa 'jam dpal	Āryamañjughoṣa
273(R93c)	782	sPyan ras gzigs	Avalokiteśvara
274(R94a)	783	Phyag na rdo rje ljang khu	Śyāma Vajrapāṇi
275(R94b)	784	'Phags ma sgrol ljang	Ārya Śyāma Tārā
276(R94c)	785	Rab tu dpa' ba'i sgrol ma	Pravīra Tārā
277(R95a)	786	dKar mo zla mdangs kyi sgrol ma	Candrakānti Gaurī Tārā
278(R95b)	787	gSer mdog can gyi sgrol ma	Kanakavarṇa Tārā
279(R95c)	788	gTsug tor rnam par rgyal ba'i sgrol ma	Uṣṇīṣavijayā Tārā
280(R96a)	789	Hūṃ sgra sgrog pa'i sgrol ma	Hūṃsvaranādinī Tārā
281(R96b)	790	'Jig rten gsum las rnam par rgyal ba'i sgrol ma	Trailokyavijayā Tārā
282(R96c)	791	rGol ba 'joms pa'i sgrol ma	Vādipramardinī Tārā
283(R97a)	792	dBang mchog ster ba'i sgrol ma	Varada Tārā
284(R97b)	793	'Od zer can ma	Mārīcī

No.	L	Tib.	Skt. etc.
285(R97c)	794	Seng ldeng nags kyi sgrol ma	Khadiravaṇī Tārā
286(R98a)	792(*sic*)	Ral gcig ma	Ekajaṭā
287(R98b)	793(*sic*)	mChog stsol ba'i sgrol ma	Varada Tārā
288(R98c)	794(*sic*)	Mya ngan sel ba'i sgrol ma	Śokavinodana Tārā
289(R99a)	795	Phongs pa sel ba'i sgrol ma	Āpadavimocanī Tārā
290(R99b)	796	bKra shis snang ba'i sgrol ma	Maṅgalāloka Tārā
291(R99c)	797	Yongs su smin par mdzad pa'i sgrol ma	Paripācaka Tārā
292(R100a)	798	Khro gnyer g'yo ba'i sgrol ma	Bhṛkuṭī Tārā
293(R100b)	799	Zhi ba chen mo'i sgrol ma	Mahāśānti Tārā
294(R100c)	800	Chags pa 'joms pa'i sgrol ma	Rāganiśūdana Tārā
295(R101a)	801	sGrol ma bde sgrub ma	Sukhasādhana Tārā
296(R101b)	802	sGrol ma rab rgyas ma	Saṃkusumita Tārā
297(R101c)	803	sGrol ma sdug bsngal bsreg ma	Duḥkhadahana Tārā
298(R102a)	804	sGrol ma dngos grub 'byung ma	Siddhisambhava Tārā
299(R102b)	805	sGrol ma yongs rdzogs byed ma	Paripūraṇa Tārā
300(R102c)	806	rNam sras ser chen lha dgu	9-deity Mahāpīta Vaiśravaṇa
301(R103a)	807	rNam sras mdun dmar rta sngon can	Nīlāśva Raktasūla Vaiśravaṇa
302(R103b)	808	rNam sras ljang ser be con can	Gadādhara Śyāmapīta Vaiśravaṇa
303(R103c)	809	rNam sras dmar po gar mkhan mchog	Nartakavara Rakta Vaiśravaṇa
304(R104a)	810	'Khor gNod sbyin brgyad	Eight Yakṣa Attendants
305(R104b)	811	rNam sras gsung mchog lus ngan po	Kubera Svarottama Vaiśravaṇa
306(R104c)	812	'Khor gNod sbyin mo brgyad	Eight Yakṣī Attendants
307(R105a-c)	813	rNam sras drag byed 'khor klu brgyad bcas	Raudra Vaiśravaṇa with Eight Nāga Attendants
308(R106a)	814	rNam sras nag po rta sngon can	Nīlāśva Kṛṣṇa Vaiśravaṇa
309(R106b)	815	rNam sras dkar po tshe 'dzin	Āyurdhara Sita Vaiśravaṇa
310(R106c)	816	rNam sras ljang gu seng zhon ma dznyā na'i lugs	Jñānakrama Siṃhavāhana Śyāma Vaiśravaṇa
311(R107a)	817	rNam sras yang gsang phyag mtshan bzhi pa	Caturāyudha Atiguhya Vaiśravaṇa
312(R107b)	818	Dzambha la ser po gtso rkyang	Ekāntanāyaka Pīta Jambhala Vaiśravaṇa
313(R107c)	819	gSang 'dus las byung ba'i dzambha la ser po	Guhyasamājavinirgata Pīta Jambhala Vaiśravaṇa
314*(R108a)	820	dPa' bo chig sgrub las byung ba'i dzambha la lha mang	Ekavīra Sādhanavinirgata Bahudeva Jambhala
315*(R108b)	821	Dzambha la nag po	Kṛṣṇa Jambhala

No.	L	Tib.	Skt. etc.
316*(R108c)	822	Dzambha la dkar po lha lnga jo bo'i lugs	5-deity Sita Jambhala of Atīśa school
317(R109a)	823	Dzambha la dmar pos sa lugs	Rakta Jambhala of Sa skya school
318(R109b)	824	Grwa pa mngon shes lugs kyi dzambha la dmar po	Abhijñakrama Rakta Jambhala
319(R109c)	825	Dzambha la ljang khu dus 'khor lugs	Kālacakrakrama Śyāma Jambhala
320(R110a)	826	gNod sbyin nor bu bzang po	Maṇibhadra Yakṣa
321(R110b)	827	Sras gar mkhan mchog	Vaiśravaṇa
322(R110c)	828	Sras rgyal ba khyu mchog	Jinarṣabha Vaiśravaṇa
323(R111a)	829	lHa mo dpal chen mo	Mahālakṣmī Devī
324(R111b)	830	gZungs las byung ba'i lha mo nor rgyun ma	Dhāraṇīvinirgata Vasu-dhārā Devī
325(R111c)	831	Nor rgyum ma dzā ma ri'i lugs	Vasudhārā of Jāmari school
326(R112a)	832	Nor rgyun ma ba lang rdzi	Gopāla Vasudhārā
327(R112b)	833	Yid 'phrog nor rgyun ma	Manoharā Vasudhārā
328(R112c)	834	Zhang blon rdo rje bdud 'dul phyi sgrub	Bāhyasādhana Zhang blon rdo rje Mārajit
329(R113a)	835	Zhang blon rdo rje bdud 'dul nang sgrub	Antarasādhana Zhang blon rdo rje Mārajit
330(R113b)	836	Zhang blon rdo rje bdud 'dul gsang sgrub	Guhyasādhana Zhan blon rdo rje Mārajit
331(R113c)	837	gNod sbyin a pa rā dzi ta	Aparājita Yakṣa
332(R114a)	838	'Jur 'gegs sel ba'i tshogs bdag	Ājñāvinivarta Gaṇapati
333(R114b)	839	Tshogs bdag dkar po phyag bzhi pa jo bo'i lugs	Four-armed Sita Gaṇapati of Atīśa school
334(R114c)	840	Tshogs bdag dmar po phyag bzhi pa	Four-armed Rakta Gaṇapati
335(R115a)	841	Klu rgyal sog ma med	Apalāla Nāgarāja
336(R115b)	842	dByug gu ma spun gsum	dByug gu ma Bhaginītraya
337(R115c)	843	Khol po kundha li	Dāsakuṇḍalī
338(R116a)	844	Jinamitra, Kṣetrapāla	Jinamitra and Kṣetrapāla
339(R116b)	845	mGon po bar chad kun sel, lHa mo	Sarvavighnavināyaka Mahākāla and Devī
340(R116c)	846	Trakṣad, Ṭakkirāja	Trakṣad and Ṭakkirāja
341(R117a)	847	mGon dkar yid bzhin nor bu	Cintāmaṇi Sita Mahākāla
342(R117b)	848	mGon ser blo 'phel	Mativardhana Pīta Mahā-kāla
343(R117c)	849	mGon dmar dbang gi rgyal po	Cintāmaṇi Rakta Mahākāla
344(R118a)	850	'Khor Ratna ḍā ki, Buddha ḍā ki	Attendant Ratnaḍāki and Buddhaḍāki
345(R118b)	851	mGon ljang tshe bdag	Āyuṣpati Śyāma Mahākāla

No.	L	Tib.	Skt. etc.
346(R118c)	852	'Khor Padma ḍā ki, Karma ḍā ki	Attendant Padmaḍāki and Karmaḍāki
347*(R119a)	853	mGon po phyag bzhi pa grub chen zhi ba sbas pa'i lugs	Four-armed Mahākāla of Mahāsiddhaśāntigupta school
348*(R119b)	854	mGon po phyag bzhi pa klu sgrub lugs	Four-armed Mahākāla of Nāgārjuna school
349*(R119c)	855	mGon po phyag bzhi pa rgwa lo'i lugs	Four-armed Mahākāla of rGwa lo tsā ba school
350*(R120a)	856	'Tshal lugs kyi mgon po phyag bzhi pa	Four-armed Mahākāla of 'Tshal school
351*(R120b)	857	Lugs gnyis gcig tu sgril ba'i mgon po phyag bzhi pa	Four-armed Mahākāla, Combination of the above two schools
352*(R120c)	858	mGon dmar rkang gling can	Rakta Mahākāla with rkang gling
353(R121a)	859	mGon po phyag bzhi pa'i 'khor lha mo tsaṇḍikā	Caṇḍikā Devī, Attendant of Four-armed Mahākāla
354(R121b)	860	Las mgon bya rog gdon can	Kākāsya Karma Mahākāla
355(R121c)	861	Gur mgoṇ lcam dral	Pañjara Mahākāla yama-yamī
356(R122a)	862	Gur mgon lha brgyad	8-deity Pañjara Mahā-kāla
357(R122b)	863	Gur mgon phur zhabs can	Garuḍapakṣavat Kīlapāda Pañjara Mahākāla
358(R122c)	864	Gur yum can klu sgrub lugs	Samātṛka Pañjara of Nāgār-juna school
359(R123a)	865	Gur rkyan rngog lugs	Ekānta Pañjara of rNgog school
360(R123b)	866	mGon po stag gzhon ma	Vyāghravāhana Mahākāla
361(R123c)	867	mGon po beng dkạ' ma	Daṇḍadhara Mahākāla
362(R124a)	868	mGon po beng gter ma	Nidhi Daṇḍadhara Mahā-kāla
363(R124b)	869	mGon po legs ldan mched gsum	Bhagavat Mahākāla Bhrātṛ-traya
364(R124c)	870	mGon po aṃ gho ra	Aṅghora Mahākāla
365(R125a)	871	mGon po lha chen dpal 'bar jo ḅo'i lugs	Mahādevaśrījvālamahākāla of Atīśa school
366(R125b)	872	mGon po gri gug dpa' gcig	Ekavīra Kartarīdhara Mahākāla
367(R125c)	873	lHo nub mgon po gri gug dmar po	Rakta Kartarīdhara Mahā-kāla dwelling at the South-west
368(R126a)	874	mGon po bzhi sprags	Four Mahākālas

No.	L	Tib.	Skt. etc.
369(R126b)	875	mGon po gri gug kha che paṇ chen lugs	Kartarīdhara Mahākāla of Kāśmīramahāpaṇḍita school
370(R126c)	876	mGon po zangs gri tsan gyi ljang lugs	Tāmrakartarīdhara Mahākāla of lJang school
371(R127a)	877	mGon po gri gug [lha dgu ma] dznyā na lugs	Jñānakrama 9-deity Kartarīdhara Mahākāla
372(R127b)	878	mGon po ber nag zangs gri can	Tāmrakartarīdhara Kṛṣṇacola Mahākāla
373(R127c)	879	mGon po gcer bu zangs gri can	Tāmrakartarīdhara Nagna Mahākāla
374(R128a)	880	Tshogs bdag mgon po seng ge'i gdan can	Siṃhāsana Gaṇapati Mahākāla
375(R128b)	881	mGon po trakṣad gnyos lugs	Trakṣad Yamayamī Mahākāla of gNyos school
376(R128c)	882	mGon po trakṣad dwags po'i lugs	Trakṣad Mahākāla of Dwags po school
377(R129a)	883	mGon po trakṣad seng zhon jo bo'i lugs	Siṃhavāhana Trakṣad Mahākāla of Atīśa school
378(R129b)	884	mGon po trakṣad gri gug sprags sgrub ma	Kartarīdhara Trakṣad Mahākāla
379(R129c)	885	mGon po trakṣad rkang thang ma	Padātika Trakṣad Mahākāla
380(R130a)	886	mGon po trakṣad ma ning ma	Paṇḍaka Trakṣad Mahākāla
381(R130b)	887	mGon po trakṣad 'brong zhal can	Camarīmukha Trakṣad Mahākāla
382(R130c)	888	mGon po trakṣad gsang sgrub shwa na'i zhal can	Ḍākamukha Guhyasādhana Trakṣad Mahākāla
383(R131a)	889	dPal mgon zhal bzhi pa bsnyen dus dang 'brel ba	Sevākālasambaddha Four-faced Śrīmahākāla
384(R131b)	890	dPal mgon zhal bzhi pa sgrub dus dang 'brel ba	Sādhanakālasambaddha Four-faced Śrīmahākāla
385(R131c)	891	Zhal bzhi pa las sbyor mgon po	Four-faced Karmayoga Mahākāla
386(R132a)	892	Zhal bzhi dkar po tshe 'phel	Four-faced Sita Āyurvardhana
387(R132b)	893	Zhal bzhi ser po nor 'phel	Four-faced Pīta Dhanavardhana
388(R132c)	894	Zhal bzhi dmar po dbang sdud	Four-faced Rakta Vaśaṃkara
389(R133a)	895	Zhal bzhi pa sngon po nyams sgrol	Four-faced Nīla Kṣatitāraka
390(R133b)	896	Zhal bzhi pa gdong gnyan can	Four-faced Caṇḍamukha
391(R133c)	897	Sha za ce spyan gdong	Śṛgālamukha Piśāca
392(R134a)	898	lHa mo dud sor ma	Dhūmavatī Devī
393(R134b)	899	dPal ldan dmag zor rgyal mo	Śrīmatī Pārvatī rājñī

No.	L	Tib.	Skt. etc.
394(R134c)	900	lHa mo srog sgrub lcags phur ma rang byung rgyal mo	Prāṇasādhana Lohakīla Svayambhūrājñī Devī
395(R135a)	901	lHa mo dung skyong ma	Śaṅkhapālī Devī
396(R135b)	902	bDud mo re ma ti	Mahākālī Rematī
397(R135c)	903	Klu mo re ma ti	Nāgī Rematī
398(R136a)	904	gNod sbyin re ma ti	Yakṣī Rematī
399(R136b)	905	Re ma ti rdo rje gshog rgod ma	Uddhatavajrapakṣā Rematī
400(R136c)	906	lHa mo e ka dza ti	Ekajaṭī Devī
401(R137a)	907	lHa mo nam mkha'i gos can	Digambarā Devī
402(R137b)	908	Chos rgyal las kyi gshin rje mthing ga	Nīla Dharmarāja Karmayama
403(R137c)	909	Las gshin dmar po ma ru rtse bzhis bskor ba	Rakta Karmayama surrounded by four Ma ru rtses
404(R138a)	910	Las gshin dmar po khrag mdog	Rudhiravarṇa Rakta karmayama
405(R138b)	911	Dur khrod bdag po	Citipati
406(R138c)	912	Pu tra lcam dral	Putra and Yamayamī
407(R139a)	913	Bran bdud gshin rje nag po	Bran bdud and Kṛṣṇayama
408(R139b)	914	dKar mo nyi zla lcam dral	Sūryacandra Gaurī and Yamayamī
409(R139c)	915	rNam thos sras	Vaiśravaṇa
410(R140a)	916	Yul 'khor bsrung	Dhṛtarāṣṭra
411(R140b)	917	'Phags skyes po	Virūḍhaka
412(R140c)	918	sPyan mi bzang	Virūpākṣa
413(R141a)	919	Rin chen mkha' 'gro, rDo rje mkha' 'gro	Ratnaḍākinī and Vajraḍākinī
414(R141b)	920	Sangs rgyas mkha' 'gro	Buddhaḍākinī
415(R141c)	921	Padma mkha' 'gro, Las kyi mkha' 'gro	Padmaḍākinī and Karmaḍākinī
416(R142a)	922	Mi g'yo glang bzang ma, mThing gi zhal bzang ma	
417(R142b)	923	bKra shis tshe ring ma	
418(R142c)	924	gTad dkar 'gro bzang ma, Cod paṇ mgrin bzang ma	

sNar thang

No.	L	Tib.	Skt. etc.
419(N1a-c)	925	Thub pa gnas bcus bskor ba	Aṣṭādaśasthaviraparivāra Muni
420(N2a)	926	gTsug tor gdugs dkar	Uṣṇīṣasitātapatrā
421(N2b)	927	gTsug tor rnam rgyal lha dgu	9-deity Uṣṇīṣavijayā
422(N2c)	928	'Jam dbyangs dkar po	Sita Mañjughoṣa

No.	L	Tib.	Skt. etc.
423(N3a)	929	'Jam dbyangs a ra pa tsa na	Arapacana Mañjughoṣa
424(N3b)	930	'Jam dbyangs smra ba'i seng ge	Vādisiṃha Mañjughoṣa
425(N3c)	931	So sor 'brang ma lha lnga	5-deity Pratisarā
426(N4a)	932	'Od zer can ma	Mārīcī
427(N4b)	933	rJe btsun byams pa	Bhaṭṭāraka Maitreya
428(N4c)	934	Mi g'yo ba dkar po	Sita Acala
429(N5a)	935	Mi g'yo ba sngon po	Nīla Acala
430(N5b)	936	Thugs rje chen po bcu gcig zhal	Eleven-faced Mahākāruṇika
431(N5c)	937	sPyan ras gzigs phyag bzhi pa	Four-armed Avalokiteśvara
432(N6a)	938	Kha sarpa ṇi	Khasarpaṇa
433(N6b)	939	Seng ge sgra	Siṃhanāda
434(N6c)	940	sGrol dkar	Sita Tārā
435(N7a)	941	sGrol ljang.	Śyāma Tārā
436(N7b)	942	rTa mgrin	Hayagrīva
437(N7c)	943	Lo ma gyon ma	Parṇaśabarī
438(N8a)	944	dByangs can ma	Sarasvatī
439(N8b)	945	Mi 'khrugs pa	Akṣobhya
440(N8c)	946	Phyag rdor mdo lugs	Sūtrakrama Vajrapāṇi
441(N9a)	947	Khro gnyer can ma	Bhṛkuṭī
442(N9b)	948	sTobs po che	Mahābala
443(N9c)	949	Khro bo sme brtsegs	Krodha Sme brtsegs
444(N10a)	950	bGegs mthar byed	Vighnāntaka
445(N10b)	951	rNam sras	Vaiśravaṇa
446(N10c)	952	Dzambha la	Jambhala
447(N11a)	953	Nor rgyun ma	Vasudhārā
448(N11b)	954	Sher phyin ma	Prajñāparamitā
449(N11c)	955	Bla med phyag rdor 'byung po 'dul byed	Bhūtaḍāmara Anuttara Vajrapāṇi
450(N12a)	956		Daśākāro vaśī
451(N12b)	957	Gri gug mgon po	Kartarīdhara Mahākāla
452(N12c)	958		Prajñākhaḍga

rDor phreng

No.	L	Tib.	Skt. etc.
453(D1a)	959	gSang 'dus 'jam rdor	Guhyasamāja Mañjuvajra
454(D1b)	960	rNam snang 'jam rdor	Vairocana Mañjuvajra
455(D1c)	961	gSang 'dus mi bskyod pa	Guhyasamāja Akṣobhya
456(D2a)	962	dGra nag gshin rje gshed	Kṛṣṇāri Yamāntaka
457(D2b)	963	sNying po kyai rdor	sNying po Hevajra
458(D2c)	964	Thugs kyai rdor	Citta Hevajra

No.	L	Tib.	Skt. etc.
459(D3a)	965	gSung kyai rdor	Vāg Hevajra
460(D3b)	966	sKu kyai rdor	Kāya Hevajra
461(D3c)	967	rDo rje mkha' 'gro	Vajraḍāka
462(D4a)	968	rDo rje bdag med ma	Vajranairātmā
463(D4b)	969	rDo rje bdag med phyag gnyis ma	Two-armed Vajranairātmā
464(D4c)	970	Ku ru ku le	Kurukullā
465(D5a)	971	rDo rje sgrol ma	Vajratārā
466(D5b)	972	Kyai rdor	Hevajra
467(D5c)	973	Thugs kyai rdor	Citta Hevajra
468*(D6a)	974	gSung kyai rdor	Vāg Hevajra
469*(D6b)	975	sKu kyai rdor	Kāya Hevajra
470*(D6c)	976	bDe mchog rdo rje sems dpa'	Vajrasattva Saṃvara
471(D7a)	977	bDe mchog	Saṃvara
472(D7b)	978	bDe mchog.phyag gnyis	Two-armed Saṃvara
473(D7c)	979	'Khor lo sdom pa ser po	Pīta Cakrasaṃvara
474(D8a)	980	Phag mo dmar mo	Rakta Vārāhī
475(D8b)	981	Phag mo sngon mo	Nīla Vārāhī
476(D8c)	982	Phag mo ser mo	Pīta Vārāhī
477(D9a)	983	Khro bo hūṃ mdzad	Krodhahūṃkāra
478(D9b)	984	rDo rje sems dpa'	Vajrasattva
479(D9c)	985	rNam par snang mdzad	Vairocana
480(D10a)	986	Rin 'byung	Ratnasambhava
481(D10b)	947	sNang mtha'	Amitābha
482(D10c)	988	Mi bskyod pa	Akṣobhya
483(D11a)	989	Don yod grub pa	Amoghasiddhi
484(D11b)	990	rDo rje bdud rtsi	Vajrāmṛta
485(D11c)	991	rDo rje hūṃ mdzad	Vajrahūṃkāra
486(D12a)	992	Khrag 'thung	Heruka
487(D12b)	993	bDud rtsi 'khyil ba	Amṛtakuṇḍalin
488(D12c)	994	Sangs rgyas thod pa	Buddhakapāla
489(D13a)	995	Sangs rgyas thód pa	Buddhakapāla
490(D13b)	996	Ma hā ma ya	Mahāmāyā
491(D13c)	997	rNal 'byor nam mkha'	Yogāmbara
492(D14a)	998	Ye shes mkha' 'gro	Jñānaḍākinī
493(D14b)	999	Dus 'khor	Kālacakra
494(D14c)	1000	sNang mdzad rdor dbyings	Vajradhātu Vairocana
495(D15a)	1001	Shākya seng ge	Śākyasiṃha
496(D15b)	1002	Chos dbyings gsung dbang	Dharmadhātuvāgīśvara
497(D15c)	1003	'Byung po 'dul byed	Bhūtaḍāmara
498(D16a)	1004	'Od zer can ma	Mārīcī

No.	L	Tib.	Skt. etc.
499(D16b)	1005	So sor 'brang ma	Pratisarā
500(D16c)	1006	Nor rgyun ma	Vasudhārā
501(D17a)	1007	gZa' yum rig pa chen mo	Grahamātṛkā Mahāvidyā
502(D17b)	1008	rNam rgyal ma	Vijayā
503(D17c)	1009	rGyan drug phyag mtshan	Ṣaḍābharaṇa

Bibliography

Lokesh Chandra (reproduced), *Sadhana-mala of the Panchen Lama, bsTan pa' i nyi ma phyogs las rnam rgyal, Yi dam rgya mtsho'i sgrub thabs rin chen 'byung gnas kyi lhan thabs rin 'byung don gsal*, 2 parts, New Delhi: International Academy of Indian Culture, 1974.

Lokesh Chandra, *Buddhist Iconography of Tibet*, Kyoto: Rinsen, 1986.

Raghu Vira & Lokesh Candra, *A New Tibet- Mongol Pantheon*. Śata-piṭaka Series, Indo-Asian Literatures Vol.21(8), New Delhi: International Academy of Indian Culture, 1963.

Lokesh Chandra, *A New Tibet-Mongol Pantheon*. Śata-piṭaka Series Indo-Asian Literatures Vol. 22(9), New Delhi: International Academy of Indian Culture, 1964.

Tāranātha, Jo nan rJe btsun, *Yi dam rgya mtho'i sgrub thabs rin chen 'byung gnas:A Collection of Sādhanas for Invoking the Various Tutelary Deities of Lamaism*, 2 vols., New Delhi, 1974 (vol.1), 1976 (vol.2).

Figures and Mantras

1*(R0a) 511

rGyal tshab rje

2*(R0b) 512

rJe rin po che

3*(R0c) 513

mKhas grub rje

4(R1a) 514

Jo lugs sgrol dkar

Sita Tārā of Atīśa school

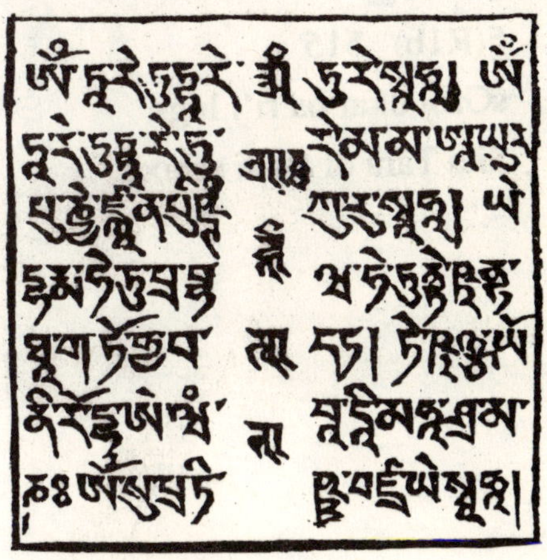

5(R1b) 515
sGrol dkar ba ri'i lugs
Sita Tārā of Ba ri school

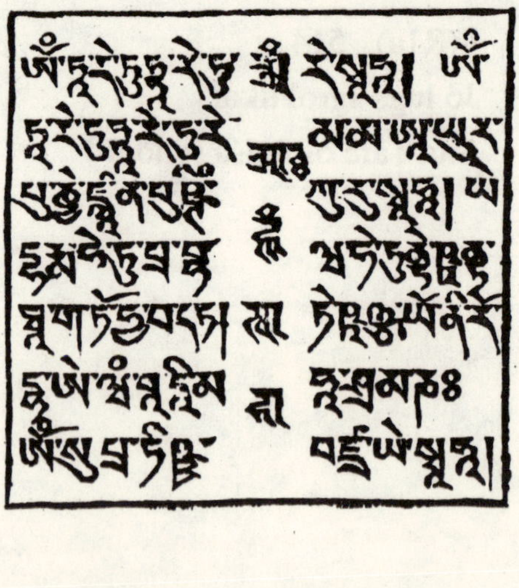

6(R1c) 516

gNyan lugs sgrol dkar

Sita Tārā of gNyan school

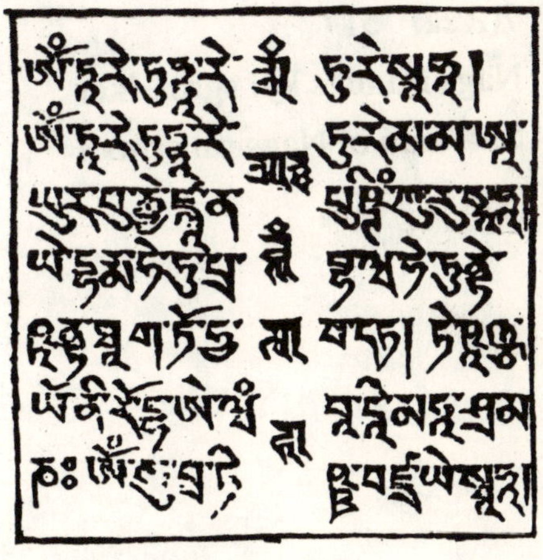

7(R2a) 517

Nags rin lugs kyi sgrol dkar

Sita Tārā of Nags rin school

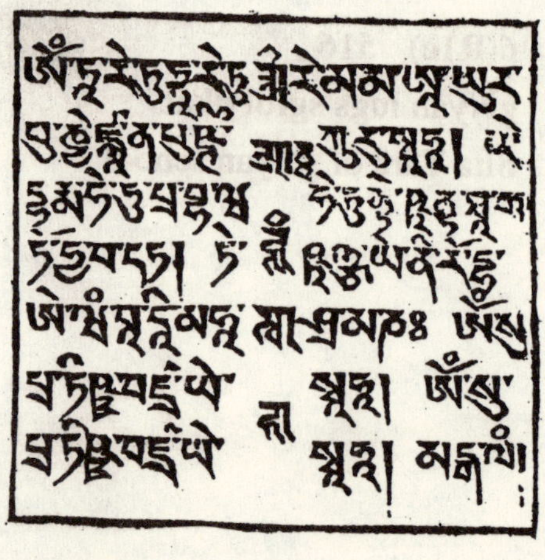

8(R2b) 518

dByangs can ma dkar mo

Sita Sarasvatī

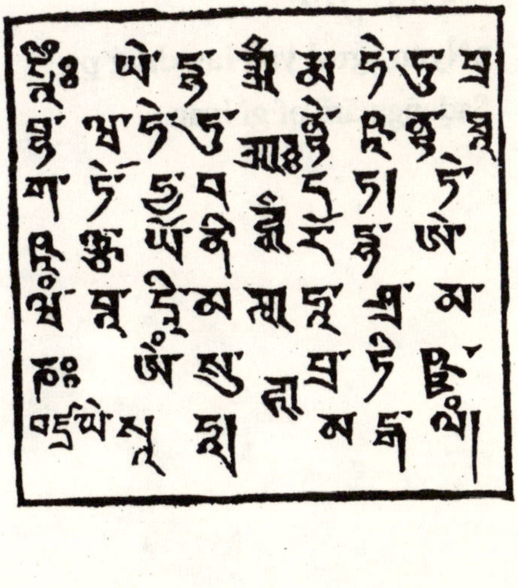

9(R2c) 519

gNyan sgrol yan lag drug pa

Ṣaḍaṅgatārā of gNyan

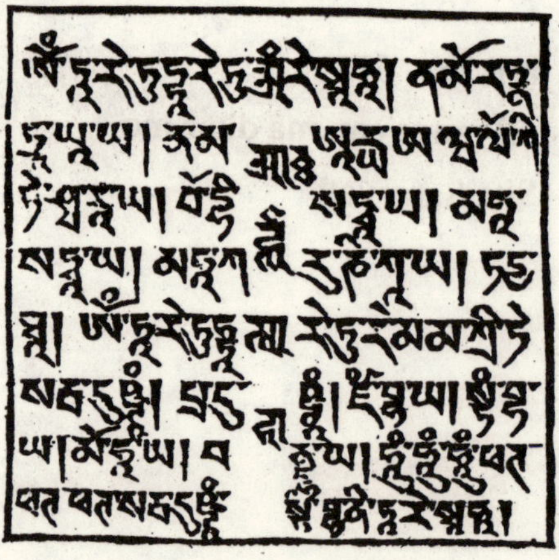

10(R3a) 520

Ku ru ku lle

Kurukullā

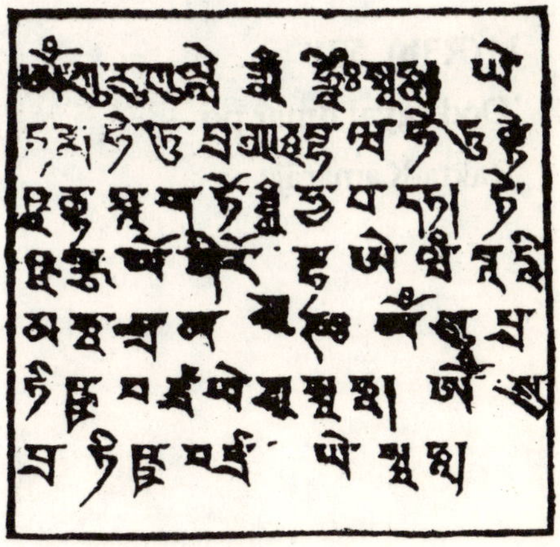

11(R3b) 521

'Dod rgyal dmar po

Rakta Kāmarāja

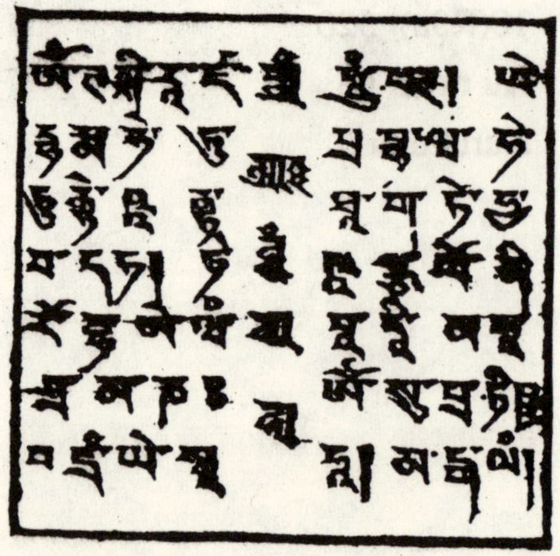

12(R3c) 522
Tshogs bdag dmar chen
Mahāraktagaṇapati

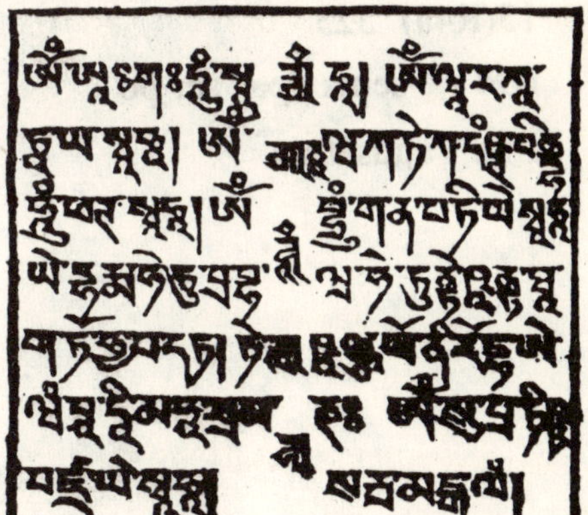

13(R4a) 523

rDo rje sems dpa' ser po

Pīta Vajrasattva

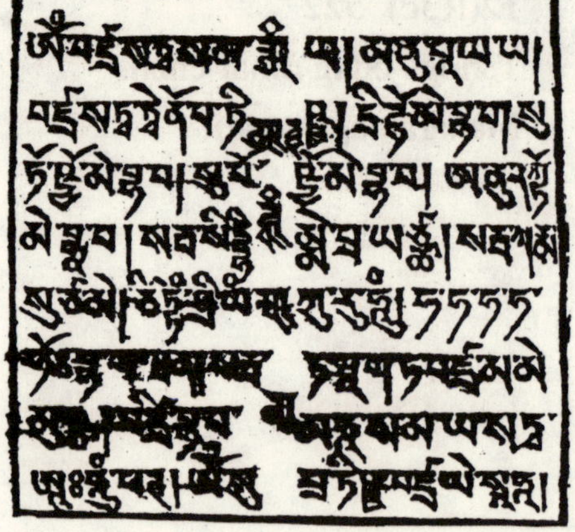

14(R4b) 524

Thub pa rdo rje gdan pa gtso 'khor gsum

Vajrāsanamuni with two disciples

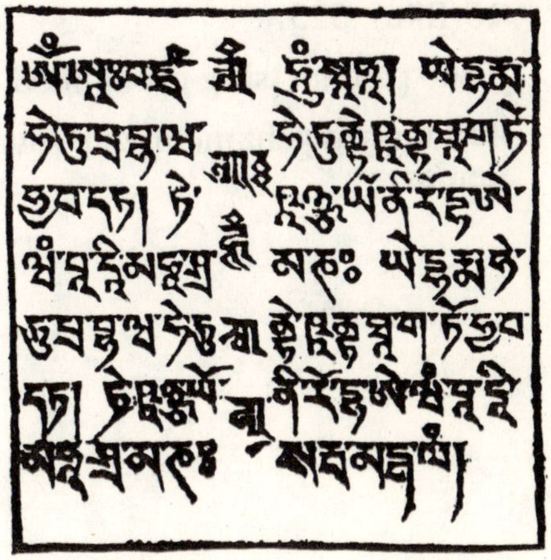

15(R4c) 525

Thub pa dam tshig gsum bkod

Trisamayavyūhamuni with four deities

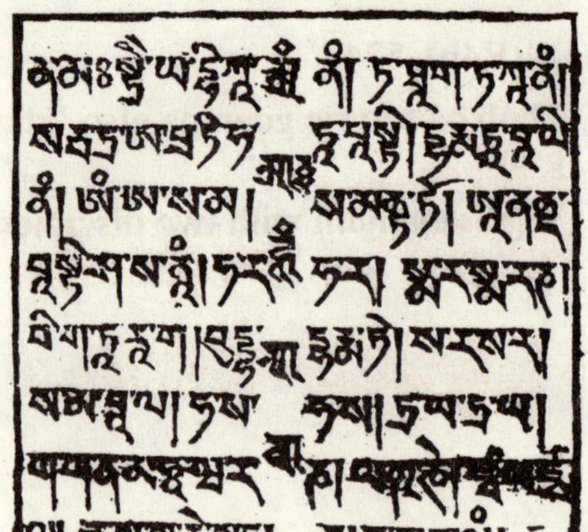

16(R5a) 526
Thub dbang
Munīndra

ཨོཾ་མུ་ནེ་མུ་ནེ་མ་ཧཱ་ཨཱཿ མུ་ནེ་ཡེ་སྭཱ་ཧཱ།
མཚུངས་མེད་ལྷ་ ཨཱ་ཧ་ བས་མི་དམིགས་ཞིང་།།
གསེར་གྱི་མདོག་ ཅན་མཛེས་པའི་སྐུ།།
ཞལ་གཅིག་ཕྱག་ཧཱུྃ གཉིས་སྐྱིལ་དཀྲུང་
བཞུགས།།ས་ སྭཱ་ གནོན་མཉམ་བཞག
མཛད་ཕྱག་རྒྱ་ཆེ་ ཧཱ་ ལ།།ཁྲ་མའི་སྐུ་ཆེ་
བརྟན་པ་དང་།།བསྐྱུན་པ་རྒྱས་པར་བྱིན་གྱིས
རློབས།།

17(R5b) 527

Yan lag 'byung

Aṅgaja

གངས་རི་ཆེན་པོ་ ཨོཾ ཏི་སེ་ལ།།འཕགས
པ་གནས་བརྟན་ མ་ཧཱ ཡན་ལག་འབྱུང༌།
དགྲ་བཅོམ་སྟོང་དང༌ སུམ་བརྒྱས
བསྐོར།། ཕྱོགས ཧཱུྃ ཕྱོ་ར་ཧ་ཡབ་འཛིན
ཕྱག་འཚལ། ། སྭཱ བླ་མའི་སྐུ་ཚེ…
བརྟན་པ་དང༌། ། ཧཱ བསྟན་པ་རྒྱས
པར་བྱིན་གྱིས་ རློབས།།མངྒ་ལཾ།།

མ་ཕམ་པ

18(R5c) 528

Ma pham pa

Ajita

དྲང་སྲོང་རི་ཡི་རྗེ་ ཨོཾ་ སྭཱ་ཧཱ་ ཨཱ །
འཕགས་པ་གནས་ ཨཱཿཧཱུྃ་ བརྟ ། ཕམ་
པ་ཿཿ དགྲ་བཅོམ་ བཛྲ་ གཅིག
གིས་བསྐོར། ། ཧཱུྃ་ ཕྱག་གཉིས་མཉམ་
བཞག་མཛད་ཕྱག ཧཱ་ འཚལ། །སྨམའི
སྐྱུ་ཆེ་བརྡན་པ་དགས ཧྲཱི ། བསྟན་པ་སྲུས་
བར་ཕྲིན་གྱིས་སྣོ་ ཧྲཱི་ བས། །མཆོད་ཡོ།

ནགས་ན་གནས

19(R6a) 529

Nags na gnas

Vanavāsin

ལོ་མ་བརྟན་པའི་ཀྲྀ་རི་ཁྲོད་ན། །ཕ་བ་སྦྲ་
པགས་ནས་བཅད་ན་ཀཱ་ཨ་ནགས་ན་གནས། །
རྒྱ་བ་ཚོམ་སྟོང་ དང་བཅས་བཀྲུས་
བསྐོར་བ། །ཕྱོགས་ཏྲཱི་མཛུབ་རྔ་ཡབ་འཛིན་
ཕྱག་འཚལ། །ཀྲྀ་ཀྲཱྀ་མའི་ལྷ་ཆེན་བརྟན་པ
དང་། །དགེ་སྟོན་པ་ཀྲ་ཀཱ་ས་པར་ཕྱིན་སྤྱོད་
རྟོགས། །ཡབ་ མཐའ་ཡཾ། །

20(R6b) 530

Dus ldan

Kālika

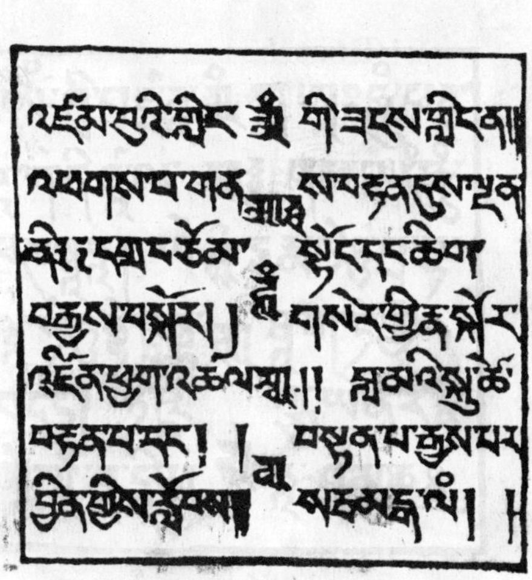

འཛམ་བུའི་གླིང་ ཧཱུྃ་ གི་ཟླ་ཚེས་གླིང་ག
འཕགས་པ་གནས་ ཨཱཿ སབ་རྡན་དུལ་ལྡན
མི། །བསྒྲང་ཚེས་ སྤྱོད་དང་ཆེག
བརྒྱལ་བསྐོར། ། ཧྲཱིཿ གསེར་གྱི་ཉ་སྐོར
འཇོན་ཕྱུག་འཆལ་བསྐྱ། ། ཀླུ་མའི་སྐུ་ཚེ
བརྟན་པ་དང་། ། བསྟན་པ་རྒྱས་པར
བྱིན་གྱིས་བརླབས། ཧཱུྃ སརྦ་མངྒ་ལཾ། །

21(R6c) 531

rDo rje mo'i bu

Vajrīputra

མི་བརྟག་པ་ཡི་སྙིང་ ཨོཾ་ ཅན། །འཕགས་པ་ར
རྡོ་རྗེ་མོ་ཡི་བུ། །ཨཱཿ བསྐལ་བཅོམ་སྐྱོང་
ཕྱག་ག་གཅིག་གིས་ བསྐོར། །ཕྱོགས་
མཛུབ་བཞ་ཡབ ཧཱུྃ འཛིན་ཕྱག་འཚལ
ནམ་འཇི་སྐུ་ཚེ་བརྟན་ སྭཱ པ་དང་། །བསྟན་པ
རྒྱས་པར་བྱིན་གྱིས་ རློབས། །ཨོཾ་བཛྲ
པུ་ཏྲ་ཀ་བཛྲ་ཡེ་སྭཱ ཧཱ ཧཱ མཎྜལ །

22(R7a) 532

bZang po

Bhadra

རྒྱུ་བོ་ཡ་མུ་ནའི་ [illegible] གླིང་ན། །འཕགས་
པ་གནས་བརྟན་ [illegible] བཟང་པོ་ནི། །དགྲ་
བཅོམ་སྟོང་དང་ [illegible] ཉིས་བརྒྱས་བསྐོར། །
ཆོས་ཀྱི་ཚད་མ་ཉེ་ མ་བཞུགས་མཛད་
[illegible]། །[illegible] [illegible] མའི་སྐུ་ཚེ་བརྟན་པ
དག །བསྟན་པ་ [illegible] རྒྱས་པར་[illegible]
[illegible]། །[illegible] མཛད་པོ། ། །

གསེར་བེའུ་

23(R7b) ·533
gSer be'u
Kanakavatsa

གནས་མཆོག་ ཏྲཱི་ དཔལ་བ་ཁ་ཆེན། །
འཕགས་པ་གན ཨཱཿ ས་བརྟན་གསེར་
བེའུ། །དགྲ་བཅོམ་ ཆེན་པོ་ལྔ་བརྒྱས
བསྐོར། །རིན་ཆེ ཧཱུྃ ན་ཞགས་པ་འཛིན
ཕྱག་འཚལ། ། སྭཱ། བླམའི་སྐུ་ཚེ་
བརྟན་པ་དང་། །ཀླུ་ བསྟན་པ་རྒྱས་པར
བྱིན་གྱིས་བརླབས། །ས་བྷ་མ་ཧ་ཡཾ། །

24(R7c) 534

Bha ra dhva dza gser can

Kanakabharadvāja

ནུབ་ཀྱི་བ་གླང་སྤྱོད་ན་ཀྵཾ་གནས་པ།། བྷ་ར་དྷྭ་
ཛ་གསེར་ཅན་ནི།། ཀཱ་ཡ་ དགྲ་བཅོམ་ཆེན་
པོ་བདུན་བརྒྱས་ བསྐོར།། ཕྱག་
གཉིས་མཉམ་བཞག ཧཱུཾ་ ཞབས་མཛད་ཕྱག་
འཚལ།། ལྷ་མའི་ ཀླུ་ སྐུ་ཚེ་བརྟན་པ་དང་།
བསྟན་པ་རྒྱས་པར་ཤོག། ཕྱི་ནང་ཕྱིར་བསྐོར་བས།།
ཨོཾ་སུ་པྲ་ཏི་ཥྛ་བཛྲ་ ཡེ་སྭཱ་ཧཱ། མཎྜ་ལ།

བ་ཀུ་ལ

25(R8a) 535

Ba ku la

Bakula

བྱང་གི་སྒྲ་མི་སྙན་ཀྱཱཾ་ན་བཞུགས། །འཕགས་པ་
གནས་བརྟན་བ་ཀུ་ལ། །དགྲ་བཅོམ་
ཆེན་པོ་དགུ་བརྒྱ་ཧཱུཾ་བསྐོར། །ཕྱག་
གཉིས་ནེའུ་ལེ་ ཛིན་ཕྱག་འཚལ།།
བླ་མའི་སྐུ་ཚེ་བ སྭཱ རྟན་པ་དང་། །བསྟན
པ་རྒྱས་པར་བྱིན་ཀཱ་གྱིས་རློབས། །ཨོཾ་
ཨུ་བྲ་ཧེ་ཙཱ་ར་དྷཱི་ ཡེ་སྭཱཧཱ། མཎྜལཾ།

26(R8b) 536

sGra gcan 'dzin

Rāhula

གྲི་ཡང་དག་ཡེ་གྲོལ་ཅན་ཀྲཱྀཾ་ཏི། །འཕགས་པ
གནས་བརྟན་སྒྲ་ ཨཱ༔ ཅན་འཛིན། །བགྲ
བཅོམ་སྡོང་དང་ཆེ་ གཱ་བརྒྱུས་བསྐོར།
རིན་ཆེན་སྤྲེག་ཕྲུ་ ཧྲཱིཿ འཛིན་ཕྱག་ཀཾ་ཡ
སྣམ་ཤིར་སྤུ་སྟོབ་རྡ་ ཛཿ མཛད་ད། །བསྟན
བརྒྱུད་པར་ཁྲིན་ ཧཿ ཁྲིས་སྐྱོབས། །ཨོཾ
སྤ་སྲ་ཊིཏྟྲ་བརྡ་ ཡེ་སྭཱཧཱ། མཛཾ་ཡཾ།

27(R8c) 537

Lam phran bstan

Cūḍapanthaka

བྷ་ར་དྷྭ་ཛ་བསོད་སྙོམས་ལེན།

28(R9a) 538

Bha ra dhva dza bsod snyoms len

Piṇḍolabharadvāja

ཤར་གྱི་ལུས་འཕགས་ [illegible] བཞུགས་གླིང་ན

[illegible]་བྷ་ར་དྷྭ་ཛ་ [illegible] བསོད་སྙོམས་

ལེན། །དགྲ་བཅོམ་ སྟོང་ཕྲག་གཅིག

གིས་བསྐོར། ། [illegible] གླེགས་བམ་ལྷུང་

བཟེད་[illegible] [illegible]། །[illegible]

[illegible] [illegible]། །བསྟོད་པ

[illegible] [illegible]། །

29(R9b) 539

Lam bstan

Panthaka

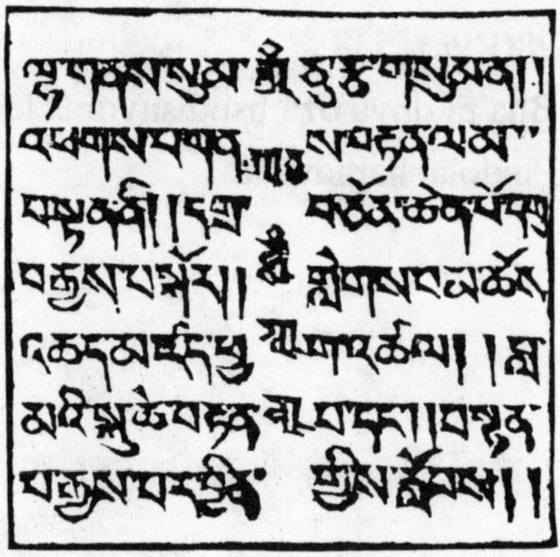

ལྷ་གནས་སུམ་ཅུ་རྩ་གསུམ་ན། །
འཕགས་པ་བཅས་ [illegible] ལ་བ་དྲུག་ལམ་
བསྟན་ནི། །དགྲ་བཅོམ་ཆེན་པོ་བརྒྱ
བརྒྱས་པ་བསྐོར། །སྐྱོབས་པ་མཆོད་
ངེས་མཛད་པ་ཀ་ཆོས། །ཐུ
མའི་སྐུ་ཚེ་བརྟན་པ་བཏག །བསྟན་
པ་རྒྱས་པ་ [illegible] གྱིས་རློབས། །

30(R9c) 540
Klu'i sde
Nāgasena

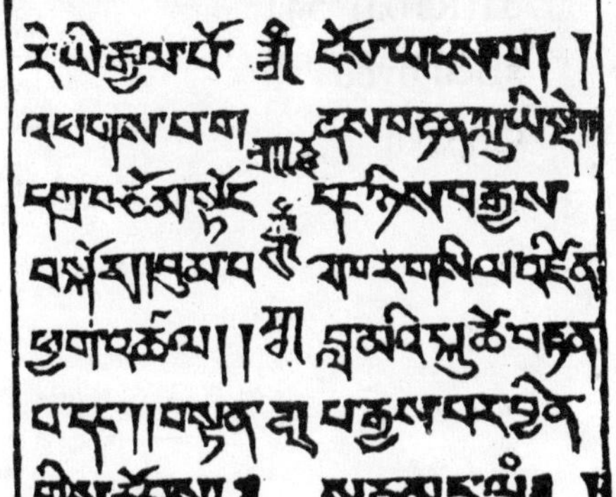

31(R10a) 541
sBed byed
Gopaka

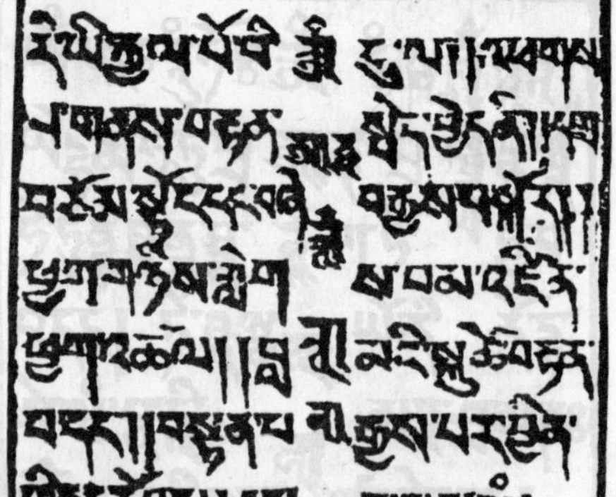

32(R10b) 542
Mi phyed
Abheda

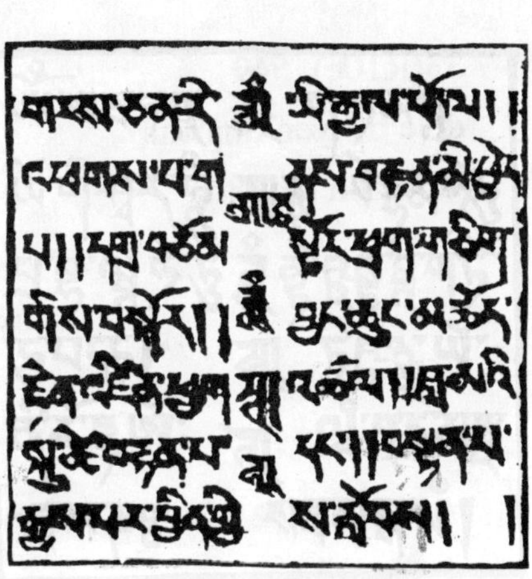

33(R10c) 543

dGe bsnyen dharma

Upāsaka Dharma

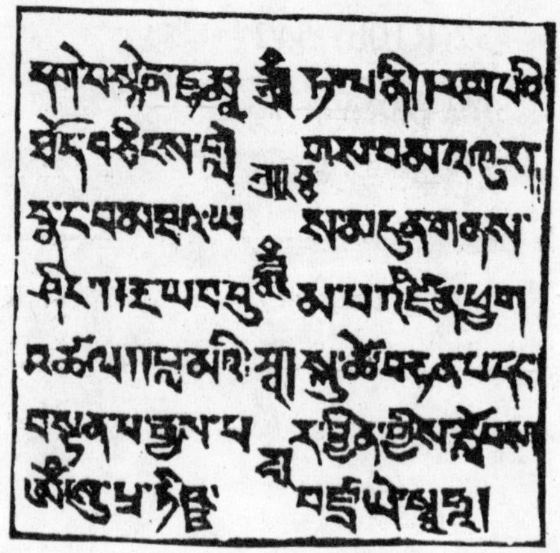

34(R11a) 544

Hwa shang

སངས་རྒྱས་གཞན་ ཧཱུྃ་ མཐུ་ལྡན་འཁོར་དང་
བཅས། །སྤྱན་དྲང་ སྟན་དུ་རྟེན་སྤྱིན་
བཞུགས་སུ་གསོལ། །ག སྨྲང་གི་བསྡུ་ཏུ
ཀྲུང་བཞེངས། ། ཧྲཱིཿ བདེན་མཐོང་ཧྭ་ཤང་
ལ་ཕྱག་འཚལ་ལོ། །སྭཱ་ དུས་ཀྱི་མཐར་
ཡང་བསྟན་པ་ སྭཱ་ མཆོག །ཕྱོགས་
བཅུར་རྒྱས་པའི་ སྦྱིན་བདག་མཛོད། །

ཡུལ་འཁོར་བསྲུང་

35(R11b) 545
Yul 'khor bsrung
Dhṛtarāṣṭra

རྒྱལ་པོ་ཆེན་པོ་ཤྲཱི་དཔལ་ལྡན་པ། །མ
ཁང་མདོག་མཆོག་[illegible]ལས་པི་ཝཾ་འཛིན། །
དྲི་ཟའི་ཚོགས་ ཧཱུྃ ལ་དབང་བསྒྱུར་
བའི། །ཡུལ་འཁོར་བསྲུང་ལ་ཕྱག་
འཚལ་ལོ། །ལྷམ་ཡཱ་འི་སྐྱེ་བོ་བརྟན་པ་
དང་། །བསྟན་པ་རྒྱས་ཞིང་པ་འི་འཕྲིན་ལས་
མཛོད། །ཨོཾ་ཛམ་བྷ་ ཧ་བཛྲ་ཡེ་སྭཱ་ཧཱ།

འཕགས་སྐྱེས་པོ

36(R11c) 546
’Phags skyes po
Virūḍhaka

དཔའ་བོ་ཆེན་པོ་ཨཱཾ སྟོབས་པོ་ཆེ། །
སྐུ་མདོག་སྔོན་པོ་ཨཱཿ རལ་གྲི་འཛིན། །
གྲུལ་བུམ་ཚོགས་ ས་ལ་དབང་བསྒྱུར
བའི། །འཕགས་ཧཱུྃ སྐྱེས་པོ་ལ་ཕྱག
འཚལ་ལོ། །ནྲྀ་ཛཿ མའི་སྐུ་ཚེ་བརྟན
པ་དང་། །བསྟན་ཛཿ པ་རྒྱས་པའི་ཕྲིན
ལས་མཛོད། ། [illegible]། །

མིག་མི་བཟང་

37(R12a) 547

Mig mi bzang

Virūpākṣa

མངའ་བདག་ཆེན་ཧཱུྃ་པོ་སྟོབས་པོ་ཆེ།།
ཁ་དོག་དམར་པོ་ [illegible] སྒྲ་ལ་ཞགས་
འཛིན།། ཀླུ་དབང་ ཚོགས་ལ་དབང་
བསྒྱུར་བའི།། ཧཱུྃ་ སྤྱན་མི་བཟང་ལ་
ཕྱག་འཚལ་ལོ།། [illegible] བླ་མའི་སྐུ་ཚེ་བརྟན་
པ་དང་།། བསྟན་པ་ [illegible] རྒྱས་པའི་འཕྲིན་
ལས་མཛོད།། ས་ ཏམ་དྲ་ཡཾ། །

རྣམ་ཐོས་སྲས་

38(R12b) 548
rNam thos sras
Vaiśravaṇa

དེ་དཔོན་ཆེན་པོ་ ཧཱུྃ་ གསེར་མདོག
ཅན། །རྒྱལ་མཚ ཨཱཿ ན་དང་ནི་ནེའུ་ལེ
འཛིན། །གནོད་སྦྱི ན་ཚོགས་ལ་
དབང་བསྒྱུར་བའི། ཨོཾ་ །རྣམ་ཐོས་སྲས
ལ་ཕྱག་འཚལ་ ལོ། །ཕྲམ་ཨིཥྨུ་ཆེ
བརྟན་པ་དང་། །བ ཀྲཱ་ཤིས་ལྷུན་པ་རྒྱས་པའི་
འབྲིན་པས་མཛོད་ དོ། །སརྦམངྒ་ལཾ།

39(R12c) 549

bKa’ gdams lha bzhi’i nang gi shākya thub pa

Śākyamuni among the four bKa’ gdams deities

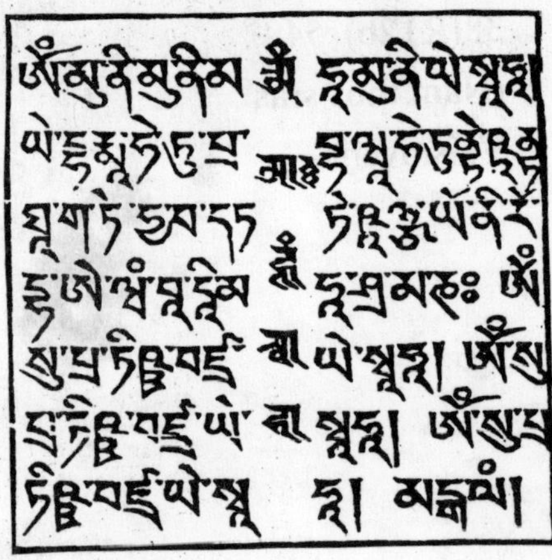

40(R13a) 550

Zla ltar snang byed

Candravairocana

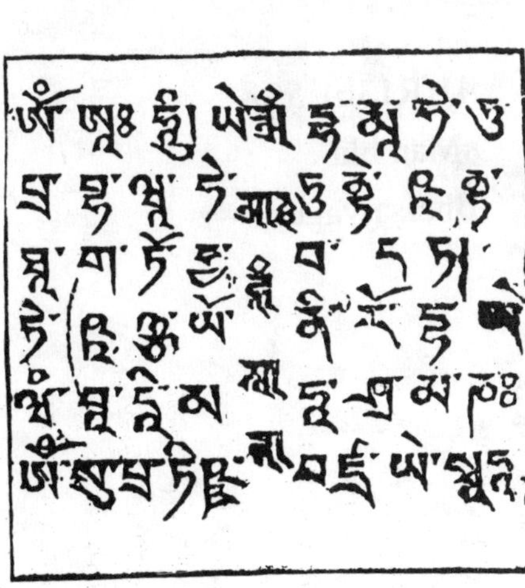

41(R13b) 551
sMan bla
Bhaiṣajyaguru

བཅོམ་ལྡན་འདས་དེ་བཞིན་གཤེགས་པ
དགྲ་བཅོམ་པ་ཡང་དག་པར་རྫོགས་པའི
སངས་རྒྱས་སྨན་གྱི་བླ་བཻ་ཌཱུརྻ་འོད་ཀྱི་
རྒྱལ་པོ་ལ་ཕྱག་འཚལ་ལོ། །མཆོད་དོ་
སྐྱབས་སུ་མཆིའོ། ། ན་མོ་བྷ་ག་ཝ་ཏེ།
བྷཻ་ཥ་ཛྱེ་གུ་རུ་བཻ་ཌཱུརྻ་པྲ་བྷ་རཱ་ཛཱ་ཡ། ཏ་ཐཱ
ག་ཏཱ་ཡ། ཨརྷ་ཏེ་སམྱཀ་སཾ་བུདྡྷཱ་ཡ། ཏདྱ
ཐཱ། ཨོཾ་བྷཻ་ཥ་ཛྱེ་བྷཻ་ཥ་ཛྱེ། མ་ཧཱ་བྷཻ་ཥ་ཛྱེ།
ས་མུདྒ་ཏེ་སྭཱ་ཧཱ། ཨོཾ་སུ་པྲ་ཏིཥྛ་བཛྲ་
ཡེ་སྭཱ་ཧཱ།

42(R13c) 552

Nyi ltar snang byed

Sūryavairocana

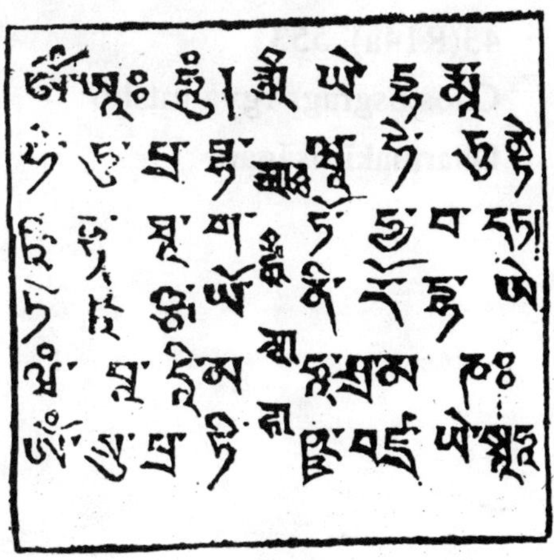

43(R14a) 553

Chos bsgrags rgya mtsho

Dharmakīrtisāgara

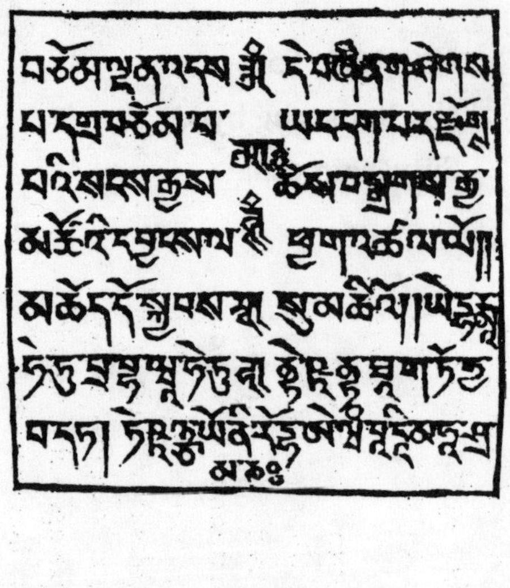

44(R14b) 554
mNgon mkhyen rgyal po
Abhijñarāja

བཅོམ་ལྡན་འདས་དེ་ཀྱི་བཞིན་གཤེགས་པ་
དགྲ་བཅོམ་པ་ཡང་དག་པར་རྫོགས་པའི་
སངས་རྒྱས་ཆོས་སྒྲ་ཀྱི་མཚོ་མཆོག་གི་བློས་
རྣམ་པར་རོལ་པས་མངོན་པར་མཁྱེན་
པའི་རྒྱལ་པོ་ལ་ཕྱག་འཚལ་ལོ།། མཆོད་
དོ་སྐྱབས་སུ་མཆིའོ།། ཨོཾ་སུ་ཀྲ་ཏི་
བཛྲ་ཡེ་སྭཱ་ཧཱ། སཙམཧྲཡཾ།

45(R14c) 555·

Mya ngan med mchog

Aśokottama

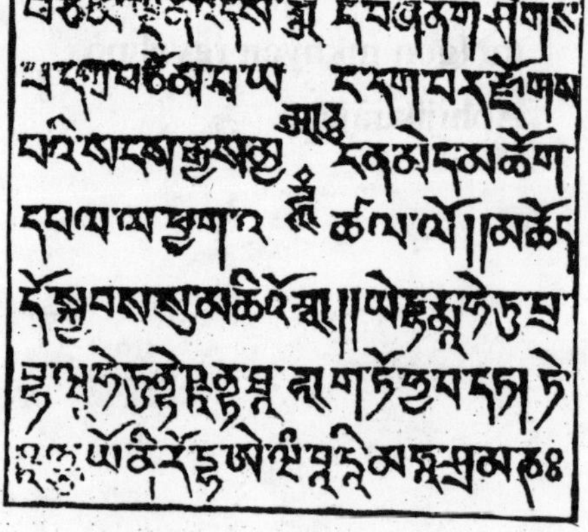

46(R15a) 556

Rin chen zla ba

Ratnacandra

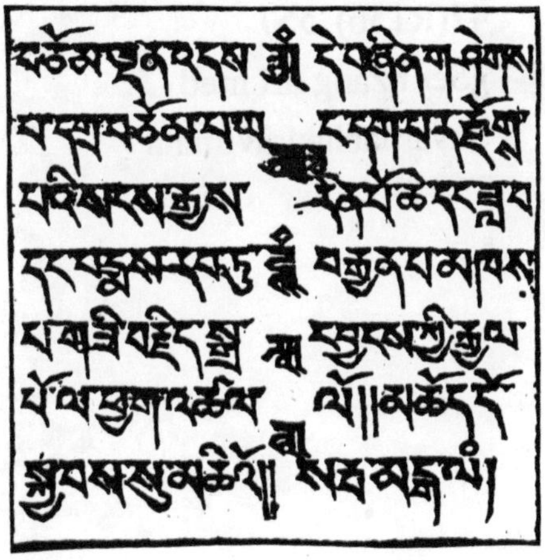
བཅོམ་ལྡན་འདས་ ༀ་ དེ་བཞིན་གཤེགས
པ་དགྲ་བཅོམ་པ་ཡང་ དག་པར་རྫོགས
པའི་སངས་རྒྱས་ རིན་པོ་ཆེ་ཟླ་བ
[illegible] ཧཱུྃ་ [illegible]
[illegible]
པོ་ལ་ཕྱག་འཚལ་ལོ། ||མཆོད་དོ
སྐྱབས་སུ་མཆིའོ|| [illegible]

47(R15b) 557

gSer bzang dri med

Suvarnabhadravimala

བཅོམ་ལྡན་འདས་ དེ་བཞིན་གཤེགས་
པ་དགྲ་བཅོམ་པ་ཡང་དག་པར་རྫོགས་
པའི་སངས་རྒྱས་ གསེར་བཟང་དྲི་མེད་
རིན་ཆེན་སྣང་བརྟུ ལ་ཞུགས་གྲུབ་པ་
ལ་ཕྱག་འཚལ་ལོ། མཆོད་དོ། སྐྱབས་
སུ་མཆིའོ། ཨོཾ་ སུ་པྲ་ཏི་ཥྛ་བཛྲེ་
ཡེ་སྭཱཧཱ། སརྦ [illegible]

48(R15c) 558
mTshan legs
Sunāman

བཅོམ་ལྡན་འདས་ཨཱཿ དེ་བཞིན་གཤེགས
པ་དགྲ་བཅོམ་པ་ཡང་[illegible] དག་པར་རྫོགས
པའི་སངས་རྒྱས་ཧཱུྃ་ མཚན་ལེགས་པར
ཡོངས་བསྒྲགས་ དཔལ་གྱི་རྒྱལ་པོ
ལ་ཕྱག་འཚལ་ལོ། [illegible] །མཆོད་དོ་སྐྱབས་སུ
མཆིའོ། །ཨོཾ་[illegible] [illegible] [illegible]
[illegible] [illegible]

49(R16a) 559

'Khor Byams pa, sGrib sel

Attendant Maitreya and Nīvaraṇa-viṣkambhin

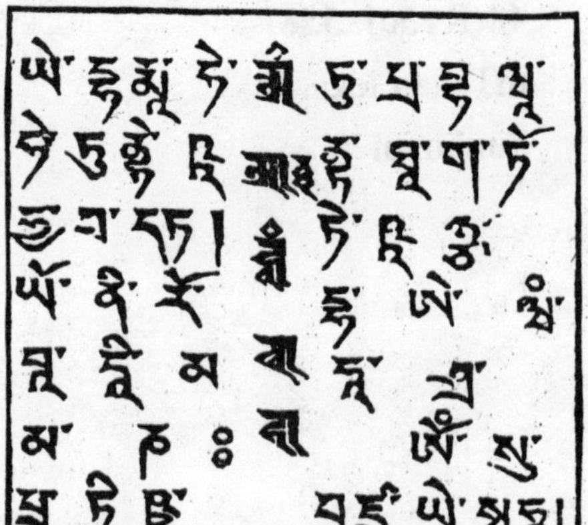

50(R16b) 560

Klu dbang rgyal po

Nāgeśvararāja

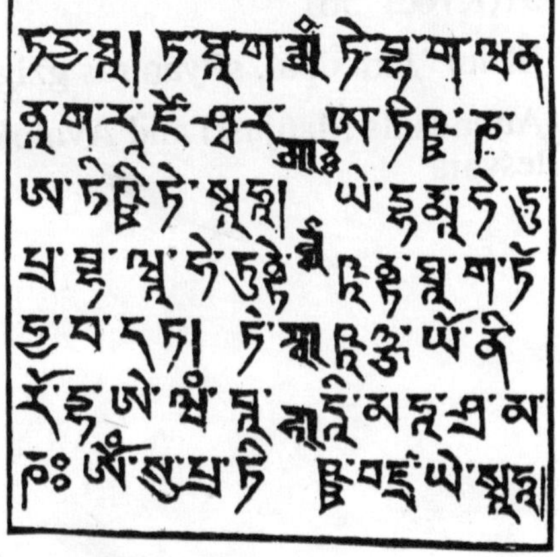
ཏདྱ་ཐཱ། ཏ་ཐཱ་ག་ཏཾ་ཏེ་ཛཱ་ག་ཤན
ནཱ་ག་ར་ཛེ་ཤྭ་ར་ ཀཱཥྛ་ ཨ་ནི་ཙྪ་ཧཱ
ཨ་ཏི་ཙྪི་ཏེ་སྭཱ་ཧཱ། ཡེ་ཛྷ་སྨཱ་ཏེ་ཙུ
པྲ་ཛཱ་ལྷཱ་ཏེ་ཙུ་ཎྜེ་ཤཱཾ་ཙྪ་ཀྲ་ཐཱ་ག་ཏོ
ཙུ་བ་ད་ཏ། ཏེ་ཀྵཱ་ཙྪ་ཨཱུཾ་ཡོ་ཀེ
རོ་ཛྷ་ཨེ་སྭཱཾ་སྭཱ་ཀྵཱ་ཏྲ་མ་ཏྲ་ཤྲ་མ
ཏཿ ཨོཾ་སུ་པྲ་ཏི་ ཙྪ་བཛྲ་ཡེ་སྭཱ་ཧཱ།

51(R16c) 561

'Khor 'Jam dpal, sPyan ras gzigs

Attendants Mañjuśrī and Avalokiteśvara

ཡེ་དྷརྨཱ་ཧེ་ཏུ་པྲ་བྷ་ཝཱ་ཧེ་
ཏུནྟེ་ཥཱན྄་ཏ་ཐཱ་ག་ཏོ་ཧྱ་ཝ་དཏ།
ཏེ་ཥཱཉྩ་ཡོ་ནི་རོ་དྷ་ཨེ་ཝཾ་
ཝཱ་དཱི་མ་ཧཱ་ཤྲ་མ་ཎཿ ཨོཾ་སུ
པྲ་ཏིཥྛ་བཛྲཱ་ཡེ་སྭཱ་ཧཱ།
ཨོཾ་སུ་པྲ་ཏིཥྛ་བཛྲ་ཡེ་སྭཱཧཱ
ཨ་ཙ་མཉྫུ་ཤྲཱི། ཧྲཱི་ཨ་ཧཱུ།

52(R17a) 562
gSang 'dus 'jam rdor
Guhyasamāja Mañjuvajra

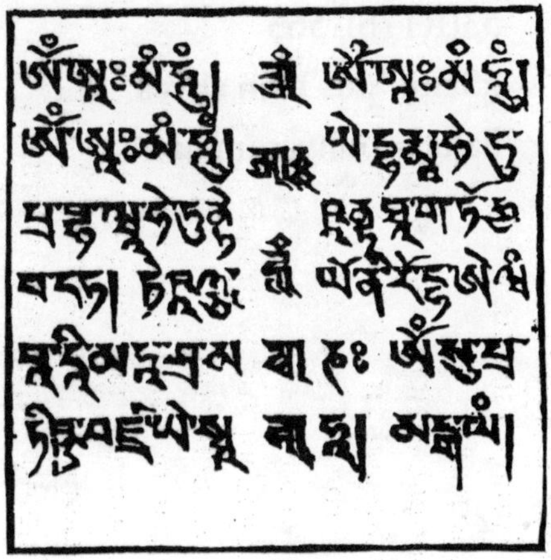

53(R17b) 563
gSang 'dus lhan skyes
Sahaja Guhyasamāja

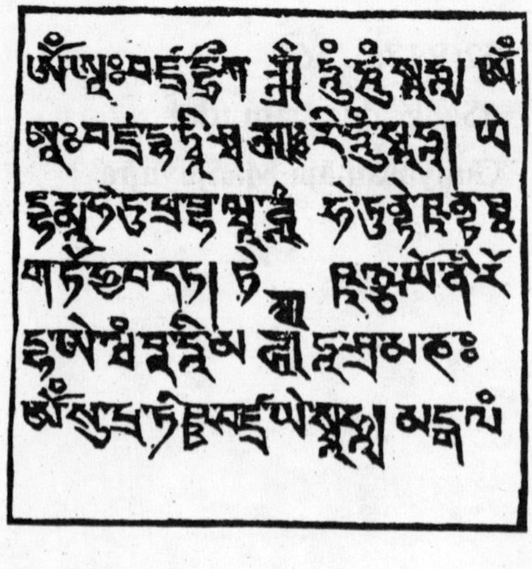

54(R17c) 564

Ma hā ma ya

Mahāmāyā

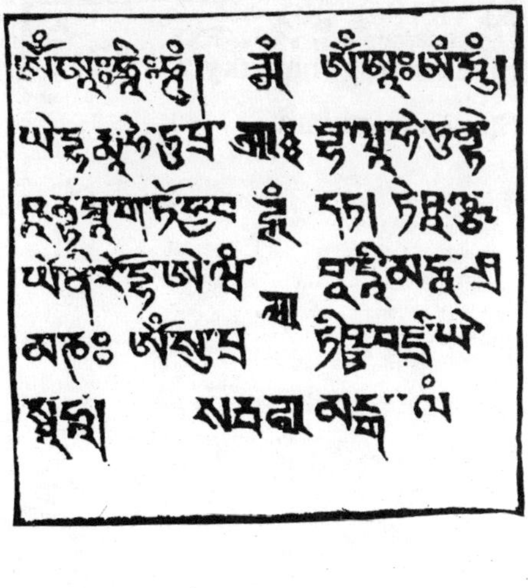

55*(R18a) 565

bDe mchog lhan skyes

Sahaja Samvara

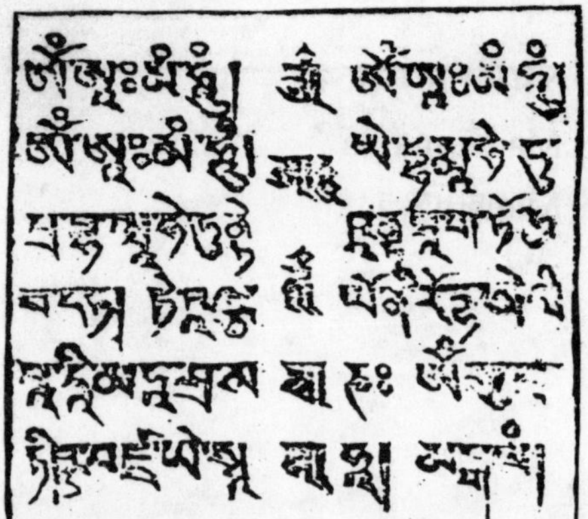

56*(R18b) 566

Go cha'i rdo rje sems dpa'

Kavaca Vajrasattva

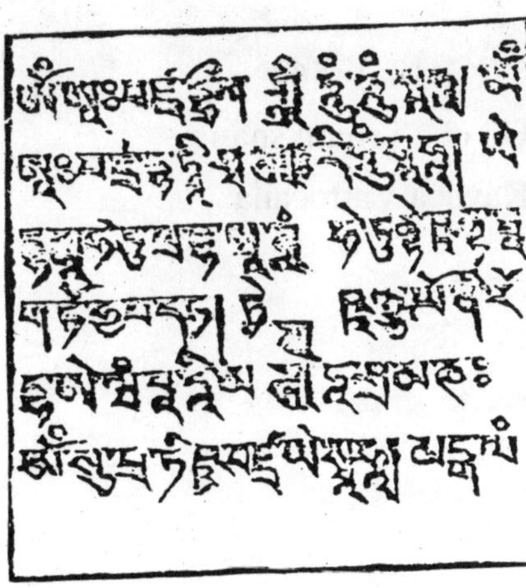

57*(R18c) 567

Go cha'i rnam snang

Kavaca Vairocana

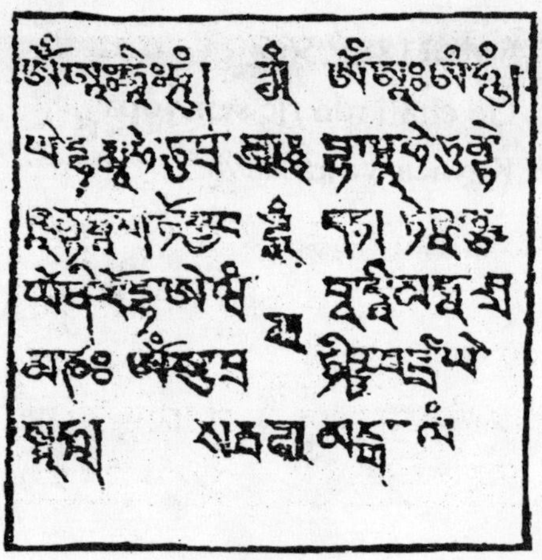

58(R19a) 568

Go cha'i padma gar dbang

Kavaca Padmanarteśvara

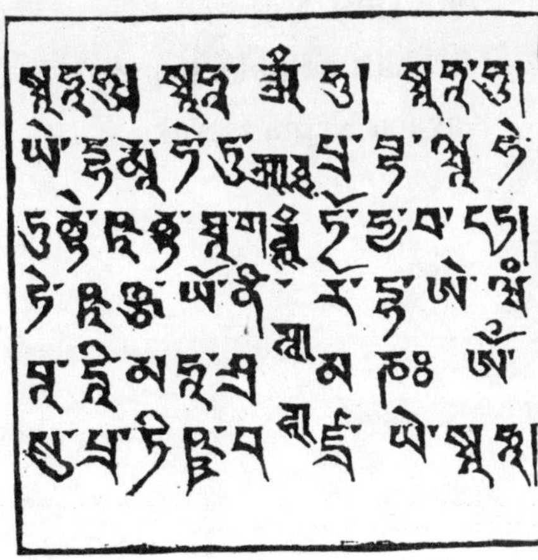

59(R19b) 569

Go cha'i he ru ka nag po

Kavaca Kṛṣṇa Heruka

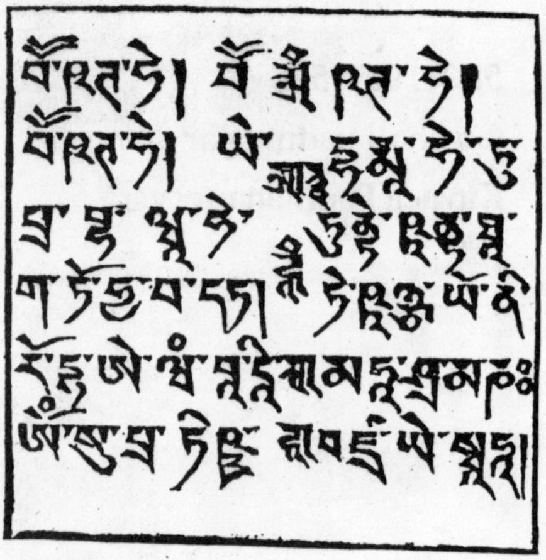

60(R19c) 570

Go cha'i rdo rje nyi ma

Kavaca Vajrasūrya

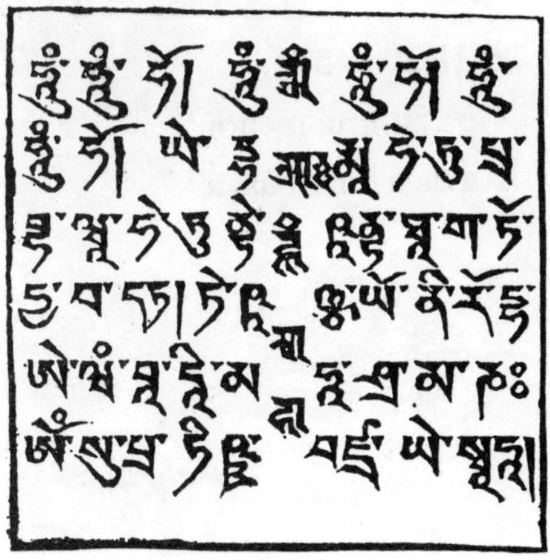

61(R20a) 571
Go cha'i rta mchog
Kavaca Paramāśva

ཕཊ་ཧཱུྃ། ཀྲཱི་ཕཊ་ཧཱུྃ། ཕཊ་
ཧཱུྃ། ཡེ་དྷརྨཱ་ཧེ་ཏུ་པྲ་བྷ་ཝཱ་ཧེ་
ཏུ་ནྟེ་ཥཱན་ཏ་ཐཱ་ག་ཏོ་ཧྱ་བ་དཏ།
ཏེ་ཥཱཾ་ཙ་ཡོ་ནི་རོ་དྷ་ཨེ་ཝཾ་
བཱ་དཱི་མ་ཧཱ་ཤྲ་མ་ཎཿ ཨོཾ་
སུ་པྲ་ཏིཥྛ་བཛྲ་ཡེ་སྭཱ་ཧཱ།

62(R20b) 572

Go cha 'i rdo rje phag mo

Kavaca Vajravārāhī

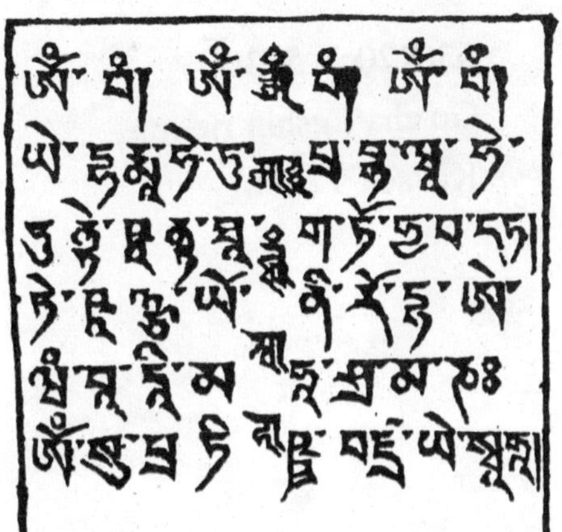

63(R20c) 573

Go cha'i gshin rje ma

Kavaca Yāminī

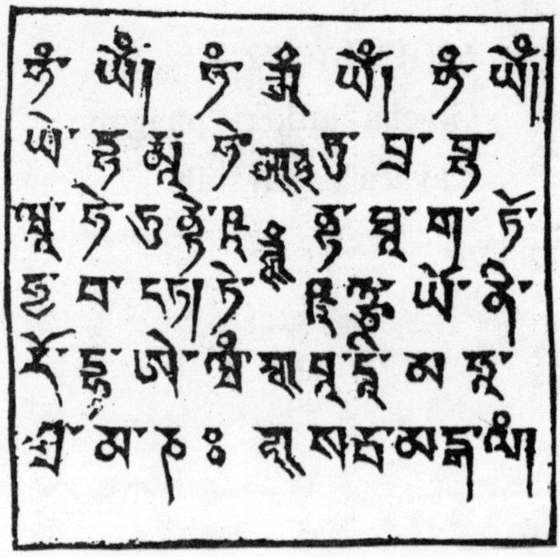

64(R21a) 574
Go cha'i rmongs byed ma
Kavaca Mohinī

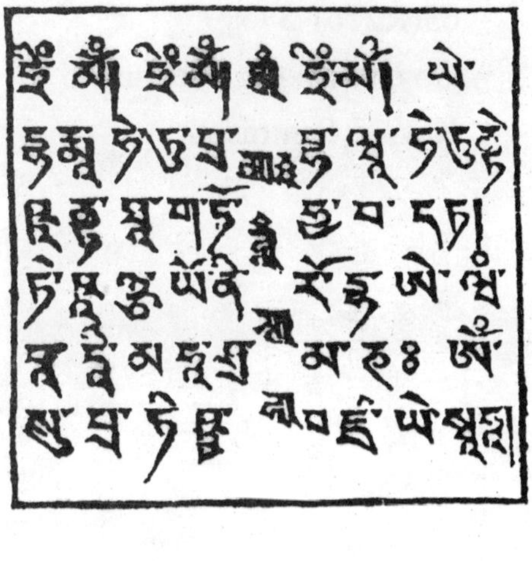

65(R21b) 575

Go cha'i skrag byed ma

Kavaca Santrāsinī

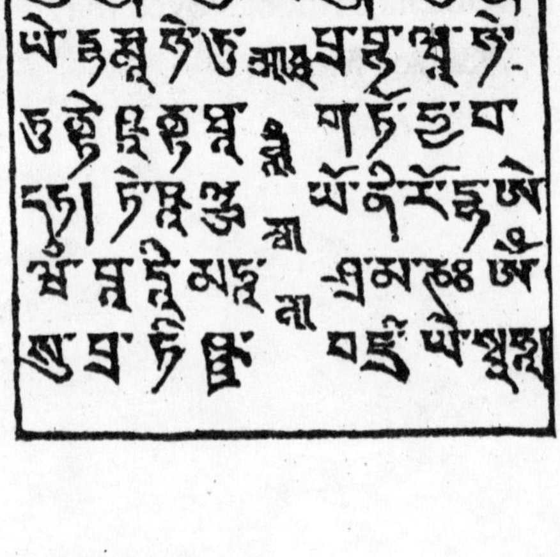

66(R21c) 576

Go cha'i bskyed byed ma

Kavaca Sañcālinī

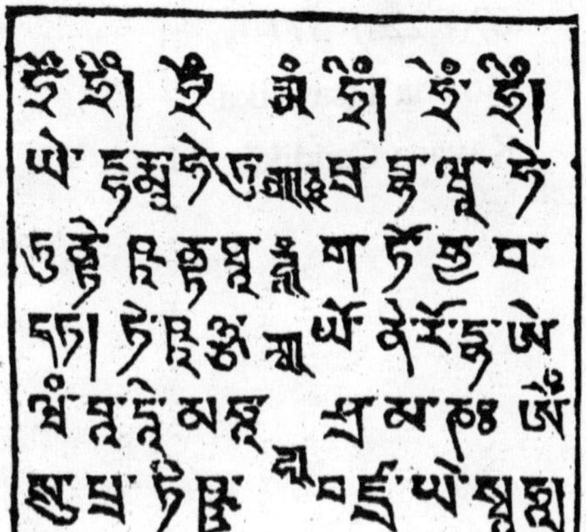

67(R22a) 577

Go cha'i tsaṇḍika

Kavaca Caṇḍikā

ཕཎ་ཕཊ། ཕ་ཊ་ཀྵཱིཾ་ཕཊ། ཕཎ་ཕཊ།
ཡེ་ རྣྨ་ དེ་ ཧུཨཱཧྲཱུྃཔྲ་ ཧྲ་ཕྲུ་ དེ་
ཧུ་ཀྵེ་ ཛྷ་ ཀྵ་ ཧྲཱུ་ཀྵཱིཾ་ ཎ་ ཏེ་ ཉྫ་ བ་
དཧ། དེ་ ཛྷ་ ཀྵྨ་ ཡོ་ ནི་ རོ་ ཧྲ་
ཨོཾ་ ཀྵཱིཾ་ ཧྲ་ དྲི་ ཀྵ་ མཧཱ་ཤྲམ་ཧཿ
ཨོཾ་ ཀྵ་ ཕྲ་ ཏྲི་ཀྵཿ བཛྲ་ཡེ་སྭཱཧཱ།

68(R22b) 578
bDe mchog dkar po
Sita Saṃvara

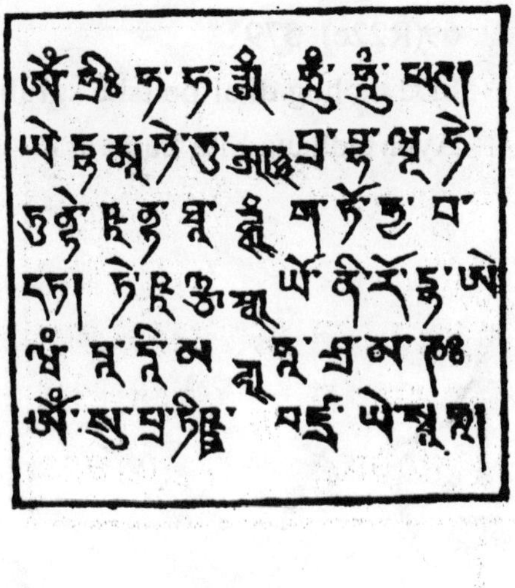

69(R22c) 579

bDe mchog dkar po tshe sgrub

Āyuḥsādhana Sita Saṃvara

ཨོཾ་ཧྲཱིཿ ཧ་ཧ་ཧྲཱི། ཧཱུཾ་ཧཱུཾ་ཕཊ་ཨ་མ
ཨཱ་ཡུར་པུཎྱེ་ཛྙཱ་ན་ཀུ་རུ་ཨོཾ་ཡེ་
དྷརྨཱ་ཧེ་ཏུ་པྲ་བྷ་ཝཱ་ཧེ་ཏུནྟེ་ཥཱན་
ཏ་ཐཱ་ག་ཏོ་ཧྱ་ཝ་དཏ། ཏེ་ཥཱཉྩ་ཡོ་ནི་
རོ་དྷ་ཨེ་ཝཾ་ཝཱ་དཱི་མ་ཧཱ་ཤྲ་མ་ཎཿ
ཨོཾ་སུ་པྲ་ཏིཥྛ་བཛྲ་ཡེ་སྭཱ་ཧཱ།

70*(R23a) 580

’Jig rten dbang phyug yi ge bdun pa

Saptākṣara Lokeśvara

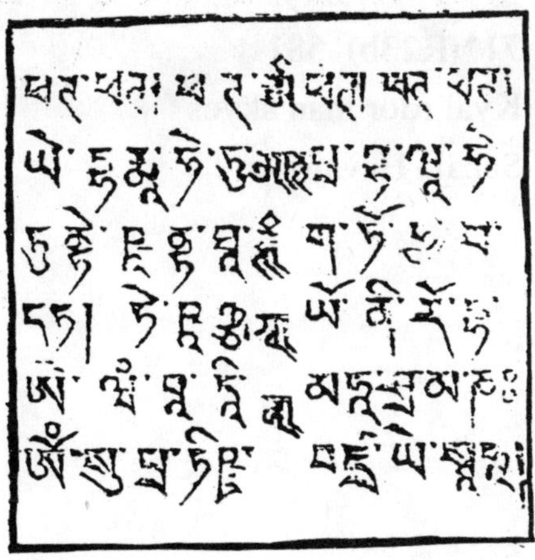

71*(R23b) 581

Kyai rdor lhan skyes

Sahaja Hevajra

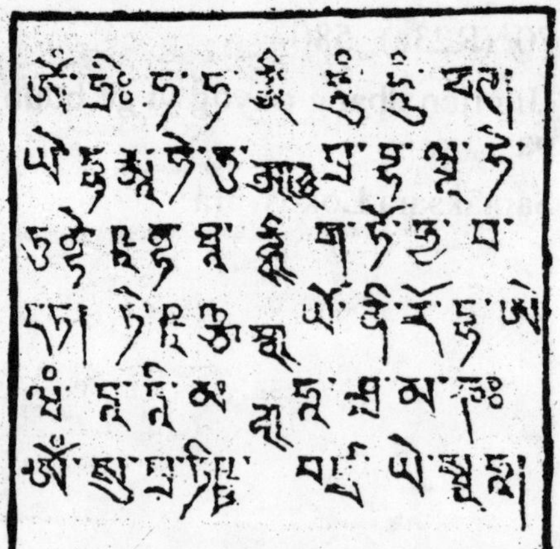

72*(R23c) 582
Dus 'khor lhan skyes
Sahaja Kālacakra

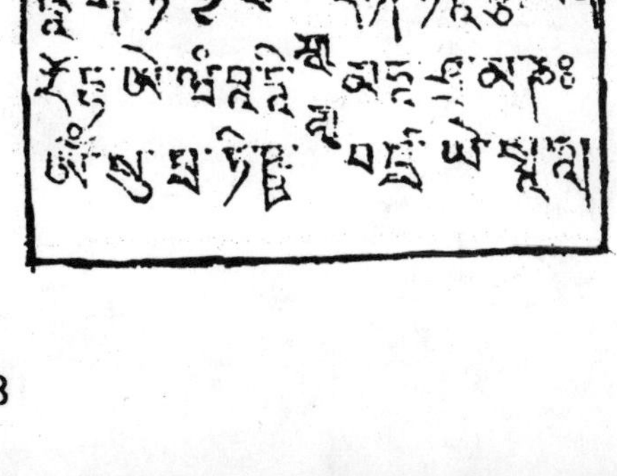

73*(R24a) 583
rDo rje shugs
Vajravega

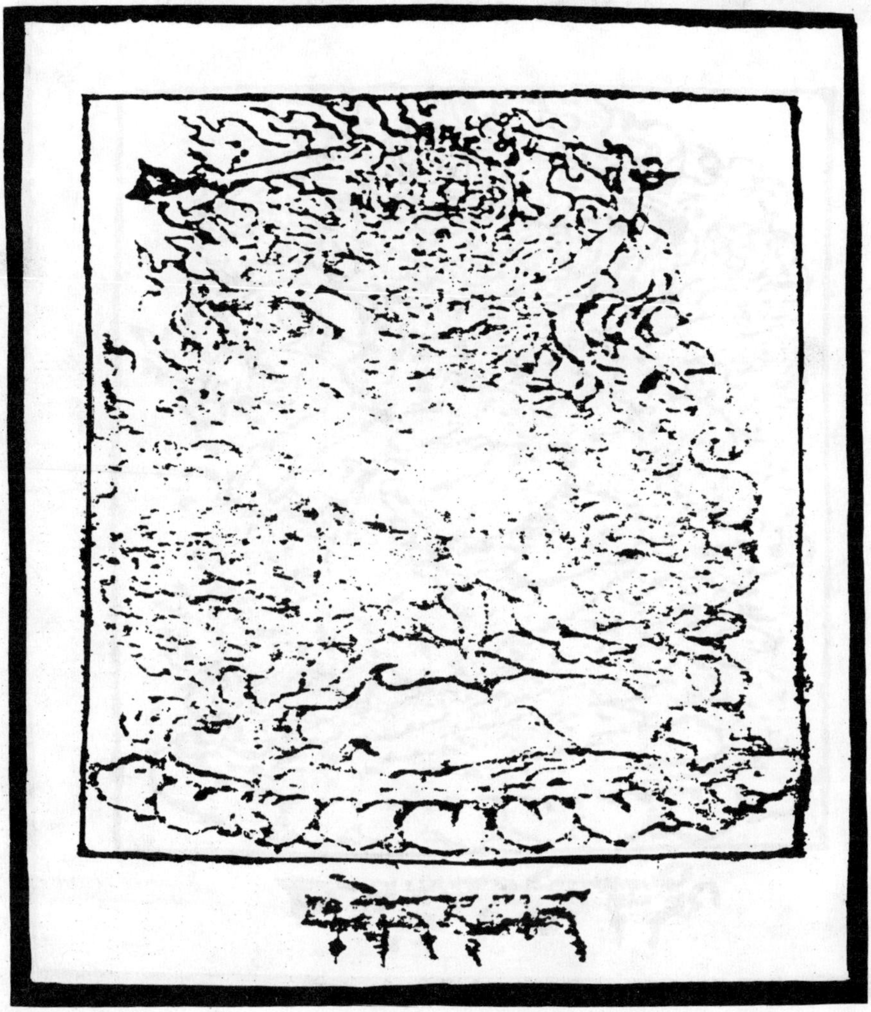

74*(R24b) 584

gShed dmar

Rakta Yamāri

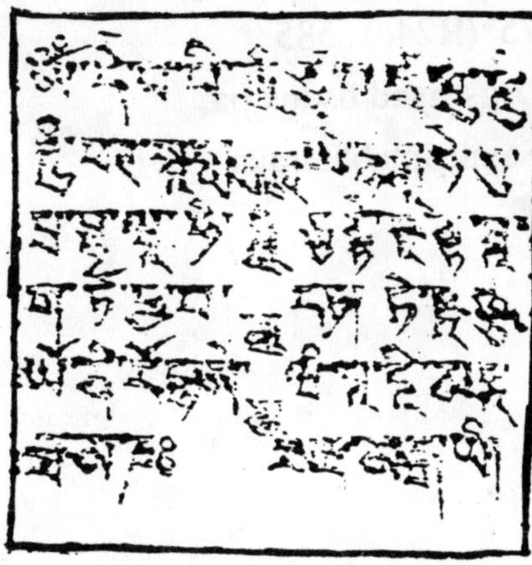

75*(R24c) 585

’Jigs byed bsdus pa

Saṃkṣiptabhairava

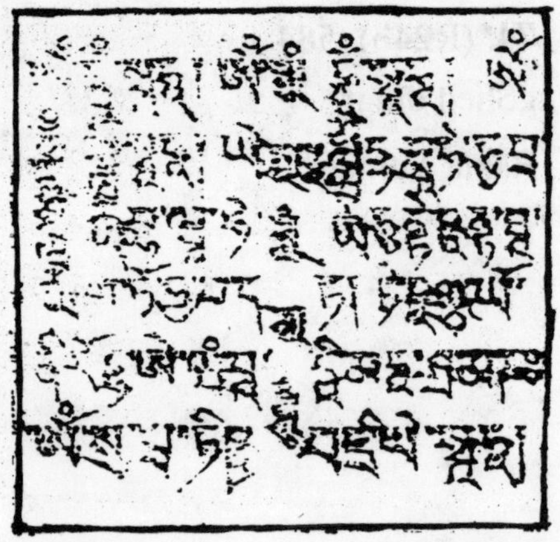

76*(R25a) 586
dPyal lugs rdo rje phag mo
Vajravārāhī of dPyal school

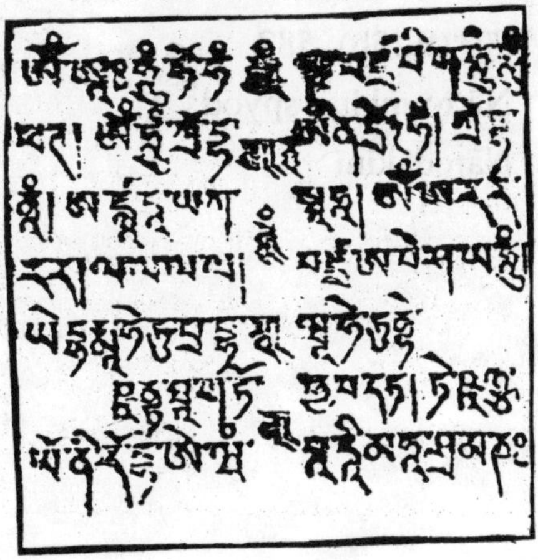

ནཱ་རོ་མཁའ་སྤྱོད་

77*(R25b) 587

Nā ro mkha' spyod

Nāroḍākinī

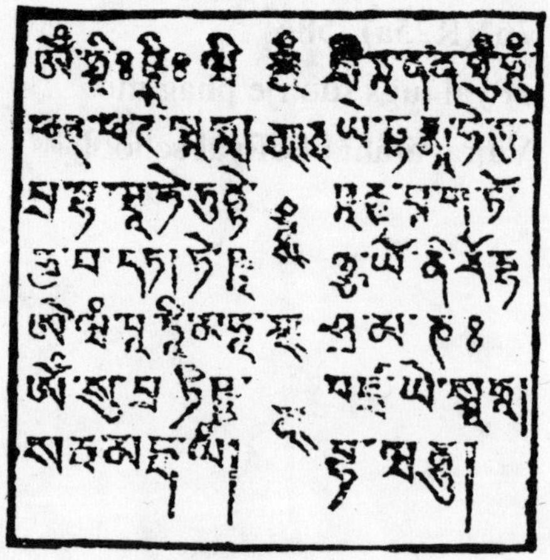

78*(R25c) 588
Mai tri mkha' spyod
Maitrīḍākinī

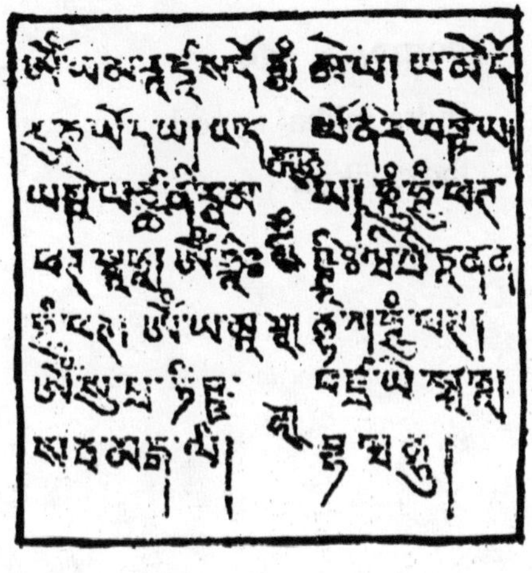

79(R26a) 589
Indra mkha' spyod
Indraḍākinī

ཨོཾ་ཨོཾ་ཨོཾ་སརྦ་ [illegible] བུདྡྷ་ཌཱ་ཀི་ནཱི་ཡེ།
བཛྲ་ཝརྞ་ནཱི་ཡེ། [illegible] བཛྲ་བཻ་རོ་ཙ་ནཱི་ཡེ།
ཧཱུཾ་ཧཱུཾ་ཧཱུཾ་ཕཊ་ཕཊ་ ཕཊ་སྭཱ་ཧཱ། ཨེ་
[illegible]
[illegible]
[illegible] ཨོཾ་[illegible]
[illegible] སྭཱ་ཧཱ། ।

80(R26b) 590
Phag mo don grub
Arthasādhanavārāhī

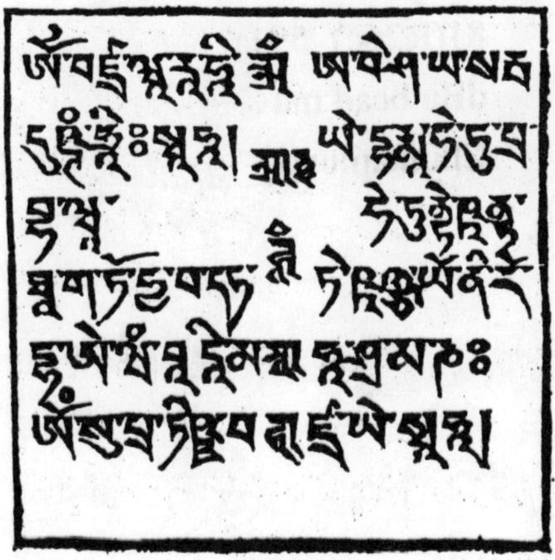

81(R26c) 591
dBu bcad ma
Chinnamuṇḍā

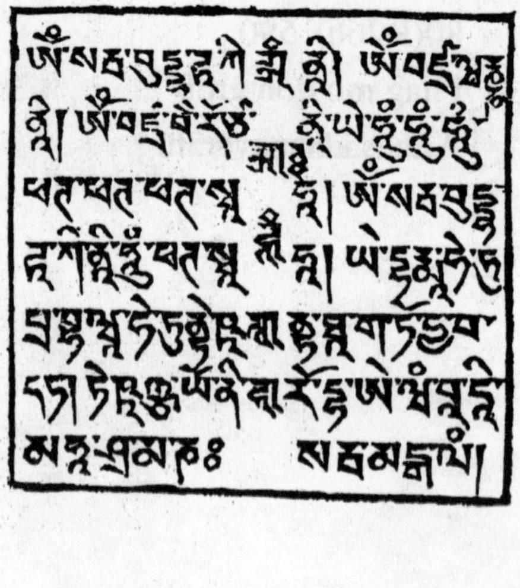

82(R27a) 592

rDo rje rab sngags ma

Vajrapraṇavā

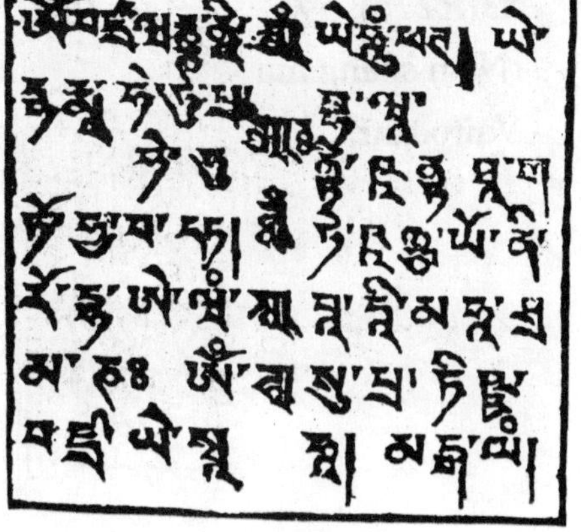

83(R27b) 593
rNam snang ma
Vairocanī

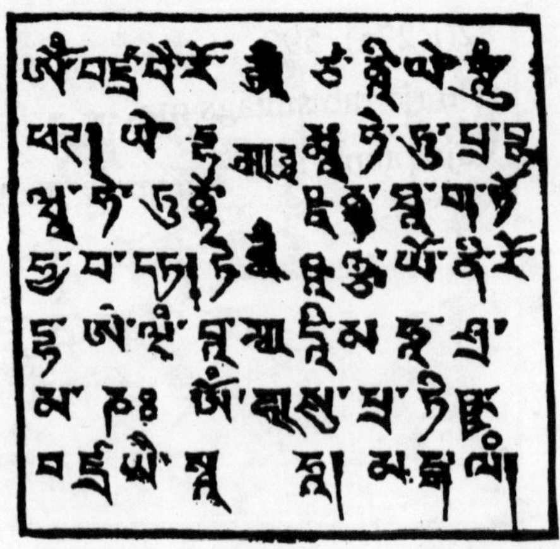

84(R27c) 594
Phag mo.gnam zhabs ma
Ūrdhvapādī Vārāhī

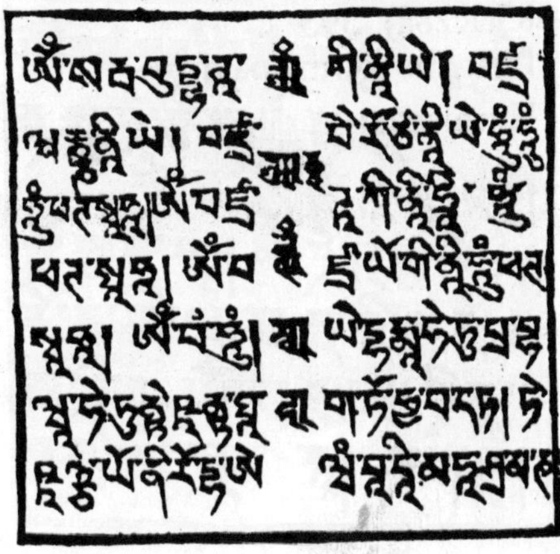

85(R28a) 595
Phag mo kurma pā dī
Kūrmapādī Vārāhī

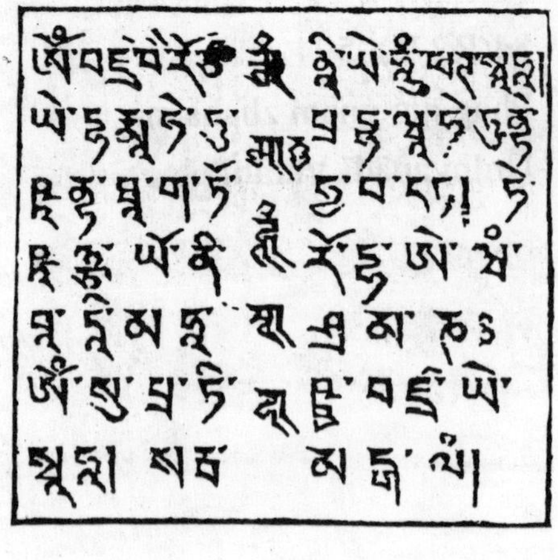

86(R28b) 596

Bram ze dPal 'dzin lugs kyi rdo rje phag mo

Varjavārāhī of Brāhmaṇa Śrīdhara school

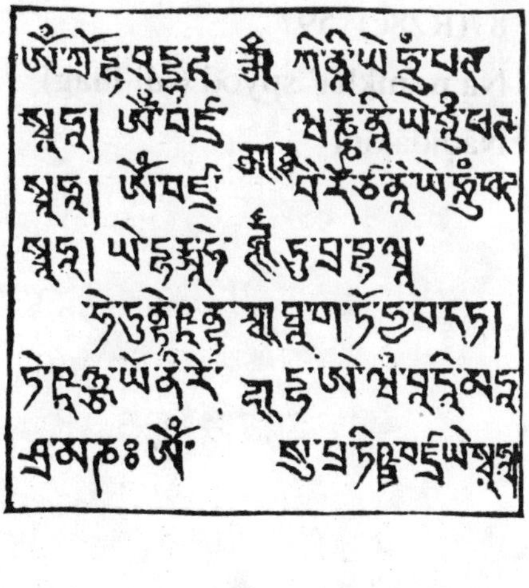

87(R28c) 597

Nā ro mkha' spyod ('di lhag)

Nāḍīḍākinī

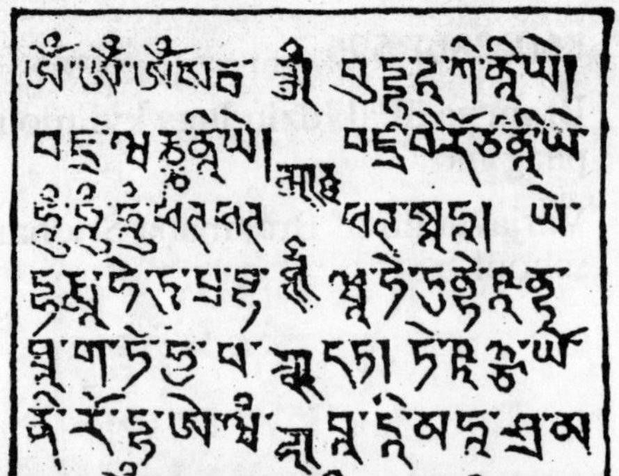

88(R29a) 598
Go bzlog lhan skyes
Sahaja Go bzlog

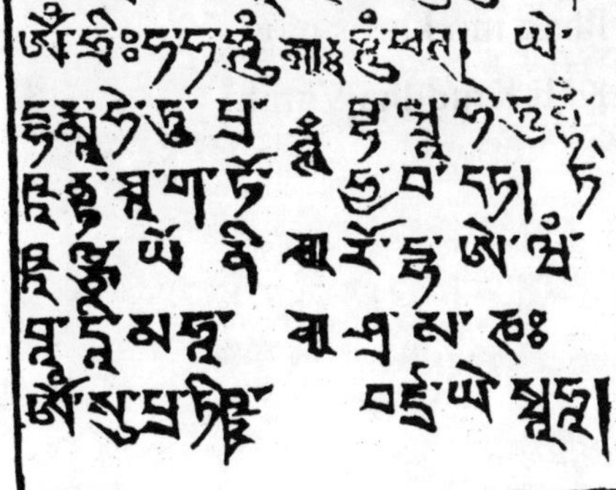

89(R29b) 599

Phag mo khros nag

Kālī Kruddha Vārāhī

ཨོཾ་ཧྲཱི་བཛྲ་ཝཱ་ར་ཧི ཧྲཱི ཧྲི་ཤྲཱི་ཧྲཱུ་ཀྲཱུ་ཧྲཱི་ཨ
ཌཱ་ཀི་ནི་ས་ཨ་བེ ཨཱཿ ཤ་ཡ། སརྦ་ཀརྨ
ཧྲཱཾ་ཧྲཱུཾ་བན་སྭཱ་ཧཱ། ཡེ་དྷརྨཱ་ཧེ་ཏུ་པྲ
བྷ་ཝཱ་ཧེ་ཏུ་ཏེ་ཥཱན྄ ཧྲཱུཾ ཏ་ཐཱ་ག་ཏོ་ཧྱ་བ་དཏ྄
ཏེ་ཥཱཉྩ་ཡོ་ནི་རོ་དྷ ཧཱུཾ ཨེ་ཝཾ་བཱ་དཱི་མ་ཧཱ
ཤྲ་མ་ཎཿ ཨོཾ་སུ ཁཱ་བ་ཏི་བཛྲ་ཡེ
སྭཱ་ཧཱ། སརྦ་མ་ཎ ཡཾ། ཧཱུཾ་ཕཊ྄།

90(R29c) 600

rDo rje mkha' 'gro ma

Vajraḍākinī

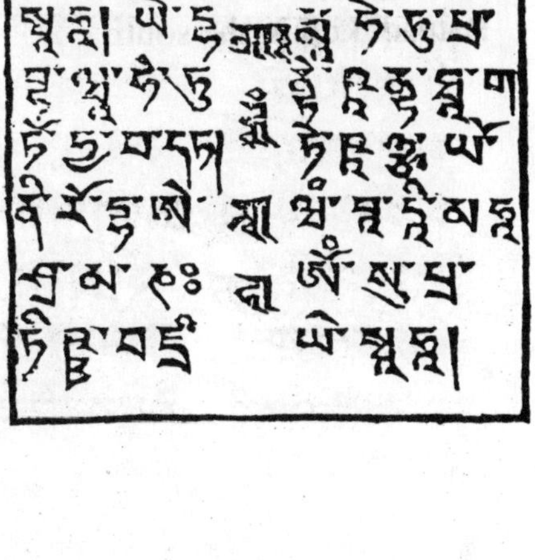

ལྷོ་རིན་ཆེན་མཁའ་འགྲོ་མ

91(R30a) 601

lHo Rin chen mkha' 'gro ma

Ratnaḍākinī in the south

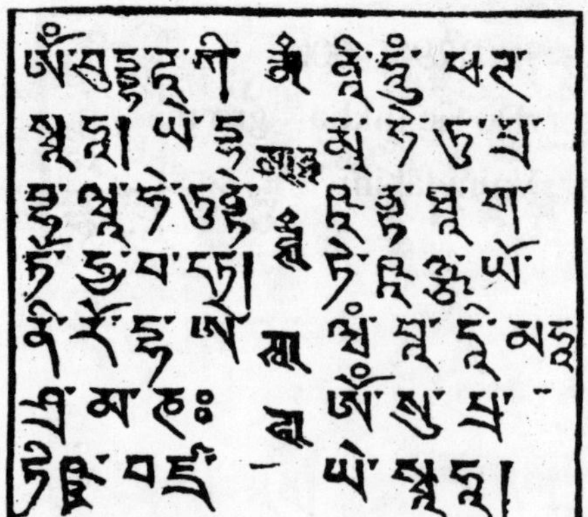

92(R30b) 602

Nub Padma mkha' 'gro ma

Padmaḍākinī in the west

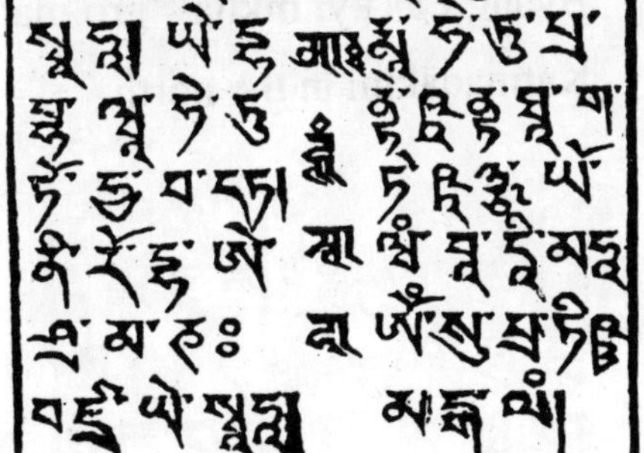

93(R30c) 603

Byang Las kyi mkha' 'gro ma

Karmaḍākinī in the north

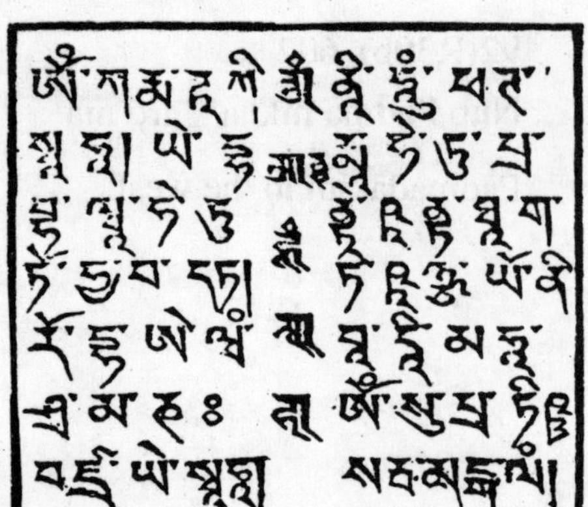

94(R31a) 604

Dam tshig mkha' 'gro

Samayaḍākinī

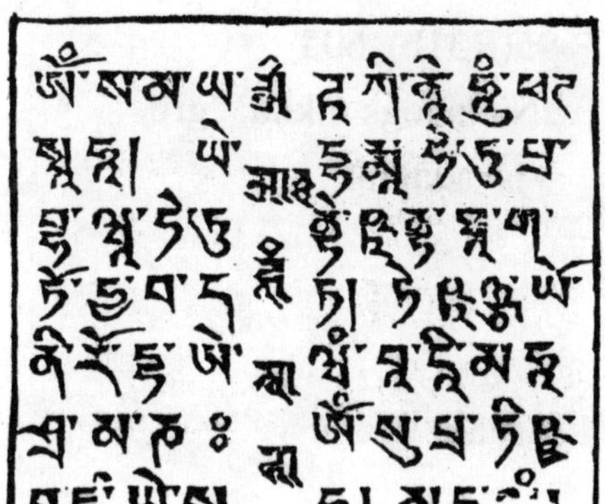

95(R31b) 605
sNa tshogs mkha' 'gro
Viśvaḍākinī

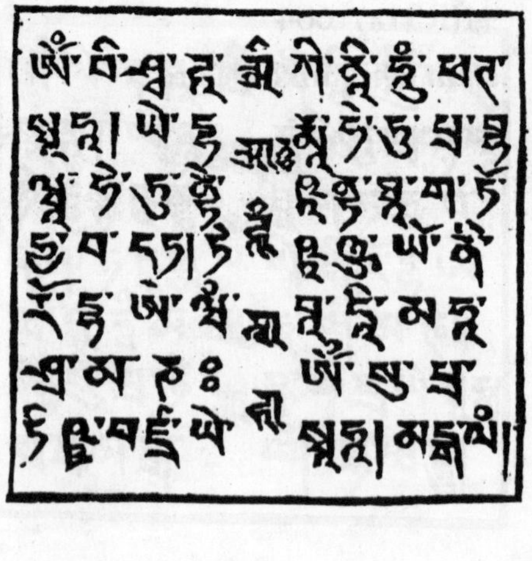

96(R31c) 606
Thams cad mkha' 'gro
Sarvaḍākinī

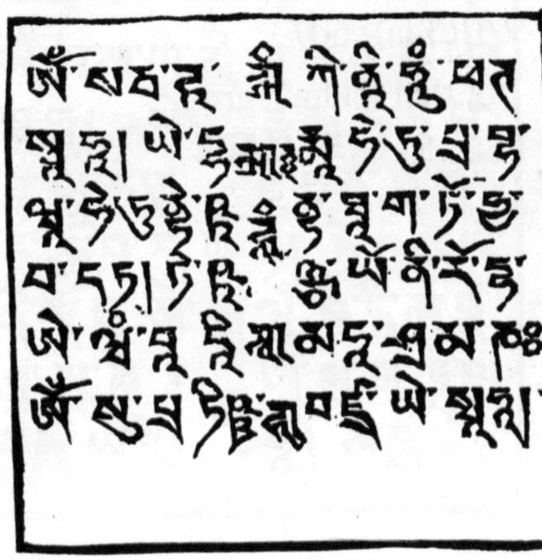

97(R32a) 607

'Jig rten mkha' 'gro

Lokaḍākinī

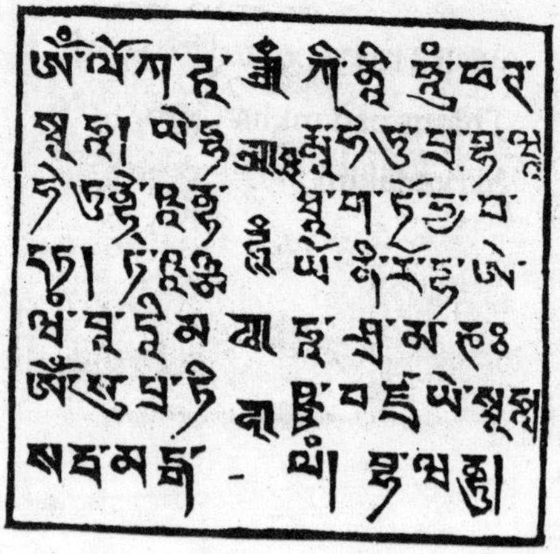
ཨོཾ་ལོ་ཀ་ཌཱ་ཀཱི་ཀི་ནི་ཧཱུྃ་ཕཊ་
སྭཱ་ཧཱ། ཡེ་དྷརྨཱ་ཧེ་ཏུ་པྲ་བྷ་ཝཱ
ཧེ་ཏུནྟེ་ཥཱན྄་ཏ་ཐཱ་ག་ཏོ་ཧྱ་ཝ
དཏ྄། ཏེ་ཥཱཉྩ་ཡོ་ནི་རོ་དྷ་ཨེ་
ཝཾ་ཝཱ་དཱི་མ་ཧཱ་ཤྲ་མ་ཎཿ
ཨོཾ་སུ་པྲ་ཏིཥྛ་བཛྲ་ཡེ་སྭཱ་ཧཱ
ས་ཏ་མ་ཏ - ཡཾ། [illegible]

98(R32b) 608

Phag dkar shes rab gsal byed

Prajñālokakṛtya Sita Vārāhī

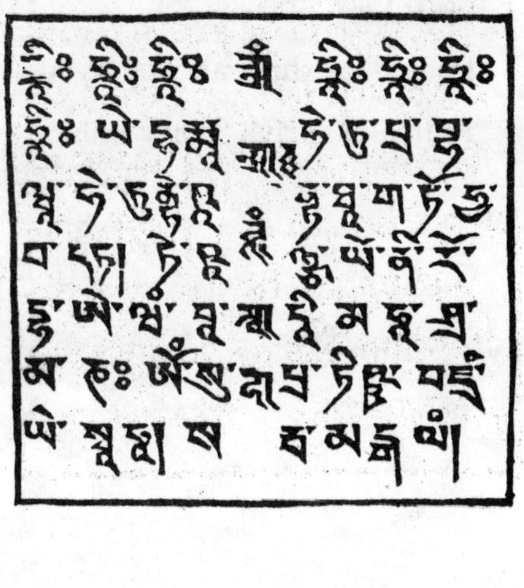

99(R32c) 609

Phag dkar shes rab gsal byed

Prajñālokakṛtya Sita Vārāhī

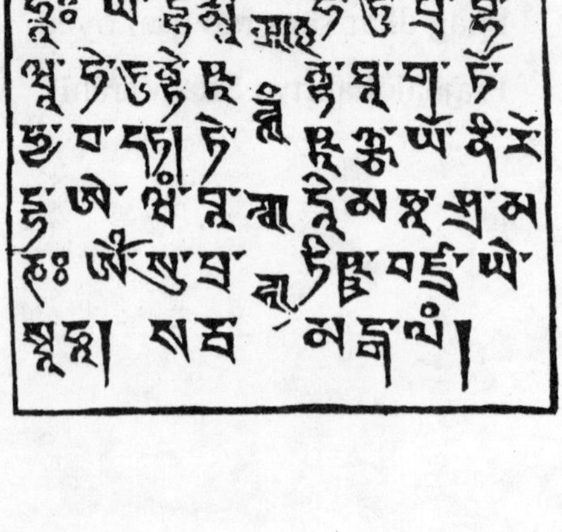

100(R33a) 610

Nor bu 'dzin pa

Maṇidhārin

ཡེ་དྷརྨཱ་ཧེ་ཏུ་པྲ་ བྷ་ ཧེ་ཏཱུན་ཏེ་ཥཱཾ
ཏ་ཐཱ་ག་ཏོ་ཧྱ་ [illegible] ཝ་ད་ཏ་ཏེ་ཥཱཾ
ཙ་ཡོ་ནི་རོ་དྷ་ ཨེ་ཝཾ་ཝཱ་དི་མ་ཧཱ
ཤྲ་མ་ཎཿ [illegible] ཡེ་དྷརྨཱ་ཧེ་ཏུ
པྲ་བྷ་ཝ་ཧེ་ཏུན་ཏེ་ ཥཱཾ་ ཏ་ཐཱ་ག་ཏོ
ཧྱ་ཝ་ད་ཏ་ཏེ་ཥཱཾ་ ཙ་ ཡོ་ནི་རོ་དྷ
ཨེ་ཝཾ་ཝཱ་དི་མ་ཧཱ ཤྲ་མ་ཎཿ

101(R33b) 611

sPyan ras gzigs yi ge drug pa jo bo lugs

Ṣaḍakṣarāvalokiteśvara of Atīśa school

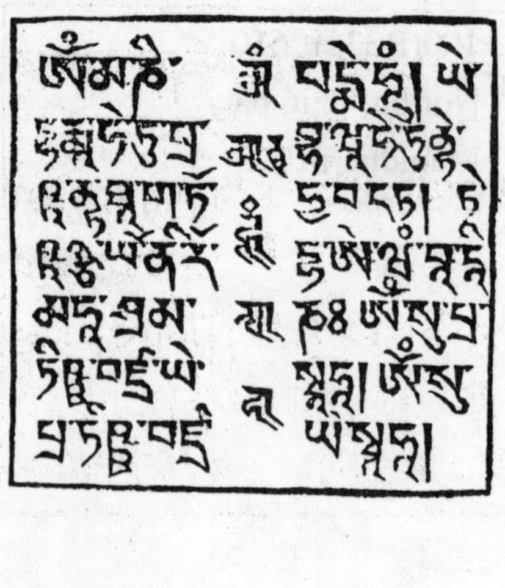

102(R33c) 612

Yi ge drug ma

Ṣaḍakṣarī

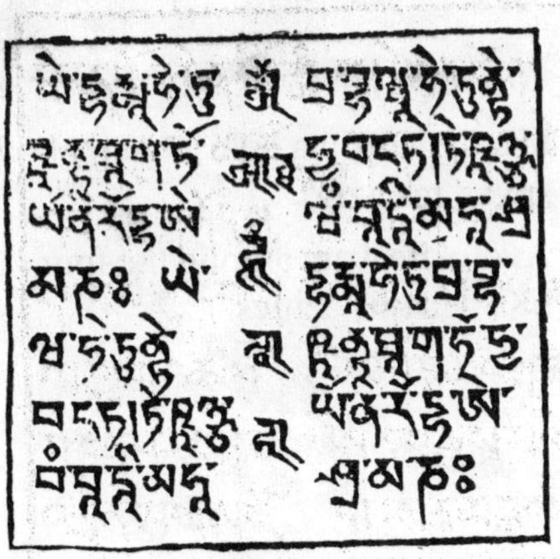

103(R34a) 613

bKa' gdams lha bzhi'i nang gi spyan ras gzigs

Avalokiteśvara among the four bKa' gdams deities

ཨོཾ་མ་ཎི་པདྨེ་ཧྲཱིཿཧཱུྃ། ཨོཾ་མ་ཎི་
པདྨེ་ཧཱུྃ། ཨོཾ་མ་ཎི་པདྨེ་ཧཱུྃ།
ཡེ་དྷརྨཱ་ཧེ་ཏུ་པྲ་བྷ་ཝཱ་ཧེ་ཏུན྄་ཏེ་
ཥཱན྄་ཏ་ཐཱ་ག་ཏོ་ཧྱ་བ་དཏ྄། ཏེ་ཥཱཉྩ་
ཡོ་ནི་རོ་དྷ་ཨེ་ཝཾ་བཱ་དཱི་མ་ཧཱ་
ཤྲ་མ་ཎཿ ཨོཾ་སུ་པྲ་ཏིཥྛ་
བཛྲ་ཡེ་སྭཱ་ཧཱ། ས་ཙ་ཀ་ཛྙ་ལོ།

104(R34b) 614

sPyan ras gzigs bcu gcig zhal dpal mo'i lugs

Eleven-faced Avalokiteśvara of Lakṣmī school

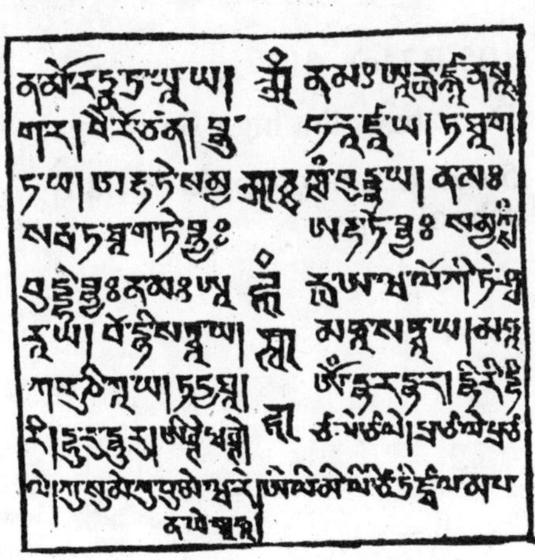

105(R34c) 615

Don zhags lha lnga Ba ri lugs

5-deity Amoghapāśa of Ba ri school

ནམཿསམནྟབུདྡྷཱ་ནཱཾ་ས ཧྲཱིཾ ཙ་ཏྲ་བྱ་ག་ཏ་ཨ་མོ་ཡོ་ག
ཏེ་སྭཱ་ཧཱ་ཨ་མ་ཡ། སྲི་ཧྣ་ཡེ ཧྲཱུཾ་ཛ་སྭཱ་ཧཱ། ཨོཾ་ཧྲཱིཿ་ཏྲི་ལོ་ཀྱ
བི་ཛ་ཡ་ཨ་མོ་གྷ་པཱ་ཤ་ཨ་ཨཱཿཧཱུཾ་ཕཊ་ཏ་ད་ཏྲི་ཏ་ད་ཧཱུཾ་ཕཊ
སྭཱ་ཧཱ། ནམཿསམནྟབུདྡྷཱ་ ཀྵཾ་ཌི་ཁ་ད་ཧཱུཾ་ཕཊ་ཏྲ་ཡ་སྭཱཧཱ
ཨོཾ་ཨ་མེ་ཤ་ཌ་ཧཱུཾ་མ་དྷ་ར་ཁ་ཧཻ། ཧཱུཾ་ཧཱུ་ས་ཡ་དྷུ་ས་ཡ། སམ་ས
མ། ཏྲ་ཤ་མ་ཏ་ཡ་སྭཱ་ཧཱ། ན་ མཿསམནྟབུདྡྷཱ་ཀྵཾ། ས་ཙ་ཏྲ
ཡ་བ་ཙུ་ར་ཏྲེ་ཧྲཱུཾ་ཧྲཱུཾ་ཕཊ་པ་ སྭཱ ཏ་ཡ་སྭཱ་ཧཱ། ཡེ་དྷརྨཱ་ཧེ་ཏུ
པྲ་བྷ་ཝཱ་ཧེ་ཏུ་ཏེ་ཥཱན་ཏ་ཐཱ་ག་ཏོ་ཧྱ་བ་དཏ། ཏེ་ཥཱཉྩ་ཡོ་ནི
རོ་དྷ་ཨེ་ཝཾ་བཱ་དཱི་མ་ཧཱ་ཤྲ་མ་ཎཿ ཡ་ཐ་མ་ཛྙཱ་ལཾ།

106(R35a) 616

'Khor Don zhags dmar po, rTa mgrin

Attendant Rakta Amoghapāśa and Hayagrīva

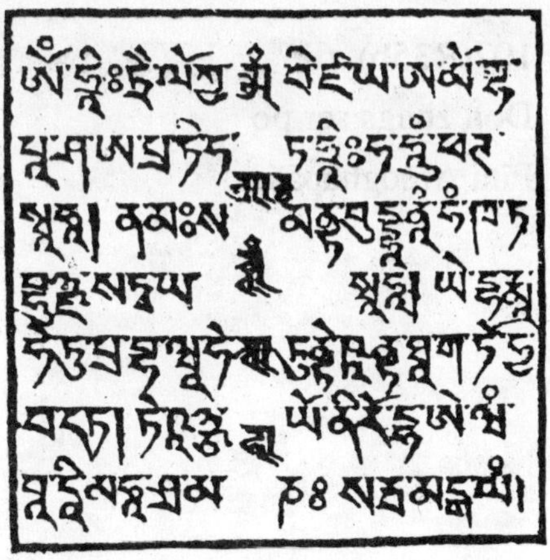

107(R35b) 617

Don zhags ser po

Pīta Amoghapāśa

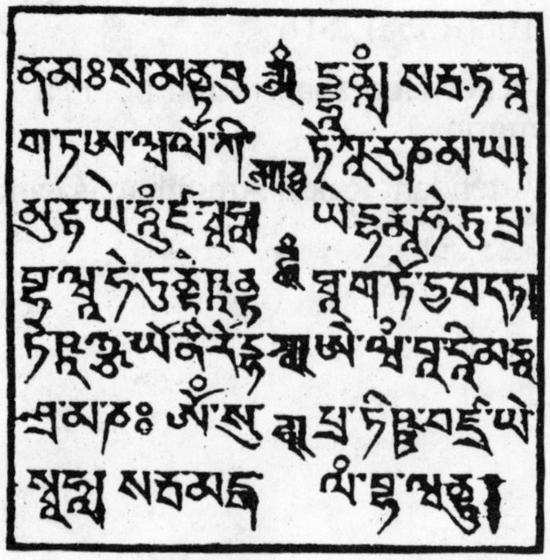

108(R35c) 618

'Khor Khro gnyer can ma, Ral gcig ma

Attendant Bhṛkuṭī and Ekajaṭā

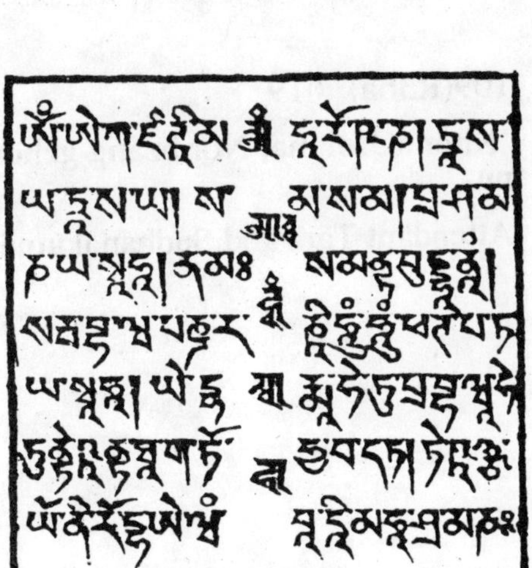

109(R36a) 619

'Khor sGrol ma, Nor bzang gzhon nu

Attendant Tārā and Sudhanakumāra

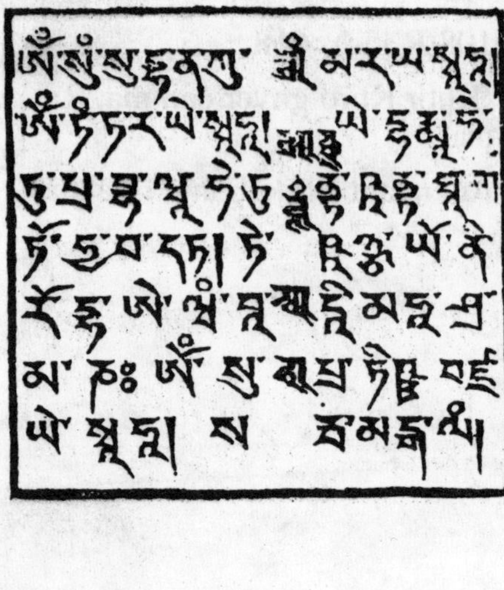

110(R36b) 620

Don zhags kha che paṇ chen lugs

Amoghapāśa of Kāśmīramahāpaṇḍita school

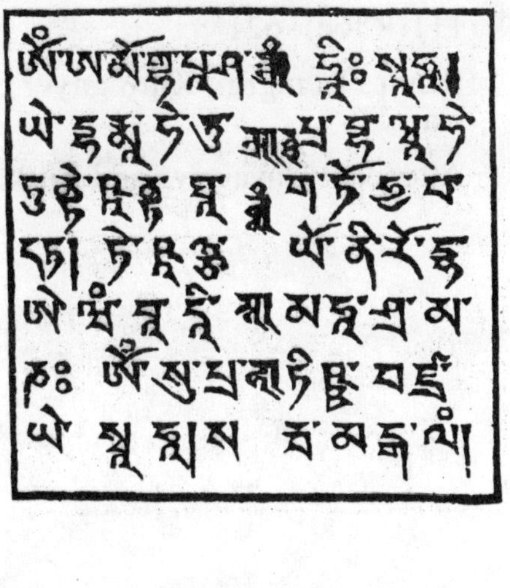

111(R36c) 621

'Khor rTa mgrin, Khro gnyer can ma

Attendant Hayagrīva and Bhṛkuṭī

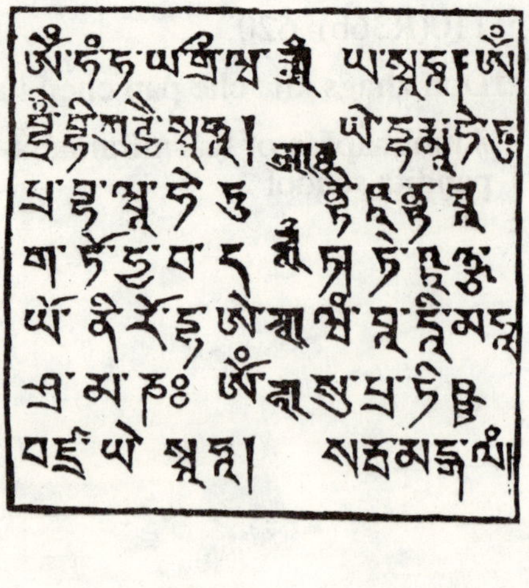

112(R37a) 622

'Khor Nor bzang, sGrol ma

Attendant Sudhana and Tārā

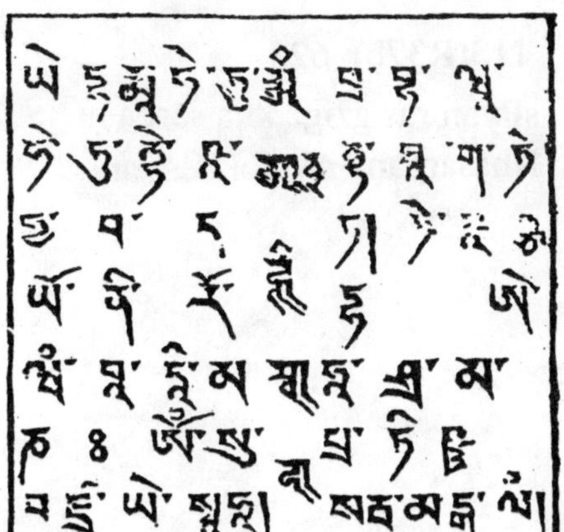

113(R37b) 623

sPyan ras gzigs kha sarpa ṇi

Khasarpaṇa Avalokiteśvara

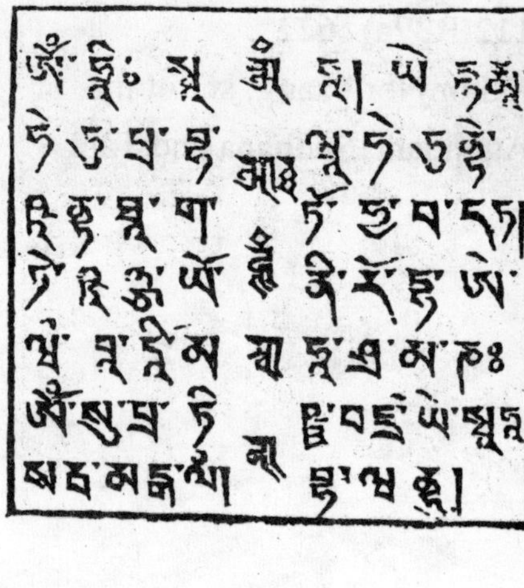

114(R37c) 624

'Khor Khro gnyer can ma, rTa mgrin

Attendant Bhṛkuṭī and Hayagrīva

115(R38a) 625
sPyan ras gzigs sems nyid ngal gso (*'di lhag*)
Cittaviśrāmaṇa Avalokiteśvara

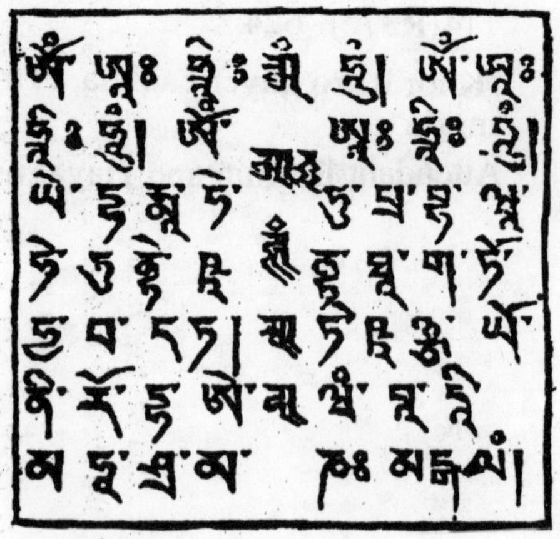

116(R38b) 626

sPyan ras gzigs yid bzhin nor bu lha lnga

5-deity Cintāmaṇi Avalokiteśvara

ན་མོ་རཏྣ་ཏྲ་ཡཱ་ཡ། ཧྲཱིཿ ན་མོ་ཨཱརྱཱ་ཝ
ལོ་ཀི་ཏེ་ཤྭ་ར་ཡ། བོ་དྷི་སཏྭཱ་ཡ།
མ་ཧཱ་སཏྭཱ་ཡ། མ་ཧཱ་ཀཱ་རུ་ཎི་ཀཱ་ཡ།
ཏ་དྱ་ཐཱ། ཨོཾ་ཙཀྲ་ཝརྟི་ཙིནྟཱ་མ་ཎི་
མ་ཧཱ་པདྨེ་རུ་རུ་ཏིཥྛ་ཛྭ་ལ་ཡ། ཨཱ་ཀརྵ་
ཡ་ཧཱུྃ་ཕཊ་སྭཱ་ཧཱ། ཨོཾ་ཝ་ར་ད་པདྨེ་ཧཱུྃ།
ཨོཾ་པདྨ་ཙིནྟཱ་མ་ཎི་ཛྭ་ལ་ཧཱུྃ། ས་ཀཱ་ཡི།

117(R38c) 627

sPyan raś gzigs sems nyid ngal gso

Cittaviśrāmaṇa Avalokiteśvara

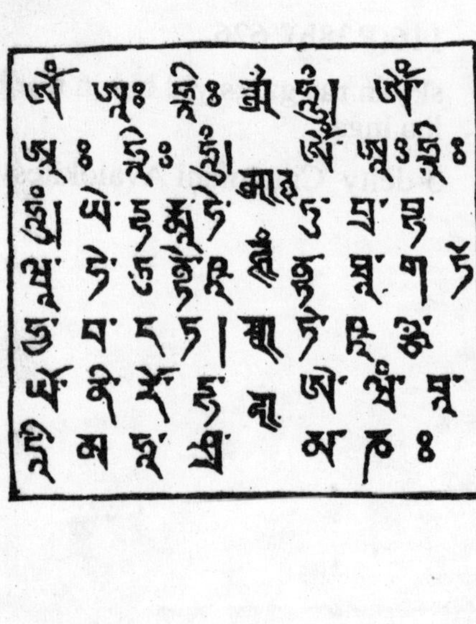

118(R39a) 628

’Jig rten dbang phyug gsang sgrub

Guhyasādhana Lokeśvara

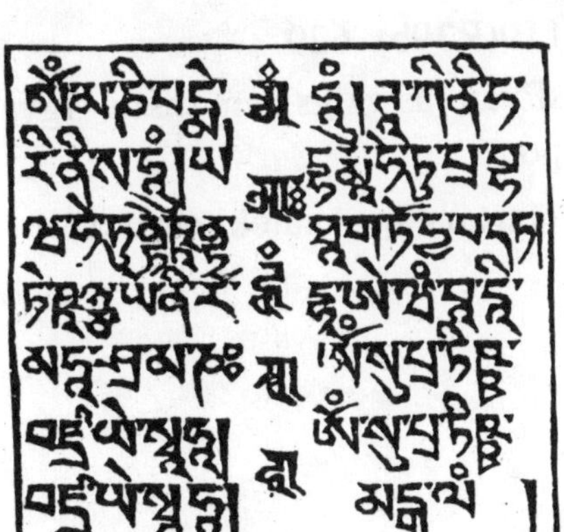

119(R39b) 629

sPyan ras gzigs nam mkha' rgyal po

Gaganarāja Avalokiteśvara

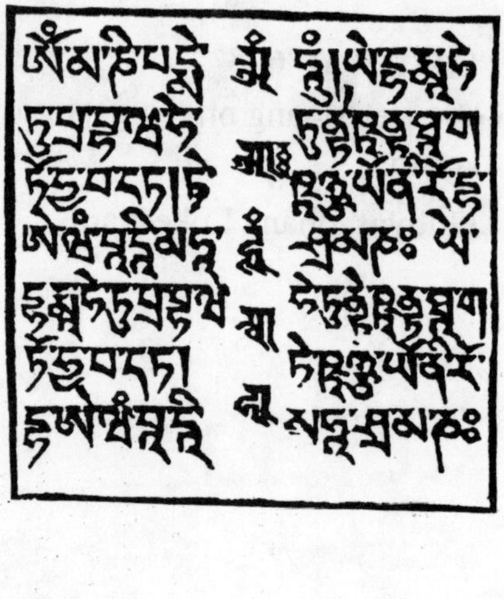

120(R39c) 630
sPyan ras gzigs yid bzhin 'khor lo
Cintāmaṇicakra Avalokiteśvara

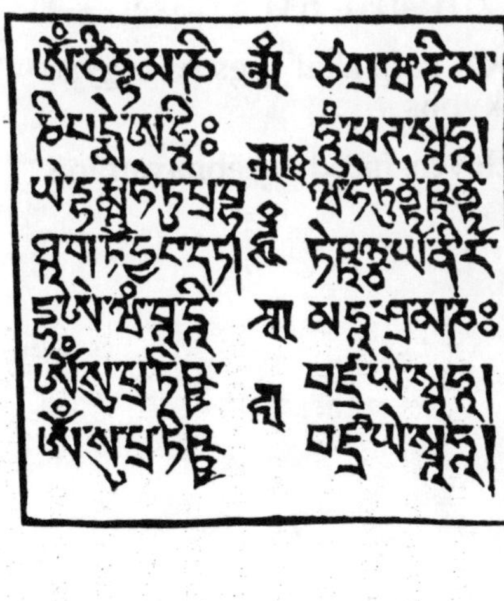

121(R40a) 631

bCu gcig zhal 'jigs pa brgyad skyobs

Eleven-faced Aṣṭābhayatrāṇa

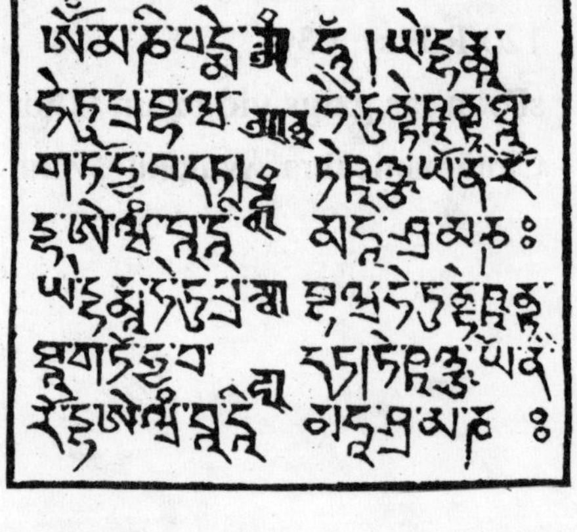

122(R40b) 632

Me'i 'jigs skyobs

Agnibhayatrāṇa

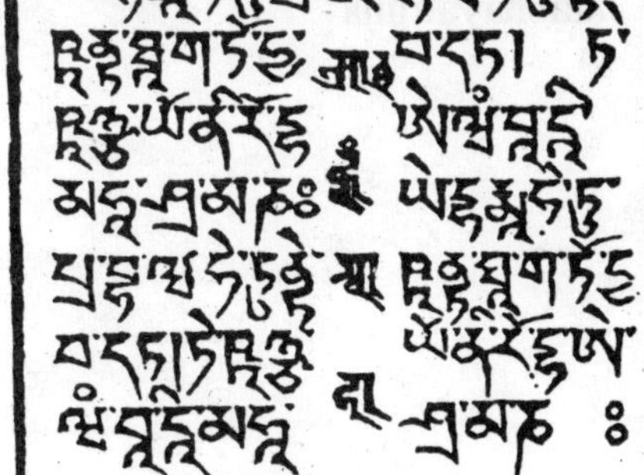

ཆུའི་འཇིགས་སྐྱོབས

123(R40c) 633
Chu'i 'jigs skyobs
Jalabhayatrāṇa

ཡེ་དྷརྨཱ་ཧེ་ཏུ་པྲ་ ༀ བྷ་ཝཱ་ཧེ་ཏུནྟེ་
ཥཱཾ་ཏ་ཐཱ་ག་ཏོ་ཧྱ་ ཝ་དཏ྄། ཏེ་ཥཱཉྩ་
ཡོ་ནི་རོ་དྷ་ཨེ་ ཨཱཿ ཝཾ་ཝཱ་དཱི་མ་ཧཱ་
ཤྲ་མ་ཎ ཿ ཧཱུྃ ཡེ་དྷརྨཱ་ཧེ་ཏུ་
པྲ་བྷ་ཝ་ཧེ་ ཧྲཱི ཏུནྟེ་ཥཱཾ་ཏ་ཐཱ་ག་
ཏོ་ཧྱ་ཝ་ད་ཏ། ཏེ་ཥཱཉྩ་ཡོ་ནི་རོ་
དྷ་ཨེ་ཝཾ་ཝཱ་དཱི་ ཧཱ མ་ཧཱ་ཤྲ་མ་ཎཿ

124(R41a) 634
Seng ge'i 'jigs skyobs
Siṃhabhayatrāṇa

ཡེ་དྷརྨཱ་ཧེ་ཏུ་ ཨཱཿ པྲ་བྷ་ཝ་ཧེ་ཏུན་ཏེ
ཥཱན་ཏ་ཐཱ་ག་ཏོ་ཧྱ་ ཝ་ད་ཏ། ཏེ་
ཥཱཉྩ་ཡོ་ནི་རོ་དྷ་ ཨེ་ཝཾ་ཝཱ་དཱི
མ་ཧཱ་ཤྲ་མ་ཎཿ ཧཱུྃ ཡེ་དྷརྨཱ་ཧེ་ཏུ་པྲ
བྷ་ཝ་ཧེ་ཏུན་ཏེ་ ཥཱན་ཏ་ཐཱ་ག་ཏོ་ཧྱ་
ཝ་ད་ཏ། ཏེ་ ཥཱཾ ཙ་ཡོ་ནི་རོ་དྷ་
ཨེ་ཝཾ་ཝཱ་དཱི ཧྲཱིཿ མ་ཧཱ་ཤྲ་མ་ཎཿ

125(R41b) 635

Glang po'i 'jigs skyobs

Hastibhayatrāṇa

ཡེ་དྷརྨཱ་ཧེ་ཏུ ༀ པྲ་བྷ་ཝཱ་ཧེ་ཏུནྟེ་
ཥཱནྟ་ཐཱ་ག་ཏོ་ཧྱ ཨཱཿ ཝ་དཏ྄། ཏེ་
ཥཱཉྩ་ཡོ་ནི་རོ་དྷ ཨེ་ཝཾ་ཝཱ་དཱི་
མ་ཧཱ་ཤྲ་མ་ཎཿ ཧཱུྃ ཡེ་དྷརྨཱ་ཧེ་ཏུ
པྲ་བྷ་ཝཱ་ཧེ་ཏུནྟེ སྭཱ ཥཱནྟ་ཐཱ་ག་ཏོ་ཧྱ
ཝ་དཏ྄། ཏེ ཥཱཉྩ་ཡོ་ནི་རོ་དྷ
ཨེ་ཝཾ་ཝཱ་དཱི ཧཱ མ་ཧཱ་ཤྲ་མ་ཎཿ

126(R41c) 636
Chad pa'i 'jigs skyobs
Daṇḍabhayatrāṇa

ཡེ་དྷརྨཱ་ཧེ་ཏུ་པྲ ཨོཾ བྷ་ཝཱ་ཧེ་ཏུནྟེ་
ཥཱན་ཏ་ཐཱ་ག་ཏོ་ཧྱ་ ཝ་དཏ། ཏེ་
ཥཱཉྩ་ཡོ་ནི་རོ་དྷ ཨཱཿ ཨེ་ཝཾ་ཝཱ་དཱི
མ་ཧཱ་ཤྲ་མ་ཎཿ ཧཱུྃ ཡེ་དྷརྨཱ་ཧེ་ཏུ
པྲ་བྷ་ཝཱ་ཧེ་ཏུནྟེ་ ཥཱ ཏ་ཐཱ་ག་ཏོ་ཧྱ
ཝ་དཏ། ཏེ་ ཥཱཉྩ་ཡོ་ནི་རོ་དྷ
ཨེ་ཝཾ་ཝཱ་དཱི ཧཱ མ་ཧཱ་ཤྲ་མ་ཎཿ

127(R42a) 636(sic)
Klu'i 'jigs skyobs
Nāgabhayatrāṇa

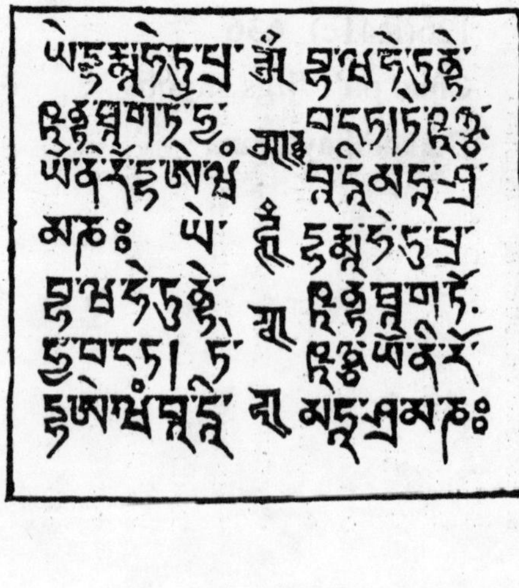

128(R42b) 637
mKha' 'gro'i 'jigs skyobs
Ḍākinībhayatrāṇa

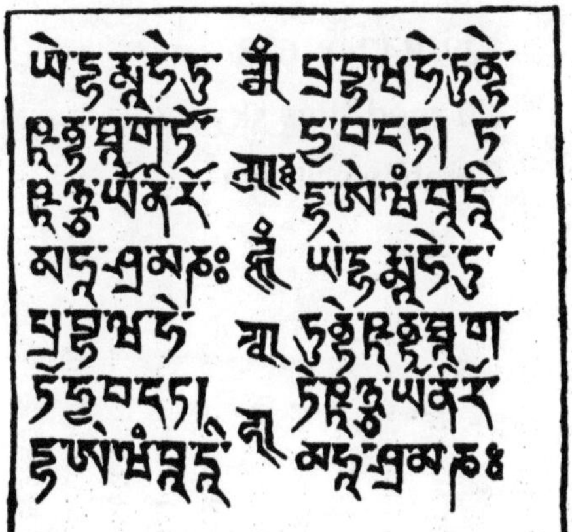

129(R42c) 638

Mi rgod 'jigs skyobs

Corabhyayatrāṇa

ཡེ་དྷརྨཱ་ཧེ་ཏུ་ ཨོཾ་ པྲ་བྷ་ཝཱ་ཧེ་ཏུནྟེ་
ཥཱན་ཏ་ཐཱ་ག་ཏོ་ཧྱ་ སྭཱཧཱ བ་ད་ཏ། ཏེ་
ཥཱཉྩ་ཡོ་ནི་རོ་དྷ་ ཨེ་ཝཾ་བཱ་དཱི་
མ་ཧཱ་ཤྲ་མ་ཎཿ ཧཱུཾ་ ཡེ་དྷརྨཱ་ཧེ་ཏུ་པྲ་
བྷ་ཝཱ་ཧེ་ཏུནྟེ་ ཧྲཱི ཥཱན་ཏ་ཐཱ་ག་ཏོ་ཧྱ་
བ་ད་ཏ། ཏེ་ ཥཱཉྩ་ཡོ་ནི་རོ་དྷ་
ཨེ་ཝཾ་བཱ་དཱི་ ཨཱ མ་ཧཱ་ཤྲ་མ་ཎཿ

130(R43a) 639
sPyan ras gzigs rdo rje snying po
Vajragarbha Avalokiteśvara

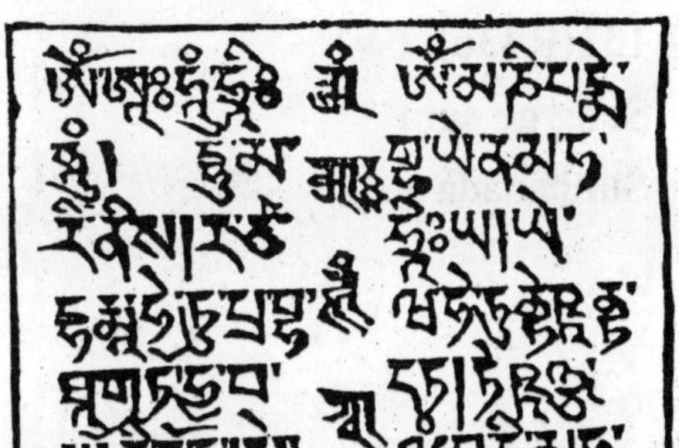

131(R43b) 640
Seng ge sgra
Simhanāda

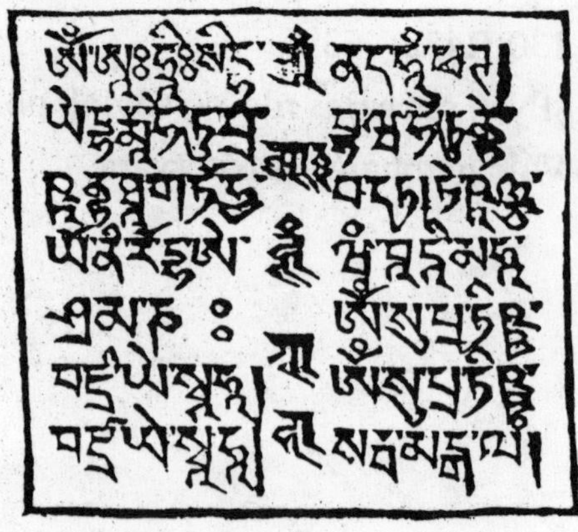

132(R43c) 641

sPyan ras gzigs rgyal ba rgya mtsho

Jinasāgara Avalokiteśvara

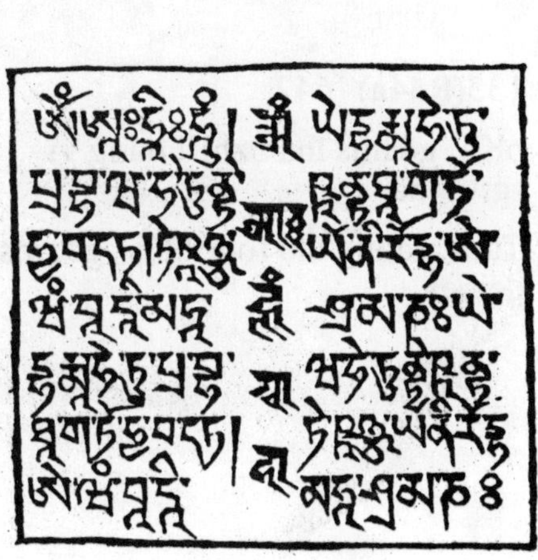

133(R44a) 642

bKa' gdams lha bzhi'i nang gi sgrol ma

Tārā among the four bKa' gdams deities

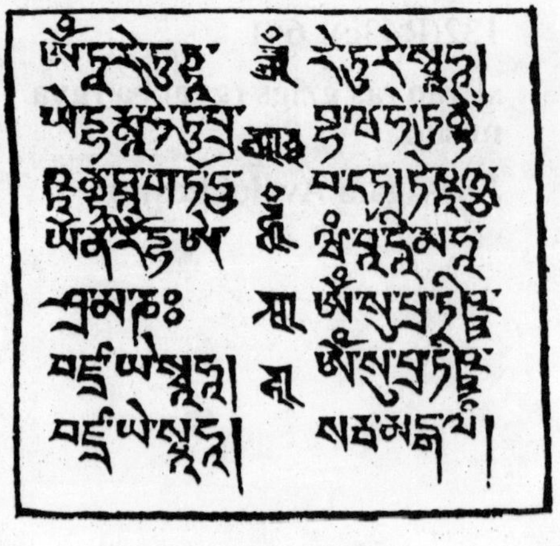

134(R44b) 643

sGrol ljang kha che paṇ chen lugs

Śyāma Tārā of Kāśmīramahā-paṇḍita school

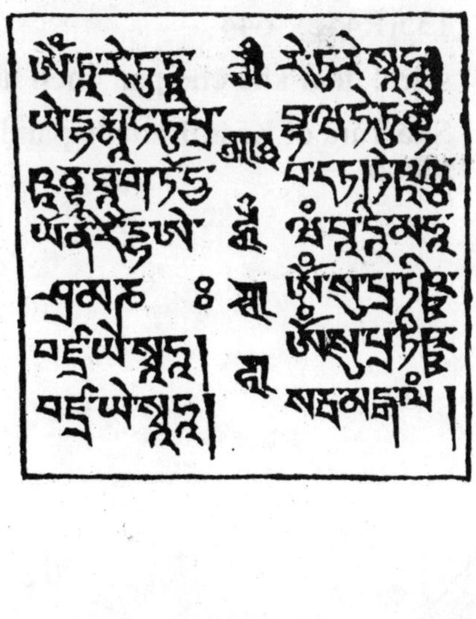

135(R44c) 644

sGrol dkar kha che paṇ chen lugs

Sita Tārā of Kāśmīramahāpaṇḍita school

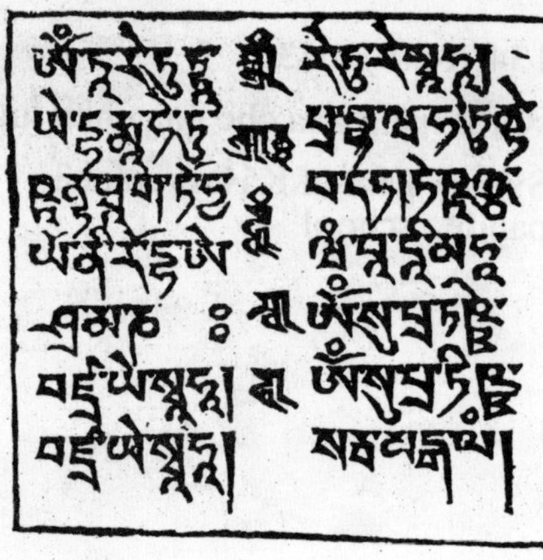

136(R45a) 645

sGrol ma nying zhi mtshan khro

Divāśāntarātrikruddha Tārā

ཨོཾ་ཏཱ་རེ་ཏུ་ཏྟཱ་རེ་ཀྲཱྀཾ ཏུ་རེ་སྭཱ་ཧཱ།
ཨོཾ་ནམ་ཏཱ་རེ། ནམཿཏཱ་རེ
ཧཱུྃ་ཏ་རེ་སྭཱ་ཧཱ། ཡེ་དྷརྨཱ་ཧེ་ཏུ
པྲ་བྷ་ཝཱ་ཧེ་ཏུནྟེ་ཥཱན྄ ཏ་ཐཱ་ག་ཏོ་ཧྱ་ཝ
དཏ྄། ཏེ་ཥཱཉྩ་ཡོ་ནི་རོ་དྷ་ཨེ་ཝཾ་ཝཱ
དཱི་མ་ཧཱ་ཤྲ་མ་ཎཿ ཡེ་སརྦ་མངྒ་ལཾ།

137(R45b) 646

O rgyan sgrol ma gnas kyi dbang phyug ma

Pīṭhīśvarī Uḍḍiyāna Tārā

ཨོཾ་ཧྲ་རེ་ཙུ་ཧྲ་ཏྲཱི་ རེ་ཙུ་རེ་ ཧྲཱུཾ་
ཕ་ཊ། ཡེ་དྷརྨཱ་ཧེ་ཏུ་པྲ་བྷ་ཝཱ་
ཧེ་ཏུནྟེ་ཥཱནྟ་ཐཱ་ག་ཏོ་ ཧྱ་བ་ད་ཏ། ཏེ
ཥཱཉྩ་ཡོ་ནི་རོ་དྷ་ཨེ་ ཝཾ་བཱ་དཱི་མ་ཧཱ་
ཤྲ་མ་ཎཿ ཨོཾ་སུ་ པྲ་ཏིཥྛ་བཛྲ་
ཡེ་སྭཱ་ཧཱ། ས་ཏ་ཀཱ་མ་ཏྲ་ལཾ།

138(R45c) 647
sGrol ma yid bzhin nor bu
Cintāmaṇi Tārā

ཨོཾ་ཏཱ་རེ་ཏུཏྟཱ་རེ་ཏུ་རེ་
སྭཱ་ཧཱ། ཡེ་དྷརྨཱ་ཧེ་ཏུ་པྲ
བྷ་ཝཱ་ཧེ་ཏུནྟེ་ཥཱཾ་ ཏ་ཐཱ་ག་ཏོ་ཧྱ
བ་དཏ། ཏེ་ཥཱཉྩ་ ཡོ་ནི་རོ་དྷ
ཨེ་ཝཾ་ཝཱ་ དཱི་མ་ཧཱ་ཤྲ་མ་ཎཿ
ཨོཾ་སུ་པྲ་ཏིཥྛ་ བཛྲ་ཡེ་སྭཱ་ཧཱ།

139(R46-48a) 648

sGrol ma dmar mo sa lugs

Rakta Tārā of Sa skya school

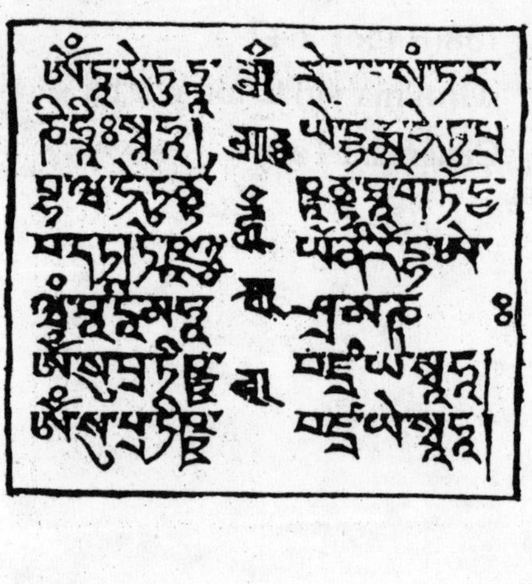

140(R46-48b) 649
sGrol ma nor sbyin ma
Dhanada Tārā

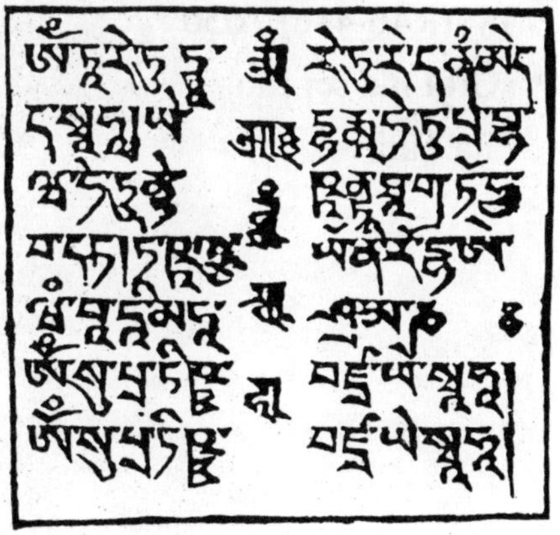

141(R46-48c) 650
sGrol ma ser mo
Pīta Tārā

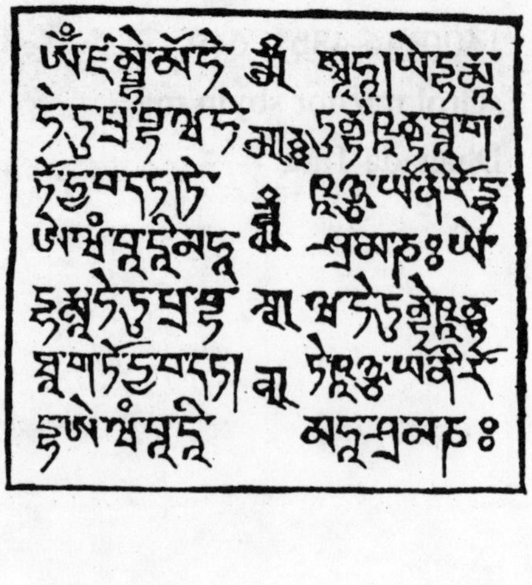

141*a**(R47a)

Rin chen grol ma

Ratnatārā

141*b**(R47b)
Padma grol ma
Padmatārā

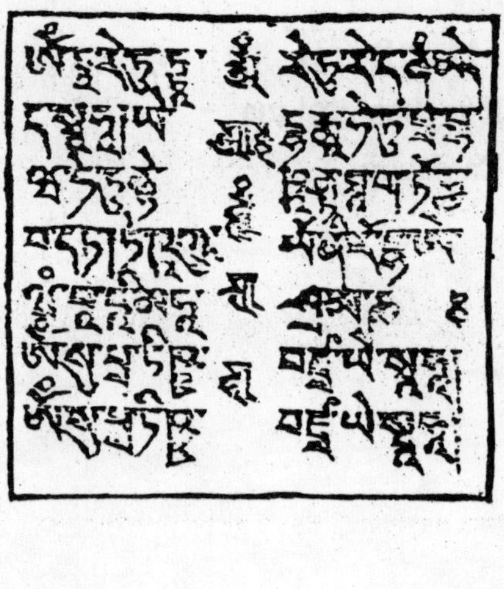

141*c**(R47c)
Sangs rgyas grol ma
Buddhatārā

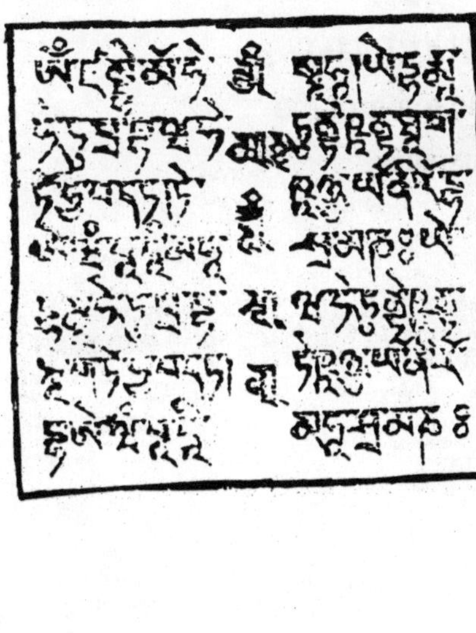

141*d**(R48a)

Me tog grol ma

Puṣpatārā

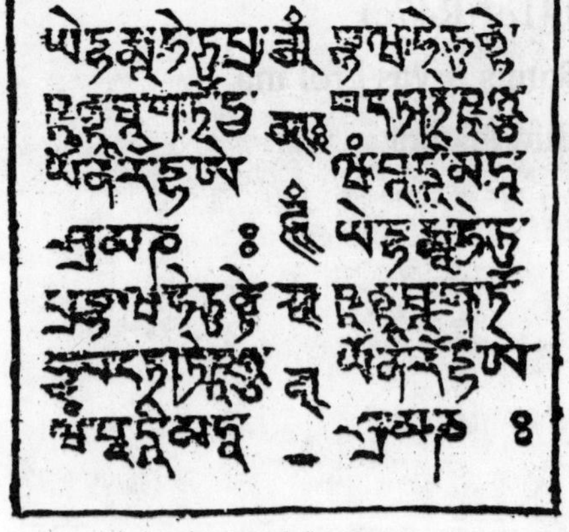

141*e**(R48b)
bDug pa grol ma
Dhūpatārā

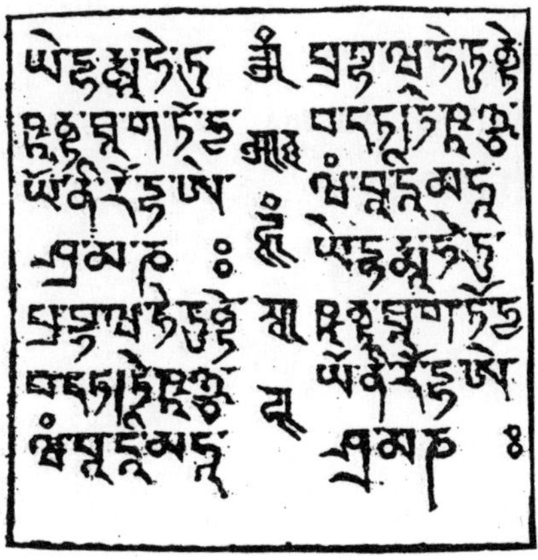

141*f**(R48c)

Mar me grol ma

Dīpatārā

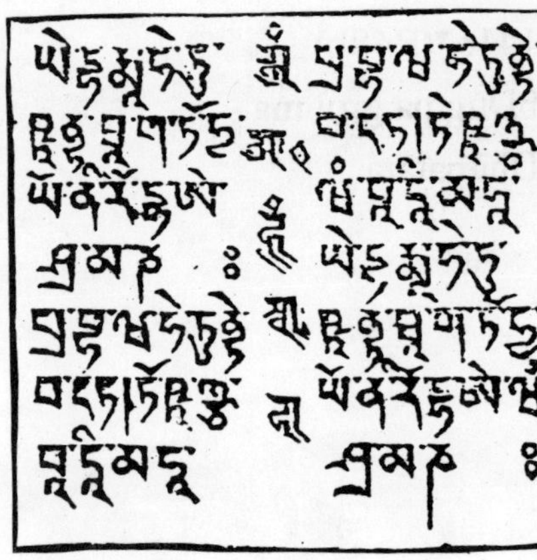

142(R49, 50a) 651
Dzambha la ser po
Pīta Jambhala

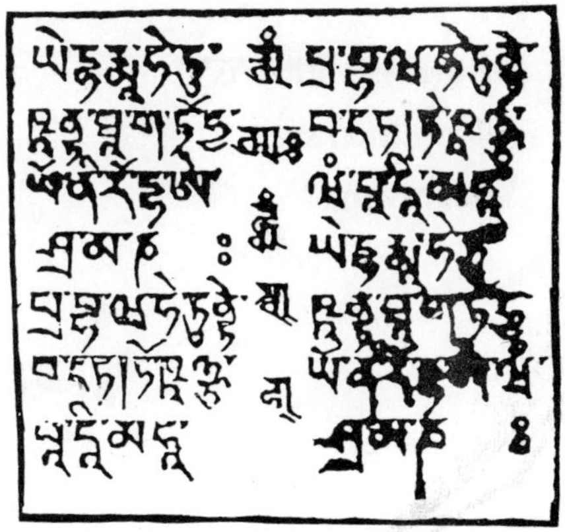

143(R49, 50b) 652

rNam thos sras

Vaiśravaṇa

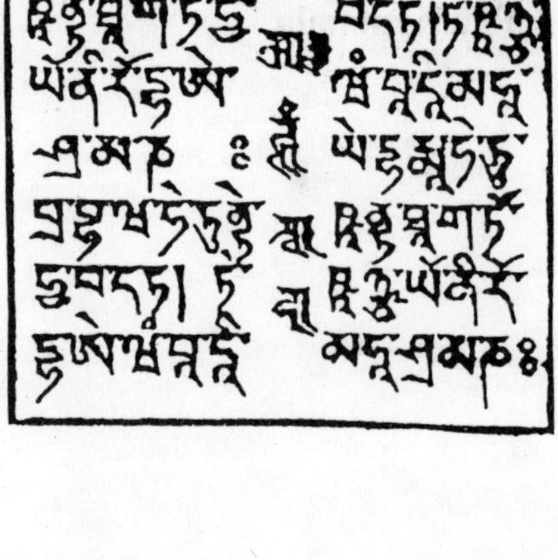

144(R49, 50c) 653
rMi lam ston pa'i sgrol ma
Svapnadeśaka Tārā

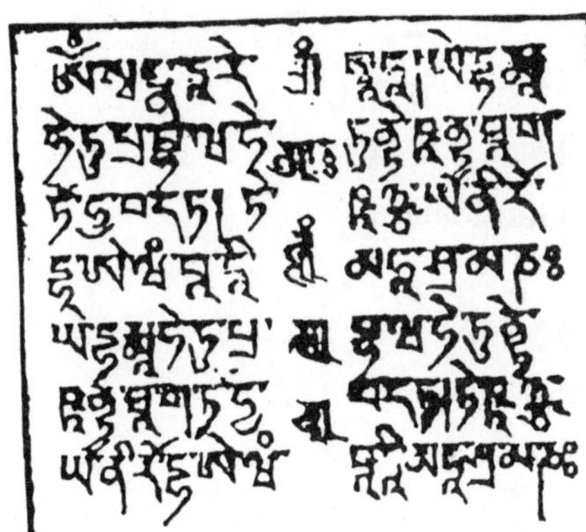

144*a**(R49a)
Dri'i grol ma
Gandhatārā

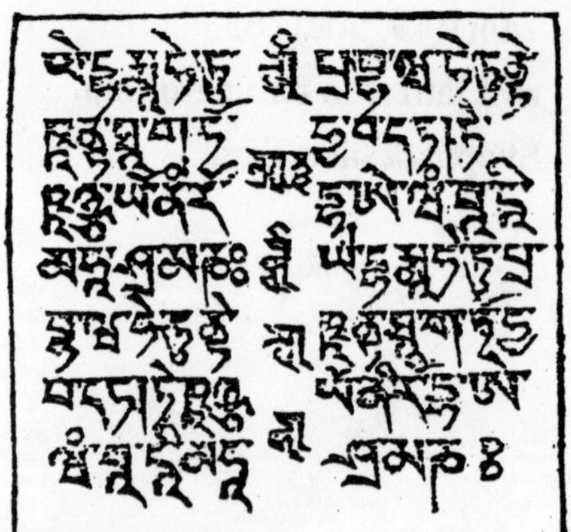

144*b**(R49b)
rDo rje lcags kyu ma
Vajrāṅkuśī

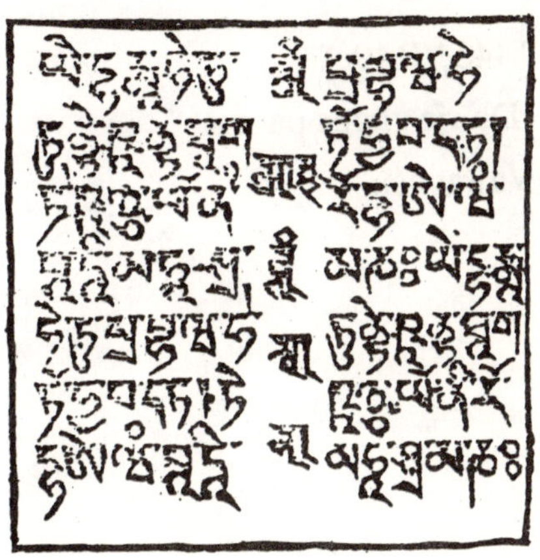

144*c* *(R49c)

rDo rje zhags pa ma

Vajrapāśī

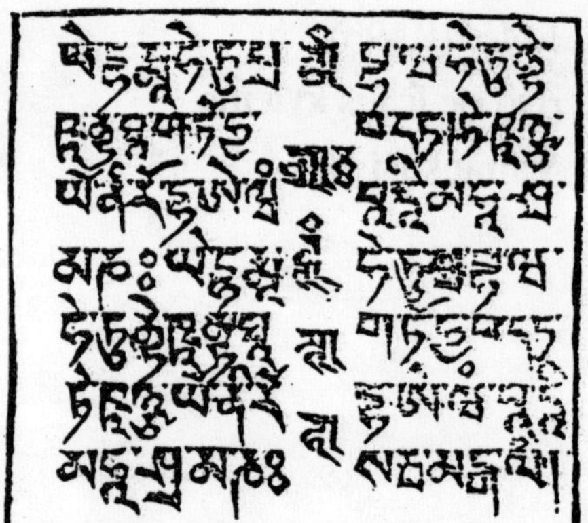

144*d**(R50a)
lCags sgrog ma
Sphoṭā

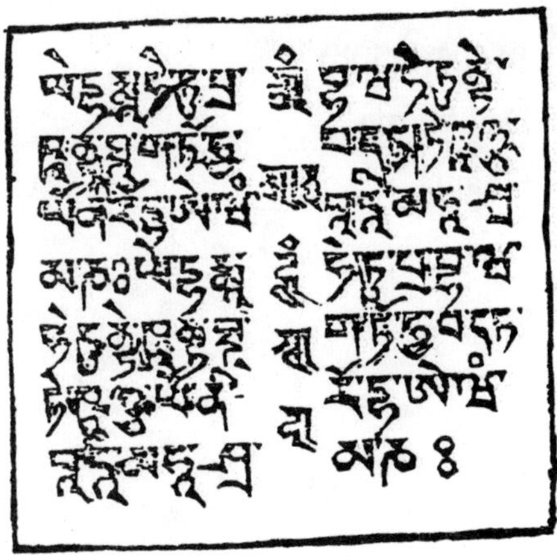

144*e* *(R50b)

Dril bu ma

Ghaṇṭā

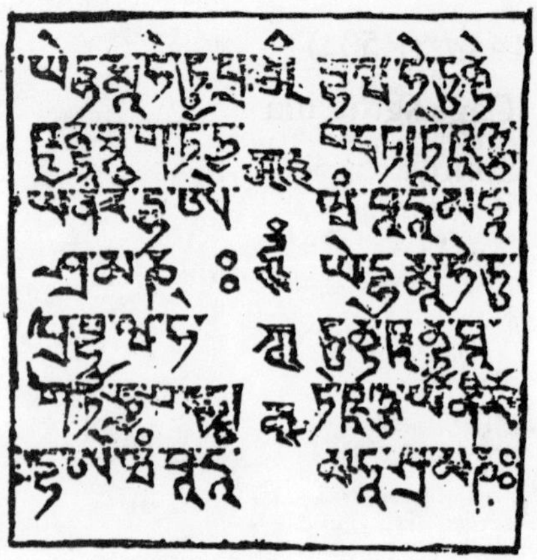

144*f**(R50c)
rDo rje sgrol ma
Vajratārā

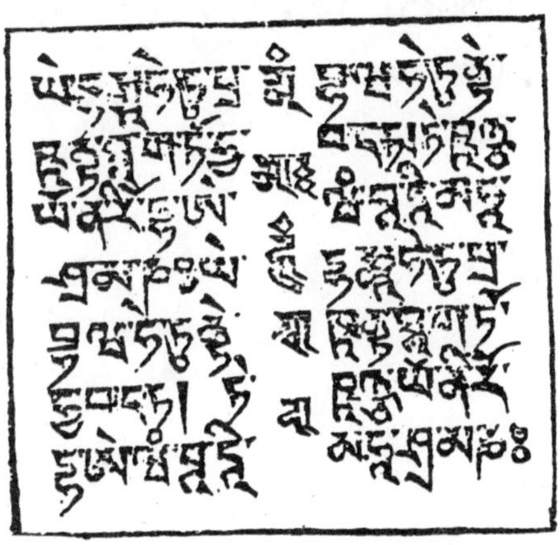

145(R51, 52a) 654

sGrol ma

Tārā

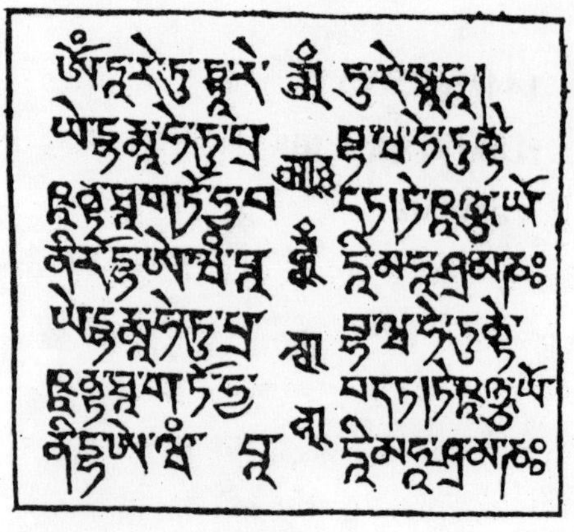

146(R51, 52b) 655
So sor 'brang ma
Pratisarā

147(R51, 52c) 656

'Od zer can ma

Mārīcī

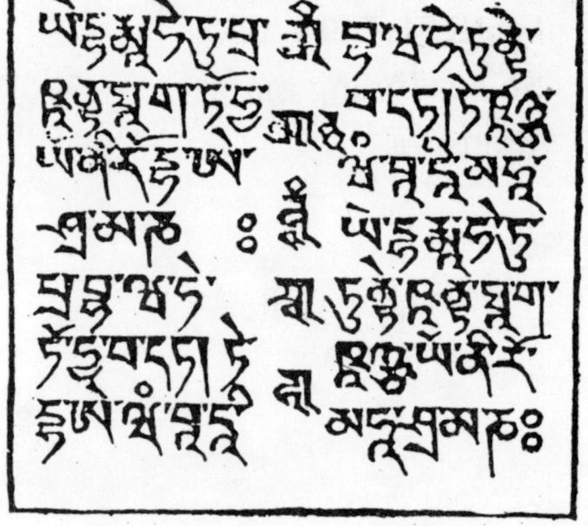

148(R53a) 657
'Khor Phag mo
Attendant Vārāhī

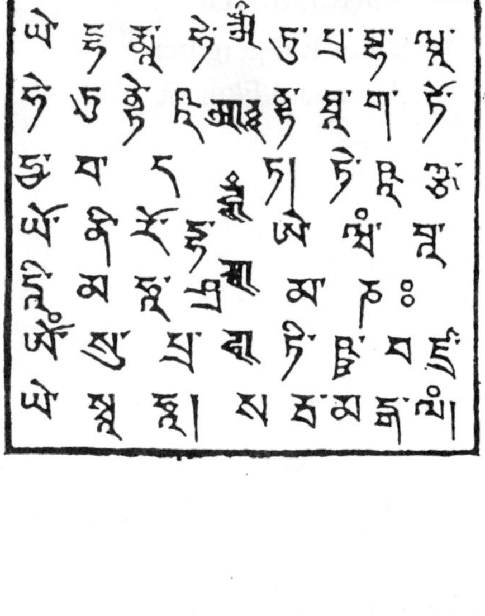

149(R53b) 658

'Khor Ral gcig ma

Attendant Ekajaṭā

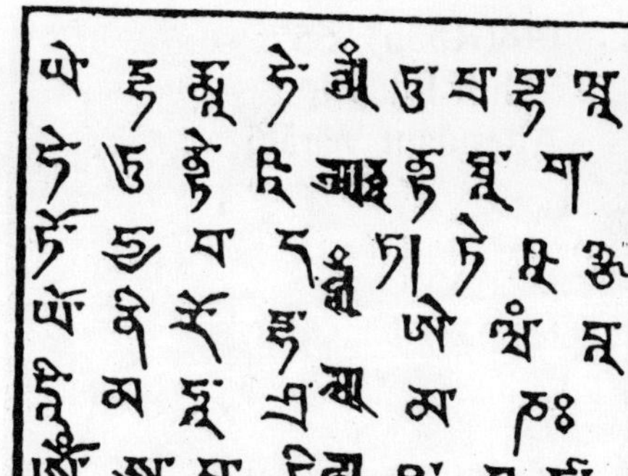

150(R53c) 659

Phyag brgyad sgrol ma

Eight-armed Tārā

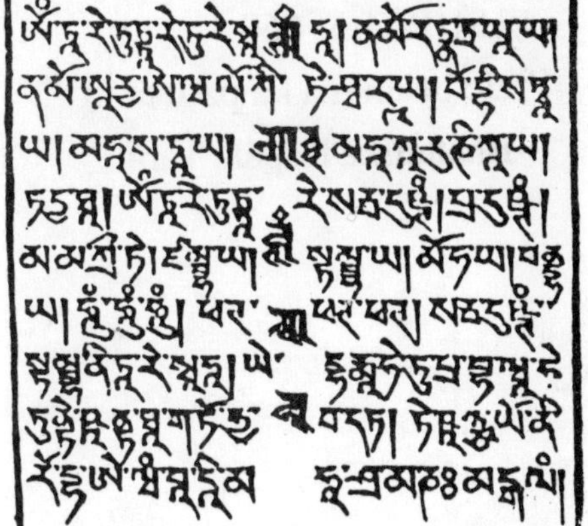
ཨོཾ་ཧྲ་རེ་ཙུཧྲ་རེ་ཙུ་རེ་སྭཱ་ཧཱ། ན་མོ་རཏྣ་ཏྲ་ཡཱ་ཡ།
ན་མོ་ཨཱརྱ་ཨ་ཝ་ལོ་ཀི་ ཏེ་ཤྭ་རཱ་ཡ། བོ་དྷི་སཏྭ
ཡ། མཧཱ་ས་ཏྭཱ་ཡ། མཧཱ་ཀཱ་རུ་ཎི་ཀཱ་ཡ།
ཏདྱ་ཐཱ། ཨོཾ་ཧྲ་རེ་ཙུཧྲ་ རེ་སརྦ་དུཥྚཾ། ཧྲ་ད་ཡཾ།
མ་མ་ཤྲཱི་ཏེ། ཛམྦྷ་ཡ། སྟམྦྷ་ཡ། མོ་ཧ་ཡ། བནྡྷ
ཡ། ཧཱུཾ་ཧཱུཾ་ཧཱུཾ། ཕཊ་ ཕཊ་ཕཊ། སརྦ་དུཥྚཾ
སྟམྦྷ་ནི་ཏ་རེ་སྭཱ་ཧཱ། ཡེ་ ཧེ་ཏུ་པྲ་བྷ་ཝཱ་ཧེ
ཏུནྟེ་ཥཱན་ཏ་ཐཱ་ག་ཏོ་ཧྱ་ ཝ་དཏ། ཏེ་ཥཱཉྩ་ཡོ་ནི
རོ་དྷ་ཨེ་ཝཾ་ཝཱ་དཱི་མ ཧཱ་ཤྲ་མ་ཎཿ མ་ཧཱ་ལི།

151(R54a) 660

rJe btsun ma kā pa li tā ra

Bhattārikā Kapāla Tārā

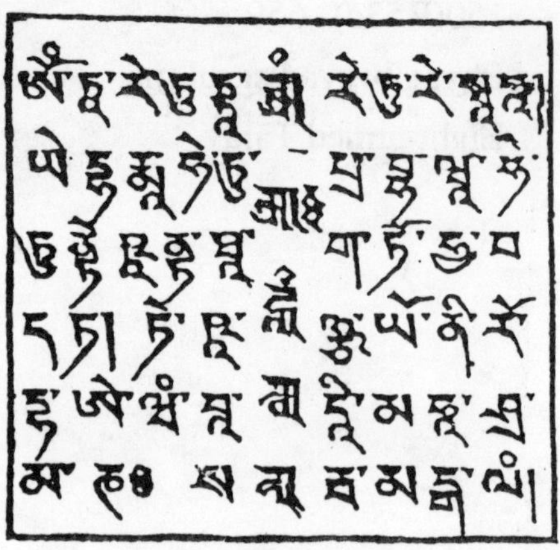

152(R54b) 661

'Phags ma tsunda tā ra

Ārya Cundā Tārā

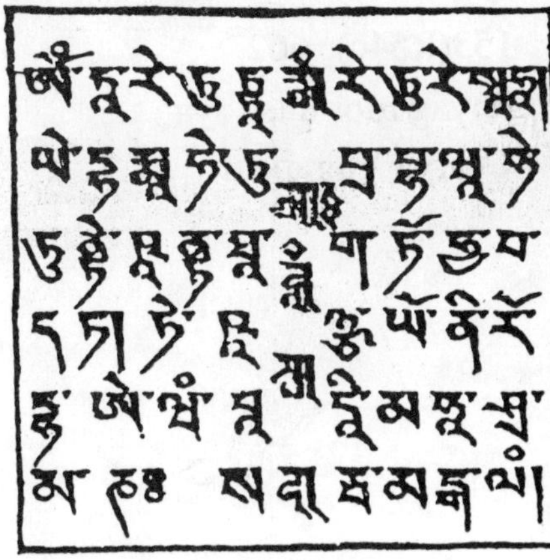

153(R54c) 662
Phyag rdor u tsa rya
Ucārya Vajrapāṇi

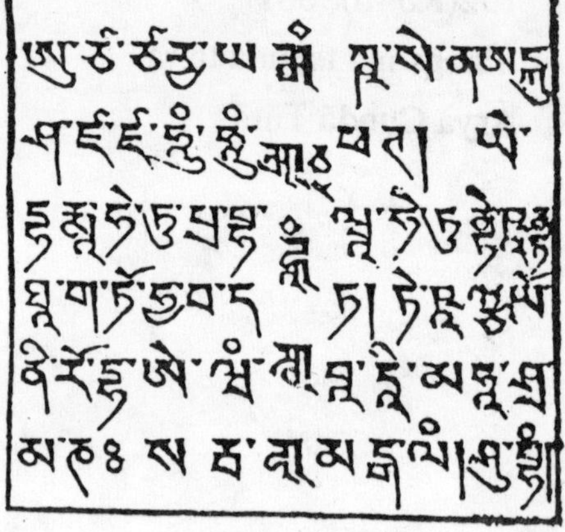

154(R55a) 663
Phyag rdor gos sngon can
Nīlāmbaradhara Vajrapāṇi

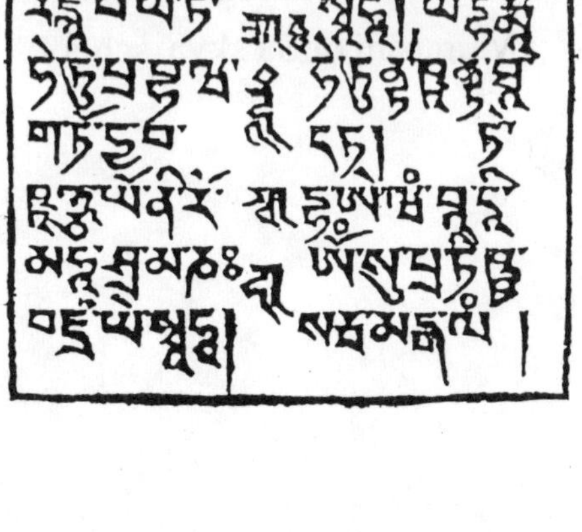

155(R55b) 664
Phyag rdor sa lugs
Vajrapāṇi of Sa skya school

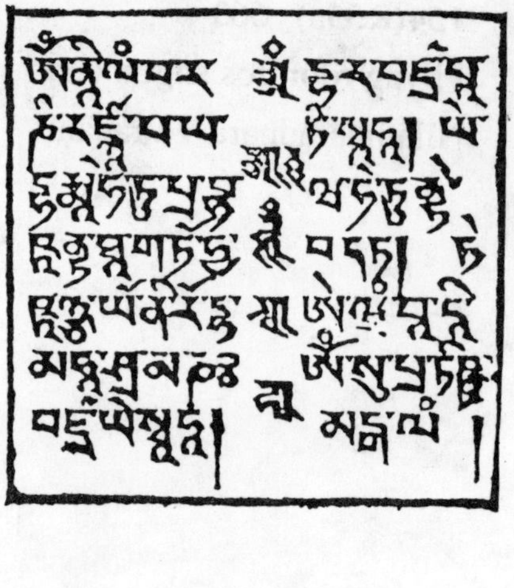

156(R55c) 665

Phyag rdor gtum chen bsrung ba'i mkhar ras chung lugs

Caṇḍamahāroṣaṇa Vajrapāṇi of Ras chung school

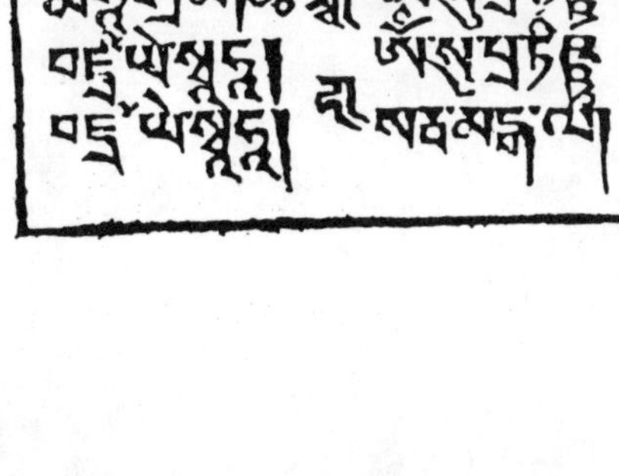

ཕྱག་རྡོར་གཏུམ་པོ་ཁྲ་ཐོགས

157(R56a) 666
Phyag rdor gtum po khra thogs
Khra thogs Caṇḍa Vajrapāṇi

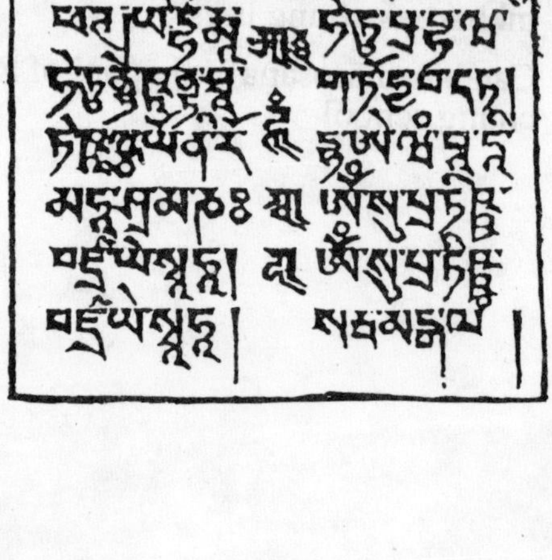

158(R56b) 667
Phyag rdor gtum chung dmar po
Rakta Alpacaṇḍa Vajrapāṇi

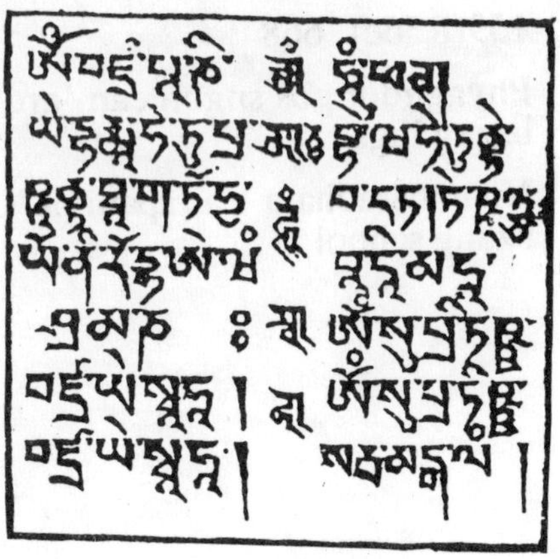

159(R56c) 668

Phyag rdor gos sngon can 'gro bzang lugs

Nīlāmbaradhara Vajrapāṇi of 'Gro bzang school

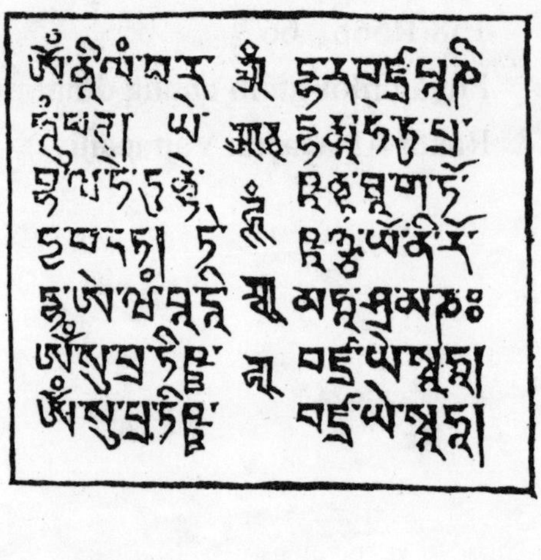

160(R57a) 669
Phyag rdor khang brtsegs
Kūṭāgāra Vajrapāṇi

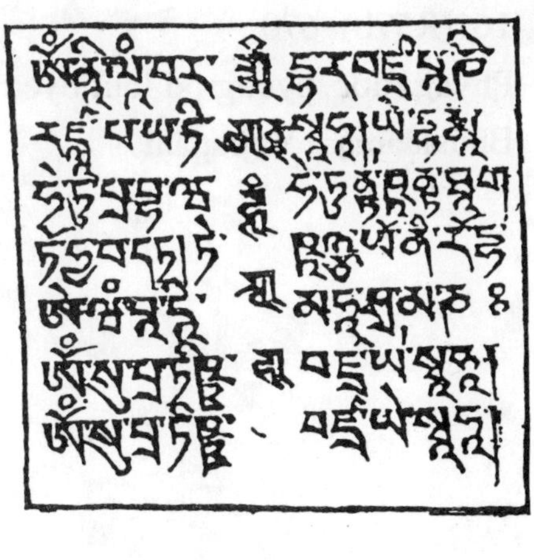

161(R57b) 670

Phyag rdor 'byung po 'dul byed

Bhūtaḍāmara Vajrapāṇi

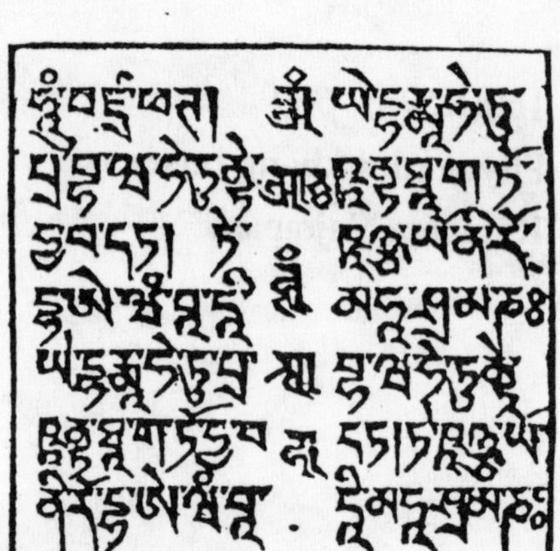

162(R57c) 671

Phyag rdor 'byung po 'dul byed gsar ma

Nava Bhūtaḍāmara Vajrapāṇi

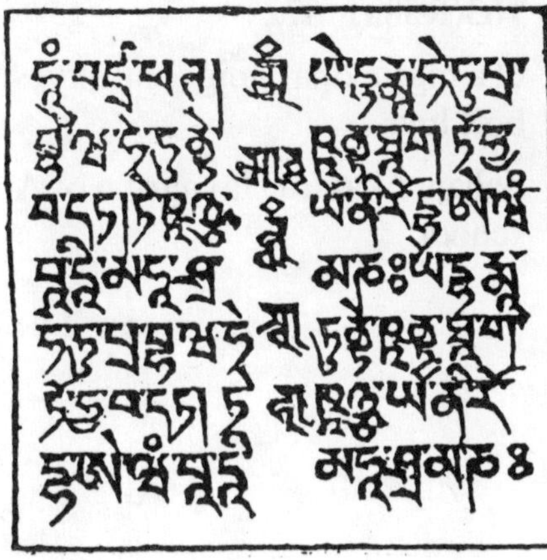

163(R58a) 672

rTa mgrin dpa' gcig lhan skyes jo bo'i lugs

Sahaja Ekavīra Hayagrīva of Atīśa school

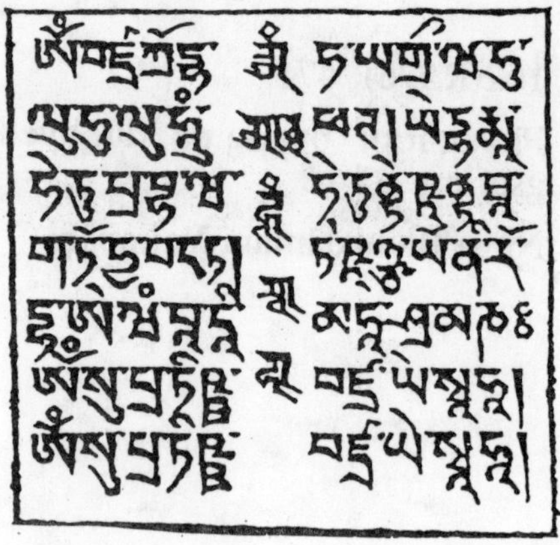

164(R58b) 673

rTa mgrin khyung gshog can jo bo'i lugs

Garuḍapakṣavat Hayagrīva of Atīśa school

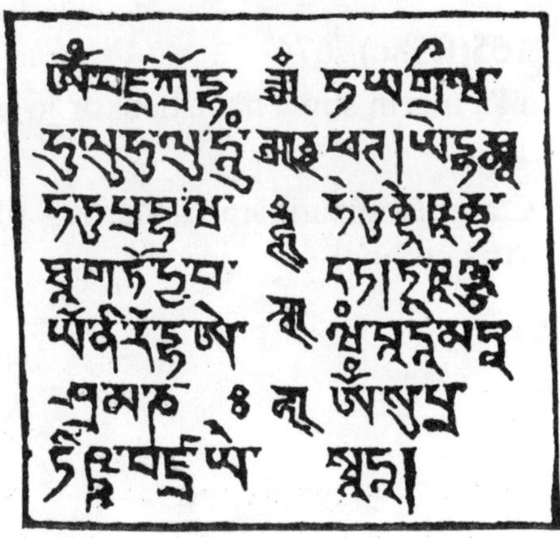

165(R58c) 674

rTa mgrin shwa na bzhi skor jo bo lugs

Caturḍākinīparivāra Hayagrīva of Atīśa school

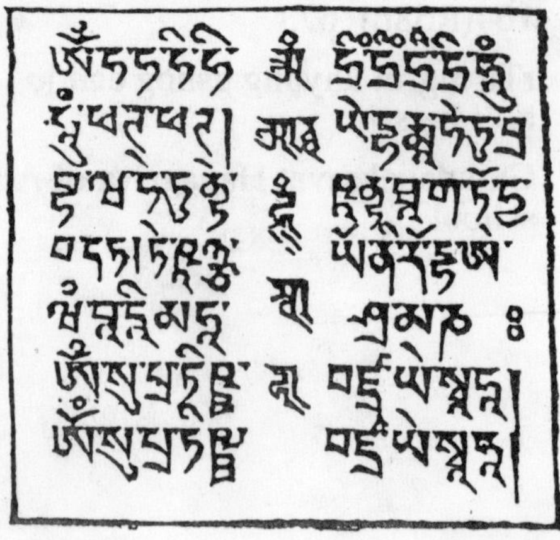

166(R59a) 675

'Khor rDo rje las byed ma

Attendant Vajrakarmakarī

ཡེ་དྷརྨཱ་ཧེ་ཏྲཱི་ཙ་པྲ་བྷ་ཝཱ
ཧེ་ཏུ་ཏེ་ཥཱནྟ་ཐཱ་ག་ཏོ་
ཧྱ་ཝ་ད་ཏ། ཏྟེ་ཥཱཉྩ་ཡོ་
ནི་རོ་དྷ་ཨེ་ཝཾ་ཝཱ་དཱི་མཧཱ་
ཤྲ་མ་ཎཿ་སྭཱ་ཧཱ་ས་ཏ་མནྟྲཾ།

167(R59b) 676

'Khor gShin rje las byed ma

Attendant Yamakarmakarī

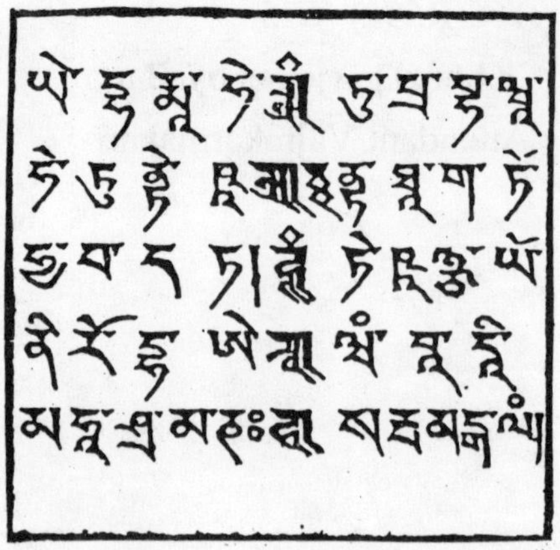

168(R59c) 677
'Khor Klu mo las byed ma
Attendant Nāgīkarmakarī

ཡེ་ དྷརྨཱ་ཧེ་ཏུ་པྲ་བྷ་ཝཱ་ཧེ་
ཏུན་ཏེ་ཥཱན་ཏ་ཐཱ་ག་ཏོ་ཧྱ་བ
ད་ཏ། ཏེ་ཥཱཉྩ་ཡོ་ནི་རོ་
དྷ་ཨེ་ཝཾ་ཝཱ་དཱི་མ་ཧཱ་ཤྲ
མ་ཎཿ ས་ཧཱ་ཧ་མ་ཧྲ་ཡཾ།

169(R60a) 678

'Khor gNod sbyin las byed ma

Attendant Yakṣakarmakarī

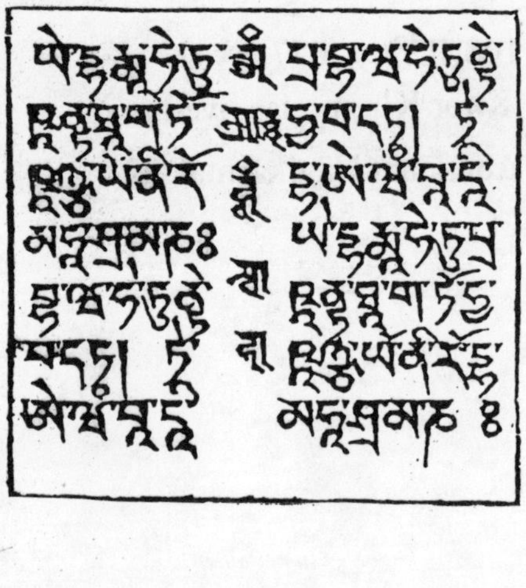

170(R60b) 679

rTa mgrin kha che paṇ chen lugs

Hayagrīva of Kāśmīramahāpaṇḍita school

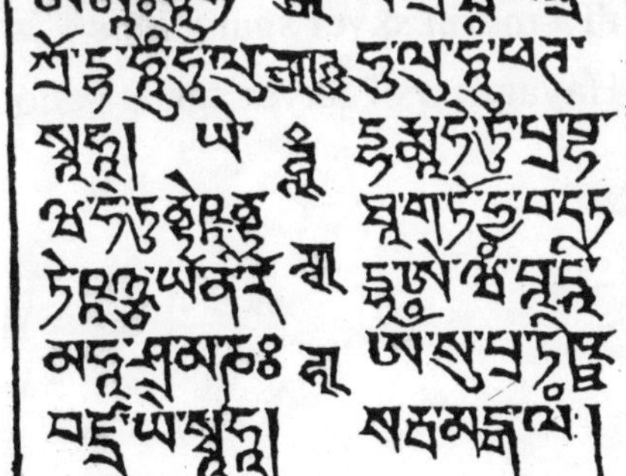

རྟ་མགྲིན་སྐྱེར་སྒང་ལུགས་

171(R60c) 680

rTa mgrin skyer sgang lugs

Hayagrīva of Skyer sgang school

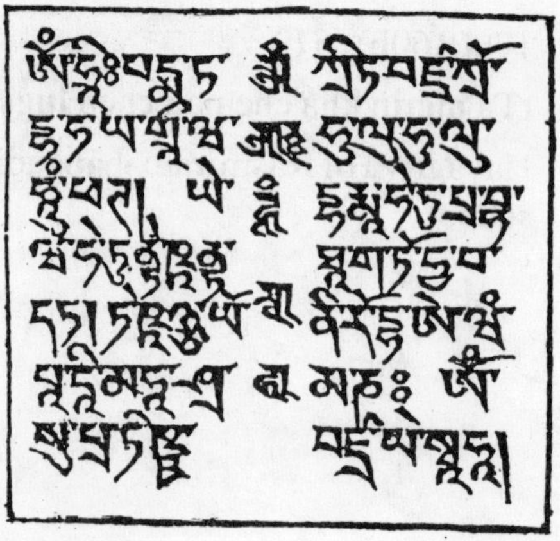

172(R61a) 681
rTa mgrin lcags ral can
Lohakhaḍga Hayagrīva

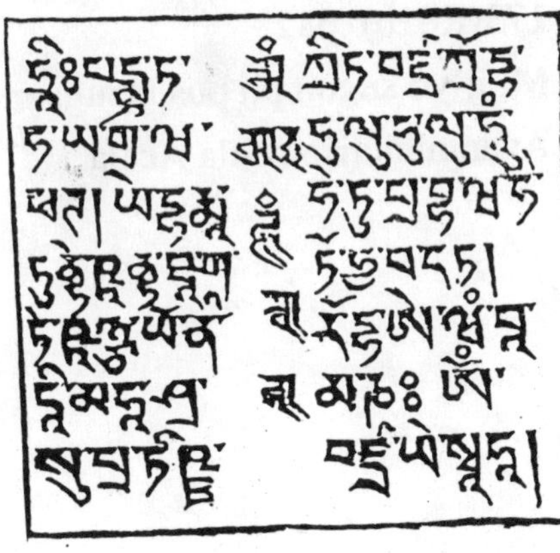

173(R61b) 682

Mi g'yo sngon po pus btsugs ma

Avaninihītajānu Nīla Acala

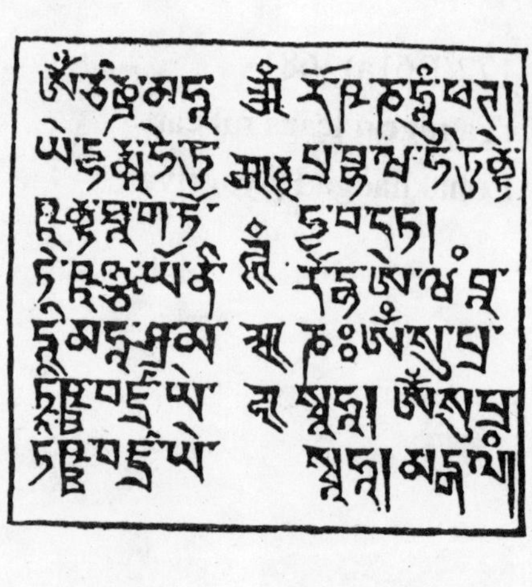

174(R61c) 683

Mi g'yo ba sngon po bka' gdams lugs

Nīla Acala of bKa' dgams school

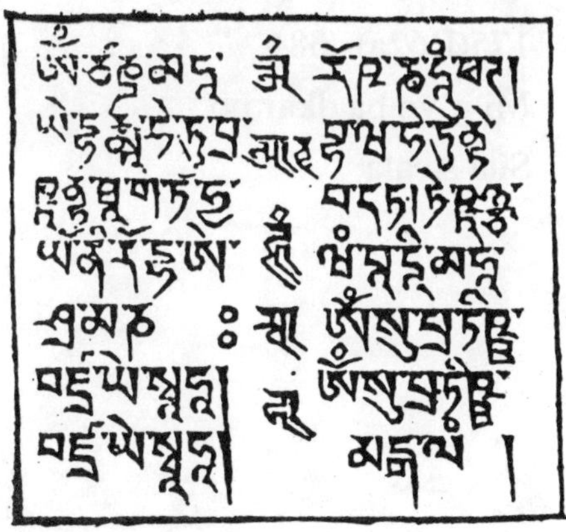

175(R62a) 684

Mi g'yo ba dkar po

Sita Acala

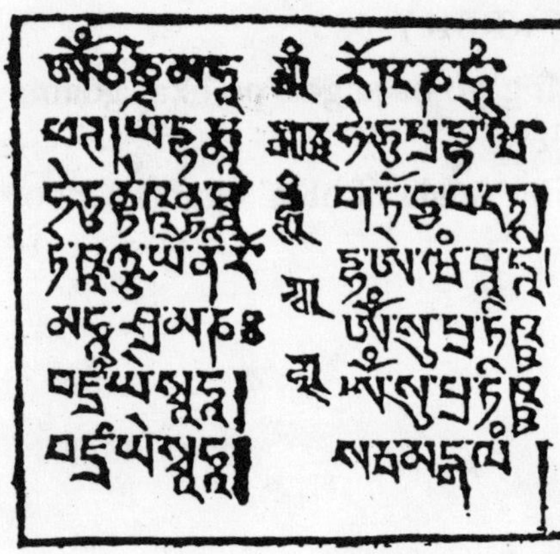

176(R62b) 685
Mi g'yo ba phyag bzhi pa
Four-armed Acala

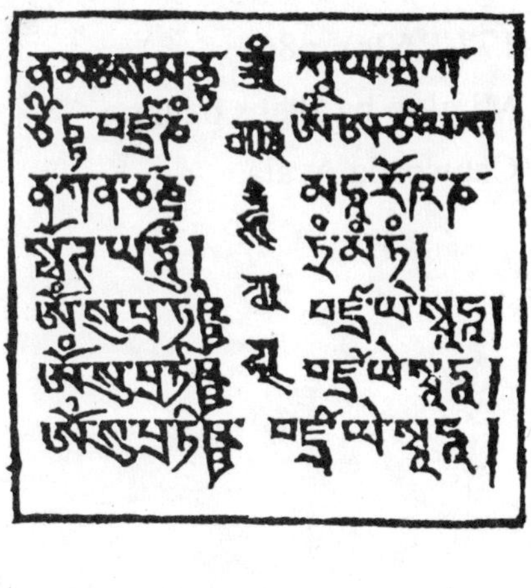

177(R62c) 686

Mi g'yo ba zhabs bzhi pa

Catuṣpada Acala

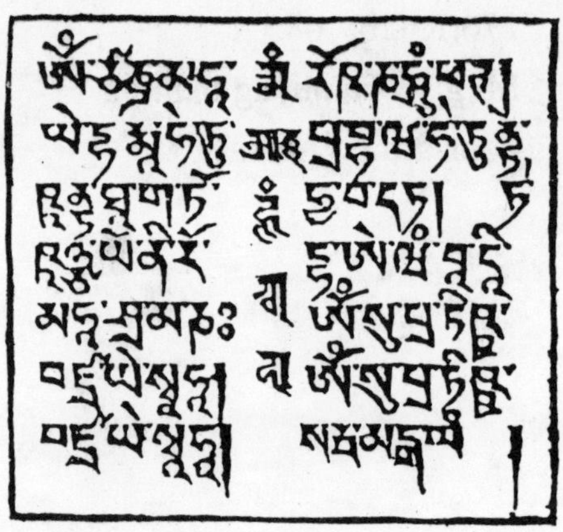

178(R63a) 687

Mi g'yo ba spre'u brgyad ma

Aṣṭakapi Acala

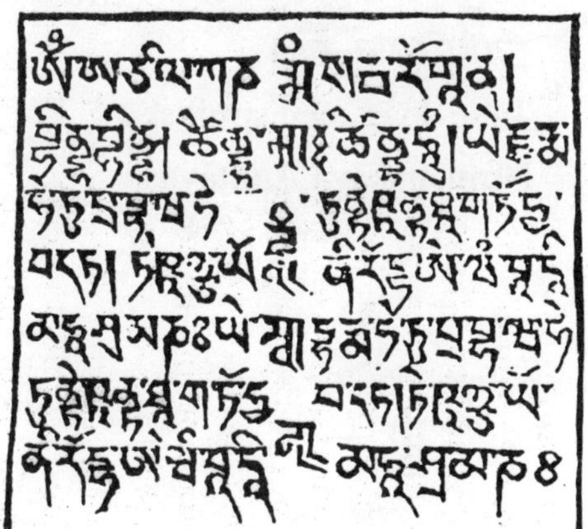

179(R63b) 688

Tshe dpag med sprul sku

Nirmāṇakāya Amitāyus

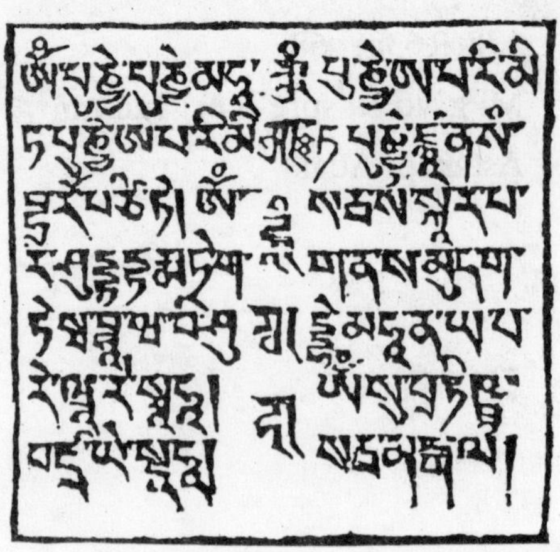

180(R63c) 689

Tshe dpag med ba ri lugs

Amitāyus of Ba ri school

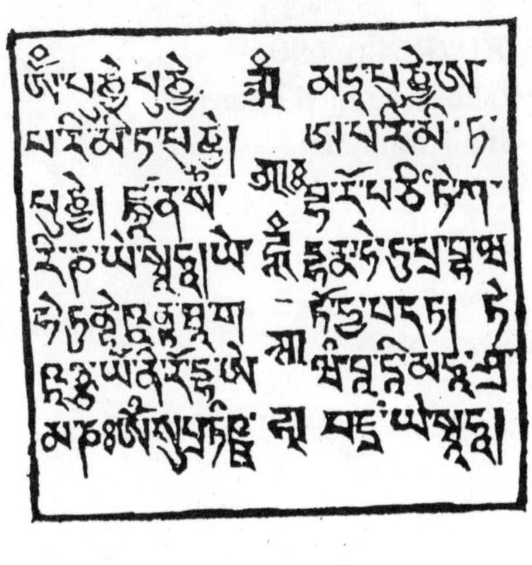

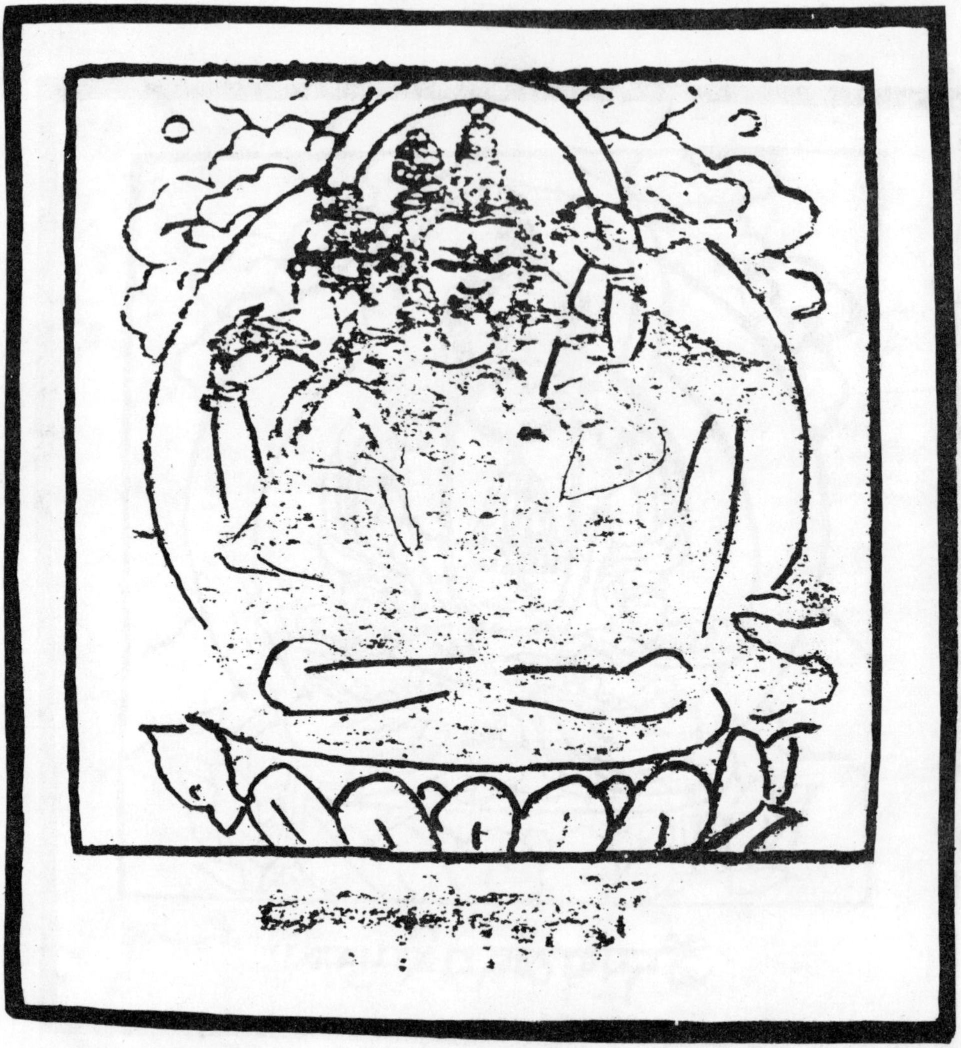

181*(R64a) 690
Tshe dpag med dkar po
Sita Amitāyus

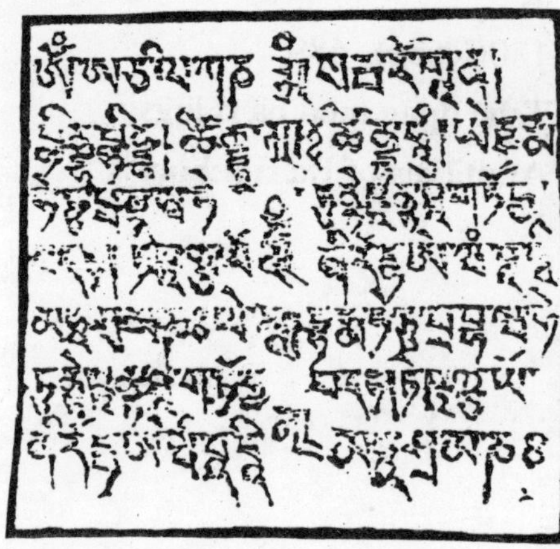

182*(R64b) 691

Tshe dpag med dkar po mi tra'i lugs

Sita Amitāyus of Mitra school

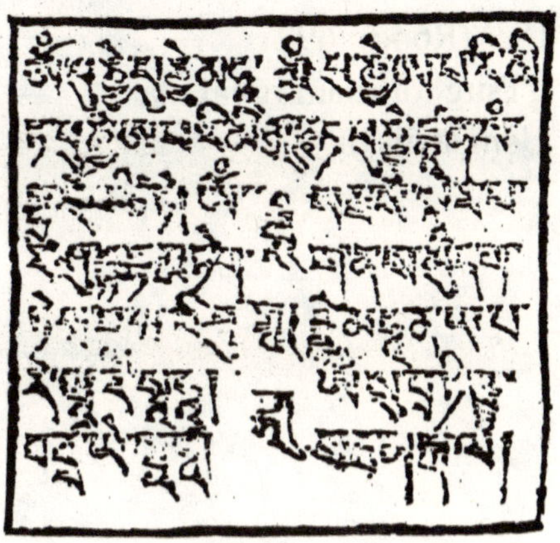

183*(R64c) 692
gTsug tor rnam rgyal ma
Uṣṇīṣavijayā

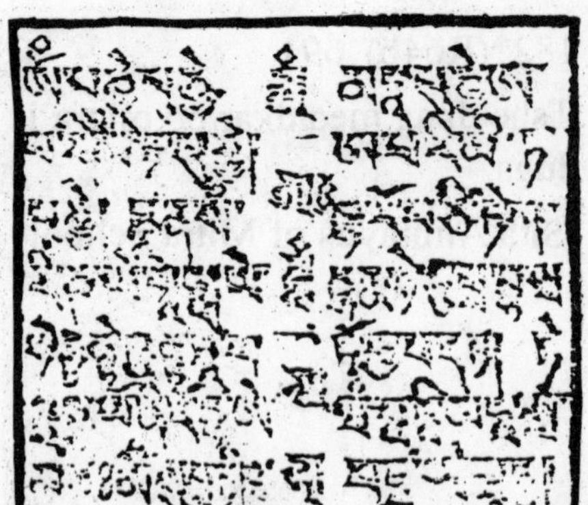

184(R65a) 693

'Chi med rdo rje lha mo

Amaravajradevī

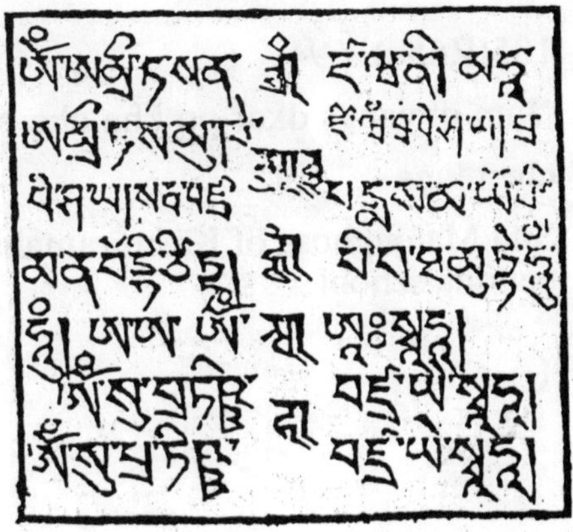

185(R65b) 694

'Jam dbyangs dkar po kha che paṇ chen lugs

Sita Mañjughoṣa of Kāśmīramahā-paṇḍita school

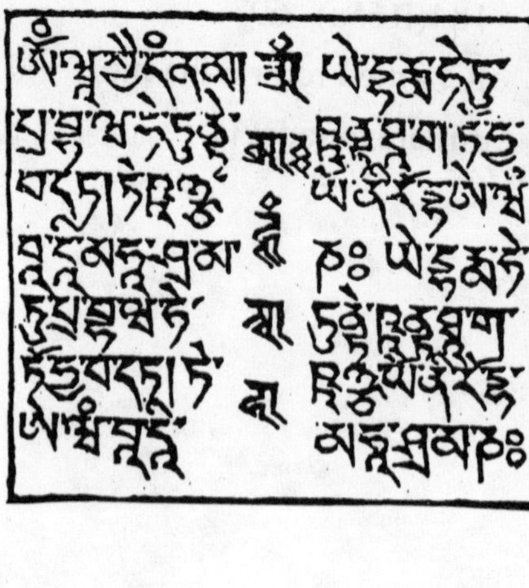

186(R65c) 695

'Jam dbyangs a ra pa tsa na dmar ser sa lugs

Raktapīta Arapacana Mañjughoṣa of Sa skya school

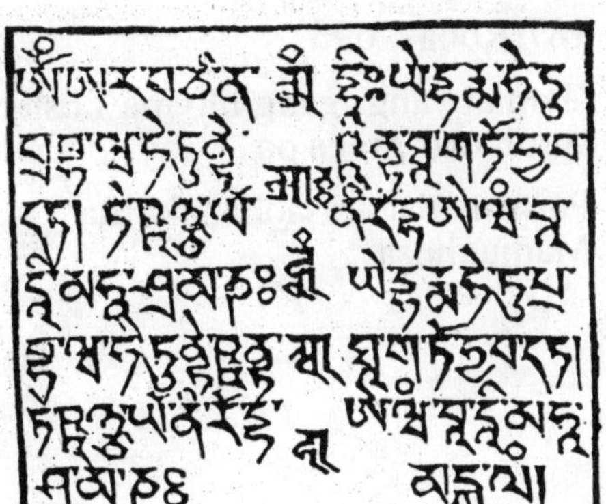

187(R66a) 696

'Jam dbyangs gang blo ma'i bstod sgrub mar grags pa

Pūrṇamatistotrasādhanakīrtita Mañjughoṣa

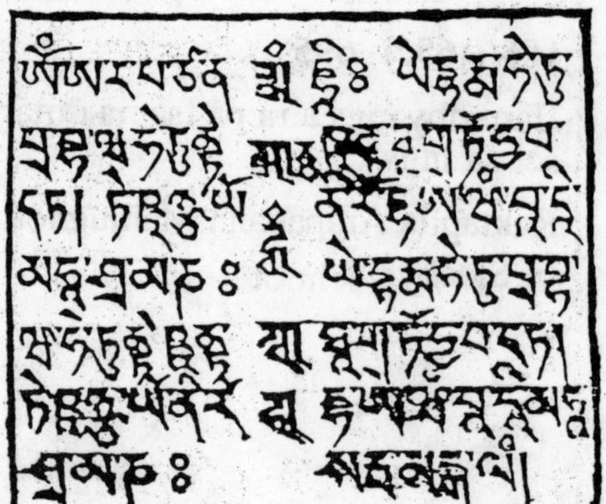

188(R66b) 697

'Jam dbyangs smra ba'i seng ge

Vādisiṃha Mañjughoṣa

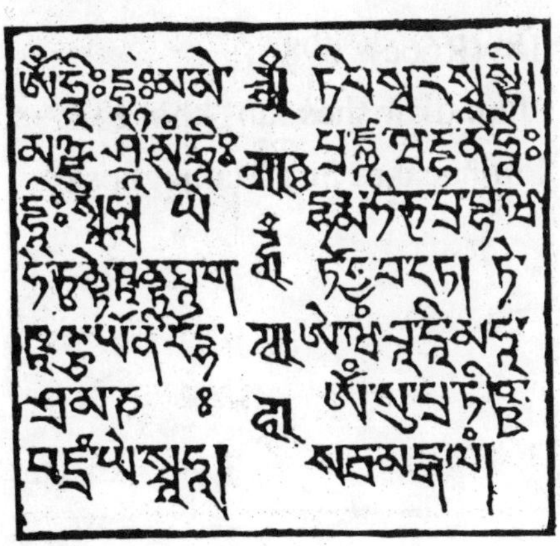

189(R66c) 698

'Jam dkar shes rab 'khor lo

Prajñācakra Sita Mañjughoṣa

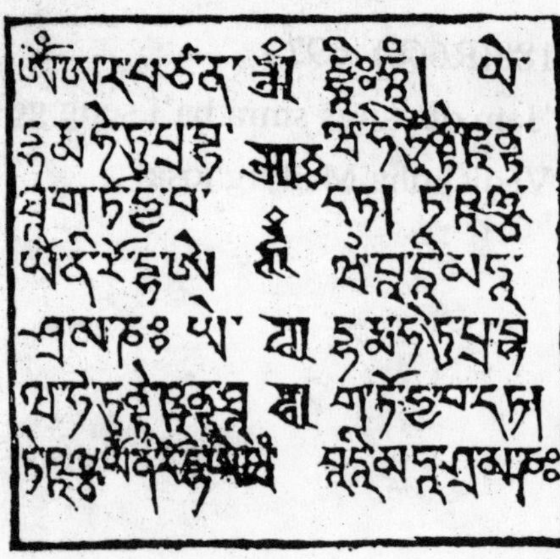

190(R67a) 699
Sher phyin ma dkar mo
Sita Prajñāpāramitā

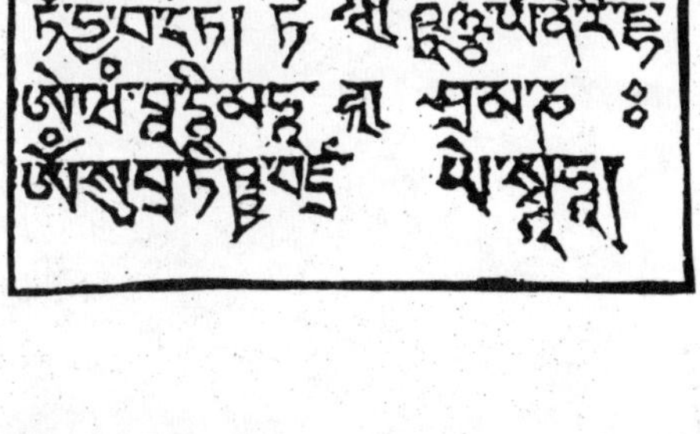

ཤེར་ཕྱིན་སེར་མོ་

191(R67b) 700

Sher phyin ser mo

Pīta Prajñāpāramitā

ཏདྱཐཱ། གཏེ་གཏེ། པཱ་ར་གཏེ། པ
རསཾ་གཏེ། བོ་དྷི་ [illegible]
[illegible]
[illegible]
[illegible]
[illegible]
[illegible]

192(R67c) 701
Byams pa
Maitreya

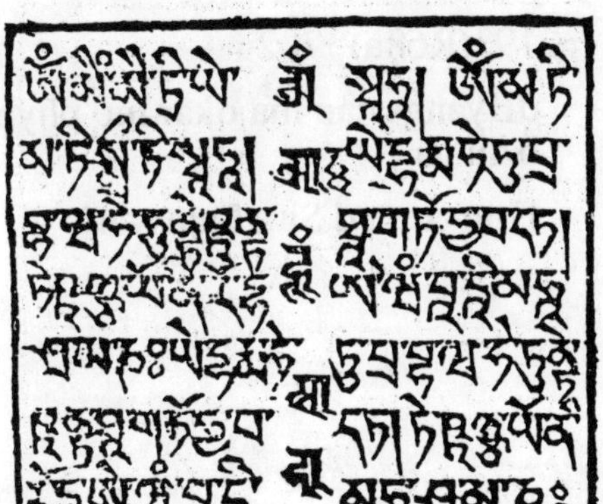

193(R68a) 702

dByangs can ma dkar mo phyag bzhi pa

Four-armed Sita Sarasvatī

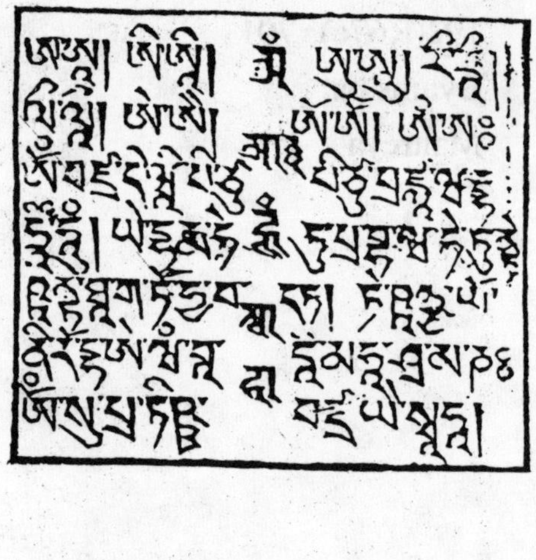

194(R68b) 703
dByangs can ma dmar po
Rakta Sarasvatī

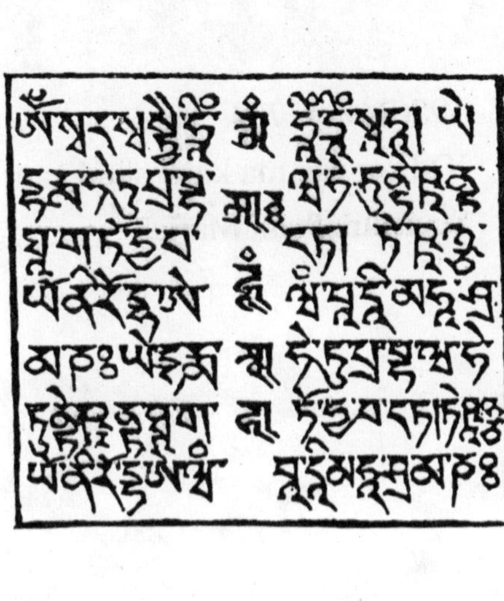

195(R68c) 704

'Od zer can ma khab skud can

Sūcīsūtradharā Mārīcī

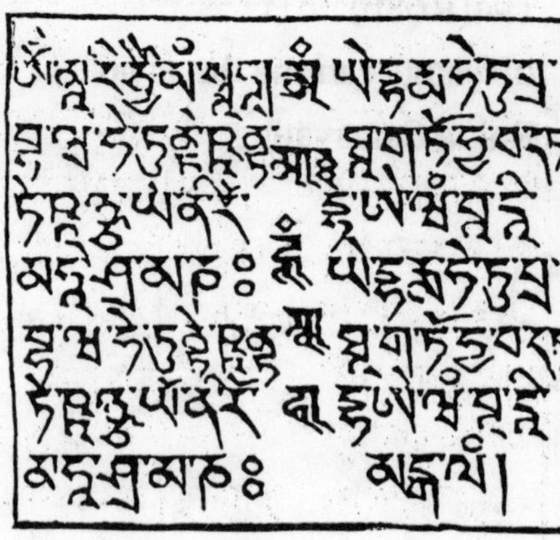

196(R69a) 705

gZungs las byung ba'i 'od zer can ma

Dhāranīvinirgatā Mārīcī

197(R69b) 706

Thub pa me ru shi ṣa

Meruśikhara Muni

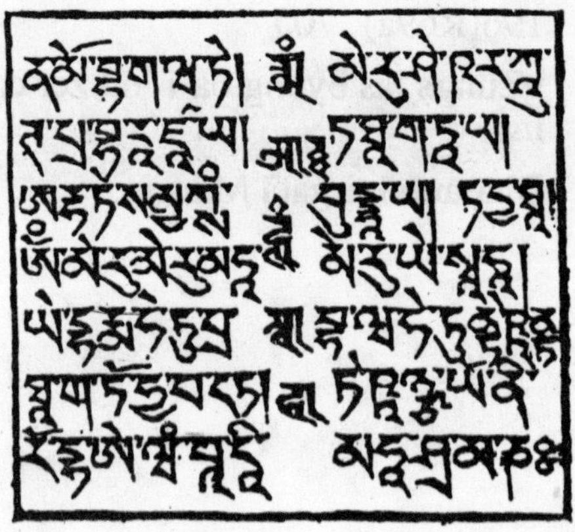

198(R69c) 707

sPyan ras gzigs yi ge phyed dang bzhi pa

Ardhacaturthākṣara Avalokiteśvara

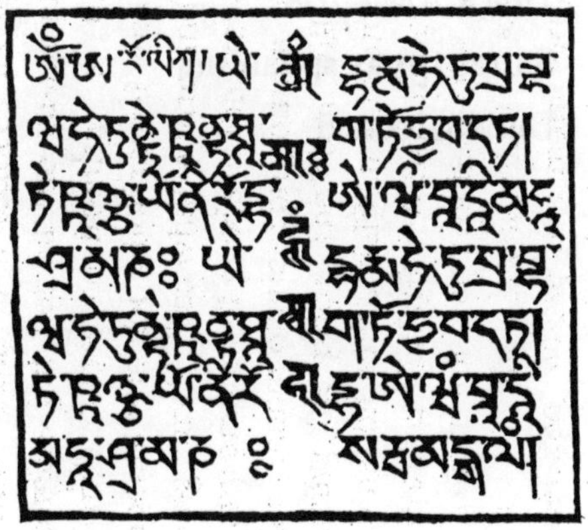

199(R70a) 708

Sangs rgyas spyan ma

Buddhalocanā

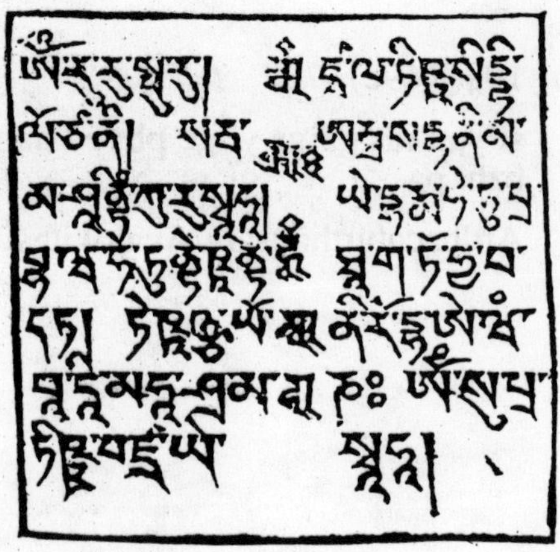

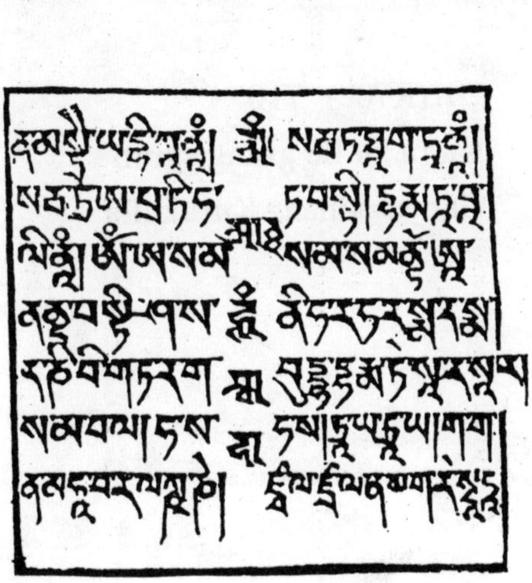

200(R70b) 709
Thub pa dam tshig gsum bkod
Trisamayavyūha Muni

201(R70c) 710

Ku ru ku lle gsang sgrub

Guhyasādhana Kurukullā

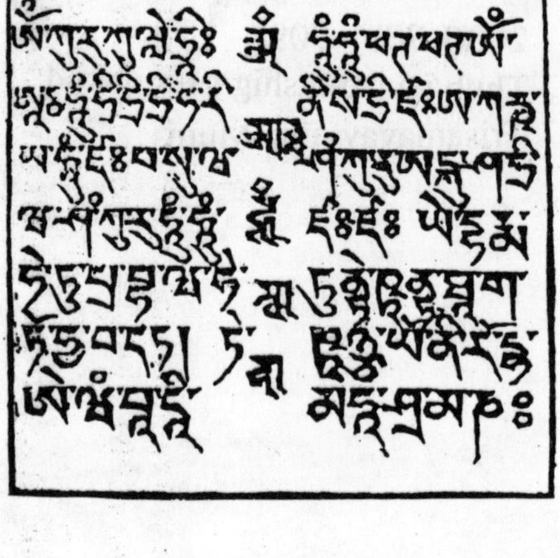

202(R70'a) 711
'Khor rDo rje mkha' 'gro ma
Attendant Vajraḍākinī

ཡེ་དྷརྨཱ་ཧེ་ཏུ་པྲ་བྷ་ཝཱ་ཧེ་
ཏུན་ཏེ་ཥཱན་ཏ་ཐཱ་ག་ཏོ་
ཧྱ་ཝ་དཏ྄་ཏེ་ཥཱཉྩ་ཡོ་
ནི་རོ་དྷ་ཨེ་ཝཾ་ཝཱ་དཱི་
མ་ཧཱ་ཤྲ་མ་ཎཿ་སྭཱ་ཧཱ།

203(R70'b) 712

Khor Rin chen mkha' 'gro ma

Attendant Ratnaḍākinī

ཡེ་ དྷརྨཱ་ཧེ་ཏྲཱུཾ་ ཏ་པྲ་བྷ་སྭཱ
ཧེ་ཏུ་ ཏྲེ་ ཥཱཾ་ཏ་ཐཱ་ག་ ཏོ
ཧྱ་ བ་ ད་ ཏཱ་ཀྵཱཾ་ ཏེ་ ཥཱཉྩ་ཡོ
ནི་རོ་ དྷ་ཨེ་ཝཾ་ཝཱ་དཱི་ མ་ ཧཱ
ཤྲ་མ་ ཎཿ་ སྭཱ་ཧཱ་ ཧ་ སརྦ་ཡཾ།

204(R70'c) 713

'Khor Padma mkha' 'gro ma

Attendant Padmaḍākinī

ཡེ་དྷརྨཱ་ཧེ་ཏུ་པྲཾ་བྷ་ཝཱ
ཧེ་ཏུ་ནྟེ་ཥཱ་ནྟ་ཐཱཿགཿཏོ་ཧྱ
ཝ་དཏ། ཏེ་ཥཱཉྩ་ཡོ་ནི
རོ་དྷ་ཨེ་ཝཾ་ཝཱ་དཱི་མ་ཧཱ
ཤྲ་མ་ཎ ཿ [illegible]

205(R71a) 714

'Khor Las kyi mkha' 'gro ma

Attendant Karmaḍākinī

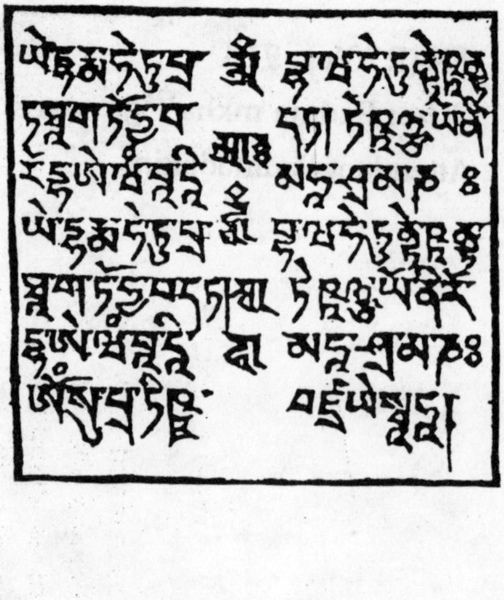

206(R71b) 715
dPal mo snying gi gser thig can
Garbhasuvarṇasūtra Śrī

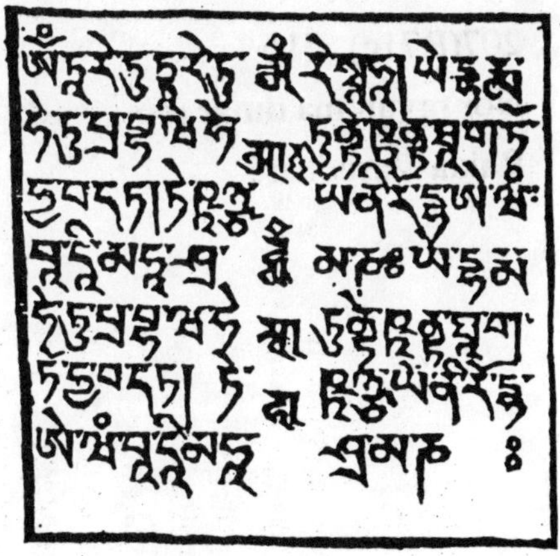

207(R71c) 716

Nor rgyun ma dmar mo

Rakta Vasudhārā

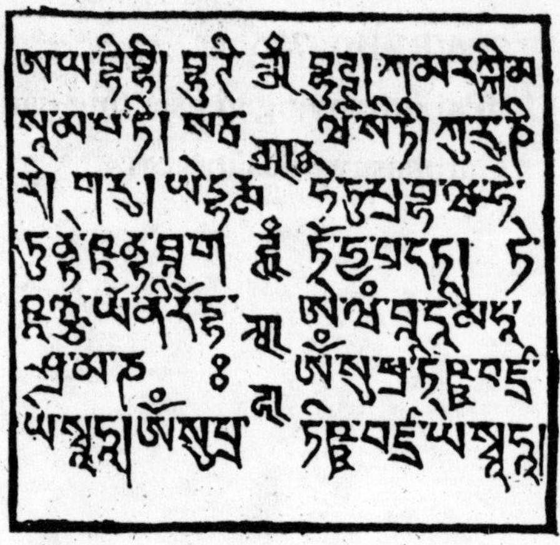

208(R72a) 717

lHa mo ti nu

Ti nu Devī

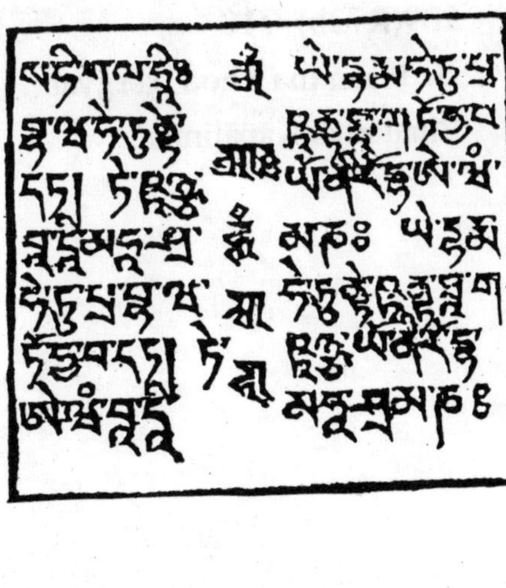

209(R72b) 718

rJe btsun ma Thod pa rgyan

Bhaṭṭārikā Kapālinī

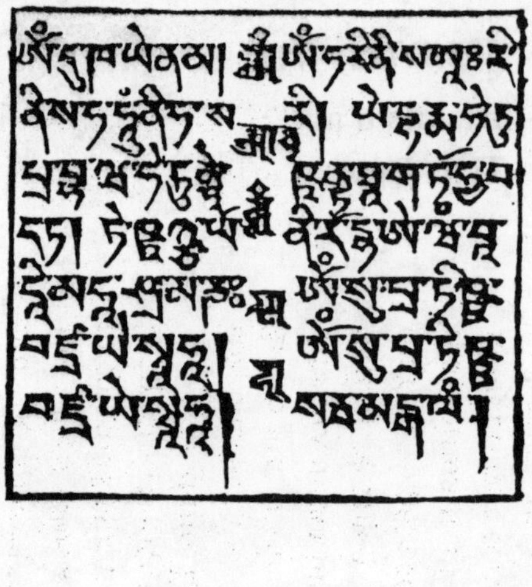

210(R72c) 719
gSang ba ye shes
Guhyajñāna

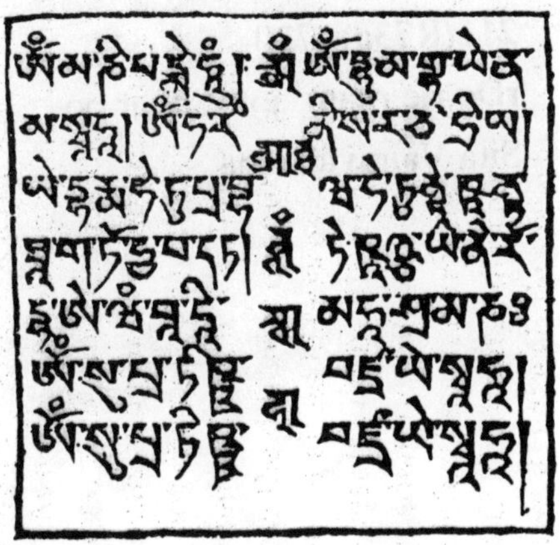

211(R73a) 720

rDo rje rnam 'joms dkar po

Sita Vajravidāraṇa

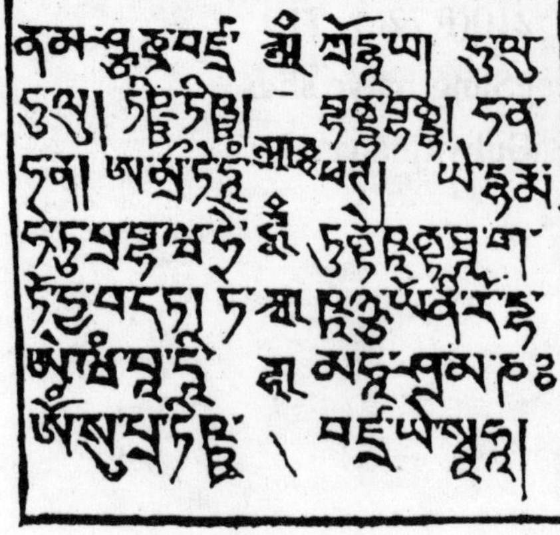

212(R73b) 721

rDo rje rnam 'joms mthing kha

Nīla Vajravidāraṇa

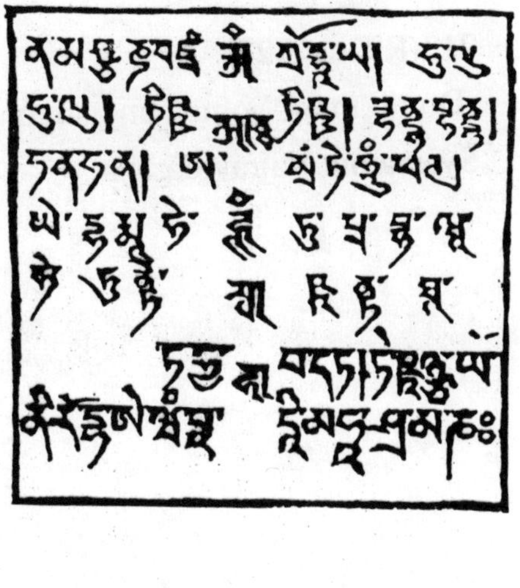

213(R73c) 722

rDo rje rnam 'joms ljang sngon

Śyāmanīla Vajravidāraṇa

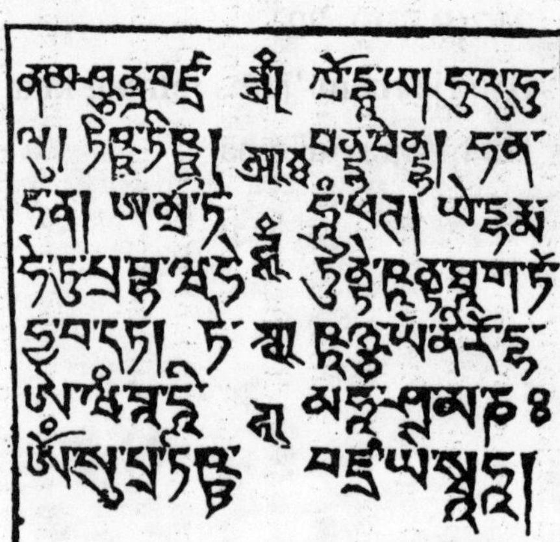

214(R74a) 723

Khro bo bgegs mthar byed

Krodha Vighnāntaka

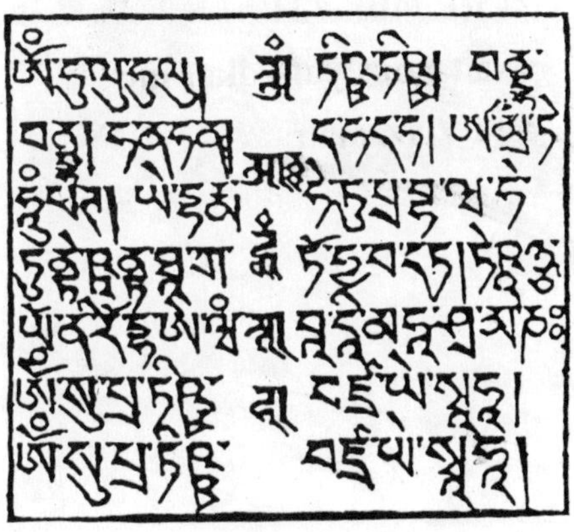

215(R74b) 724

sNa tshogs yum dkar mo

Sita Viśvamātṛ

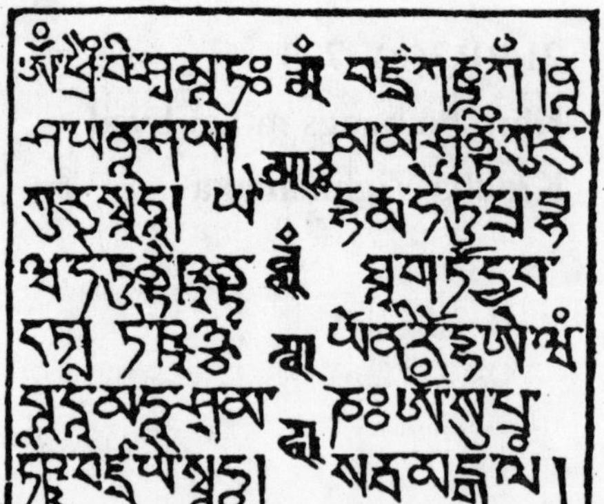

216(R74c) 725
rDo rje gur nas gsungs pa'i so sor 'grang ma
Vajrapañjarabhāṣitā Pratisarā

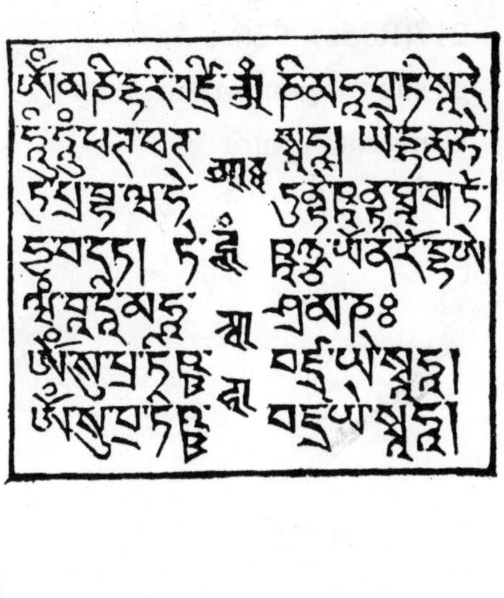

217(R75a) 726

gTsug tor gdugs dkar

Uṣṇīṣasitātapatrā

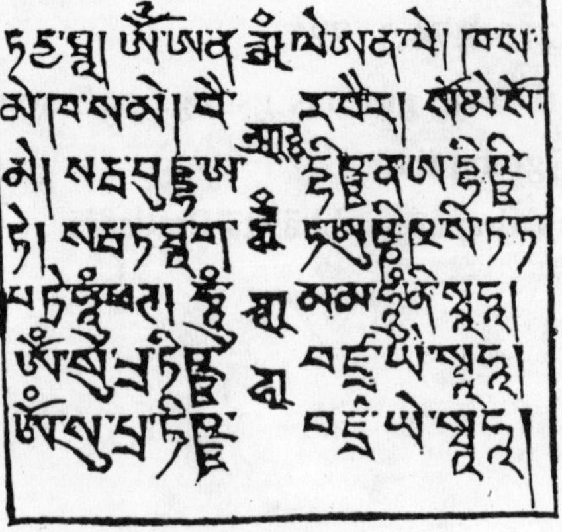

218(R75b) 727

Ri khrod lo ma gyon ma ser mo

Pīta Parṇaśabarī

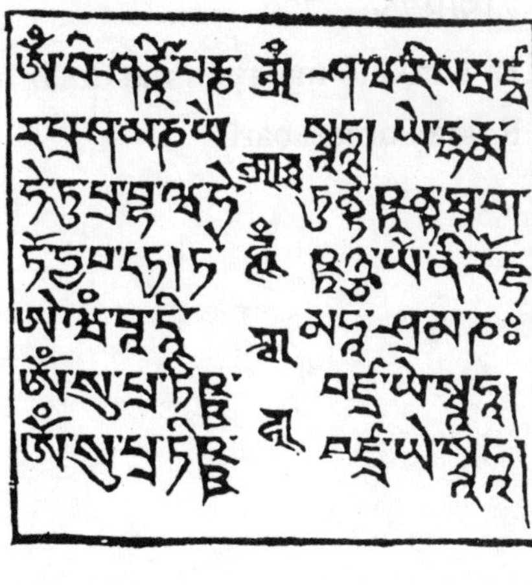

219(R75c) 728

Ri khrod lo ma gyon ma dmar mo

Rakta Parṇaśabarī

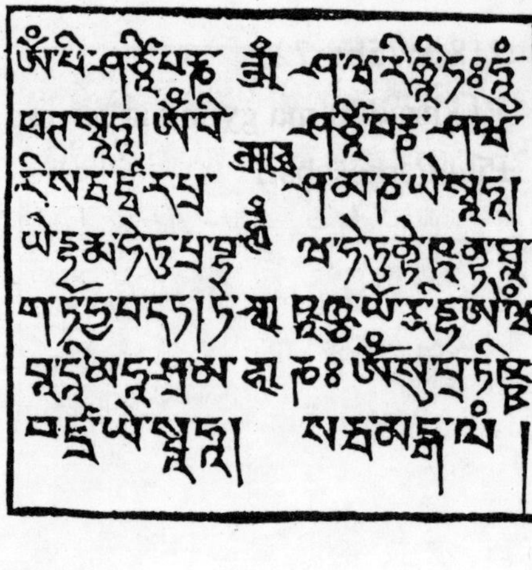

220(R76a) 729

Ri khrod lo ma gyon ma sngon po

Nīla Parṇaśabarī

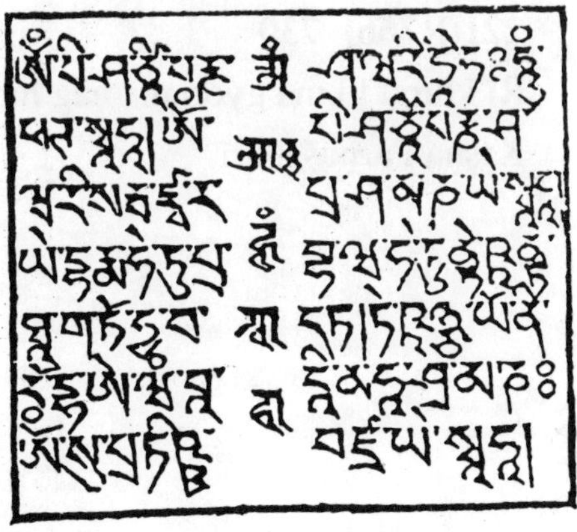

221(R76b) 730

Ri khrod lo ma gyon ma nag mo

Kṛṣṇa Parṇaśabarī

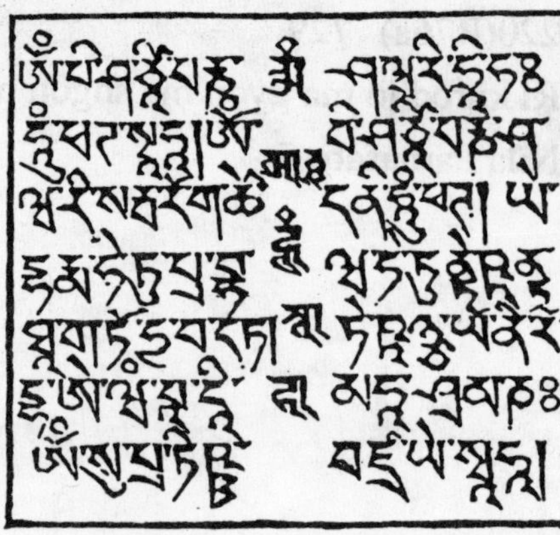

222(R76c) 731
Ri khrod lo ma gyon ma ljang gu
Śyāma Parṇaśabarī

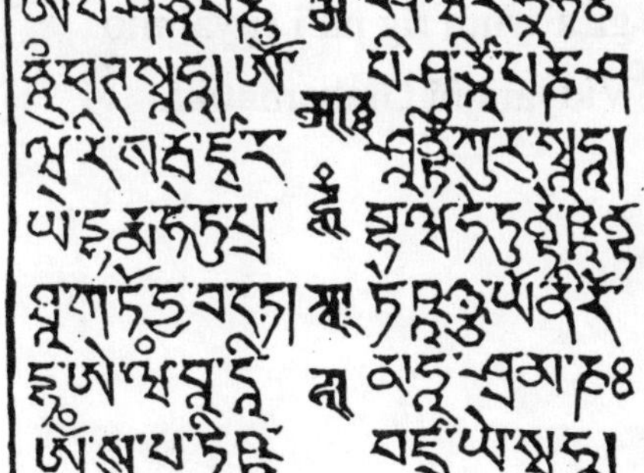

223(R77a) 732

gZa' yum rig pa'i rgyal mo

Vidyārājñī Grahamātṛkā

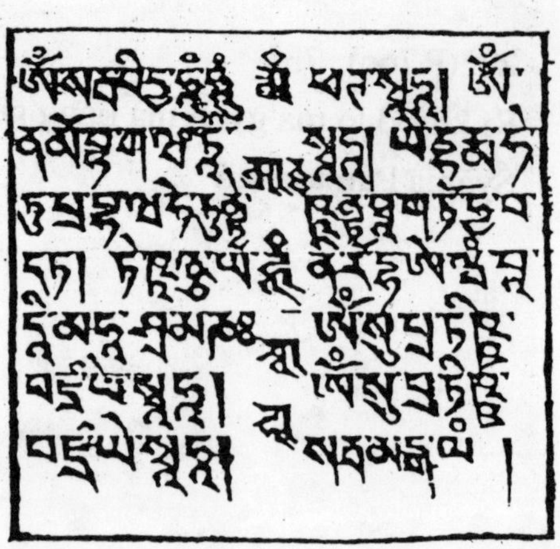

224(R77b) 733

Khro bo sme brtsegs dud kha

Dhūmavarṇa Krodha Bhurkuṃkūṭa

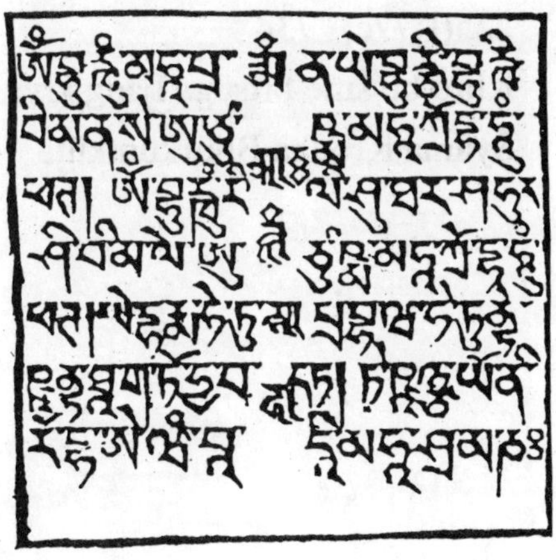

225(R77c) 734

Khro bo sme brtsegs ljang khu

Śyāma Krodha Bhurkuṃkūṭa

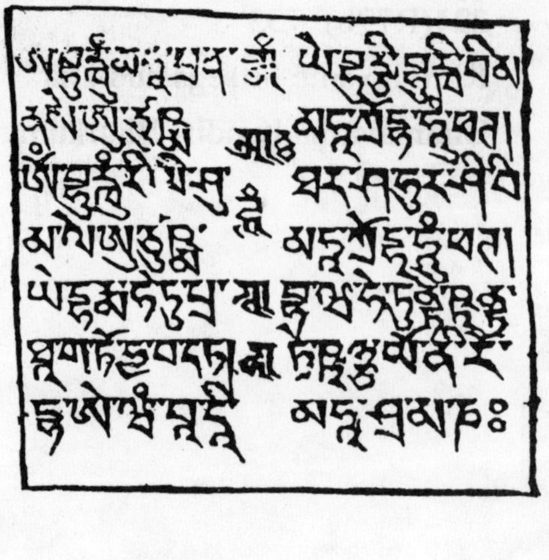

226*(R78a) 735

Khro mo sme brtsegs

Krodha Bhurkuṃkūṭī

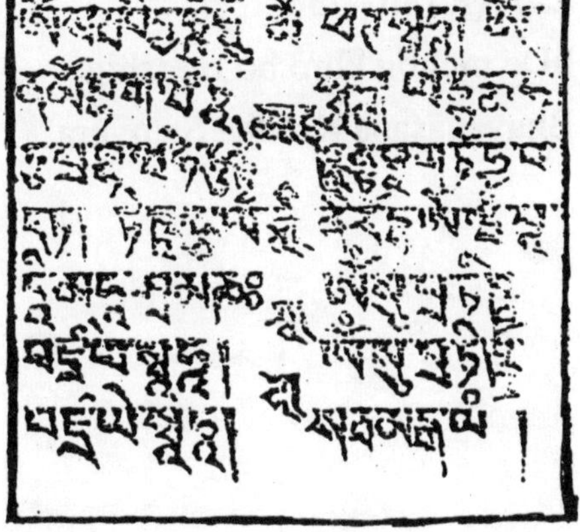

227*(R78b) 736

bDe mchog khro bo rig tshig

Bhayanāśana Krodha Saṃvara

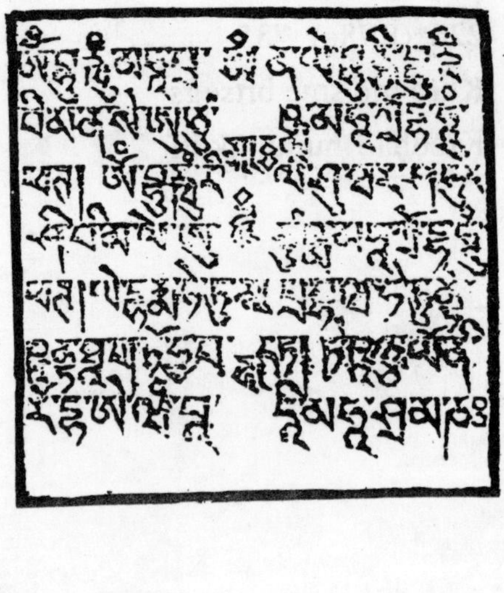

228*(R78c) 737

bDe mchog rdo rje mkha' lding

Vajragaruḍa Saṃvara

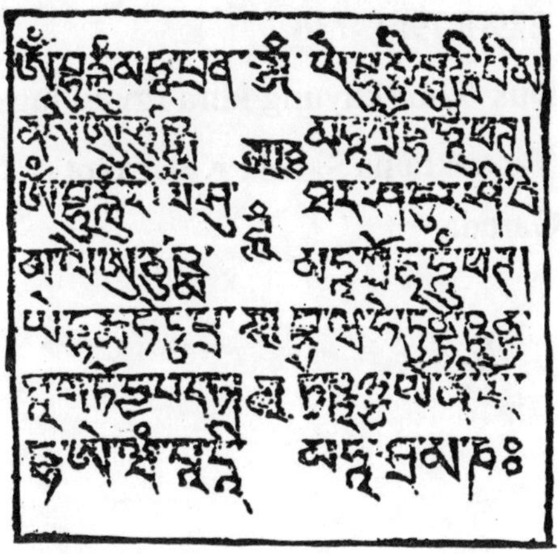

དུས་འཁོར་ཁྱུང་ཁྲ་རྒྱུད་ལུགས་

229(R79a) 738

Dus 'khor khyung khra rgyud lugs

Tantrakrama Śabala Kālacakra

Garuḍa

ཨོཾ་པཀྴིཾ་སྭཱཧཱ། ཀྵཱི ཨེ་ཧྲ་སྨུ་རེ་
ཙ་པྲ་ཧྲ་སྭ་ཀཱལ་རེ་ཙཀྲེ་ཧྲཱུ
ཀྵ་ག་ཧོ་ཛྲ བ་དད། རེ
ཧྲ་ཀྵ་ཡོ་ནི་ཀྵཱི་ཧོ་ཧྲ་ཨོ་སྶཾ
ལྲ་དྲི་མཧྲ་སྭཱ་ཤྲ་མ་ཧཿ
ཨོཾ་སྲུ་པྲ་ཧྲེ་ནཱ་ཀྵྱ་བརྡ་ཡེ
སྭཱཧཱ། སཙ་ མནྟ་ལཾ།

230(R79b) 739

Khyung khra man ngag lugs

Upadeśakrama Śabala Garuḍa

ཨོཾ་པཀྵིཾ་སྭཱ་ཧཱ། ཀྵཱཿ ཨོཾ་པཀྵིཾ་སྭཱ་ཧཱ།
ཨོཾ་པཀྵིཾ་སྭཱ་ཧཱ། ཨཱཿཧཱུྃ ཨོཾ་པཀྵིཾ་སྭཱ་ཧཱ།
ཨོཾ་པཀྵིཾ་སྭཱ་ཧཱ། ཡེ་དྷརྨཱ་ཧེ་
ཏུ་པྲ་བྷ་ཝཱ་ཧེ་ ཧཱུྃ ཏུནྟེ་ཥཱན་ཏ་
ཐཱ་ག་ཏོ་ཧྱ་ཝ་ད་ཏ། ཏེ་
ཥཱཉྩ་ཡོ་ནི་ ཝཱ་རོ་དྷ་ཨེ་ཝཾ་
ཝཱ་དཱི་མ་ཧཱ་ཤྲ་ མ་ཎཿ ཨུ་ཧཱུྃ།

ཁྱུང་སེར་བཀའ་གདམས་ལུགས

231(R79c) 740

Khyung ser bka' gdams lugs

Pīta Garuḍa of bKa' gdams school

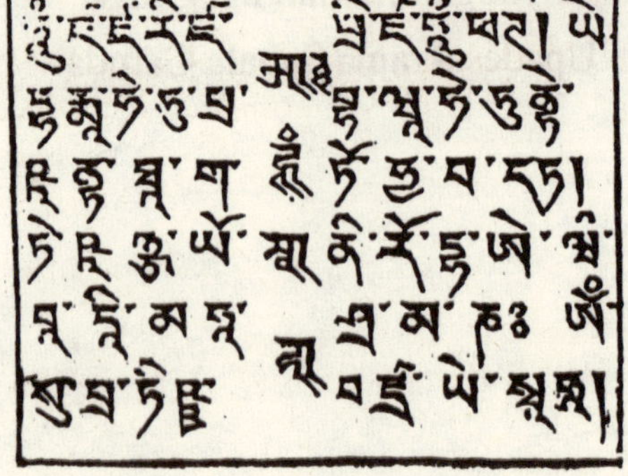

232(R80a) 741

'Jam dbyangs nag po

Kṛṣṇa Mañjughoṣa

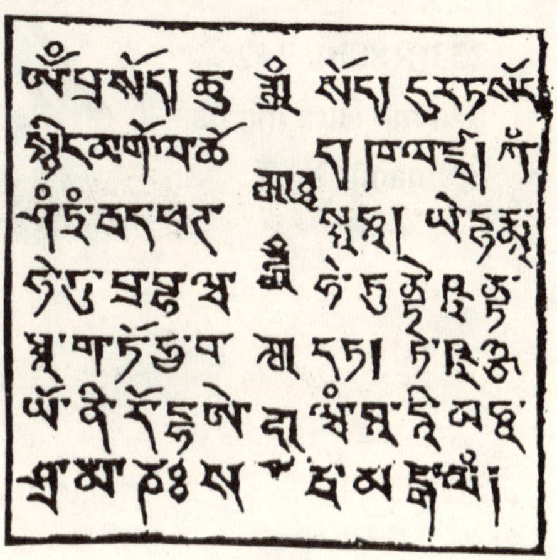

233(R80b) 742

lHa mo shra ma ṇa

Śramaṇā Devī

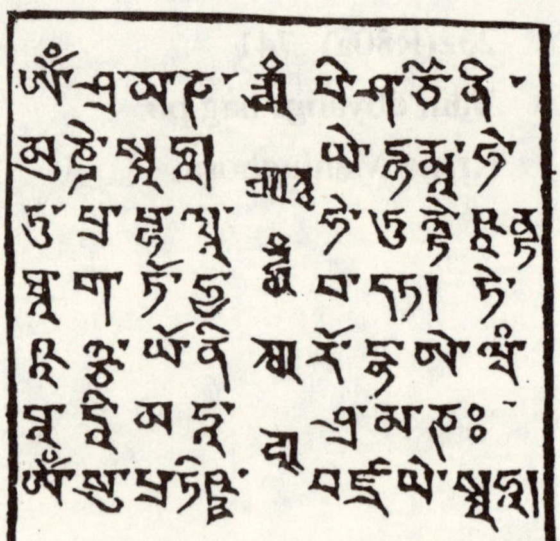

234(R80c) 743
Seng gdong ma sngon mo
Nīla Siṃhavaktrā

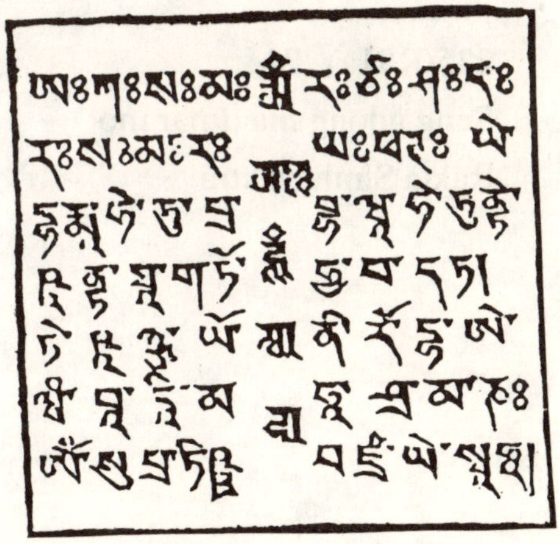

235(R81a) 744

Seng gdong ma dmar mo

Rakta Siṃhavaktrā

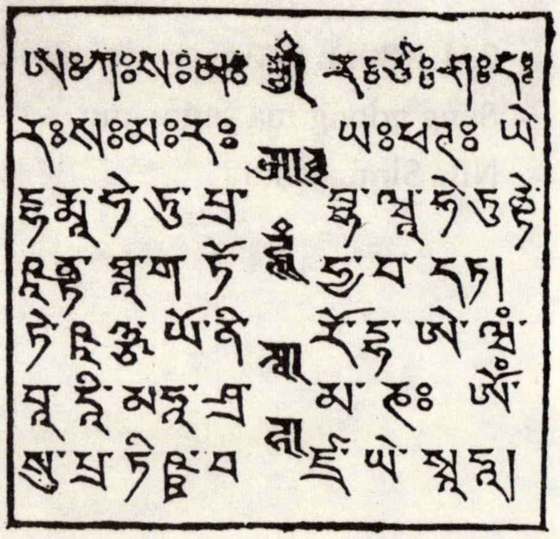

236(R81b) 745

'Jam dpal nāga rakṣa

Nāgarakṣa Mañjuśrī

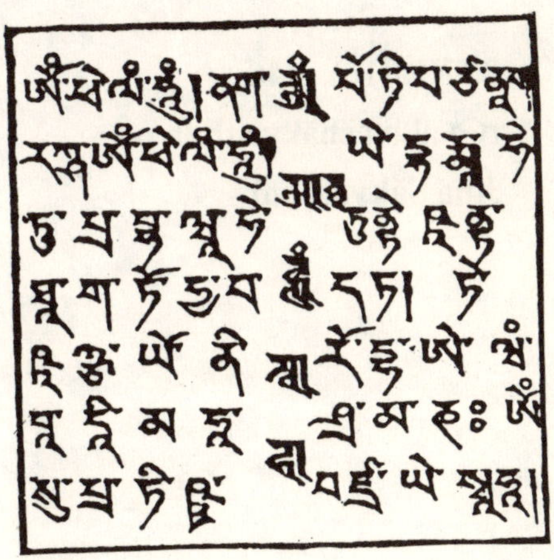

237(R81c) 746
rGyal ba shākya thub pa
Jina Śākyamuni

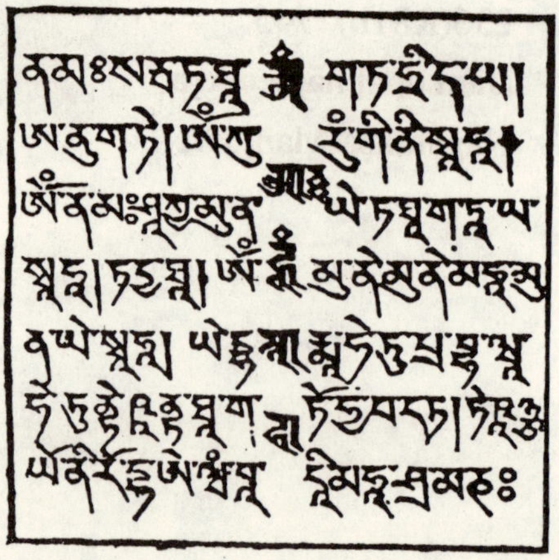

238(R82a) 747
Sangs rgyas rnam gzigs
Vaiśyin Buddha

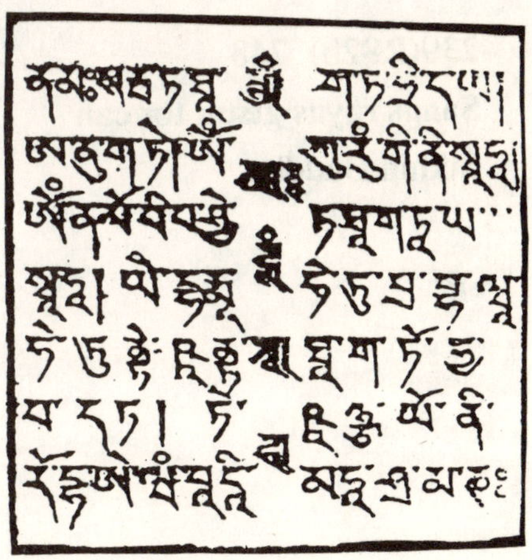

239(R82b) 748
Sangs rgyas gtsug tor can
Śikhin Buddha

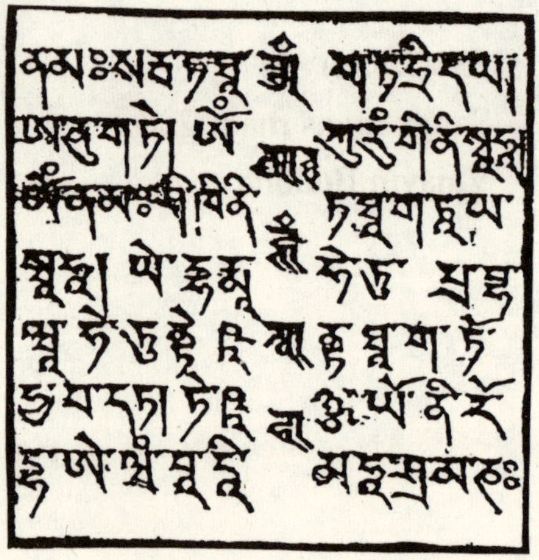

240(R82c) 749

Sangs rgyas thams cad skyob

Viśvabhū Buddha

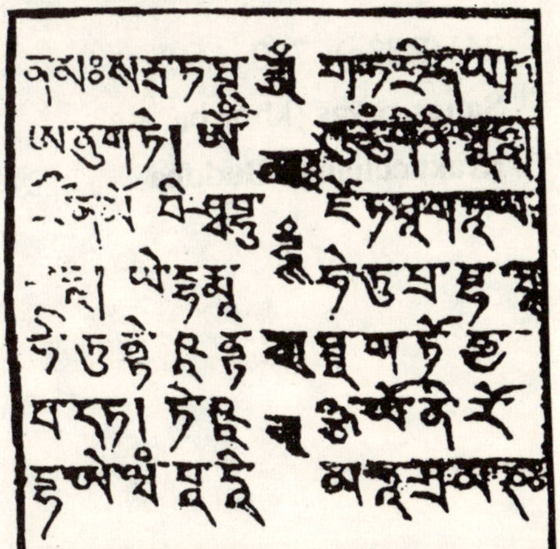

241(R83a) 750
Sangs rgyas 'khor ba 'jig
Krakucchanda Buddha

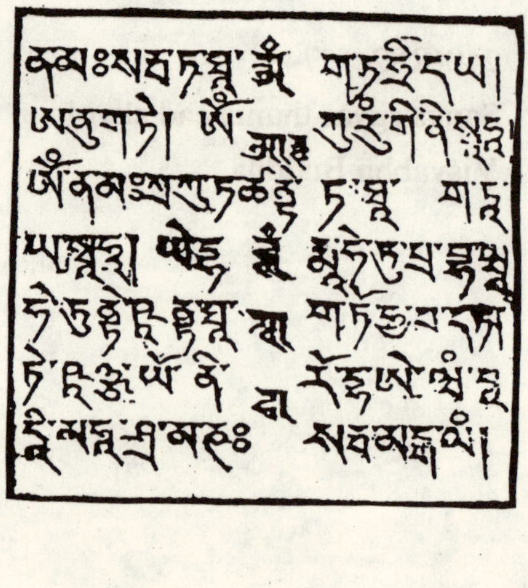

242(R83b) 751

Sangs rgyas gser thub

Kanakamuni Buddha

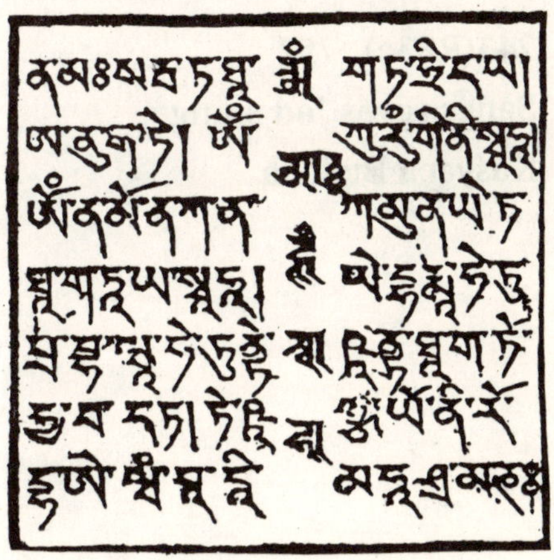

243(R83c) 752

Sangs rgyas 'od srung

Kāśyapa Buddha

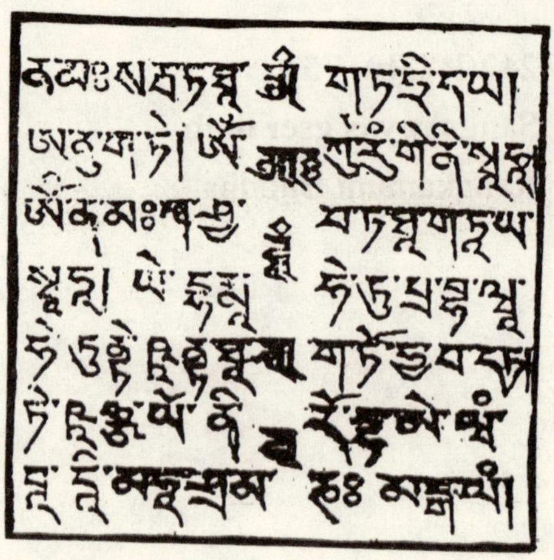

244(R84a) 753
Khro bo chen po
Mahākrodha

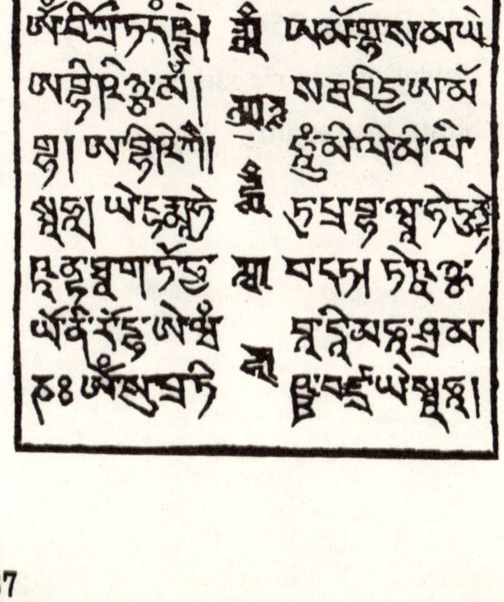

245(R84b) 754

Phyag na rdo rje zhi ba

Śānta Vajrapāṇi

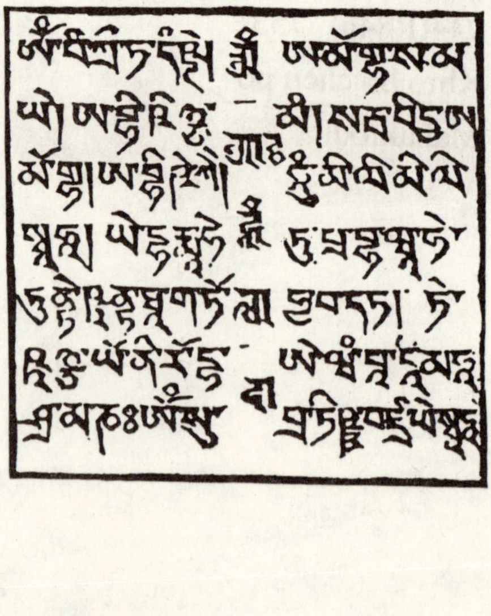

246(R84c) 755
’Od dpag med
Amitābha

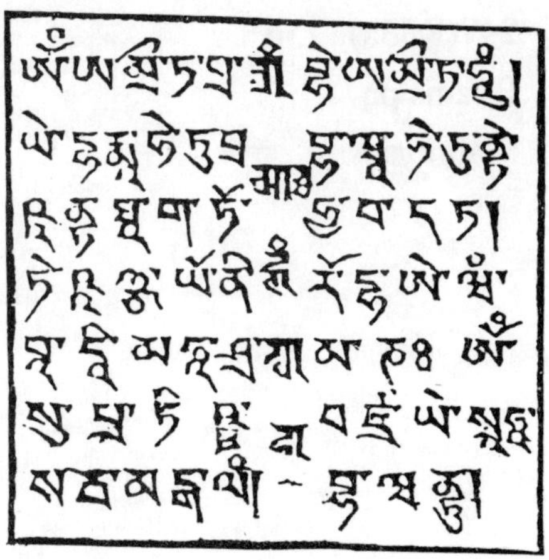

247(R85a) 756

Byams pa

Maitreya

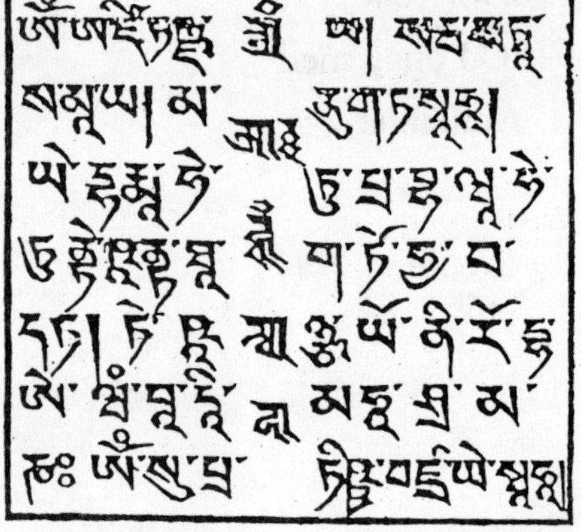

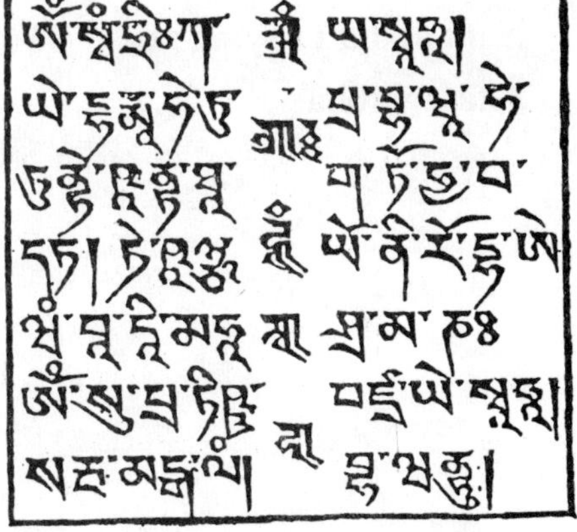

248(R85b) 757
Kun tu bzang po
Samantabhadra

249(R85c) 758

Nam mkha'i snying po

Ākāśagarbha

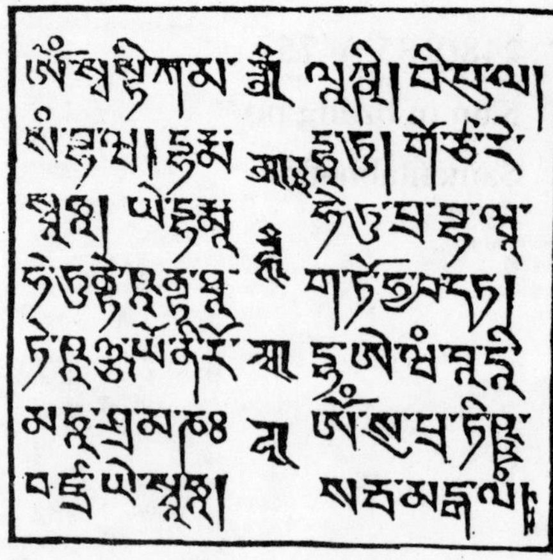

250(R86a) 759
Sa'i snying po
Kṣitigarbha

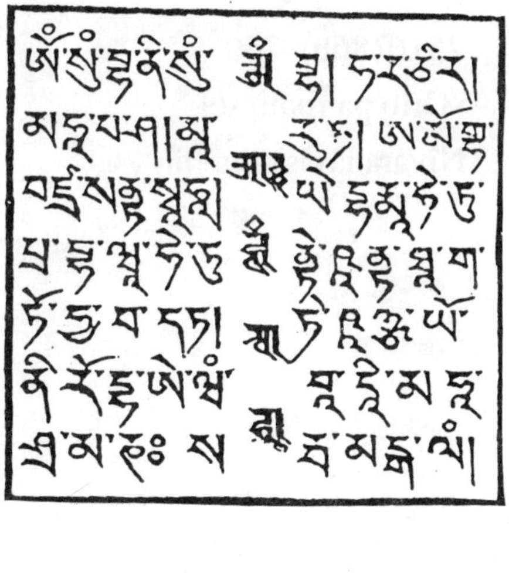

251(R86b) 760

sGrib pa rnam sel

Nīvaraṇaviṣkambhin

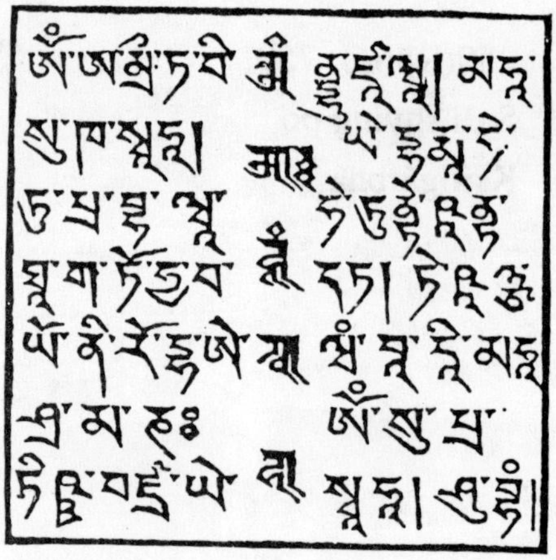

252(R86c) 761

sPyan ras gzigs 'jigs pa brgyad skyob

Aṣṭabhayatrāṇa Avalokiteśvara

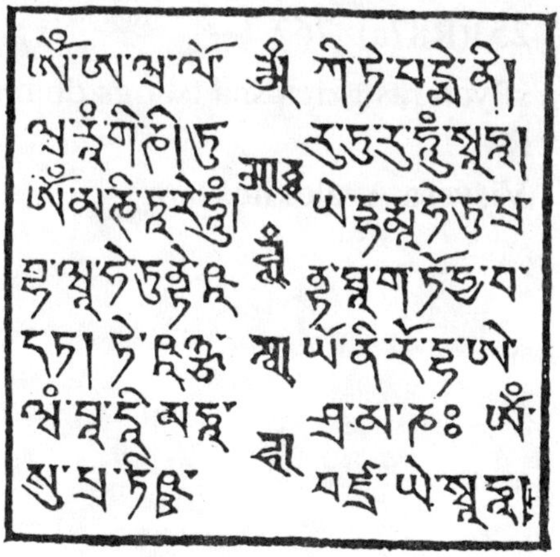

253(R87a) 762

sPyan ras gzigs sna tshogs dbang po

Viśveśa Avalokiteśvara

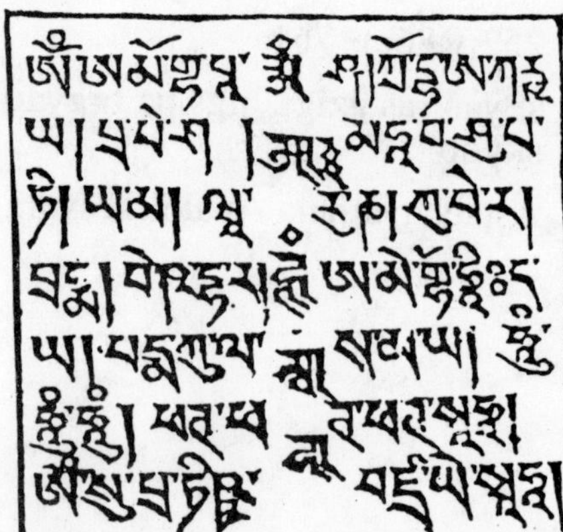

254(R87b) 763

sPyan ras gzigs padma'i phyag

Padmapāṇi Avalokiteśvara

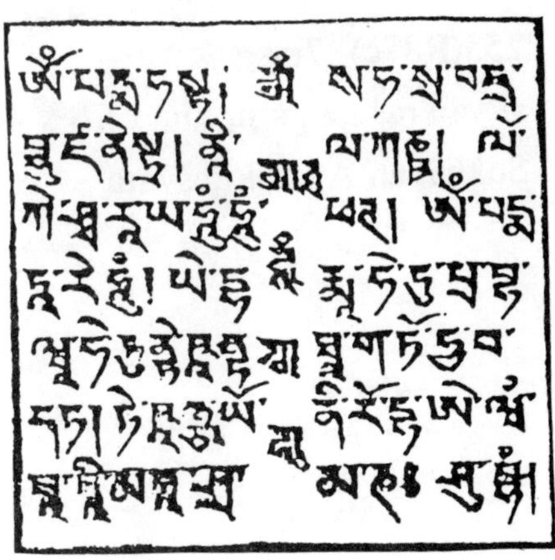

255(R87c) 764
sPyan ras gzigs su kha va ti
Sukhāvatī Avalokiteśvara

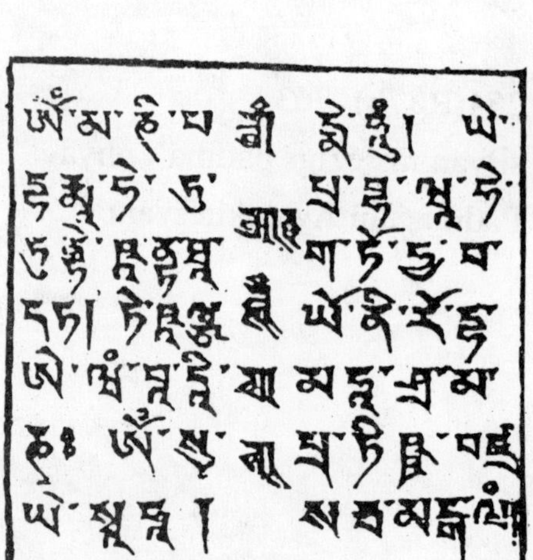

སྤྱན་རས་གཟིགས་དོན་ཡོད་ལྕགས་ཀྱུ།

256(R88a) 765

sPyan ras gzigs don yod lcags kyu

Amoghāṅkuśa Avalokiteśvara

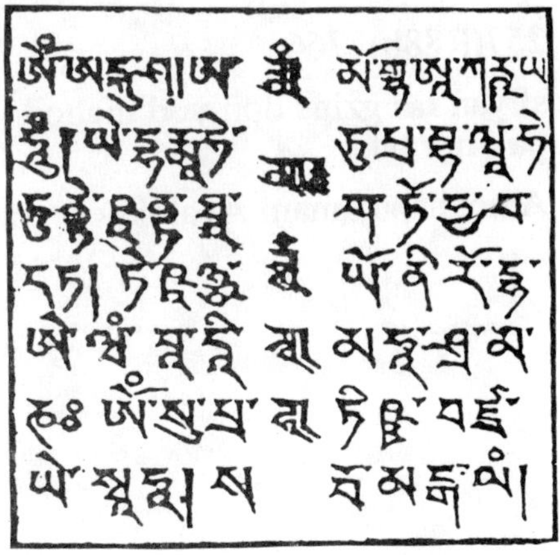

257(R88b) 766

sPyan ras gzigs don yod mchod pa'i nor bu

Amoghapūjāmaṇi Avalokiteśvara

ཨོཾ་ཨ་མོ་གྷ་པཱུ་ཛ་ [illegible] མ་ཎི་ པདྨ
བཛྲེ་ཏ་ཐཱ་ག་ཏ། [illegible] བི་ལོ་ཀི་ཏེ
ས་མནྟ་པྲ་སར [illegible] ཧཱུྃ། ཡེ་དྷརྨཱ
ཧེ་ཏུ་པྲ་བྷ་ཝཱ་ཧེ་ཏུནྟེ [illegible] ཥཱན྄་ཏ་ཐཱ་ག་ཏོ་ཧྱ་ཝ་དཏ྄
ཏེ་ཥཱཉྩ་ཡོ་ནི [illegible] རོ་དྷ་ཨེ་ཝཾ
བཱ་དཱི་མ་ཧཱ་ཤྲ [illegible] མ་ཎཿ ཨོཾ
སུ་པྲ་ཏིཥྛ་བ [illegible] ཛྲ་ཡེ་སྭཱ་ཧཱ།

258(R88c) 767
gSang bdag lhan skyes zhi ba
Śānta Sahaja Guhyapati

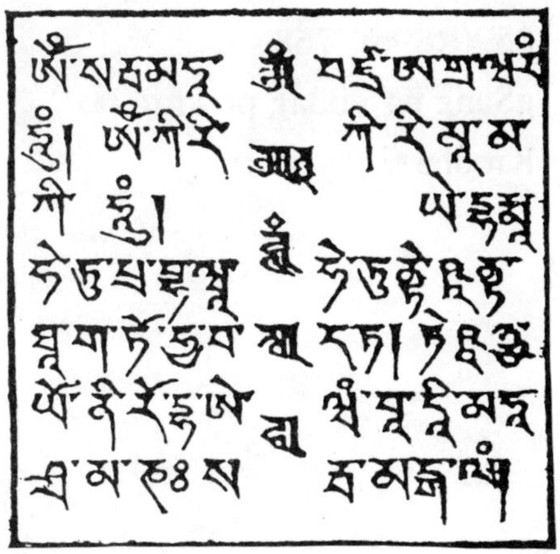

259(R89a) 768

gSang ba'i bdag po khro bo

Krodha Guhyapati

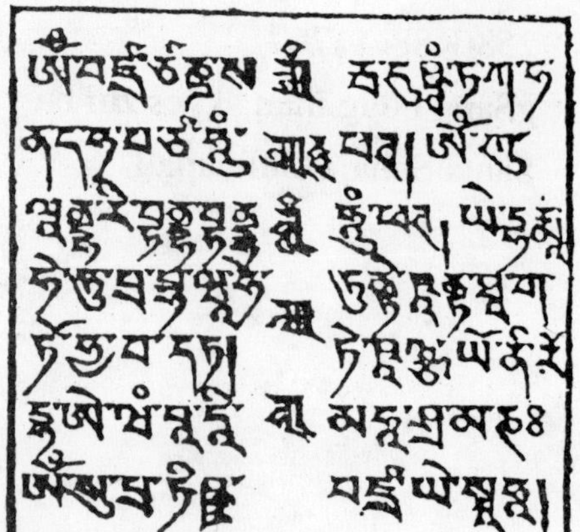

260(R89b) 769
lHa mo mā ma ki
Māmakī Devī

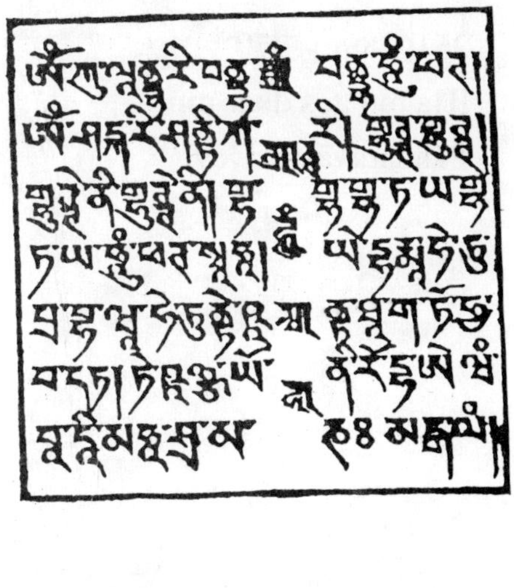

261(R89c) 770

lHa mo gos dkar mo

Pāṇḍaravāsinī Devī

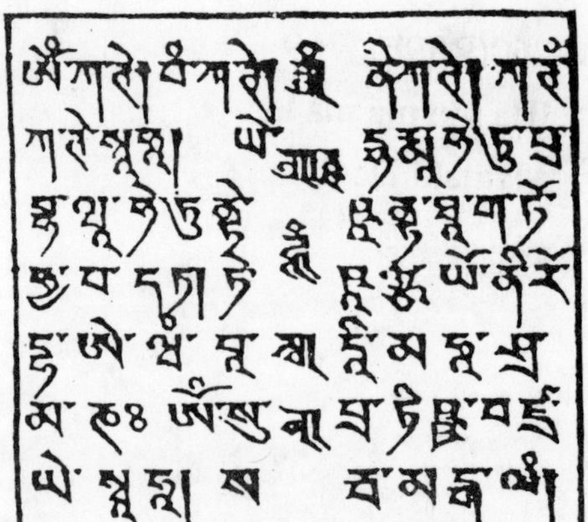

262(R90a) 771

gTsug tor rnam rgyal phyag gnyis ma

Two-armed Uṣṇīṣavijayā

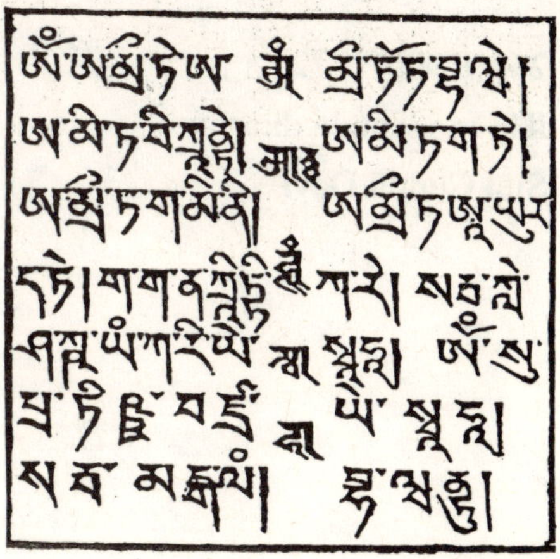

263(R90b) 772

lHa mo tsunda dkar mo

Sita Cundā Devī

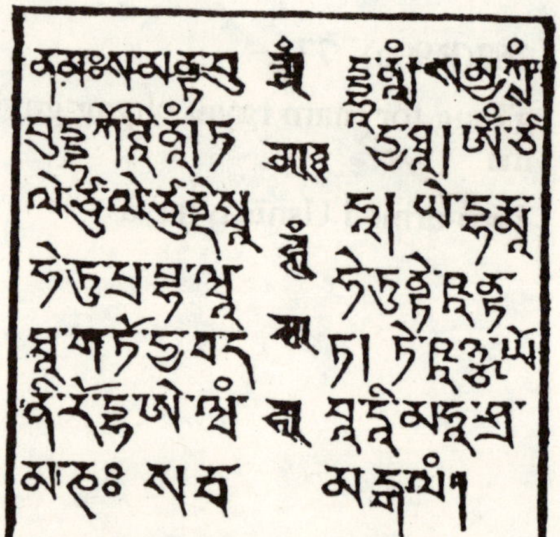

ཁྲོ་བོ་གཞན་གྱིས་མི་ཐུབ་པ་

264(R90c)   773
Khro bo gzhan gyis mi thub pa
Krodha Aparājita

ནམཿསམནྟཱ ཨོཾ ཡཀྵ་ཀ་ཙི་ཧྲ་ཕཊ
ཧཾ་ཨོཾ་ཧྲུཾ་ཧེ་ན་རི་ཏི་ ཨཱཿ ཧྲ་ཧྲུཾ་ཧྲུཾ་ཧྲུཾ་ཕཊ
སྭཱཧཱ། ཨོཾ་ཨོཾ་ཨ ཧཱུྃ པ་ར་ཧེ་ཧྲ་ཧྲི་ཀ།
སྭཱཧཱ། ཡེ་དྷརྨཱ་ཧེ་ ཧཱུྃ ཏུ་པྲ་བྷ་ཝཱ་ཧེ་
ཏུནྟེཥཱནྟཐཱགཏ སྭཱ ཧྱ་ཝ་ད་ཏ། ཏེ་
ཥཱཉྩ་ཡོ་ནི་རོ་དྷ་ ཧཱ ཨེ་ཝཾ་ཝཱ་དཱི་མ་ཧཱ
ཤྲ་མ་ཎཿ ཡ [illegible]།

265*(R91a) 774

rTa mgrin dkar po

Sita Hayagrīva

266*(R91b) 775

Mi g'yo ba dmar po

Rakta Acala

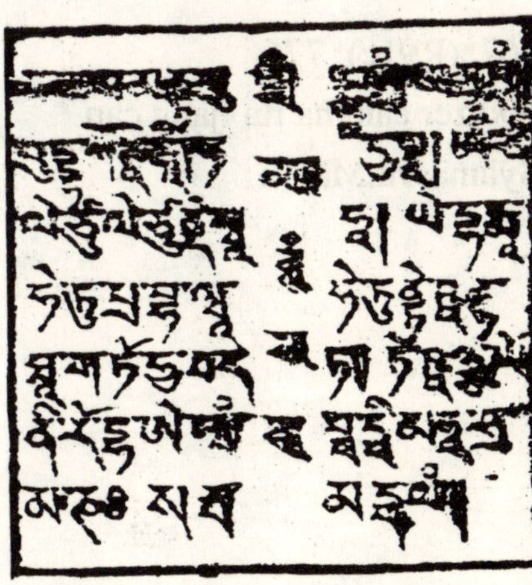

267*(R91c) 776

’Od zer can ma rta ljang can

Śyāmāśva Mārīcī

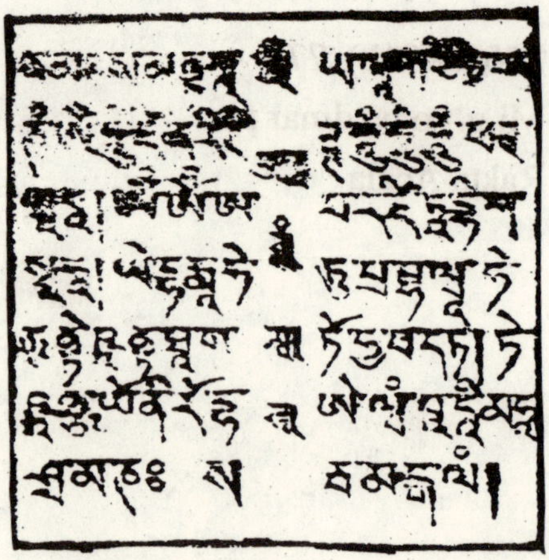

268(R92a) 777

rGyal mtshan rtse mo'i dpung rgyan

Dhvajāgrakeyūrā

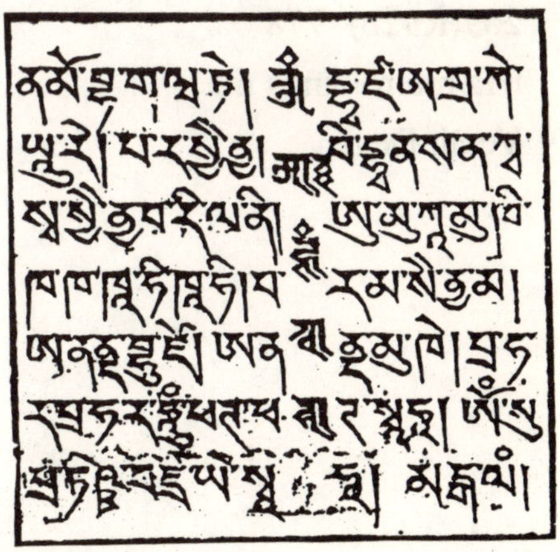

269(R92b) 778

lHa mo ro langs ma

Vetālī Devī

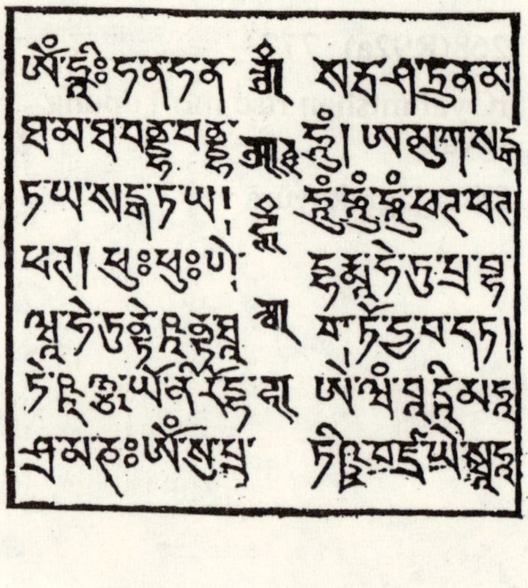

270(R92c) 779
gNod sbyin no 'brog ma
Hārītī Yakṣiṇī

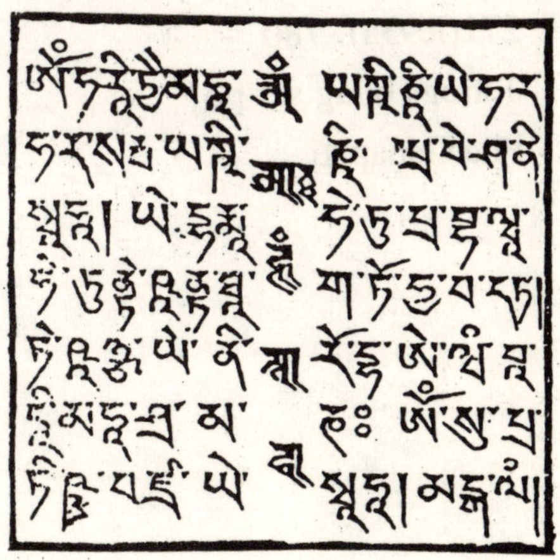

271(R93a) 780

Tshogs bdag ser po

Pīta Gaṇapati

ཨོཾ་ཊི་ཙཙཙ་ཧཱུཾ་ ཀྲཱི་ ཛཿསྭཱ་ཧཱ། ཡེ་
དྷརྨཱ་ཧེ་ཏུ་པྲ་ བྷཱ་ཝཱ་ ཧེ་ཏུ་ཏེ་ཥཱ་
ཏ་ཐཱ་ག་ཏོ་ ཧྱ་ ཝ་ད་ཏ།
ཏེ་ཥཱཉྩ་ཡོ་ ཀྲཱིཾ་ ནི་རོ་དྷ་ཨེ་
ཝཾ་ཝཱ་དཱི་མ་ ཧཱ་ ཤྲ་མ་ཎཿ
ཨོཾ་སུ་པྲ་ཏིཥྛ་ བཛྲ་ཡེ་སྭཱ་ཧཱ།
ས་ཙ་མ་ཛ་ ཞ་ ཡཾ། ཧཱུཾ་ཕཊ྄།

272(R93b) 781

'Phags pa 'jam dpal

Āryamañjughoṣa

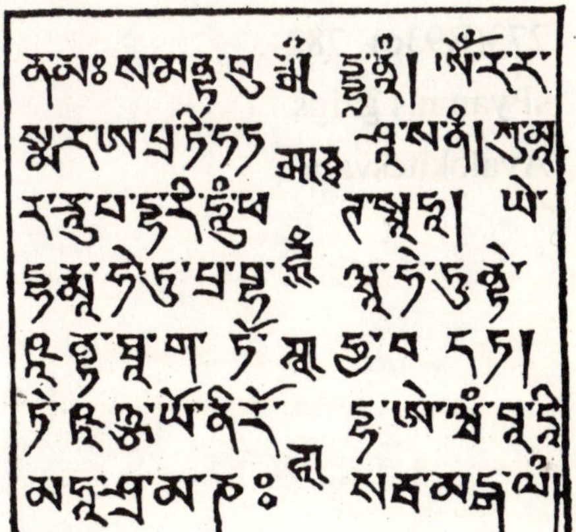

273(R93c) 782
sPyan ras gzigs
Avalokiteśvara

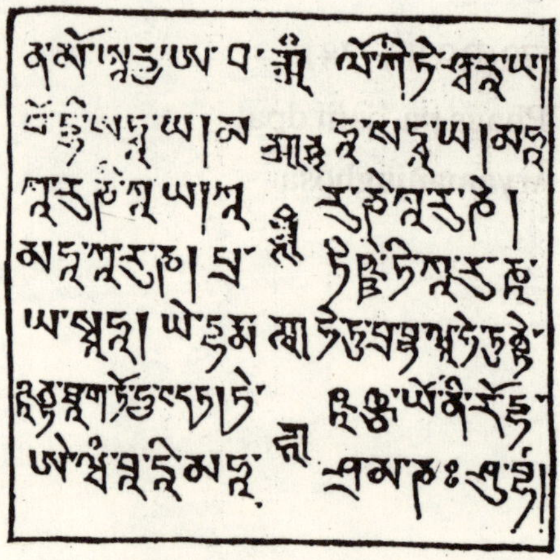

274(R94a) 783
Phyag na rdo rje ljang khu
Śyāma Vajrapāṇi

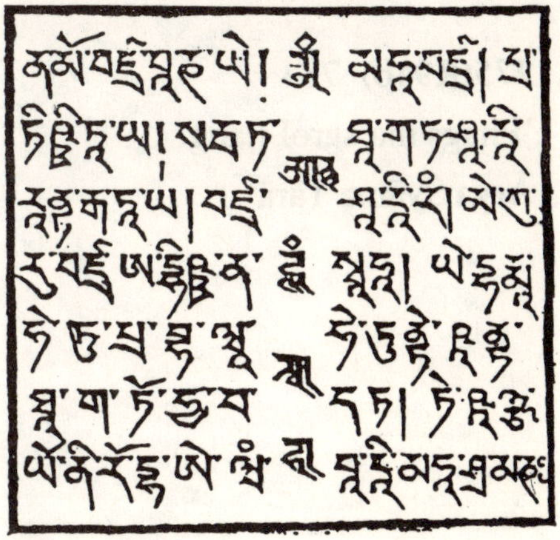

275(R94b) 784

'Phags ma sgrol ljang

Ārya Śyāma Tārā

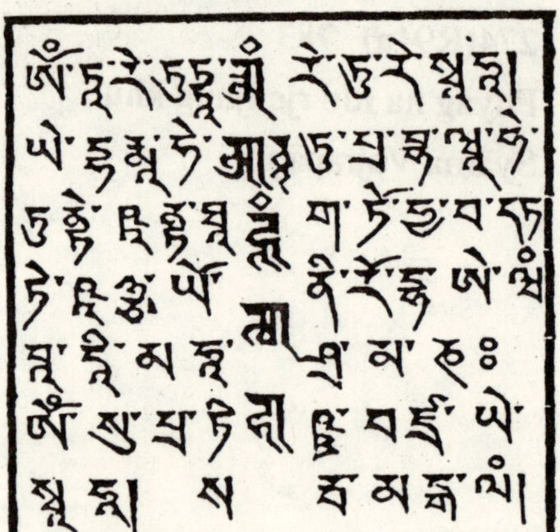

276(R94c) 785

Rab tu dpa' ba'i sgrol ma

Pravīra Tārā

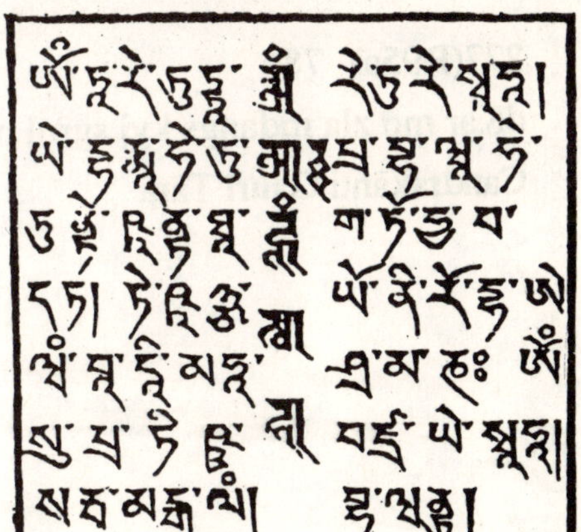

277(R95a) 786

dKar mo zla mdangs kyi sgrol ma

Candrakānti Gaurī Tārā

ཨོཾ་ཏཱ་རེ་ཏུཏྟཱ་རེ་ཏྲཱིཾ་ཏུ་རེ་སྭཱ་ཧཱ།
ཡེ་དྷརྨཱ་ཧེ་ཏུ་པྲ་བྷ་ཝཱ་ཧེ་
ཏུ་ནྟེ་ཥཱཾ་ཏ་ཐཱ་ག་ཏོ་ཧྱ་ཝ་
དཏ་ཏེ་ཥཱཾ་ཙ་ཡོ་ནི་རོ་
དྷ་ཨེ་ཝཾ་ཝཱ་དཱི་མ་ཧཱ་ཤྲ་
མ་ཎཿ ཨོཾ་སུ་པྲ་ཏིཥྛ་
བཛྲ་ཡེ་སྭཱ་ཧཱ། མངྒ་ལཾ།

278(R95b) 787

gSer mdog can gyi sgrol ma

Kanakavarṇa Tārā

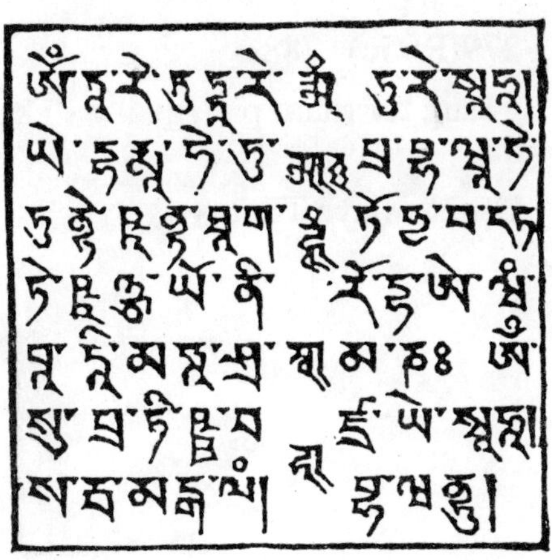

279(R95c) 788

gTsug tor rnam par rgyal ba'i sgrol ma

Uṣṇīṣavijayā Tārā

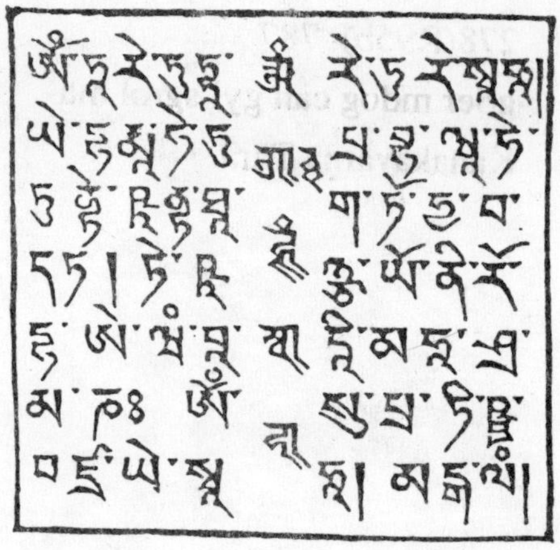

280(R96a) 789

Hūṃ sgra sgrog pa'i sgrol ma

Hūṃsvaranādinī Tārā

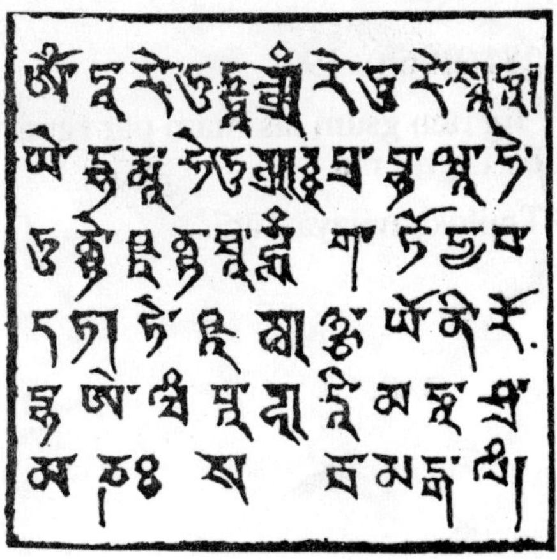

281(R96b) 790

'Jig rten gsum las rnam par rgyal ba'i sgrol ma

Trailokyavijayā Tārā

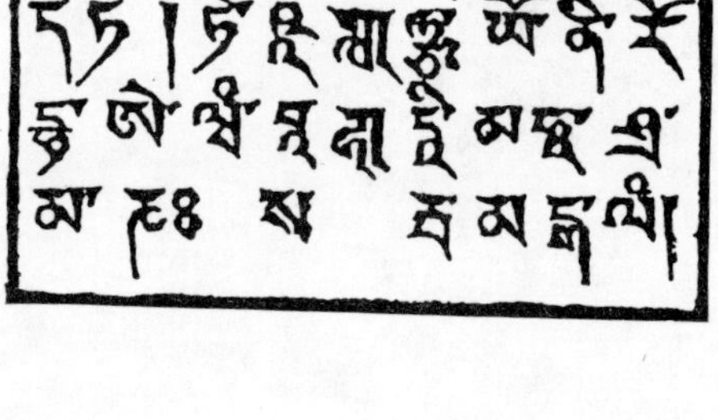

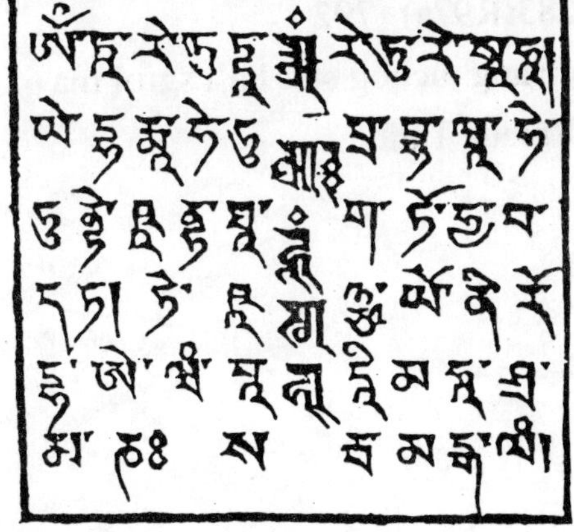

282(R96c) 791

rGol ba 'joms pa'i sgrol ma

Vādipramardinī Tārā

283(R97a) 792

dBang mchog ster ba'i sgrol ma

Varada Tārā

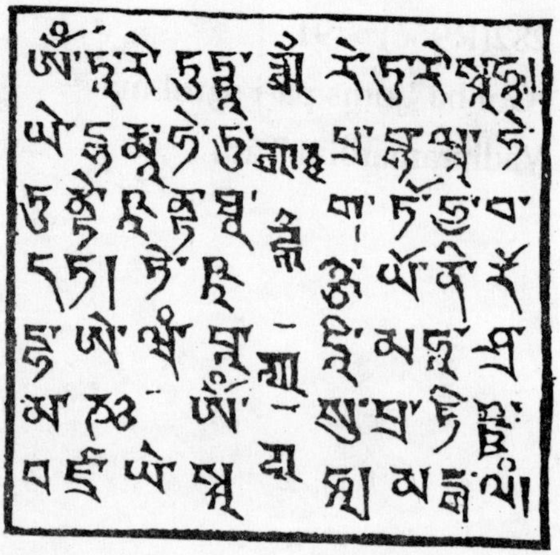

284(R97b) 793

'Od zer can ma

Mārīcī

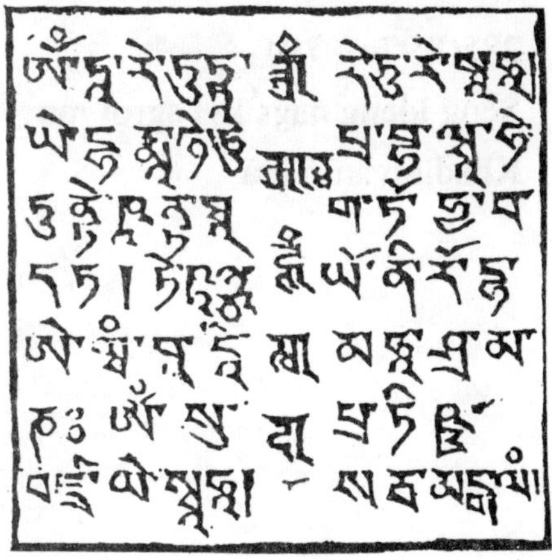

285(R97c) 794
Seng ldeng nags kyi sgrol ma
Khadiravaṇī Tārā

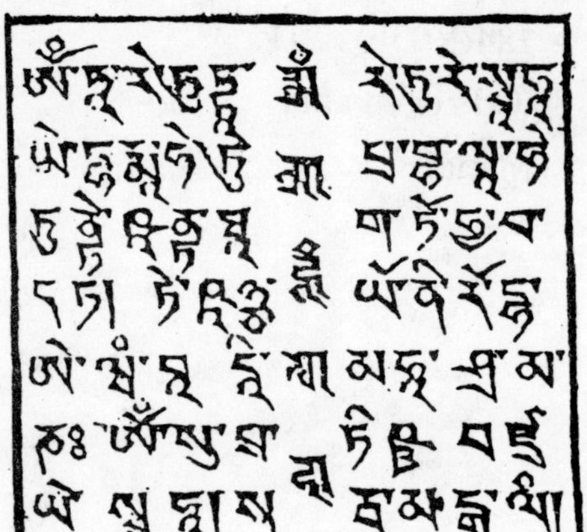

286(R98a) 792(sic)

Ral gcig ma

Ekajaṭā

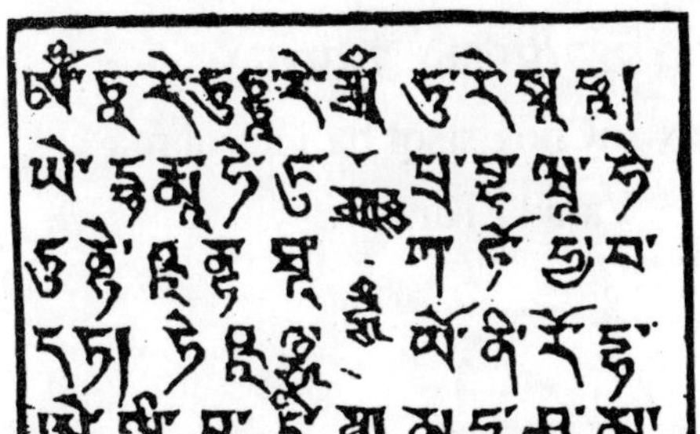

287(R98b) 793(sic)
mChog stsol ba'i sgrol ma
Varada Tārā

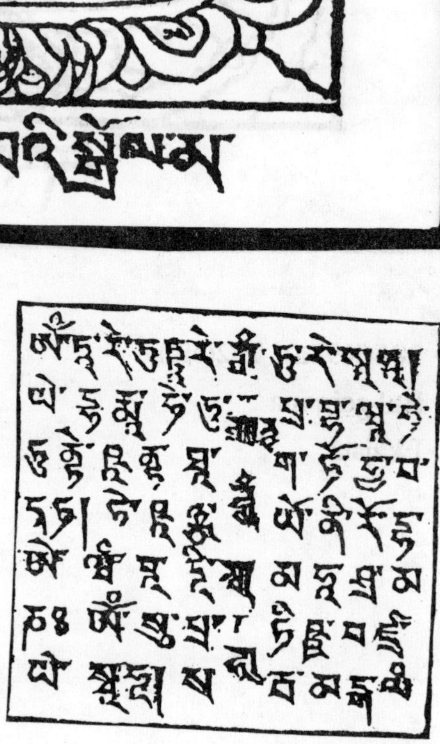

288(R98c) 794(sic)
Mya ngan sel ba'i sgrol ma
Śokavinodana Tārā

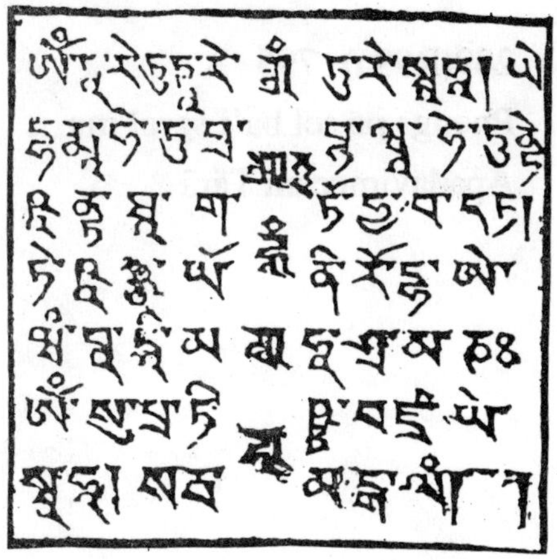

289(R99a) 795

Phongs pa sel ba'i sgrol ma

Āpadavimocanī Tārā

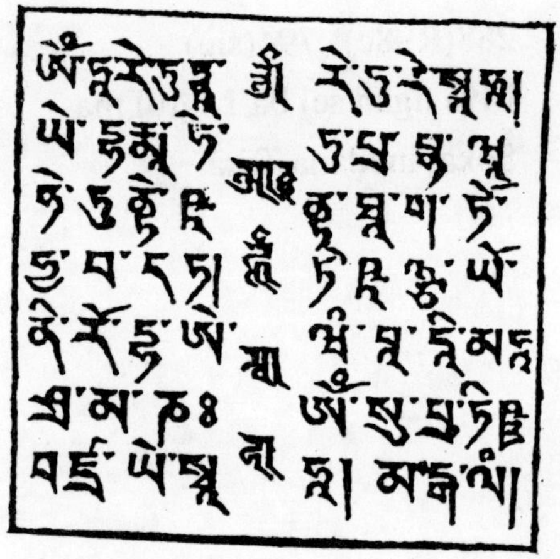

290(R99b) 796

bKra shis snang ba'i sgrol ma

Maṅgalāloka Tārā

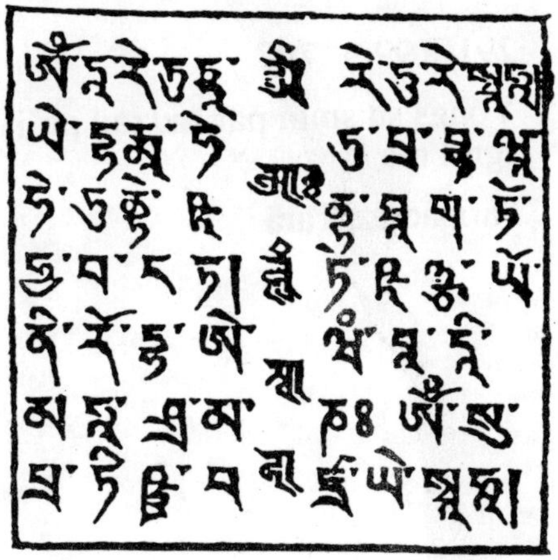

291(R99c) 797

Yongs su smin par mdzad pa'i sgrol ma

Paripācaka Tārā

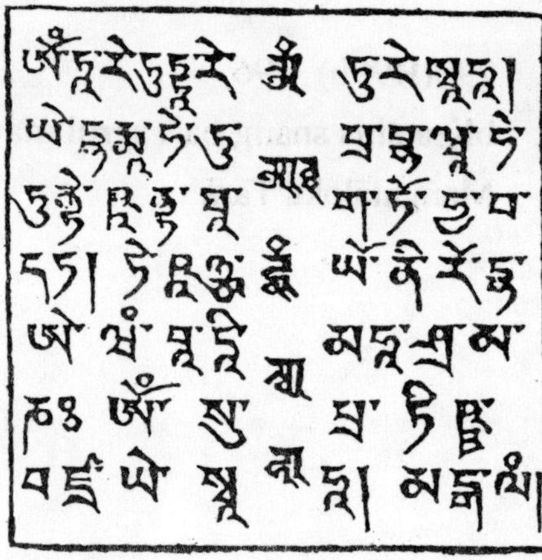

292(R100a) 798

Khro gnyer g'yo ba'i sgrol ma

Bhṛkuṭī Tārā

ཨོཾ་ཏ་རེ་ཏུཏྟ་ ཀྲཾ རེ་ཙ་རེ་སྭཱ་ཧཱ།
ཡེ་དྷརྨཱ་ཧེ་ ཨཱཿ ཏུ་པྲ་བྷ་ཝཱ་
ཧེ་ཏུནྟེ་ཥཱཾ་ ཏ་ཐཱ་ག་ཏོ་
ཧྱ་བ་ད་ཏ། ཧཱུཾ ཏེ་ཥཱཾ་ཙ་ཡོ་
ནི་རོ་དྷ་ཨེ་ སྭཱ ཝཾ་བཱ་དཱི་མཧཱ་
ཤྲ་མ་ཎཿ ཨོཾ་སུ་པྲ་
ཏིཥྛ་བཛྲ་ ཧཱ ཡེ་སྭཱ་ཧཱ།

ཞི་བ་ཆེན་མོའི་སྒྲོལ་མ་

293(R100b) 799

Zhi ba chen mo'i sgrol ma

Mahāśānti Tārā

ཨོཾ་ཏཱ་རེ་ཏུཏྟཱ་ ཏྲཱཾ་ རེ་ཏུ་རེ་སྭཱ་ཧཱ།
ཕེ་ཧྲཱ་སྭཱ་ཧེ་ཏུ་ ཨཱཿཧཱུཾ་ བྲ་ཧྨ་ལྷཱ་ཧེ་
ཏུ་ཧྲཱྀཾ་ཛ་ཧྲཱྀཾ་སྭཱ་ ག་ཧོ་ཧྲཱུ་བ་
དགཿ ཧེ་ཛ་ཀྲྀཾ་ ཧྲཱྀཿ ཡོ་ཧེ་རོ་ཧ་
ཨེ་ཕཾ་སྭཱ་ཧཱི་ སྭཱ་ མ་ཧཱ་ཤྲཱ་མ་
ཧཱུཿ ཨོཾ་ ཧྲ་ བྲ་ཧེ་ཧཱུཾ་བརྡ་
ཡེ་སྭཱ་ཧཱ་ཨཱཿ ཧཱུཾ་ ཙ་མནྡ་ལཾ།

294(R100c) 800

Chags pa 'joms pa'i sgrol ma

Rāganiśūdana Tārā

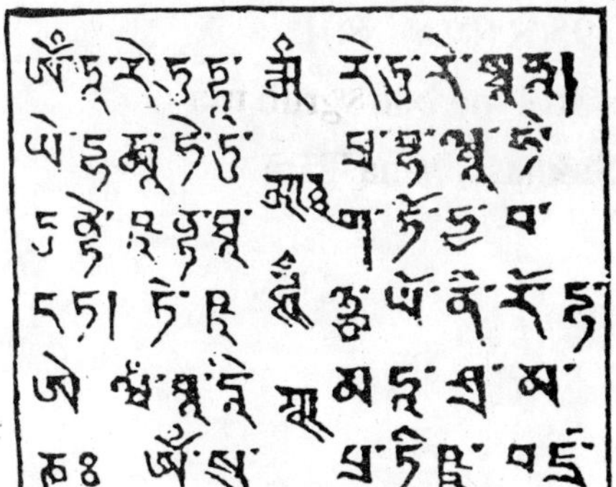

295(R101a) 801

sGrol ma bde sgrub ma

Sukhasādhana Tārā

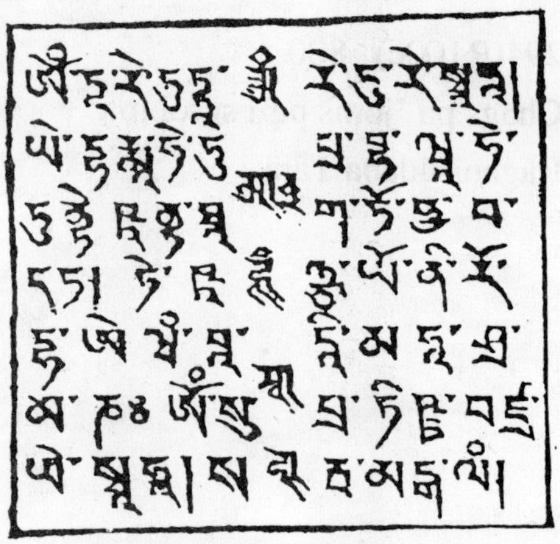

296(R101b) 802
sGrol ma rab rgyas ma
Saṃkusumita Tārā

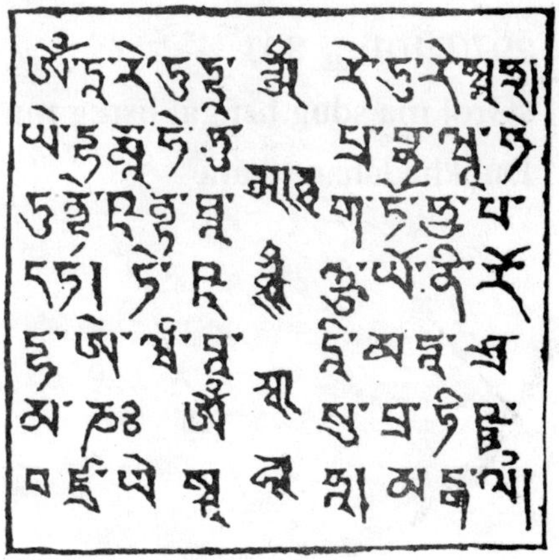

297(R101c)   803

sGrol ma sdug bsngal bsreg ma

Duḥkhadahana Tārā

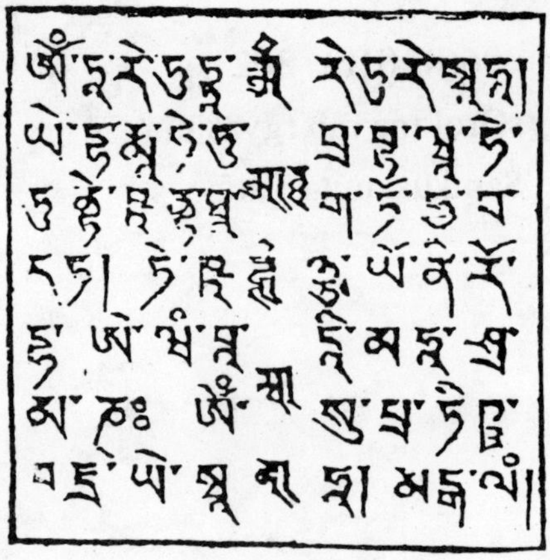

298(R102a) 804

sGrol ma dngos grub 'byung ma

Siddhisambhava Tārā

ཨོཾ་ཏཱ་རེ་ཏུཏྟཱ་རེ་ ཏྲཱཾ་ ཏུ་རེ་སྭཱ་ཧཱ།
ཡེ་དྷརྨཱ་ཧེ་ཏུ་པྲ་ ཨཱཿ་ བྷཱ་ཝཱ་ཧེ་ཏུནྟེ
ཥཱཾ་ཏ་ཐཱ་ག་ཏོ་ཧྱ་ བ་ད་ཏ། ཏེ
ཥཱཾ་ཙ་ཡོ་ནི་རོ་དྷ་ ཧཱུཾ་ ཨེ་ཝཾ་ཝཱ་དི
མ་ཧཱ་ཤྲ་མ་ཎཿ ཨོཾ་སུ་པྲ
ཏི་ཥྛ་བཛྲེ་ཡེ་ སྭཱ་ཧཱ། སརྦ
མངྒ་ལཾ། ཧཱ་ ཨ་ཧཱུཾ།

སྒྲོལ་མ་ཡོངས་རྫོགས་བྱེད་མ

299(R102b) 805

sGrol ma yongs rdzogs byed ma

Paripūraṇa Tārā

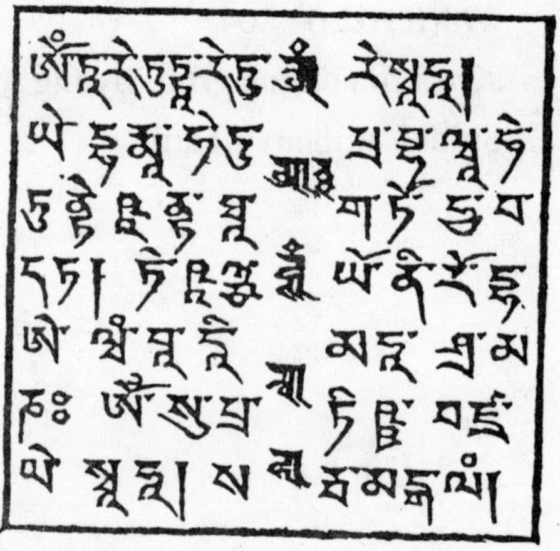

300(R102c) 806
rNam sras ser chen lha dgu
9-deity Mahāpīta Vaiśravaṇa

ཨོཾ་ཧྲཱི་ཤྲ་མ་ཎ་ཡེ་ སྭཱ་ཧཱ། ཨོཾ་ཛམྦྷ་
ལ་ཡེ་སྭཱ་ཧཱ། ཨོཾ་པཱུ ཎྞ་བྷ་དྲ་ཡེ་སྭཱ་ཧཱ།
ཨོཾ་མ་ཎི་བྷ་དྲ་ཡེ་སྭཱ ཧཱ། ཨོཾ་ཀུ་བེ་ར་ཡེ
སྭཱ་ཧཱ། ཨོཾ་སཾ་པྲ་ཛི་ཏ ཡེ་སྭཱ་ཧཱ། ཨོཾ་ཙུཌ
བ་ན་ཡེ་སྭཱ་ཧཱ། ཨོཾ་པ ཉྩི་ཀ་ཡེ་སྭཱ་ཧཱ།
ཨོཾ་པི་ཏྲེ་ཀུ་ཎྜ་ལི་ཡེ་ སྭཱ་ཧཱ། ཨོཾ་ཤུ་པྲ
ཏི་ཥྛ་བཛྲ་ཡེ་སྭཱ་ཧཱ། ས་ཏྲ་མ་ནྟྲ་ཡཾ།

301(R103a) 807

rNam sras mdun dmar rta sngon can

Nīlāśva Raktasūla Vaiśravaṇa

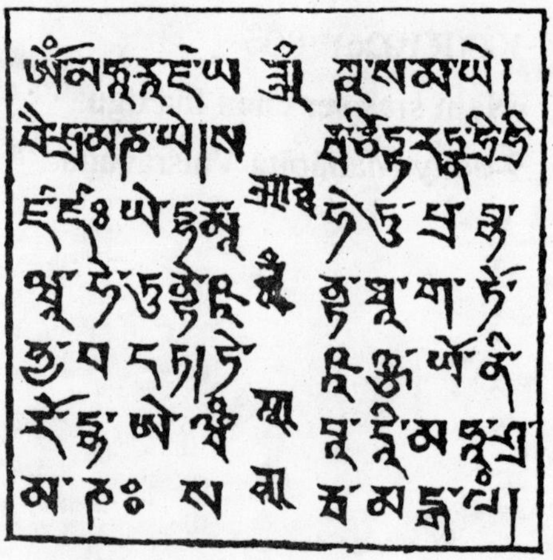

302(R103b) 808
rNam sras ljang ser be con can
Gadādh̤ara Śyāmapīta Vaiśravaṇa

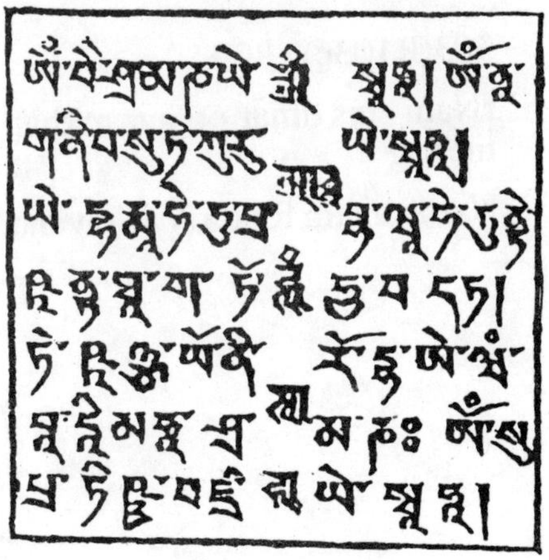

303(R103c) 809

rNam sras dmar po gar mkhan mchog

Nartakavara Rakta Vaiśravaṇa

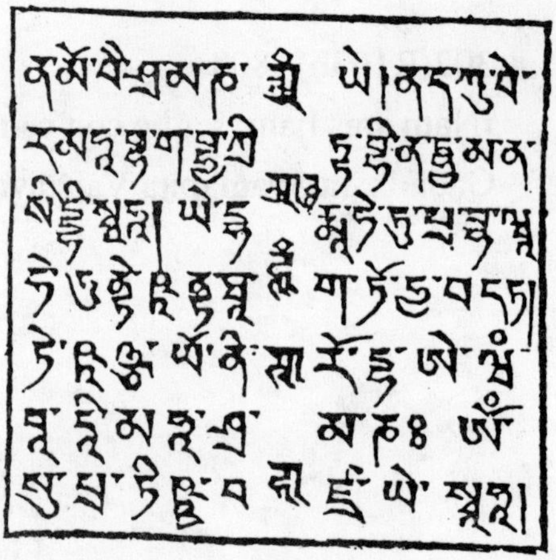

304(R104a) 810
'Khor gNod sbyin brgyad
Eight Yakṣa Attendants

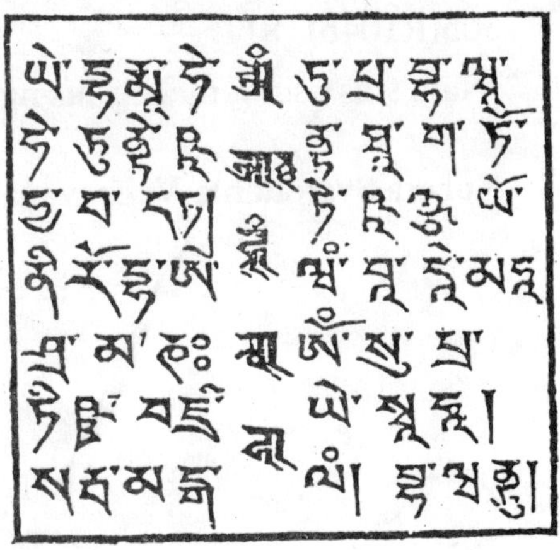

305(R104b) 811

rNam sras gsung mchog lus ngan po

Kubera Svarottama Vaiśravaṇa

ཨོཾ་བཻ་ཤྲ་མ་ཎ་ [illegible] མ་མ་སྐུ་རྡེ
པུ་ཏྲི་ཀ་ཧ་སྭཱ་ཧཱ། [illegible] ཡེ་དྷརྨཱ་ཧེ་
ཏུ་པྲ་བྷ་ཝཱ་ཧེ་ ཏུནྟེ་ཥཱཾ་ཏ་ཐཱ
ག་ཏོ་ཧྱ་ཝ་ [illegible] དཏ། ཏེ་ཥཱཉྩ
ཡོ་ནི་རོ་དྷ་ཨེ་ [illegible] ཝཾ་ཝཱ་དཱི་
མ་ཧཱ་ཤྲ་མ་ [illegible] ཎཿ ཨོཾ་སུ་
པྲ་ཏིཥྛ་བཛྲ་ ཡེ་སྭཱ་ཧཱ།

306(R104c) 812
'Khor gNod sbyin mo brgyad
Eight Yakṣī Attendants

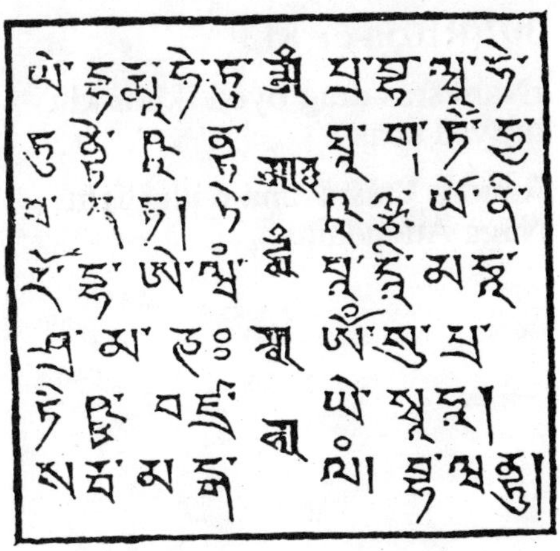

307(R105a-c) 813

rNam sras drag byed 'khor klu brgyad bcas

Raudra Vaiśravaṇa with Eight Nāga Attendants

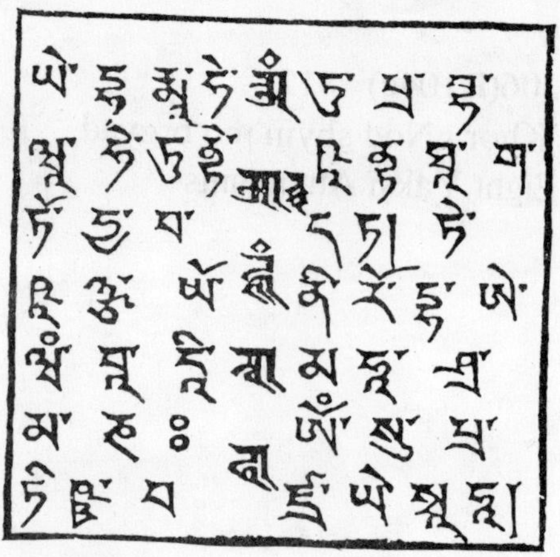

307(R105a-c) 813

rNam sras drag byed 'khor klu brgyad bcas

Raudra Vaiśravaṇa with Eight Nāga Attendants

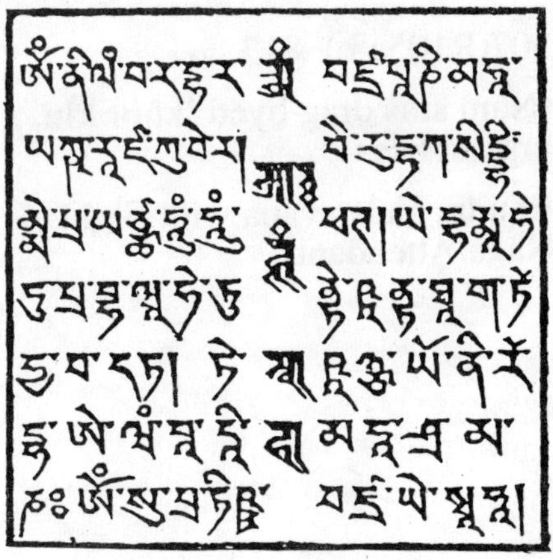

307(R105a-c) 813

rNam sras drag byed 'khor klu brgyad ḅcas

Raudra Vaiśravaṇa with Eight Nāga Attendants

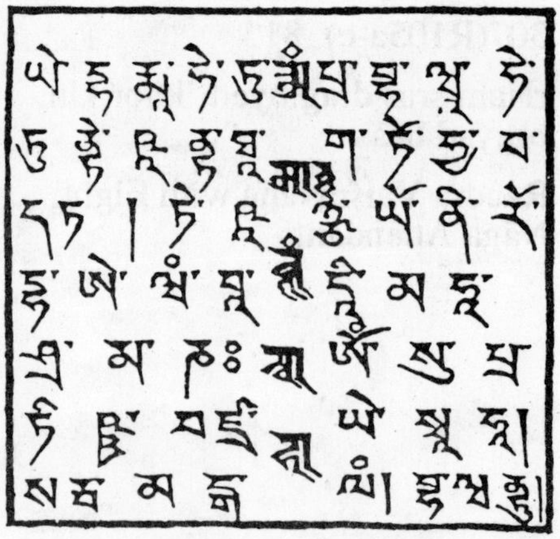

རྣམ་སྲས་ནག་པོ་རྟ་སྔོན་ཅན

308(R106a) 814

rNam sras nag po rta sngon can

Nīlāśva Kṛṣṇa Vaiśravaṇa

ཨོཾ་བེ་ཏྲཀ་ར་ཨཱཿ ཀླ་རྒྱ། ཡེ
ཛ་མྦྷ་ཧེ་ཙུ་ཕྲ་ ཏྲ་སྣྲ་ཏ་ཙུ་ཏྲེ
ཀྲ་ཏྲ་སྣ་ག་ནྟ་ཨཱཿ ཧྲུ་བ་ཏཏ།
ཏ་ཀྲ་ཀྵ་ཡོ་ཧཱུཾ་ཤི་ར་ཧྲ་ཨེ་
ཁཾ་ཏྲ་རྡེ་མ ཧ་ཕྲ་མ་ཧཿ
ཨོཾ་སུ་ཕྲ་ཏྲི ཨཱ ཧྱ་བ་རྡེ་ཡེ་སྭཱ
ས་ཙ་མ་ཧ་ ཧཱུཾ་ཡཾ། ཧྲ་ཡ་ཀྲུ།

309(R106b) 815

rNam sras dkar po tshe 'dzin

Āyurdhara Sita Vaiśravaṇa

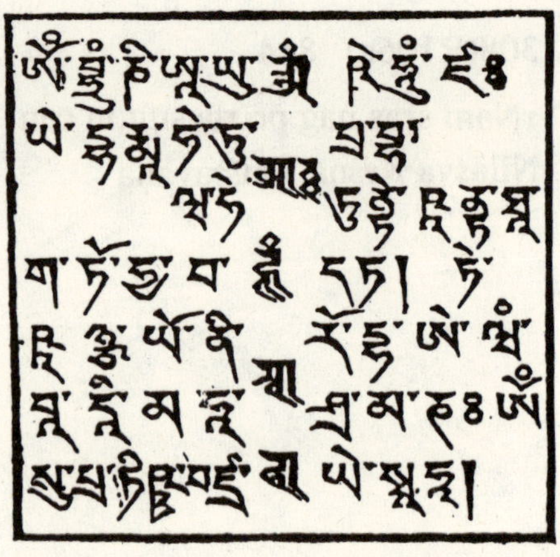

310(R106c) 816

rNam sras ljang gu seng zhon ma dznyā na'i lugs

Jñānakrama Siṃhavāhana Śyāma Vaiśravaṇa

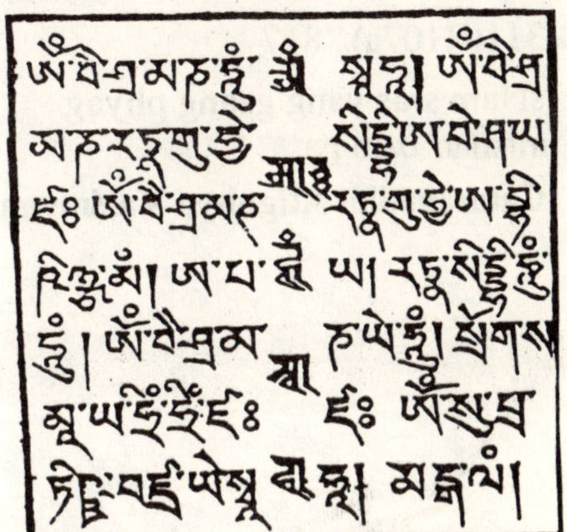

311(R107a) 817

sNam sras yang gsang phyag mtshan bzhi pa

Caturāyudha Atiguhya Vaiśravaṇa

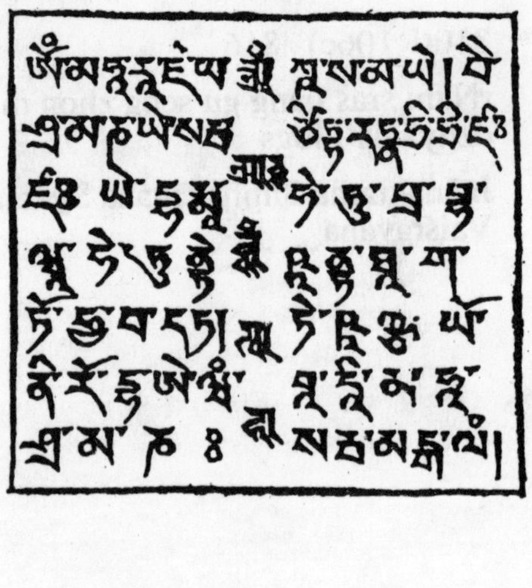

312(R107b) 818

Dzambha la ser po gtso rkyang

Ekāntanāyaka Pīta Jambhala Vaiśravaṇa

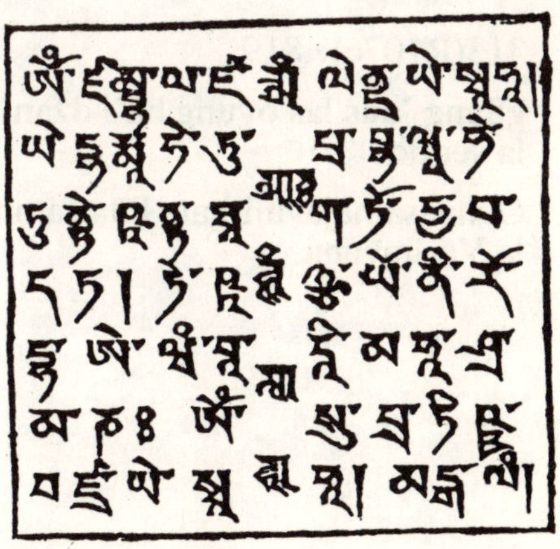

313(R107c) 819

gSang 'dus las byung ba'i dzambha la ser po

Guhyasamājavinirgata Pīta Jambhala Vaiśravaṇa

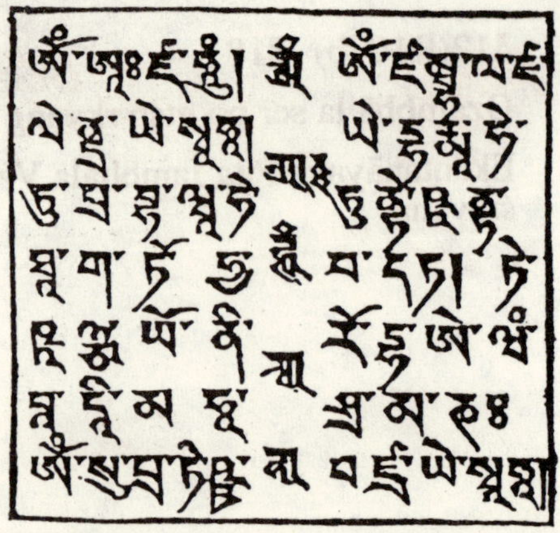

314*(R108a) 820

dPa' bo chig sgrub las byung ba'i dzambha la lha mang

Ekavīra Sādhanavinirgata Bahudeva Jambhala

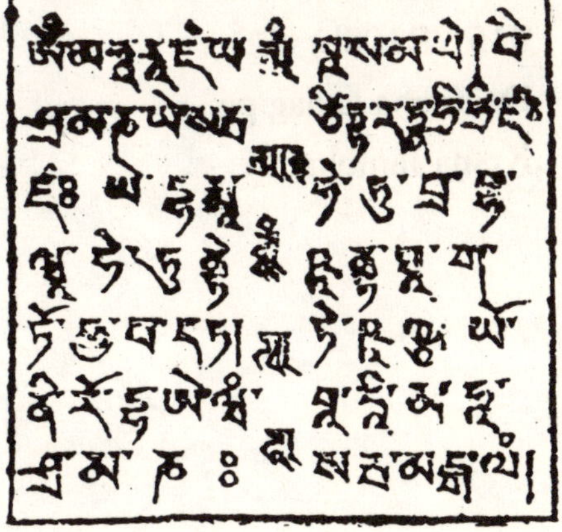

315*(R108b) 821

Dzambha la nag po

Kṛṣṇa Jambhala

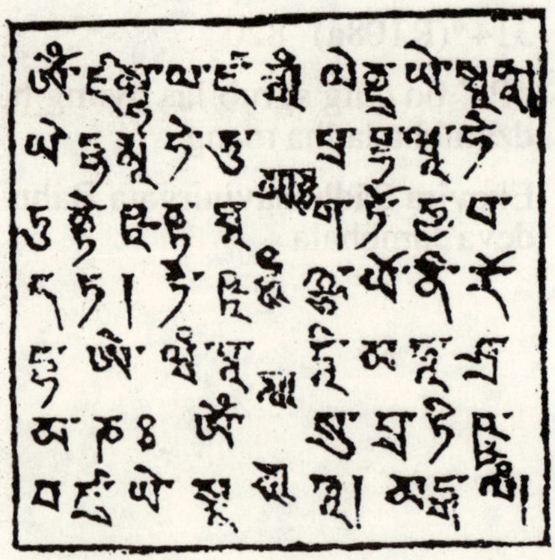

316*(R108c) 822

Dzambha la dkar po lha lnga jo bo'i lugs

5-deity Sita Jambhala of Atīśa school

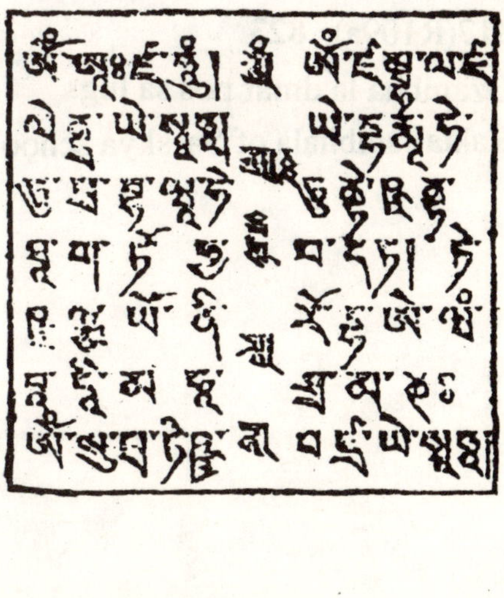

317(R109a) 823

Dzambha la dmar pos sa lugs

Rakta Jambhala of Sa skya school

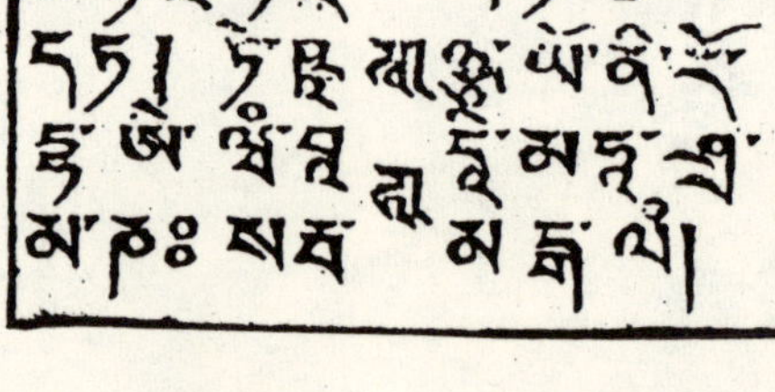

318(R109b) 824

Grwa pa mngon shes lugs kyi dzambha la dmar po

Abhijñakrama Rakta Jambhala

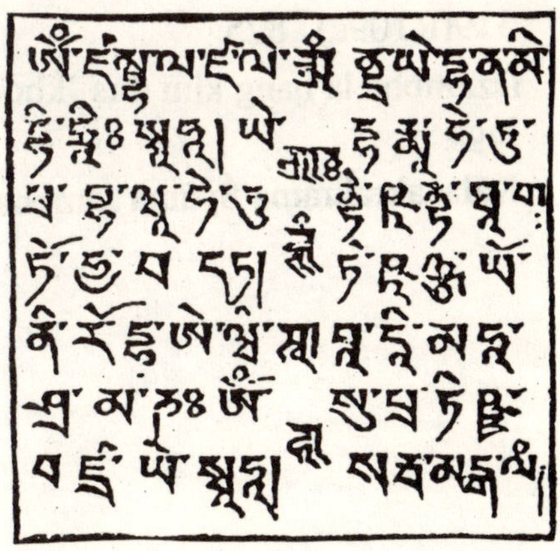

319(R109c) 825

Dzambha la ljang khu dus 'khor lugs

Kālacakrakrama Śyāma Jambhala

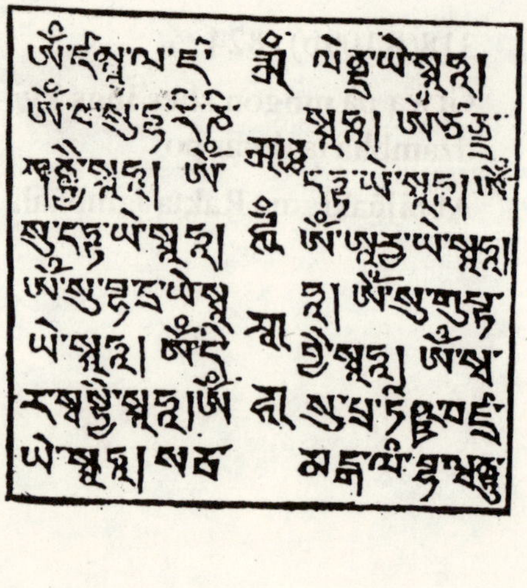

320(R110a) 826

gNod sbyin nor bu bzang po

Maṇibhadra Yakṣa

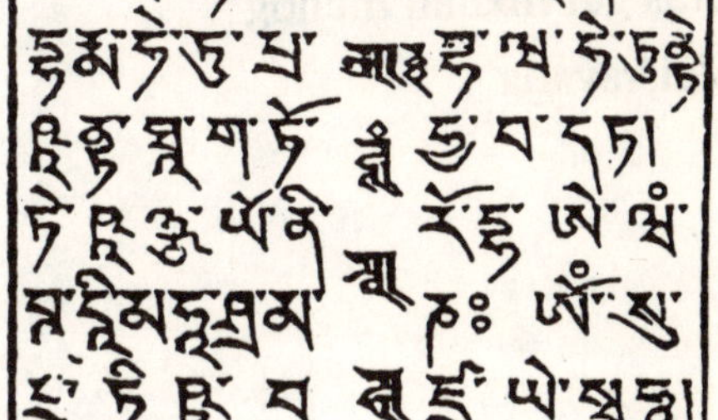

སྲས་གར་མཁན་མཆོག

321(R110b) 827

Sras gar mkhan mchog

Vaiśravaṇa

ན་མོ་ཝཻ་ཤྲ་མ་ཎ་ཡེ། ༀ ན་ད་ཀུ་བེ་ར་མ་ཧཱ
ཛྙ་ག་ཛྙ་ཤྲི་ཧྲི་ཧྲི་ནཱ་ཧཱུཾ ཨཱཿཧཱུཾ མ་ན་ཥི་ཧྲཱི་ཧྲཱ་ཧཱ།
ན་མོ་ར་ཏྣ་ཏྲ་ཡཱ་ཡ་ན་ མོ་ཝཻ་ཤྲ་མ་ཎ་ཡ།
ན་ཏ་ཀུ་བ་རཻ། གུ་ཧྱ ཧྲཱིཿ ཀླུ། ནརྟ་པ་དེ་མ
ཧཱ་ར་ཏ་ཡེ་ཧཱུཾ། ཨ་ནུ་ཏྲཱ་ སྭཱ་ ཡ་སུ་རྟཱུ་པ་ནཾ
ཀུ་པ་ར། ཙཏྲ་ཧཾ། ནཙཾ ཧཱ གཾ། དེ་མ་ཧཱ་ཤྲཱི་ན
ཏ་ཀུ་པ་ར། ཧེ་མ་གཾ། ཀ་ཏཾ། ཙཾ་ཡ་ཙཾ
ཡ་པ་ཙ་པ་ཙཾ། སྭ་ཧཱ་ ཀུ་ཀུ་པ་ར།

322(R110c) 828

Sras rgyal ba khyu mchog

Jinarṣabha Vaiśravaṇa

ནམོ་ཝཻ་ཤྲ་བ་ཎཱ་ཡ། ཧཱུཾ་ཊཙྪཱ། ཤི་མི་ཤི་མི།
སུ་མུ་ཤུ་མུ། ཙ་ཊུ་ཙ་ཊུ། ཙ་ར་ཙ་ར།
ས་ར་ས་ར། ག་ར་ག་ར ཛཿཧཱུཾ གི་རི་གི་ཏི་གི་ལི
ཀི་ལི། ཀུ་རུ་ཀུ་རུ། སུ ཧཱུཾ རུ་སུ་རུ། ཙུ་རུ
ཙུ་རུ། མ་ཧཱ་ཡ། ཨ་ཏྲ་ཧོ ཛཱ ནི་ཀྲི་ཏྭཱ། ཨ་ཧཱ་ར
ཧཱུ་ཏུ་སྭཱ་ཧཱ། ནམོ་ཝཻ་ཤྲ་ བ་ཎ་ཡ་སྭཱ་ཧཱ།
རཏྣ་ད་ཡ་སྭཱ་ཧཱ། མོ་ནི་ ཛཱ ར་ཐ་པ་རི་པཱུ་ར་
ཡ་སྭཱ་ཧཱ། ཨོཾ་ཤྲཱི་བྲ་ཧི ཀྲྀ་བཛྲ་ཡེ་སྭཱ་ཧཱ།

323(R111a) 829

lHa mo dpal chen mo

Mahālakṣmī Devī

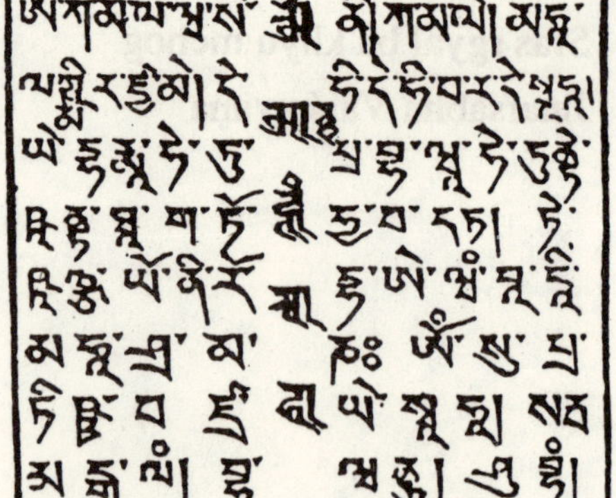

324(R111b) 830

gZungs las byung ba'i lha mo nor rgyun ma

Dhāraṇīvinirgata Vasudhārā Devī

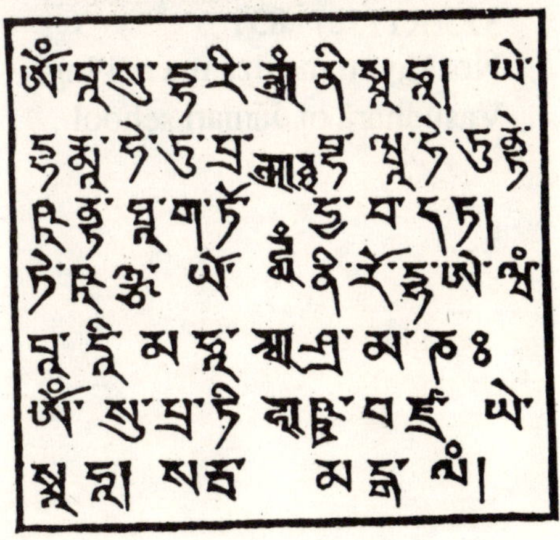

325(R111c) 831
Nor rgyun ma dzā ma ri'i lugs
Vasudhārā of Jāmari school

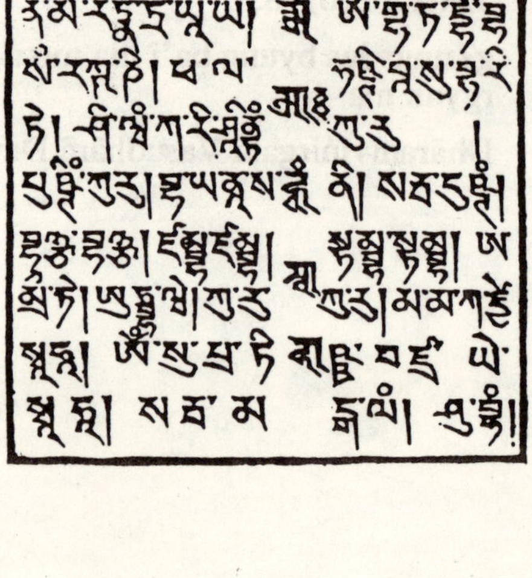

326(R112a) 832

Nor rgyun ma ba lang rdzi

Gopāla Vasudhārā

ཨོཾ་ཧྲཱིཿཧྲཱི་ཀ་པ་ས་ ཤྲཱི་ ནོ་ཏ་ར་ས་ཙ་ཛ
ན་པ་དྲྀ་ར་ཏྣེ་ཧྲཱུཾ་ཧྲཱིཾ་ཨཱཿཧ་ ཧཱུཾ་ཧཱུཾ་སྭཱ་ཧཱ།
ཡེ་དྷརྨཱ་ཧེ་ཏུ་པྲ་བྷ་ཝཱ་ ཧེ་ཏུན་ཏེ་ཥཱན་ཏ
ཐཱ་ག་ཏོ་ཧྱ་ཝ་ད་ཏ། ཏེ་ཥཱཉྩ་ཡོ
ནི་རོ་དྷ་ཨེ་ཝཾ་ཝཱ་དཱི་མ་ཧཱ་ཤྲ
མ་ཎཿ ཨོཾ་སུ་པྲ་ཏིཥྛ་བཛྲ་ཡེ
སྭཱ་ཧཱ། སརྦ་མངྒ་ལཾ། ཤུ་བྷཾ།

327(R112b) 833

Yid 'phrog nor rgyun ma

Manoharā Vasudhārā

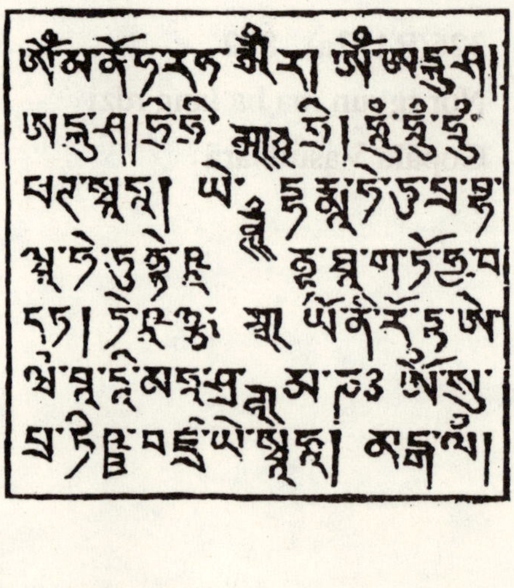

ཞང་བློན་རྡོ་རྗེ་བདུད་འདུལ་ཕྱི་སྒྲུབ

328(R112c) 834

Zhang blon rdo rje bdud 'dul phyi sgrub

Bāhyasādhana Zhang blon rdo rje Mārajit

ༀ་བཛྲ་རཀྵ་ཧཱུྃ་ཕཊ་ ཨཱཿ ར་ག་ར་གོ་ཀྲཱི་པ་ར།
ༀ་བཛྲ་ཀྲོ་དྷ་ཨ་མྲྀ་ཏ་ ཀྲཱིཾ ཛྫ་ལ་ཀྲི་ད་ཡ་
སྭཱ་ཧཱ། ༀ་མ་ཧཱ་ཀཱ་ལ་ ཏ་ན་ཏ་ན་བཛྲ་ཏ་
སྭཱ་ཧཱ། ༀ་ཨ་ཧཱ་ཡ་ ཧྲཱི་ ཀཱ་ལ་ཏྲཾ་རེ་ད་ནྲ་ཛ་ཡ
སྭཱ་ཧཱ། ༀ་བཻ་ཤྲ་མ་ ཛཱ་ ཏ་ཡེ་སྭཱ་ཧཱ། ཡེ་དྷརྨཱ
ཧེ་ཏུ་པྲ་བྷ་ཝཱ་ཧེ་ཏུནྟེ་ ཥཱནྟ་ཐཱ་ག་ཏོ་ཧྱ་ཝ་དཏ྄
ཏེ་ཥཱཉྩ་ཡོ་ནི་རོ་དྷ་ཨེ་ཝཾ་ ཧྲཱི་ ཝཱ་དཱི་མ་ཧཱ་ཤྲ་མ་ཎཿ

ཞང་བློན་རྡོ་རྗེ་བདུད་འདུལ་ནང་སྒྲུབ

329(R113a) 835

Zhang blon rdo rje bdud 'dul nang sgrub

Antarasādhana Zhang blon rdo rje Mārajit

ཨོཾ་བཛྲ་རུདྲ་ ཀྲཾ་ ཙཎྜ་རཱ་ག་ར་
ཎེ་ཧཱུྃ་ཕཊ། ཀྲཱཿ ཨོཾ་བཛྲ་རཀྵ་ཙཎྜ་
བརྐྱ་བདུད་མ་ ཧྲཱིཾ་ ཧིང་སྒྲོལ་ཧིང་ཧིང་
ཛཿཛཿ ཡེ་ ཧྲཱིཾ་ ཧ་ཀྲྀ་ཏི་ཙ་བྲ་ཧ་ཀྵ་
ཏེ་ཙ་ཧྲི་ཛཿཧ་སྭ་ཡ་ ཀྵ་ ཏྲེ་ཌ་བ་ཏ། ཏེ་
ཧྲཱུ་རུ་ཡོ་ཨི་རེ་ཧུ་ཨེ་ ཧཱིཾ་ཧྲི་མ་ཧ་ཤྲཱ་མ་རཀྵ

ཞང་བློན་རྡོ་རྗེ་བདུད་འདུལ་གསང་སྒྲུབ

330(R113b) 836

Zhang blon rdo rje bdud 'dul gsang sgrub

Guhyasādhana Zhan blon rdo rje Mārajit

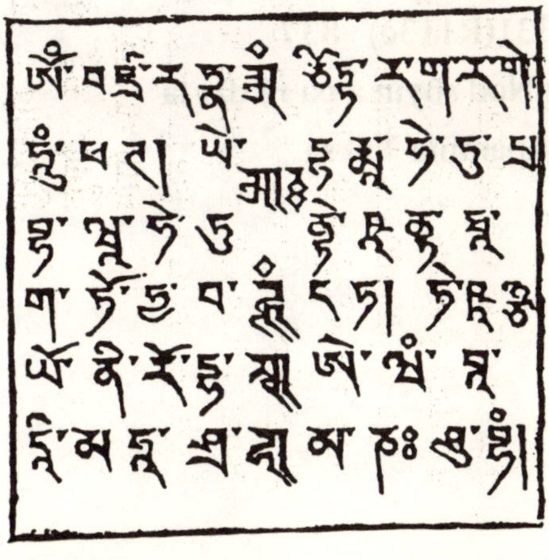

331(R113c) 837
gNod sbyin a pa rā dzi ta
Aparājita Yakṣa

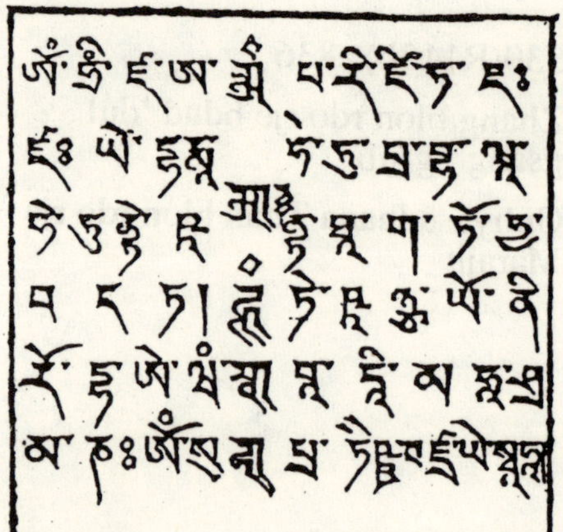

332(R114a) 838

'Jur 'gegs sel ba'i tshogs bdag

Ājñāvinivarta Gaṇapati

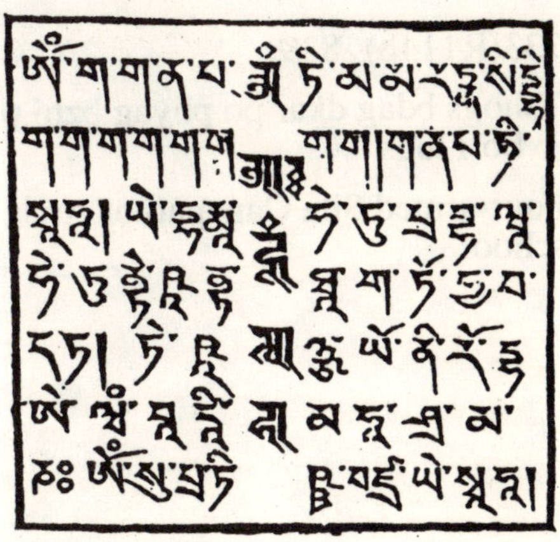

333(R114b) 839

Tshogs bdag dkar po phyag bzhi pa jo bo'i lugs

Four-armed Sita Gaṇapati of Atīśa school

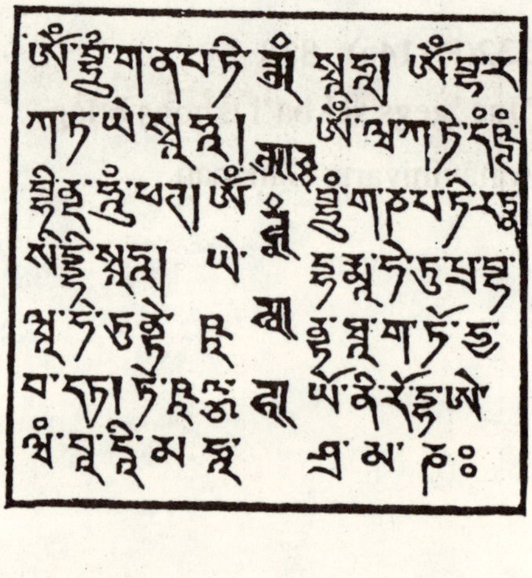

ཚོགས་བདག་དམར་པོ་ཕྱག་བཞི་པ་

334(R114c) 840

Tshogs bdag dmar po phyag bzhi pa

Four-armed Rakta Gaṇapati

ཨོཾ་རཏྣ་རཏྣ། རཏྣཾ་ཛྲཱིཾ་ རཏྣཾ། གཎཔ་ཏེ།
ག་ག་ག་ག་ག་ག་ ཨཱཿཧཱུཾ་ གགཱ། གཎཔ་ཏེ།
ཧཱུཾ་རུ་རུ་རུ། མཧཱ་ ཧཱུཾ་ ཕཊ། རུ་རུ་རུ། ག
ག་ཎ་ཡ། གཎཔ་ཏེ་ ཧྲཱི་ ཡེ་སྭཱཧཱ། ཡེ་ཧུམ་ཎ
ཏེ་ཙ་པྲ་ཧྲ་ཀླ་ཏེ་ ཧྲཱི་ ཏུ་ཧེ་ཊཱ་ཧཱུ་སྭཱ་གཎ
ཏུ་པ་ཏཾ། ཏེ་ཊཱ་ཀྟ་ཧྲཱི་ ཡོ་ནི་རོ་ཧ་ཨེ་སྭཾ
སྭཱ་ཧཱ་མ་ཧ་ཀྲ་མ་ ཏཿ མཧཱ་ཡཾ།

ཀླུ་རྒྱལ་སོག་མ་མེད་

335(R115a) 841

Klu rgyal sog ma med

Apalāla Nāgarāja

ཨོཾ་བྷུཿབྷུཿབྷུ་ཏ་ཀྵཾ་བྷུ་ཏམ་ཧ་གྲེ་ཧ་ཧཱུཾ
ཤི་ཀྲི་ཤི་ཀྲི་སྭཱ་ར་ [illegible] ཡ་ཧཱུཾ་ཕཊ་སྭཱ་ཧཱ།
ཡེ་དྷརྨཱ་ཧེ་ཏུ་ [illegible] པྲ་བྷ་ [illegible] ཧེ་ཏུནྟེ
ཥཱན་ཏ་ཐཱ་ག་ཏོ་ ཧྱ་བ་ད་ཏ།
ཏེ་ཥཱཾ་ཙ་ཡོ་ནི་རོ་དྷ་ཨེ་ཝཾ་
བཱ་དཱི་མ་ཧཱ་ཤྲ་མ་ཎཿ ཨོཾ་སུ་
པྲ་ཏིཥྛ་བཛྲ་ཡེ་ སྭཱ་ཧཱ། མངྒ་ལཾ།

336(R115b.) 842

dByug gu ma spun gsum

dByug gu ma Bhaginītraya

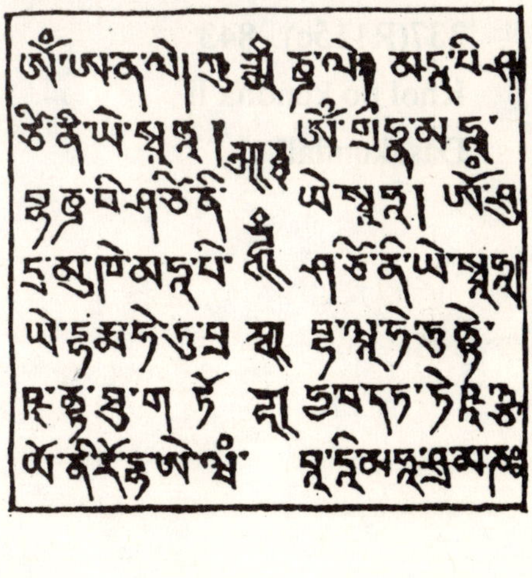

337(R115c) 843

Khol po kundha li

Dāsakuṇḍalī

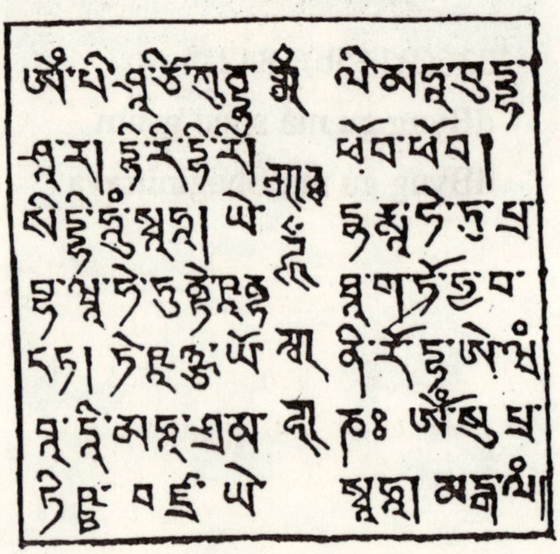

338(R116a) 844

Jinamitra, Kṣetrapāla

Jinamitra and Kṣetrapāla

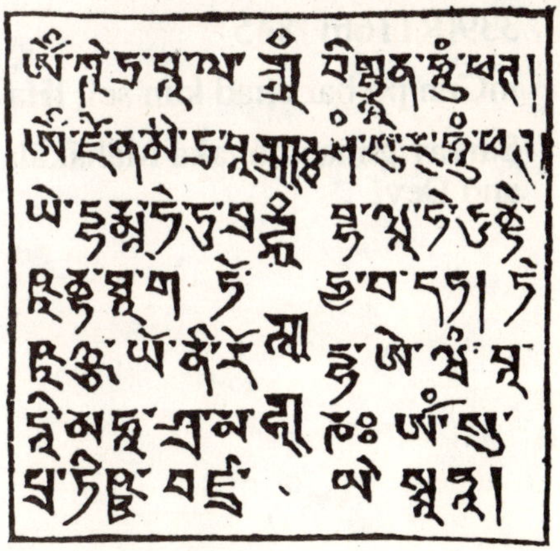

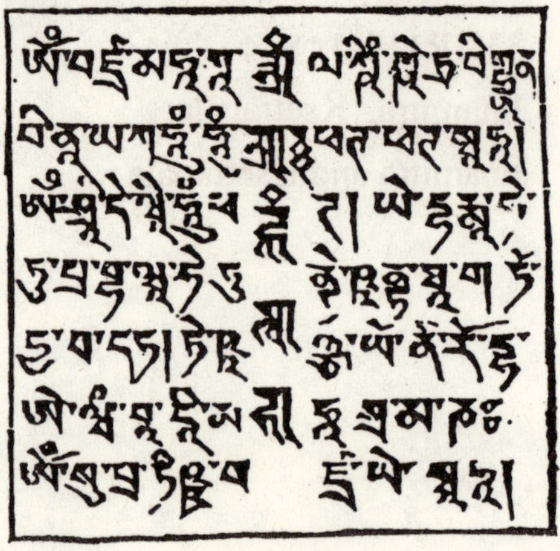

339(R116b) 845

mGon po bar chad kun sel, lHa mo

Sarvavighnavināyaka Mahākāla and Devī

340(R116c) 846

Trakṣad, Ṭakkirāja

Trakṣad and Ṭakkirāja

ཨོཾ་ཊཀྐི་རཱ་ཛཱ་ཡ་ཏྲཱཾ་མ་ཡ་སྭཱ༔ཧཱུཾ་ཛཿ
ཧཱུཾ་ཕཊ། ཨོཾ་ཧ་[illegible]ཡ་བ་ཛྲ་མ་ཧཱ་ཀཱ
ལ་ཏྲཱ་ཊཀྐི་ཧཱུཾ་ཕ་ཊ་ཏ། ཡེ་དྷརྨཱ
ཧེ་ཏུ་པྲ་བྷ་ཝཱ་ཧེ་ཏུནྟེ
ཥཱཾ་ཏ་ཐཱ་ག་ཏོ་ཧྱ་ཝ་དཏ།
ཏེ་ཥཱཉྩ་ཡོ་ནི་རོ་དྷ་ཨེ
ཝཾ་ཝཱ་དཱི་མ་ཧཱ་ཤྲ་མ་ཎཿ

341(R117a) 847

mGon dkar yid bzhin nor bu

Cintāmaṇi Sita Mahākāla

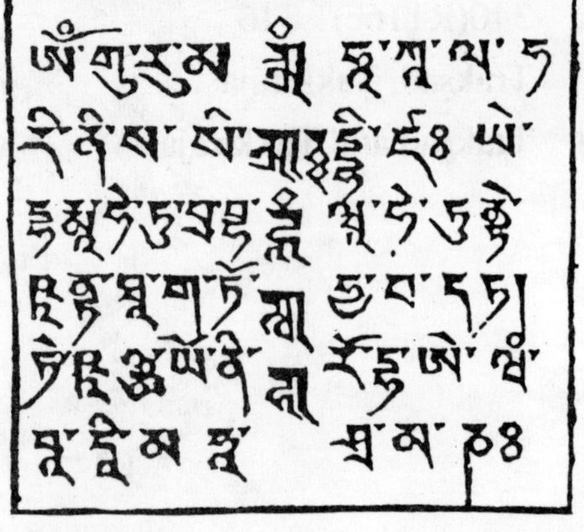

342(R117b) 848
mGon ser blo 'phel
Mativardhana Pīta Mahākāla

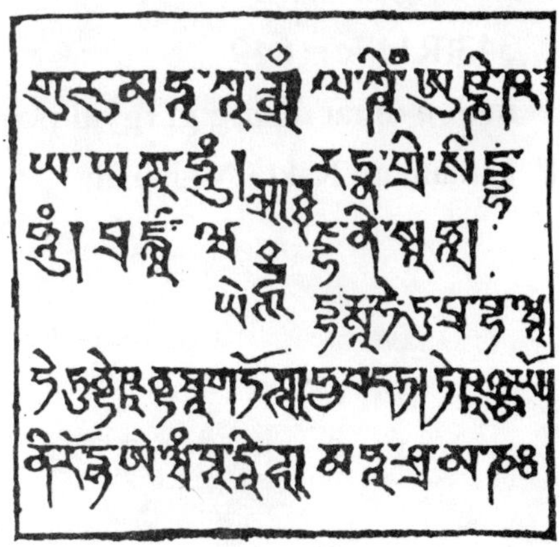

343(R117c) 849
mGon dmar dbang gi rgyal po
Cintāmaṇi Rakta Mahākāla

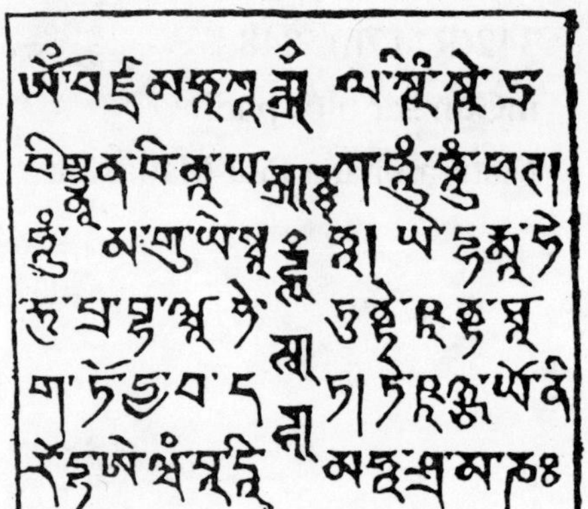

344(R118a) 850

'Khor Ratna ḍā ki, Buddha ḍā ki

Attendant Ratnaḍāki and Buddha-ḍāki

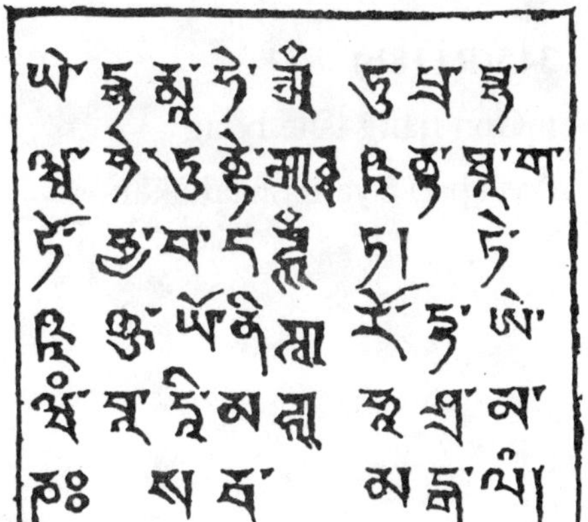

345(R118b) 851
mGon ljang tshe bdag
Āyuṣpati Śyāma Mahākāla

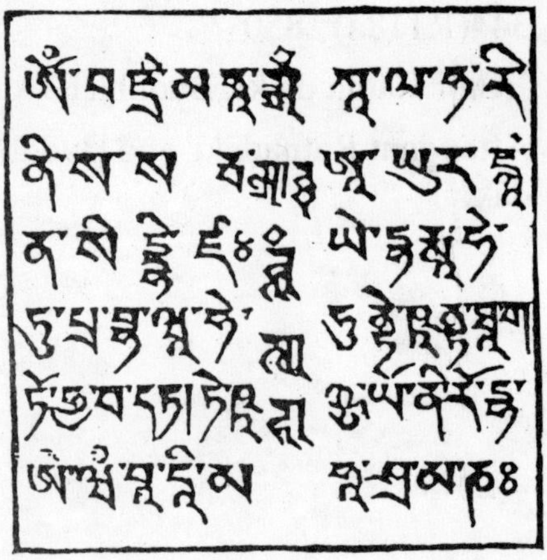

346(R118c) 852

'Khor Padma ḍā ki, Karma ḍā ki

Attendant Padmaḍāki and Karmaḍāki

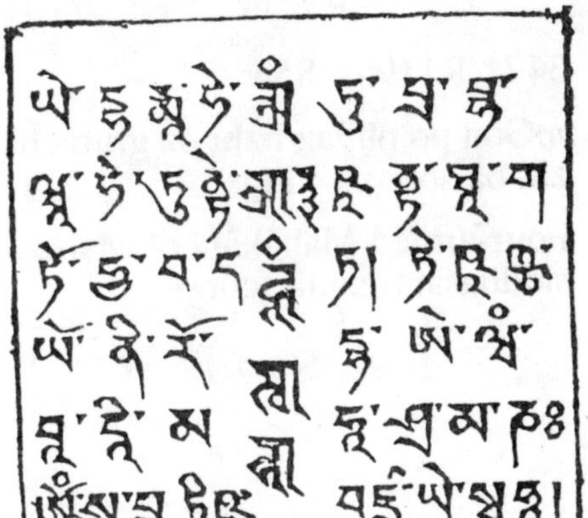

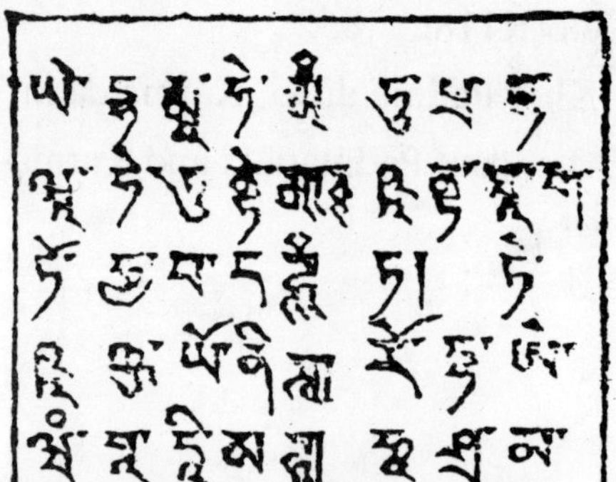

347*(R119a) 853

mGon po phyag bzhi pa grub chen zhi ba sbas pa'i lugs

Four-armed Mahākāla of Mahāsiddhaśāntigupta school

348*(R119b) 854

mGon po phyag bzhi pa klu sgrub lugs

Four-armed Mahākāla of Nāgārjuna school

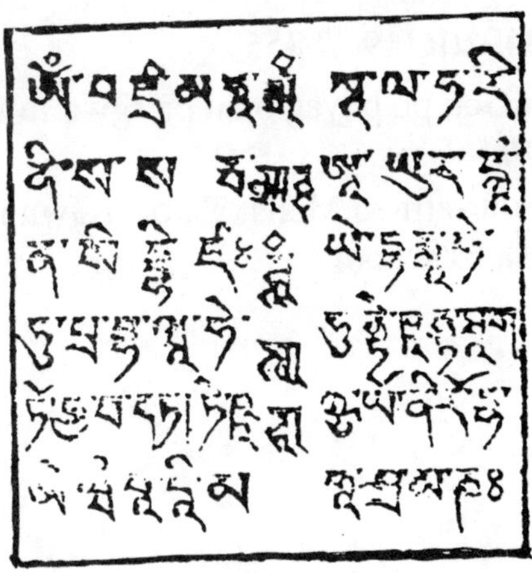

349*(R119c) 855

mGon po phyag bzhi pa rgwa lo'i lugs

Four-armed Mahākāla of rGwa lo tsā ba school

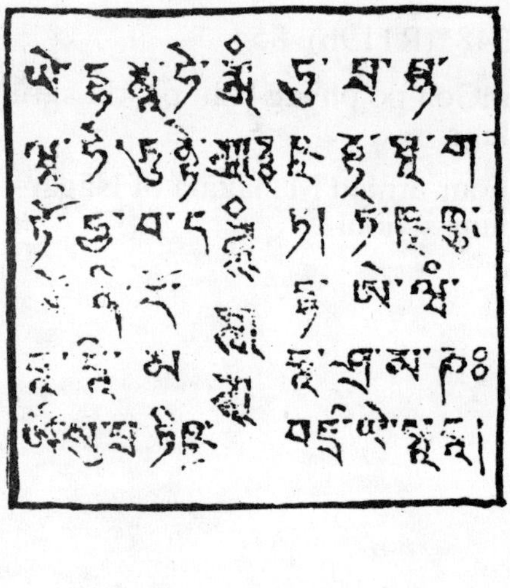

350*(R120a) 856

’Tshal lugs kyi mgon po phyag bzhi pa

Four-armed Mahākāla of ’Tshal school

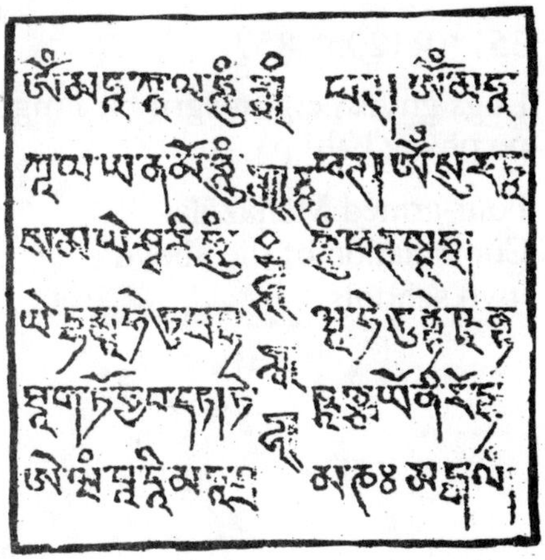

351*(R120b) 857

Lugs gnyis gcig tu sgril ba'i mgon po phyag bzhi pa

Four-armed Mahākāla, Combination of the above two schools

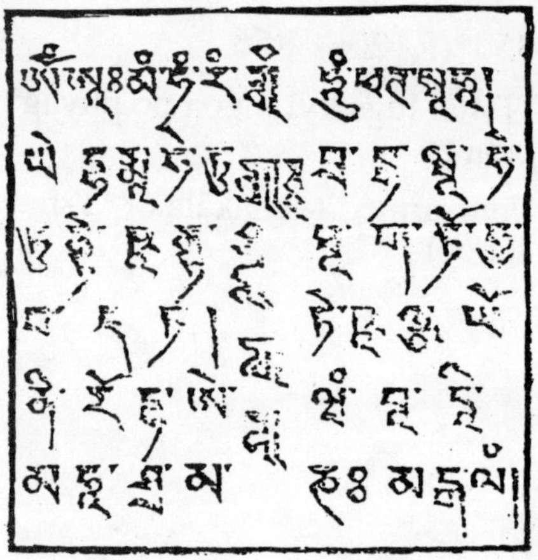

352*(R120c) 858

mGon dmar rkang gling can

Rakta Mahākāla with rkang gling

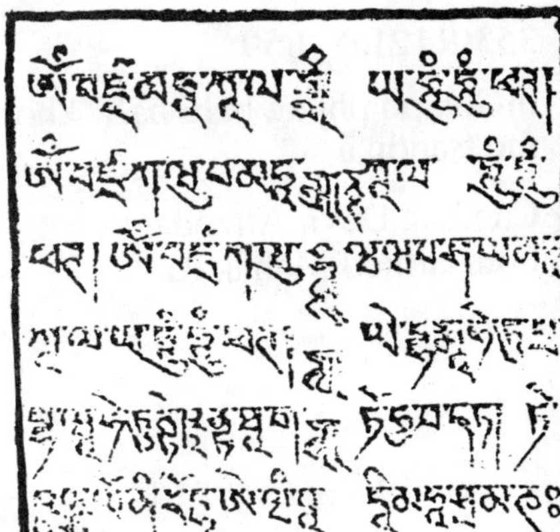

353(R121a) 859

mGon po phyag bzhi pa'i 'khor lha mo tsaṇḍikā

Caṇḍikā Devī, Attendant of Four-armed Mahākāla

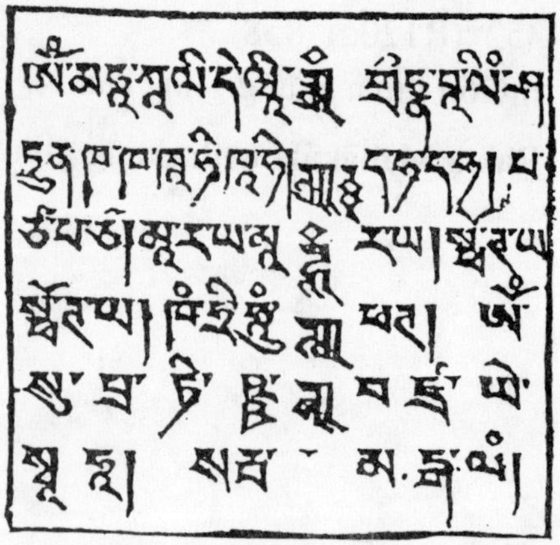

354(R121b) 860
Las mgon bya rog gdon can
Kākāsya Karma Mahākāla

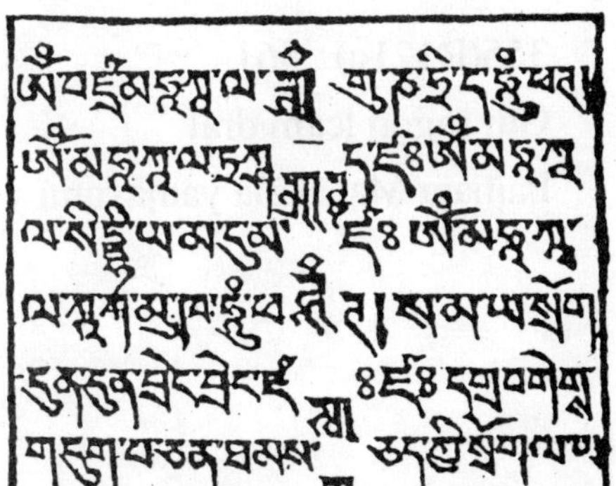

355(R121c) 861
Gur mgon lcam dral
Pañjara Mahākāla yamayamī

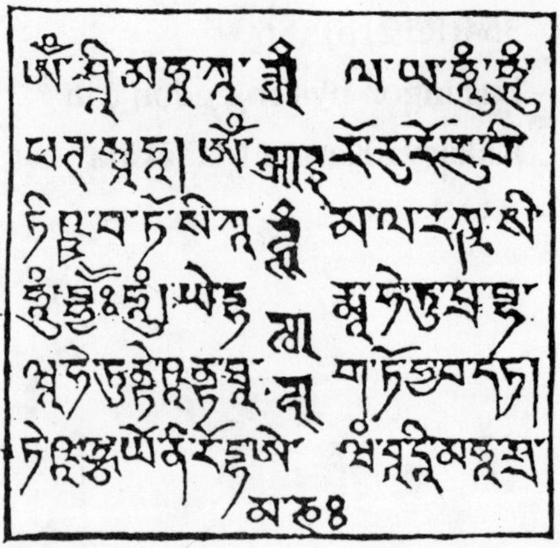

356(R122a) 862
Gur mgon lha brgyad
8-deity Pañjara Mahākāla

ཨོཾ་མ་ཧཱ་ཀཱ་ལ་ཧཱུྃ་ཧྲཱིཾ་ ཕཊ། ཨོཾ་ཤྲཱི་
མ་ཧཱ་ཀཱ་ལ་ཡ་ཧཱུྃ་ཀྵཱིཾ་ ཧཱུྃ་ཕཊ་སྭཱ་ཧཱ།
ཡེ་དྷརྨཱ་ཧེ་ཏུ་པྲ་ བྷ་ཝཱ་ཧེ་ཏུན་ཏེ་
ཥཱན་ཏ་ཐཱ་ག་ཏོ་ ཧྱ་ཝ་དཏ། ཏེ་
ཥཱཉྩ་ཡོ་ནི་རོ་ དྷ་ཨེ་ཝཾ་བཱ་དཱི་
མ་ཧཱ་ཤྲ་མ་ཎཿ ཡེ་སྭཱ་ཧཱ།

357(R122b) 863

Gur mgon phur zhabs can

Garuḍapakṣavat Kīlapāda Pañjara Mahākāla

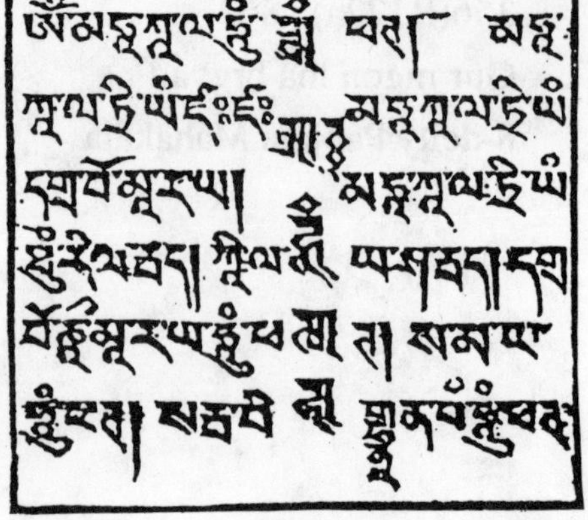

གུར་ཡུམ་ཅན་ཀླུ་སྒྲུབ་ལུགས

358(R122c) 864

Gur yum can klu sgrub lugs

Samātrka Pañjara of Nāgārjuna school

ཨོཾ་ཧྲཱིཿམ་ཧཱ་ཀཱ་ལ་ཤྲཱི ཧཱུཾ་ཧཱུཾ་པ་ཏ་ཕར་
སྭཱ་ཧཱ། ཡེ་དྷརྨཱ་ཀཱ་ཧེ་ཏུ་པྲ་བྷ་ཝཱ
ཧེ་ཏུནྟེ་ཥཱན་ཏ་ཐཱ་ག་ཏོ་ཧྱ་ཝ་དཏ།
ཏེ་ཥཱཉྩ་ཡོ་ནི་ལི་རོ་དྷ་ཨེ་ཝཾ་
ཝཱ་དཱི་མ་ཧཱ་ཤྲ་མཱ་ཎཿ ཨོཾ་སུ
པྲ་ཏིཥྛ་བཛྲ་ཡེ་སྭཱ་ཧཱ།

གུར་རྐྱང་རྔོག་ལུགས།

359(R123a) 865

Gur rkyan rngog lugs

Ekānta Pañjara of rNgog school

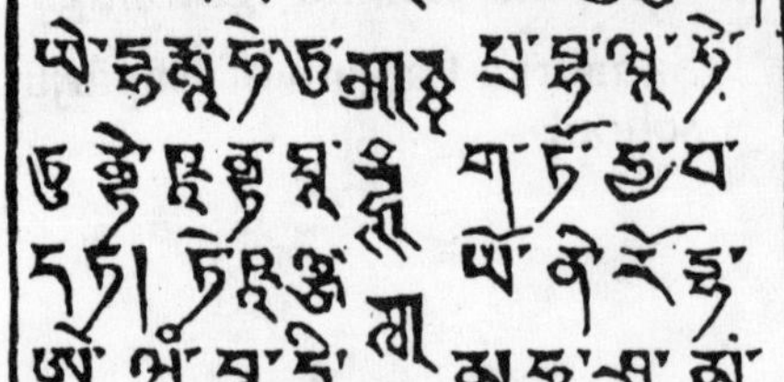

360(R123b) 866
mGon po stag gzhon ma
Vyāghravāhana Mahākāla

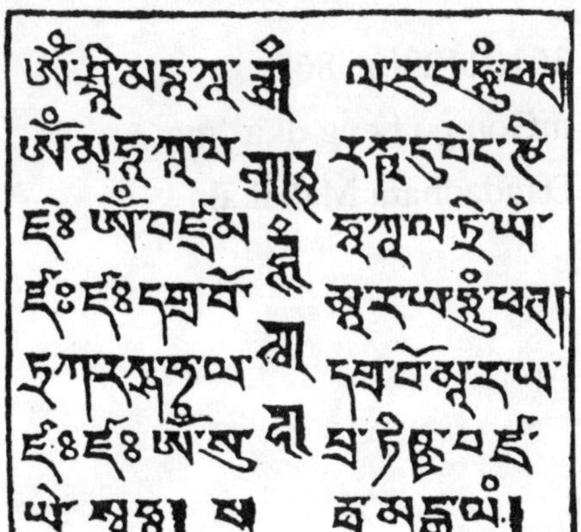

361(R123c) 867

mGon po beng dka' ma

Daṇḍadhara Mahākāla

ཨོཾ་མཧཱ་ཀཱ་ལ་ར་ཀྵི་ ཀྵ་ཧུ་བེ་ད་ཏི་
ཧཱུཾ༔ ཨོཾ་བཛྲ་ཡཀྵ་ཀྵ་ཀྵ༔ དེ་བ་མཧཱ་ཀཱ་ལ
ཁ་གོ་ཧཱུྃ་ཕཊ། སྭཱ་ཧཱ་ ཡ་ཛཿཛཿ
ཤྲཱི་ཀཱ་ལ་ར་ཀྵ། ཧཱུྃ་ ཧེ་ཛ་བད།
ཡེ་དྷརྨཱ་ཧེ་ཏུ་པྲ་བྷ་ཝཱ། ཧེ་ཏུནྟེ་ཥཱན་ཏ
ཐཱ་ག་ཏོ་ཧྱ་བ་དཏ། ཏེ་ ཥཱཾ་ ཙ་ཡོ་ནི་རོ་དྷ་ཨེ
ཝཾ་ཝཱ་དཱི་མཧཱ་ཤྲ་མ་ཎ༔ མངྒ་ལཾ།

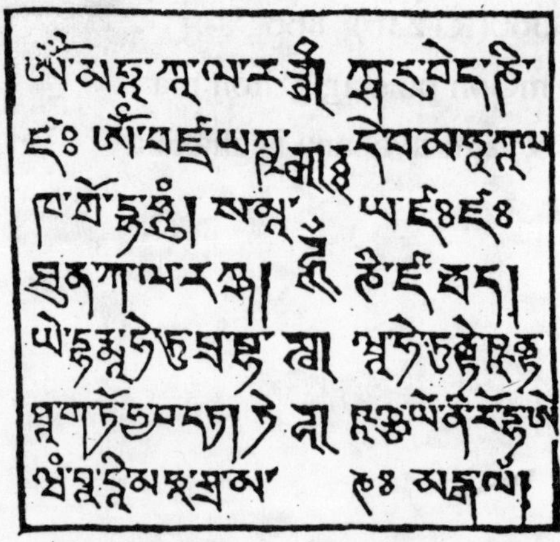

362(R124a) 868

mGon po beng gter ma

Nidhi Daṇḍadhara Mahākāla

མ་ཧཱ་ཀཱ་ལ་ཤྲཱི། ཏྲི་ད་ཧཱུྃ་
ཛཿ ཨོཾ་མ་ཧཱ་ཀཱ་ཀཱ་ཡ་ཏི་ཧྲཱུྃ་ཡི་ཧྲཱུྃ
ཧི་ཡ་བད། པུ་ཥྨེ་ཧྲཱིཿ ཛཿ དགྲ་བོའི
སྙིང་ལ་ཛཿ ཏ ཀྲཱ ཀ་ར་ཀྲ་ཧཱུྃ་རོ་ལ་
བད། དགྲ་བོའི་ཀྲཱ སྙིང་ཁ་རག་ཛཿ
ཨོཾ་བྷྱཱ་ཤྲཱ་ཏི་ཧཱུྃ བཛྲ་ཡེ་སྭཱ་ཧཱ།

མགོན་པོ་ལེགས་ལྡན་མཆེད་གསུམ་

363(R124b) 869

mGon po legs ldan mched gsum

Bhagavat Mahākāla Bhrātṛtraya

ཨོཾ་མཧཱ་ཀཱ་ལ་ཧྲཱིཾ་ཤྲཱི་ཧྲཱུཾ། ཨོཾ་
མཧཱ་ཀཱ་ལ་ཌ་ཀྲཱཾ་ཌཾ་ཧྲཱུཾ། ཨོཾ་
མཧཱ་ཀཱ་ལ་ཌ་ཧྲཱིཾ་ཌཾ་ཧྲཱུཾ། ཡེ་དྷརྨཱ
ཧེ་ཏུ་པྲ་བྷ་ཝཱ་ཧེ་ ཏུནྟེ་ཥཱན྄་ཏ་ཐཱ་ག
ཏོ་ཧྱ་ཝ་དཏ྄། ཏེ་ ཥཱཉྩ་ཡོ་ནི་རོ་དྷ
ཨེ་ཝཾ་ཝཱ་དཱི་མ་ཧཱ་ ཤྲ་མ་ཎཿ

མགོན་པོ་ཨཾ་གྷོ་ར

364(R124c) 870
mGon po aṃ gho ra
Aṅghora Mahākāla

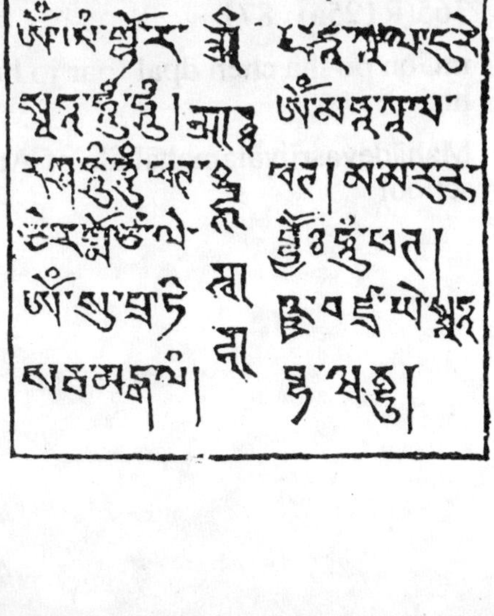

365(R125a) 871

mGon po lha chen dpal 'bar jo bo'i lugs

Mahādevaśrījvālamahākāla of Atīśa school

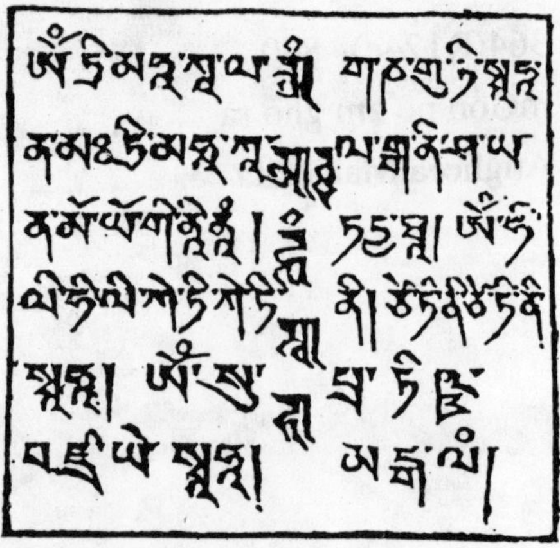

366(R125b) 872

mGon po gri gug dpa' gcig

Ekavīra Kartarīdhara Mahākāla

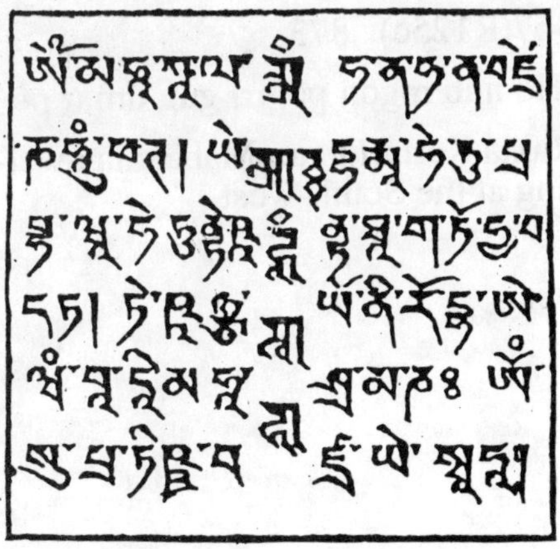

367(R125c) 873

lHo nub mgon po gri gug dmar po

Rakta Kartarīdhara Mahākāla dwelling at the South-west

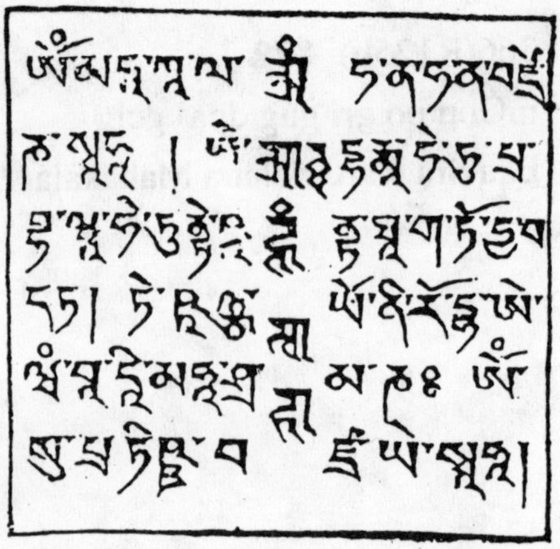

368(R126a) 874
mGon po bzhi sprags
Four Mahākālas

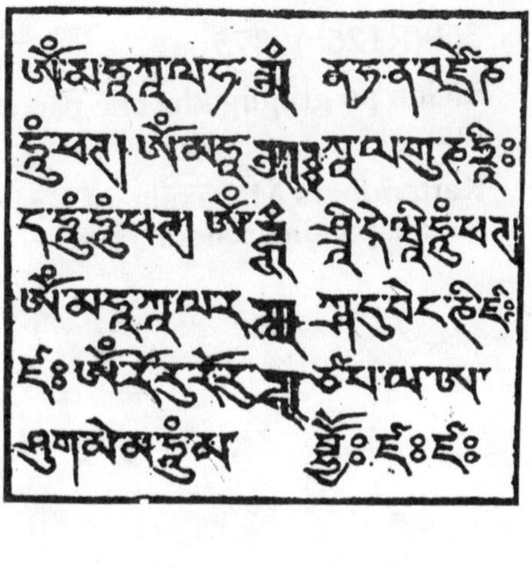

369(R126b) 875

mGon po gri gug kha che paṇ chen lugs

Kartarīdhara Mahākāla of Kāśmīramahāpaṇḍita school

ཨོཾ་མ་ཧཱ་ཀཱ་ལ་ཡ་ཏྲཱཾ། ན་ཏ་ན་བརྡཱི
ཧ་སྭཱ་ཧཱ། ཨོཾ་ཨ་ཏྲཱ་ཊ་ཤི་ཤུ་ཤ་ཡ།
ཊི་ཤུ་ཡ། ཨེ་ཧྱེ་ཧི་ཧྲཱིཿ མ་ཧཱ་ཀཱ་ཡ།
སརྦ་ཤ་ཏྲུན་ནི་རྐྵ་[illegible] ཏ་ཡ། ཧཱུཾ་ཕ
ཊ། ཤྲཱི་ཧེ་རུ་ཀ་ཡ། ཤྲཱི་ཧེ་རུ་ཀ་ཡ
ཧཱུཾ་ཕཊ། སརྦ་ མ་ཧཱ་ཀཱ་ལཾ།

370(R126c) 876

mGon po zangs gri tsan gyi ljang lugs

Tāmrakartarīdhara Mahākāla of lJang school

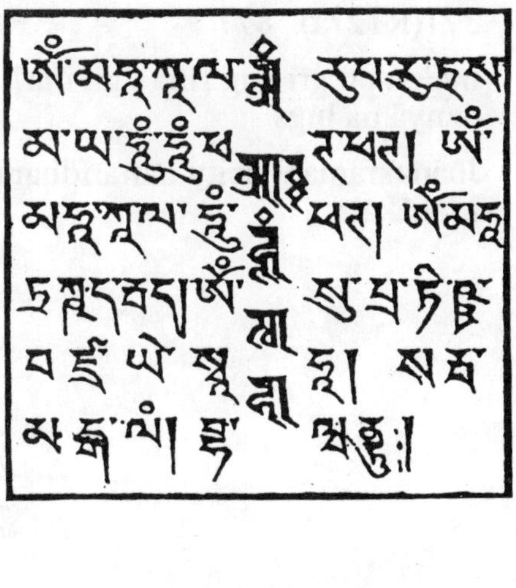

371(R127a) 877

mGon po gri gug [lha dgu ma]
dznyā na lugs

Jñānakrama 9-deity kartarīdhara
Mahākāla

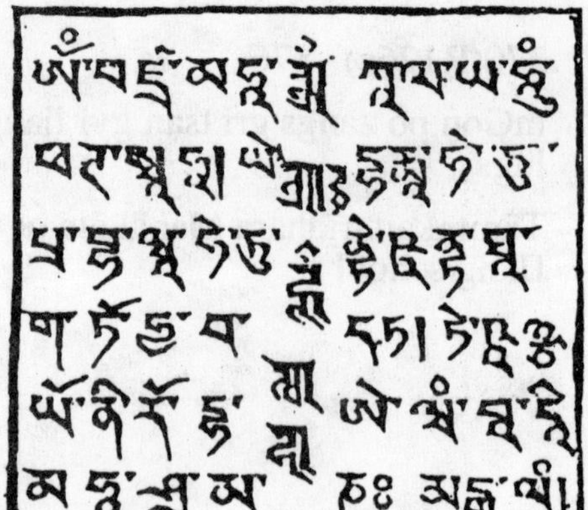

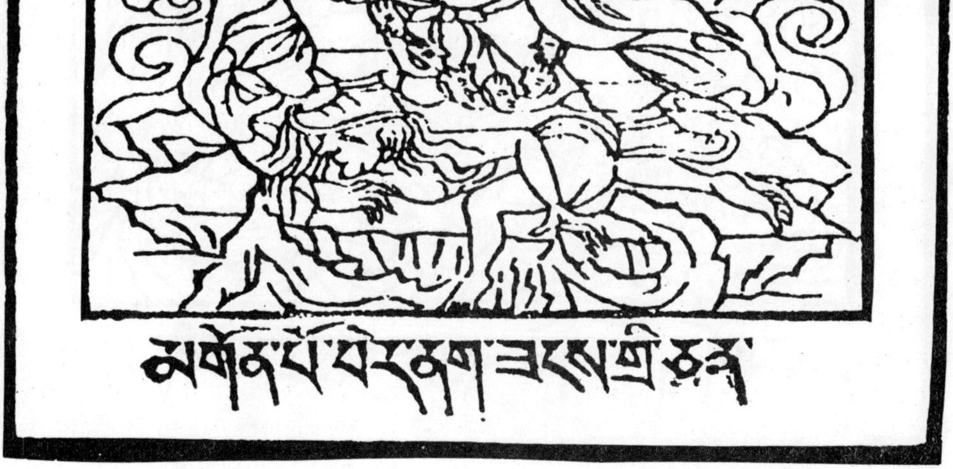

372(R127b) 878

mGon po ber nag zangs gri can

Tāmrakartarīdhara Kṛṣṇacola Mahākāla

ཨོཾ་མ་ཧཱ་ཀཱ་ལ་ཏྲཱི་ ཀཱ་ལ་རཱུ་པ
ཡ་ མ་ ཡ་ ཧཱུཾ་ཨཱཿ ཧཱུཾ་ཕཊ་ཕཊ་
ཡེ་ཧྲ་ཀྲ་ཏེ་ཙ་ཧཱུཾ་ ཕྲ་ཛྲ་སྭ་ཏེ
ཙ་ཏྟེ་ ཚ་ཧྲ་ ཐ་མ་ ག་ཏོ་ཙ་བ་ཙ
ཏེ་ཚ་ཀྵ་ཡ་ ཀེ་ཝཱ་ ཀོ་ཧྲ་ཨེ་ཤཾ
ཤ་ཏྲི་མ་ཧཱ་ཕྲ་མ་ཊཿ ཤ་ཐ་མ་ཀྵ་སཾ།

373(R127c) 879
mGon po gcer bu zangs gri can
Tāmrakartarīdhara Nagna Mahākāla

ཨོཾ་མ་ཧཱ་ཀཱ་ལ་ཧྲཱིཾ་ ཧུ་བ་ཤ་ཧཱུྃ་
ཕཊ། ཨོཾ་མ་ཧཱ་ཀྲོ་དྷ་ཀཱ་ལ་ཧུ་ཏ་ཤ
ན་ཤཱུ་རི། ཙཎྜ་ཧཱུྃ་ ཤཱུ་རི། ཞ་མ་རེ
ཤ་ལ་བ་ཡེ་ཀེ་ཏྲི་ཊ་ཀྵ་སུ་ཀི། ཤཾ་ར
ཤཾ་ཏ། ཛ་ན་ཛ་ས། ཀྵ། ཛྷ་ག་ཛྷ་ག་ཛྷ
ག་ཊ་ཡ། ཧཱུྃ་ཧཱུྃ་ཕ ཊ་ཕཊ།

374(R128a) 880

Tshogs bdag mgon po seng ge'i gdan can

Siṃhāsana Gaṇapati Mahākāla

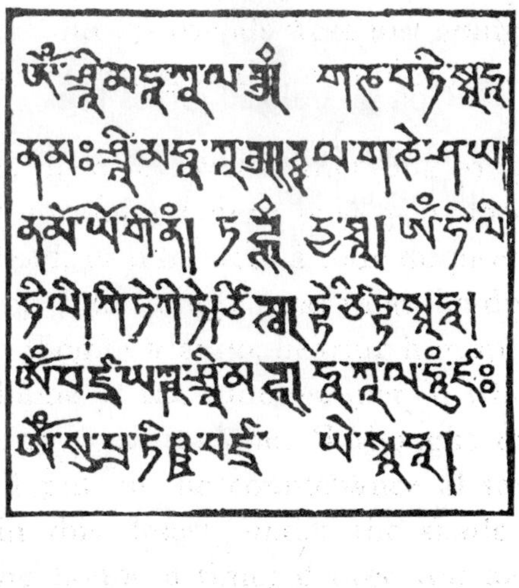

མགོན་པོ་ཏྲཀྵད་གཉོས་ལུགས

375(R128b) 881

mGon po trakṣad gnyos lugs

Trakṣad Yamayamī Mahākāla of gNyos school

ཨོཾ་ཤྲཱི་མ་ཧཱ་ཀཱ་ལ ཀྵཾ ཡཀྵ་མ་ཧཱ་ཀཱ་ལ
ཏེ་ཧྲཱི་ཀྲི་ཡཾ་ཧྲཱུཾ་ཛཿ ཀྵ ཛཿ་ཨོཾ་ར་ཏུ་ར་ཏུ
ཙ་པ་ལ་ཨ་ཤུ་ཀེ ཧཱུཾ ས་ཧཱུཾ་ས་ཧྲཱུཾ་ཛཿ
ཛཿ་མ་ཐོད། མ་ཐོད། མ་ཤོར་མ་ཤོར།
གཟུང་། གཟུང་། མ ལས་ཐམས་ཅད་
སྒྲུབ་པ་མཛོད་དྷི ཤ། སྭཱ་ཧཱ།

མགོན་པོ་ཏྲཀྵད་དྭགས་པོའི་ལུགས།

376(R128c) 882

mGon po trakṣad dwags po'i lugs

Trakṣad Mahākāla of Dwags po school

ཨོཾ་མཧཱ་ཀཱ་ལ་ ཏྲཾ་ ཧཀྵ་ར་མཧཱ་ཀཱ
ལ་ཤྲཱི་ཧྲཱིཾ་ཧྲི་ཡཾ་ ཨཱ་ཀྲྀཥྚ་ ཛཿ ཛཿ ཡེ
དྷརྨཱ་ཧེ་ཏུ་པྲ་བྷཱ་ཝཱ་ ཧེ་ཏུནྟེ་ཥཱན་ཏ
ཐཱ་ག་ཏོ་ཧྱ་ཝ་དཏ་ ཏེ་ཥཱཉྩ
ཡོ་ནི་རོ་དྷ་ཨེ་ཝཾ་ ཝཱ་དཱི་མ་ཧཱ
ཤྲ་མ་ཎཿ སཧ་མཎྜ་ལཾ།

377(R129a) 883

mGon po trakṣad seng zhon jo bo'i lugs

Siṃhavāhana Trakṣad Mahākāla of Atīśa school

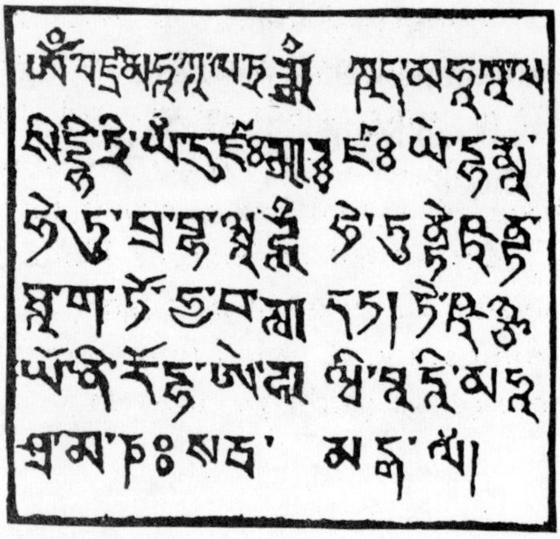

378(R129b) 884

mGon po trakṣad gri gug sprags sgrub ma

Kartarīdhara Trakṣad Mahākāla

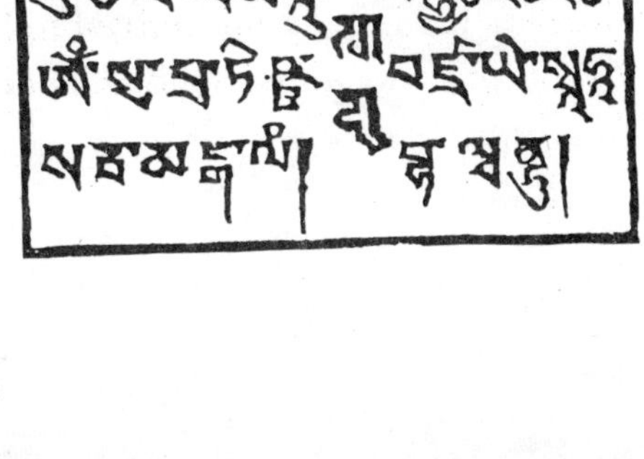

379(R129c) 885

mGon po trakṣad rkang thang ma

Padātika Trakṣad Mahākāla

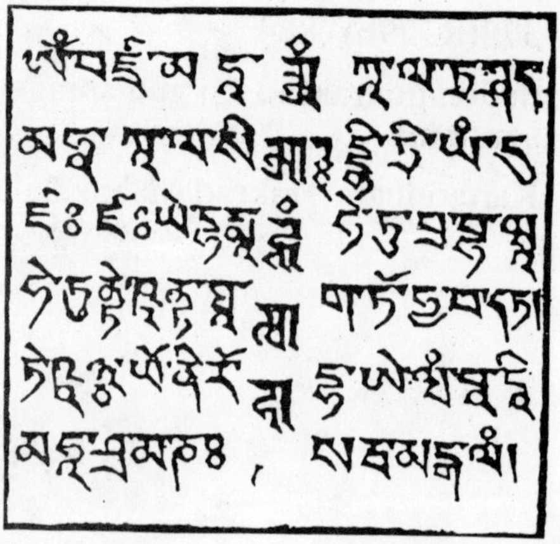

380(R130a) 886

mGon po trakṣad ma ning ma

Paṇḍaka Trakṣad Mahākāla

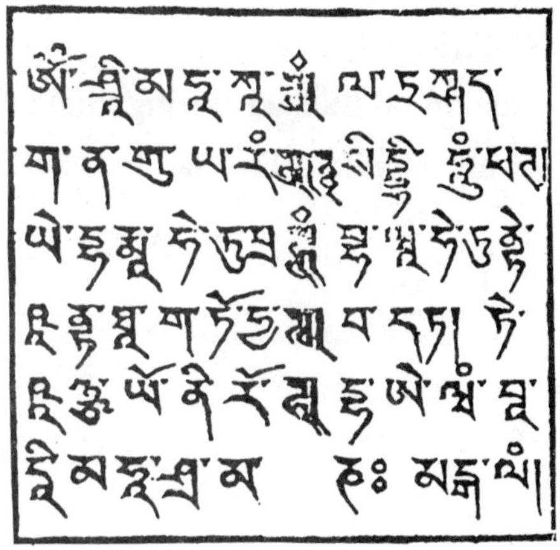

381(R130b) 887

mGon po trakṣad 'brong zhal can

Camarīmukha Trakṣad Mahākāla

ཨོཾ་བཛྲ་མ་ཧཱ་ཀྵྨཾ ཀཱ་ལ་ཏྲཀྵད་
ཏྲི ཡཾ་ཧྲཱུཾ༔ ཧྲི་ཀྵྨཱ་ཚོ་ལ་པ་ཏྲི་ཡཾ
ཛཿ ཛཿ རུ་རུ་ཧཱུཾ་རུ་རུ་ཙེ་པ་ལ
ཨ་ཤུག་མེ་ཧྲཱུཿ ཀྵ ཨོཾ་སུ་པྲ་
ཏི་ཥྛ་ བཛྲ་ཡེ་ སྭཱ་ཧཱ། སྭ་ཧྲ
མ་ཧ་ ཡཾ། ཧྲ ཀྵཱུྃ། ཤུཾ།

382(R130c) 888

mGon po trakṣad gsang sgrub shwa na'i zhal can

Ḍākamukha Guhyasādhana Trakṣad Mahākāla

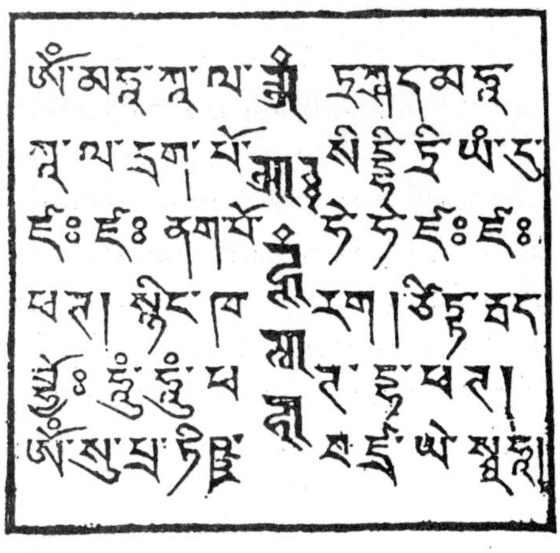

དཔལ་མགོན་ཞལ་བཞི་པ་བསྙེན་དུས་དང་འབྲེལ་བ

383(R131a) 889

dPal mgon zhal bzhi pa bsnyen dus dang 'brel ba

Sevākālasambaddha Four-faced Śrīmahākāla

ཨོཾ་མ་ཧཱ་ཀཱ་ལ་ཀྲཱྀཾ ཀཱ་ལ་བི་ཀཱ
ལ་ར་ཏྲི་ད་ཧཱུྃ་[illegible]ཕཊ། ཨོཾ་མ་ཧཱ
ཀཱ་ལ་ཀཱ་ལ་བི་[illegible] ཀཱ་ལ་ར་ཏྲི
ད། ཧཱུྃ་ཧྲི་ཧྲི། [illegible] ཙ་ཏྲ་ལི། རཀྵ
ཤི། ཤི་དྷ་ལི། [illegible] [illegible] [illegible] ཧཱུྃ་ཧཱུྃ
ཕཊ་[illegible] [illegible] མ་དྷ་ལིཾ།

དཔལ་མགོན་ཞལ་བཞི་པ་སྒྲུབ་དུས་དང་འབྲེལ་བ་

384(R131b) 890

dPal mgon zhal bzhi pa sgrub dus dang ’brel ba

Sādhanakālasambaddha Four-faced Śrīmahākāla

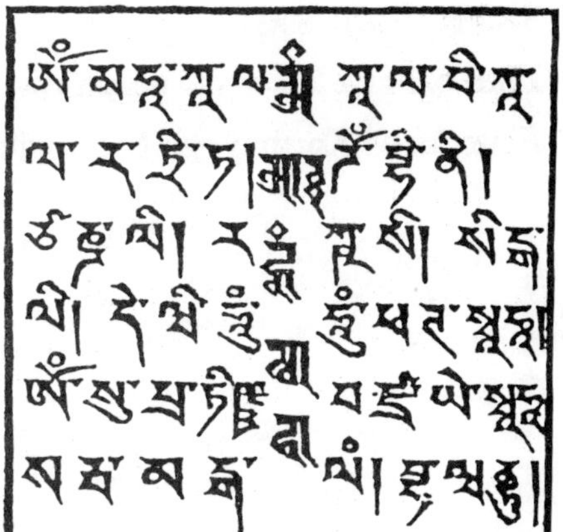

ཞལ་བཞི་པ་ལས་སྦྱོར་མགོན་པོ་

385(R131c) 891

Zhal bzhi pa las sbyor mgon po

Four-faced Karmayoga Mahākāla

ཨོཾ་མ་ཧཱ་ཀཱ་ལ་ཀྲོཾ་ཀཱ་ལ་ཙེ་ཀཱ་
ལ་ར་ཌི་ཏ་ཧཱུྃ་ཀྲཱ་ཕཊ། ཨོཾ་
མ་ཧཱ་ཀཱ་ལ་ཀཱ་ཧྲཱིཾ་ལ་ཙེ་ཀཱ་ལ་
ར་ཌི་ཏ། ཧཾ་ཀྲི་ཏི། ཙ་ཧྲུ་ལི། རཀྵ
སི། སི་ཀྵ་ལི། ཧཱུྃ་ཧཱུྃ་
ཕཊ་སྭཱཧཱ། ས མ་ཀྵ་ཡཾ།

386(R132a)   892
Zhal bzhi dkar po tshe 'phel
Four-faced Sita Āyurvardhana

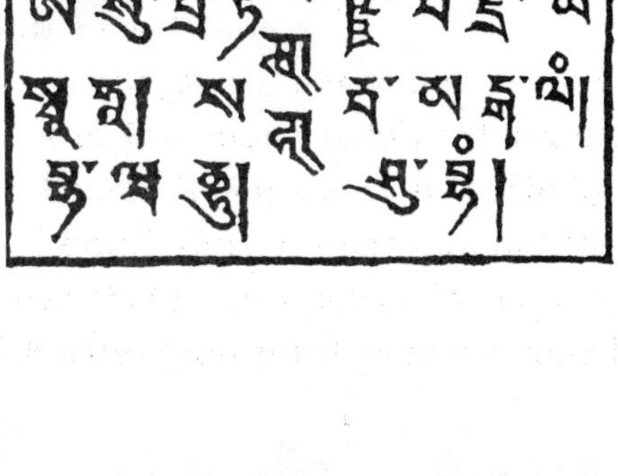

ཞལ་བཞི་སེར་པོ་ནོར་འཕེལ་

387(R132b) 893

Zhal bzhi ser po nor 'phel

Four-faced Pīta Dhanavardhana

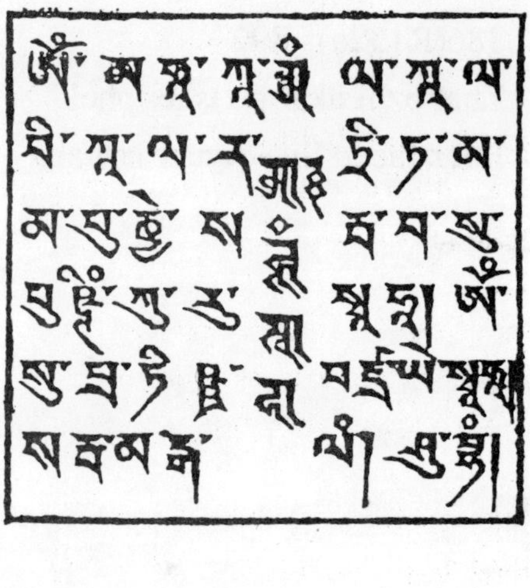

388(R132c) 894

Zhal bzhi dmar po dbang sdud

Four-faced Rakta Vaśaṃkara

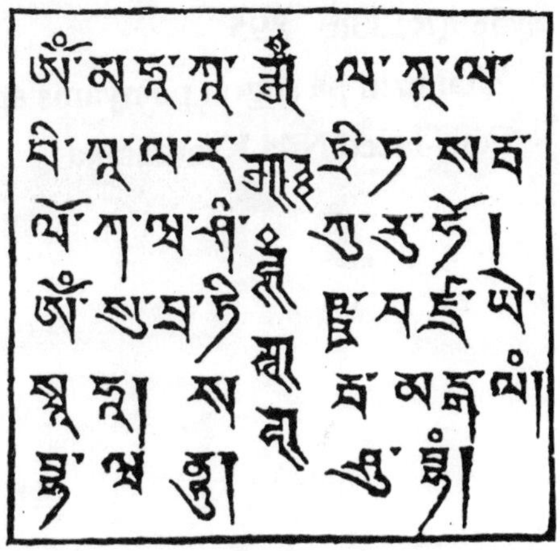

389(R133a) 895

Zhal bzhi pa sngon po nyams sgrol

Four-faced Nīla Kṣatitāraka

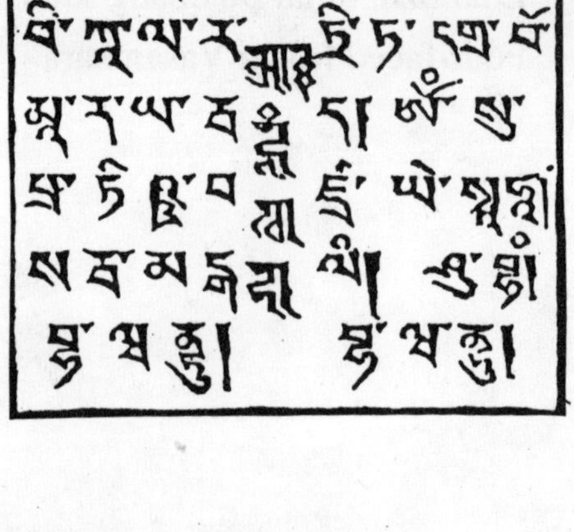

ཞལ་བཞི་པ་གདོང་གཉན་ཅན

390(R133b) 896

Zhal bzhi pa gdong gnyan can

Four-faced Caṇḍamukha

ཨོཾ་མཉྫུ་ཤྲཱི་ཡ་ - ཤྲཱི་ཡ་གུ་ཧ་ཧི
ད་ཨེ་ཀ་ཪྻ་ ཏི་ཧཱུཾ་ཕཊ།
ཡེ་དྷརྨཱ་ཧེ་ཏུ་ པྲ་བྷ་ཝཱ་ཧེ་
ཏུ་ཏེ་ཥཱཾ་ཏ་ཐཱ་ ག་ཏོ་ཧྱ་ཝ
ད་ཏ། ཏེ་ཥཱཉྩ་ ཡོ་ནི་རོ་དྷ་
ཨེ་ཝཾ་ཝཱ་དཱི་ མ་ཧཱ་ཤྲ་མ་ཎཿ

391(R133c) 897

Sha za ce spyan gdong

Śṛgālamukha Piśāca

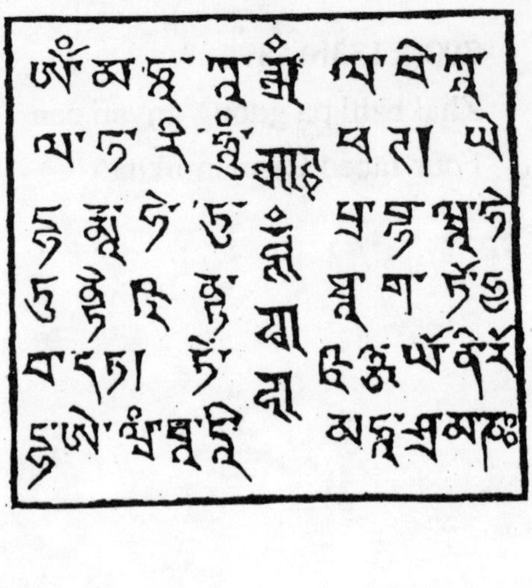

392(R134a) 898
lHa mo dud sor ma
Dhūmavatī Devī

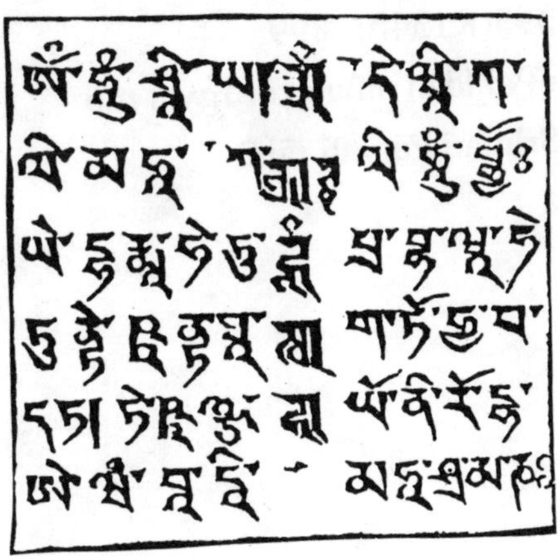

དཔལ་ལྡན་དམག་ཟོར་རྒྱལ་མོ་

393(R134b) 899

dPal ldan dmag zor rgyal mo

Śrīmatī Pārvatī rājñī

ཧཱུྃཿ རཀ་མོ་ཧཱུྃ་ ཧཱུྃ། རཀ་མོ
ཧཱུྃ་ ཧཱུྃ། རཀ་ཀྵ་མོ་སྟན་ ཧཱུྃ།
ཁ་ལ་ རཀ་ཀྵ་ ཆེན་མོ།
རཀ་མོ་ཨ་ཏྲ་ ཀྲ་ཏྲ་ སྟན
ཧཱུྃ། ཙ་ལ་ཙ་ ཧཱུྃ་ ཧཱུྃ་ ཧཱུྃ
ཧཱུྃ། ལ་ཅ་མ་ ཡཾ། ཧཱུྃ་ཧཱུྃ

394(R134c) 900

lHa mo srog sgrub lcags phur ma rang byung rgyal mo

Prāṇasādhana Lohakīla Svayambhūrājñī Devī

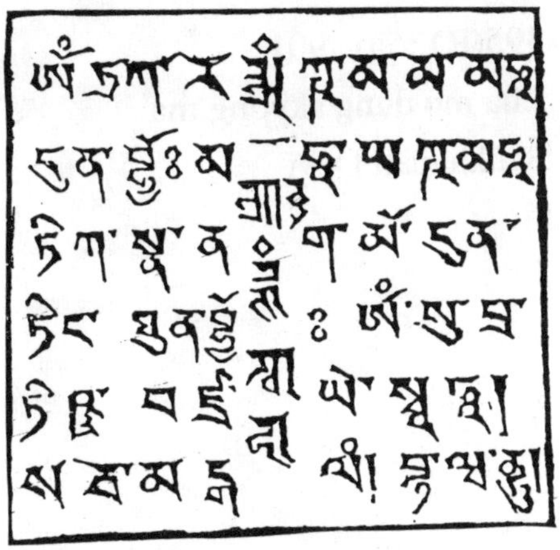

ལྷ་མོ། དུང་སྐྱོང་མ

395(R135a) 901

Lha mo dung skyong ma

Śaṅkhapālī Devī

ཧཱུྃ༔ ཛཿ༔ ཨོཾ་ཤྲཱི ཙཾ་པ་ལ་ཨ
ཧྲ་ག་མ་ཧཱུྃ༔ཕཊ༔ ཨོཾ་རེ་ཏ་རེ
ཏ་ཙཾ་པ་ལ་ཧྲཱི ཨ་ཧྲ་ག་མེ
ཧཱུྃ༔ ཛཿ༔ ཛཿ༔སྭཱ ཨོཾ་སུ་བྲ
ཏ་ཀྵ་བཛྲ་ཀྐ ཡེ་སྭཱ་ཧཱ།
ས་ཙ་མ་ཧཱ ཡཾ། ཧྲཱུྃ།

396(R135b) 902
bDud mo re ma ti
Mahākālī Rematī

ཨོཾ་མ་ཧཱ་ཀཱ་ལཱིཾ་ཡེ་རེ་མ་ཏི
ཤ་མ་ཤཱ་ན་ཀཱ་ལཱ་རཱ་ཏྲི་རེ་མ
ཏཱི་ཧཱ་ལཱ་ཧཱ་ཧྲཱིཾ་ལཱ་ཧཱུྃཿཛ
ཛཿཨོཾ་སུ་ཀྵཱ་བྲ་ཏི་ཙྪ
བ་ཛྲེ་ཡེ་སྭཱ་ཧཱ། ས་བ
མ་ཧྨ་ལཾ། ཧ་སུ་ཏྲུ།

397(R135c) 903

Klu mo re ma ti

Nāgī Rematī

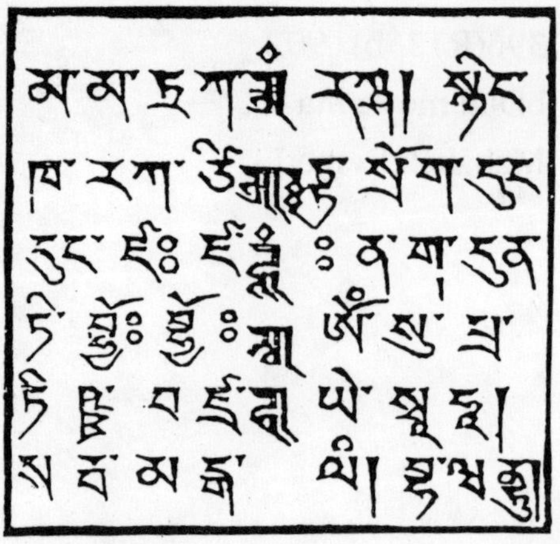

གནོད་སྦྱིན་རེ་མ་ཏི

398(R136a) 904
gNod sbyin re ma ti
Yakṣī Rematī

བྷྱོཿཛཿཨོཾ་ཙ་པ་ལ་ཀྲོཾ། ཨ་ཤུ་ཀ་མེ
བྷྱོཿཨོཾ་རོ་རུ་རོ་རུ་ཙ་ཀྲ་ཧྲཱུཾ་པ་ལ་ཨ
ཤུ་ཀ་མ་བྷྱོཿཛཿཛཿཧྲཱུཾ ཡེ་དྷརྨཱ་ཧེ
ཏུ་པྲ་བྷ་ཝཱ་ཧེ་ཏུན་ཏེ་ཥཱན་ཏ་ཐཱ་ག་ཏོ་ཧྱ
ཝ་དཏ། ཏེ་ཥཱཉྩ་ཡོ་ནི་རོ་དྷ་ཨེ
ཝཾ་ཝཱ་དཱི་མ་ཧཱ་ཤྲ་ མ་ཎཿ

399(R136b) 905

Rema ti rdo rje gshog rgod ma

Uddhatavajrapakṣā Rematī

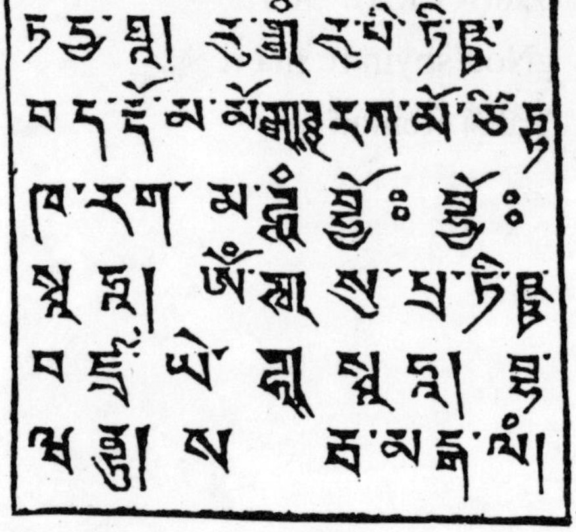

400(R136c) 906
lHa mo e ka dza ti
Ekajaṭī Devī

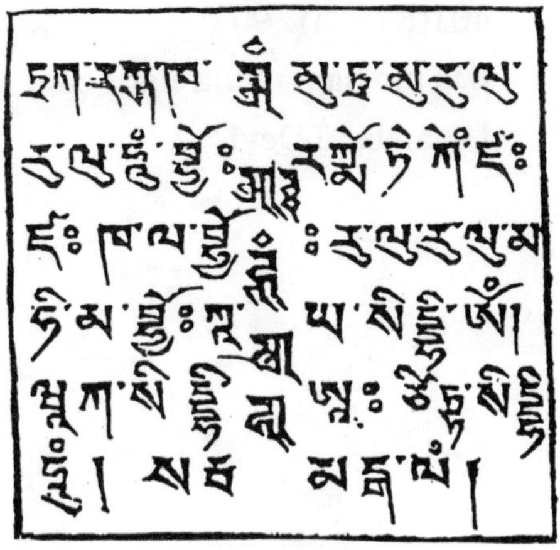

401(R137a) 907

lHa mo nam mkha'i gos can

Digambarā Devī

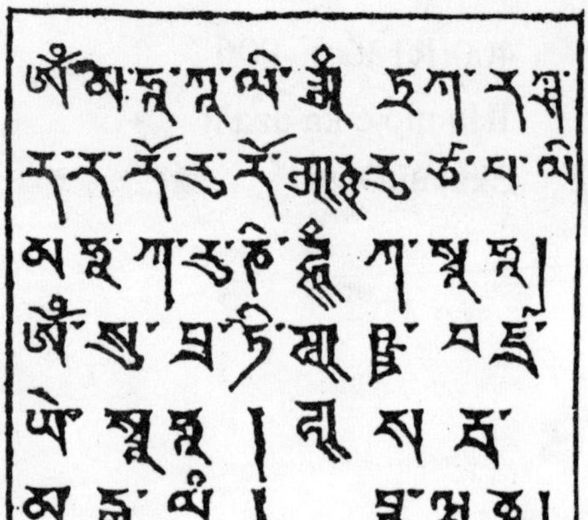

402(R137b) 908

Chos rgyal las kyi gshin rje mthing ga

Nīla Dharmarāja Karmayama

ཨོཾ་ཀཱ་ལ་རཱུ་པ་ཧྲཱིཾ་ ཧཱུཾ་ཕཊ།
ཨོཾ་ཀཱ་ལ་རཱུ་པ་ཡ་ཨཱཿ་མ་ནྟ་ཡ་
ཧཱུཾ་ཕཊ། ཨོཾ་ཧྲཱིཿ ཀཱ་ལ་རཱུ་པཀྵི
མ་ཡ་ཀྵ་ཧཱུཾ་མ་ཧཱ་སྭཱ་རོ་ཙ་ན་ར་ཤི་ཧྲཱི་
ཡེ་ཡ་མ་ནྟ་ཀ་པ་ཏྲཱ་ཧྲཱུཾ་ཧཱུཾ་ཕཊ་ཕཊ་
སྭཱ་ཧཱ། ཨོཾ་ཌྲིཿསྟི་ སྟྲི་ཧཱུཾ་ཕཊ།

ལས་གཤིན་དམར་པོ་མ་རུ་རྩེ་བཞིས་བསྐོར་བ་

403(R137c) 909

Las gshin dmar po ma ru rtse bzhis bskor ba

Rakta Karmayama surrounded by four Ma ru rtses

ཨོཾ་ཡ་མ་རཱ་ཛྲཱི་ ཛ་ཨེ་ཀ་ཛ
ཊི་ཡ་ཧོ་ ཤཏྲཱུན། མ་ཧོ་
ཕ་ཊ། སུ་ཧོ་ཧྲཱི་ ཕ་ཊ། མ
རུ་རྩེ་ཕ་ཊ །ཧྲཱ་ཧཾ་ཧཱི་ཕ་ཊ།
ཧེ་ཕ་ཊ། ཧཱུྃ་དྲཱ་ཧཱུྃ་ཕ་ཊ།
ས་ཏ་མ་ཏྲ་ ཡེ། སུ་ཧཱ།

404(R138a) 910

Las gshin dmar po khrag mdog

Rudhiravarṇa Rakta Karmayama

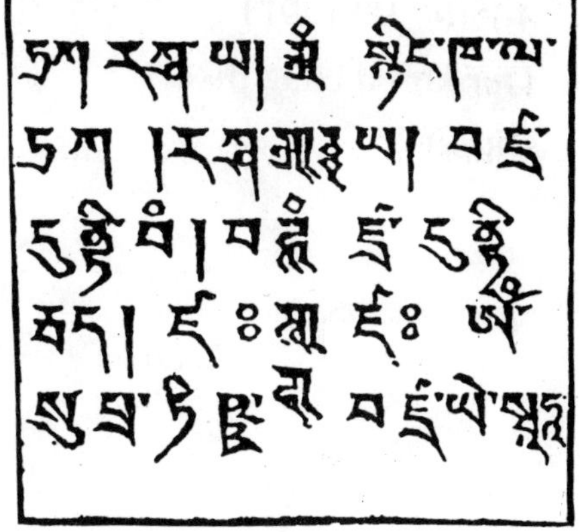

405(R138b) 911
Dur khrod bdag po
Citipati

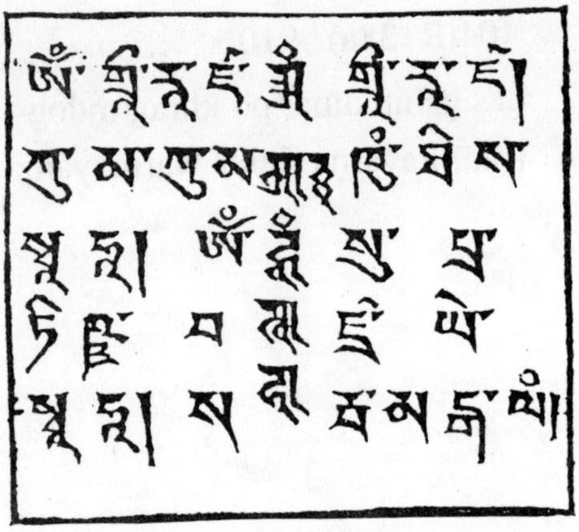

406(R138c) 912

Pu tra lcam dral

Putra and Yamayamī

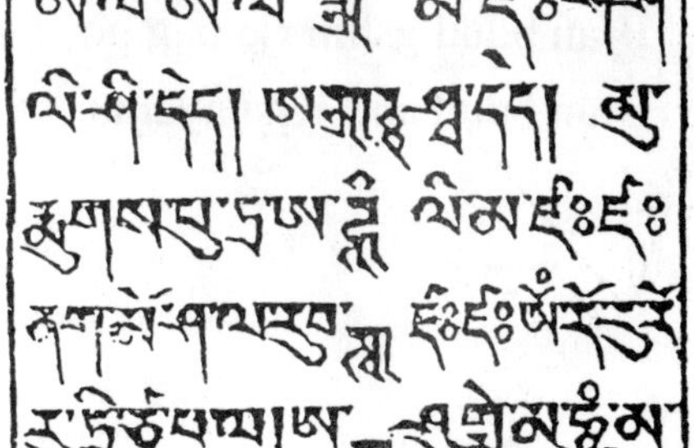

407(R139a) 913

Bran bdud gshin rje nag po

Bran bdud and Kṛṣṇayama

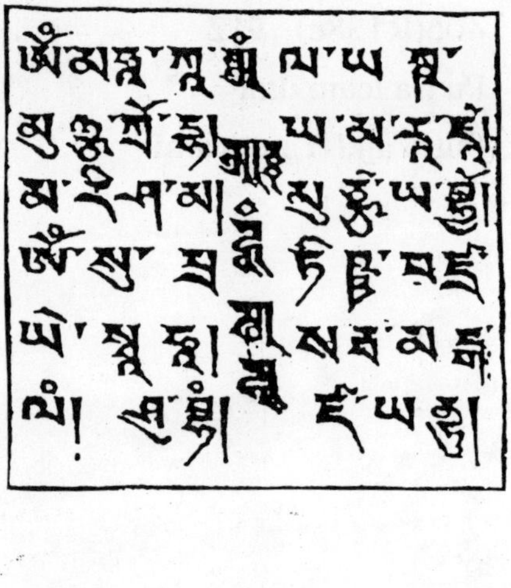

408(R139b) 914
dKar mo nyi zla lcam dral
Sūryacandra Gaurī and Yamayamī

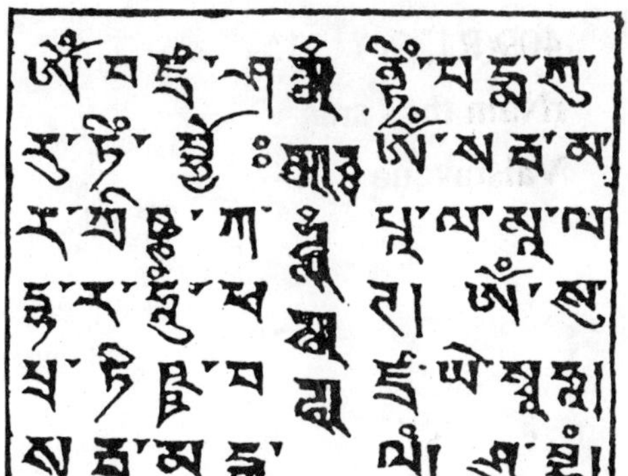

རྣམ་ཐོས་སྲས

409(R139c) 915
rNam thos sras
Vaiśravaṇa

ཨོཾ་བཻ་ཤྲ་མ་ཎཱ་ཡ་སྭཱ་ཧཱ།
ཨོཾ་བཻ་སྲ་ཝ་ཎཱ་ཡ་རྟ་སྲུ་ཏེ་
ཙ་བྲ་ཧྨ་སྒྲ་རྣ་ཏེ་ཙ་ཧེ་ཁྲ་ཏ
བྲ་ག་ཧཱ་ཙ་བ་རྣ་དཏ། ཏེཀྲུ་རྒྱ
ཡོ་ཉི་རེ་ཧུ་ཙ་ཨེ་ཕྲཾ་བྲ་དྲ
ས་ཧཱ་ཤྲ་ས་ཀྱ་ཧཿ སྭཱ་ཧཱ།

410(R140a) 916
Yul 'khor bsrung
Dhṛtarāṣṭra

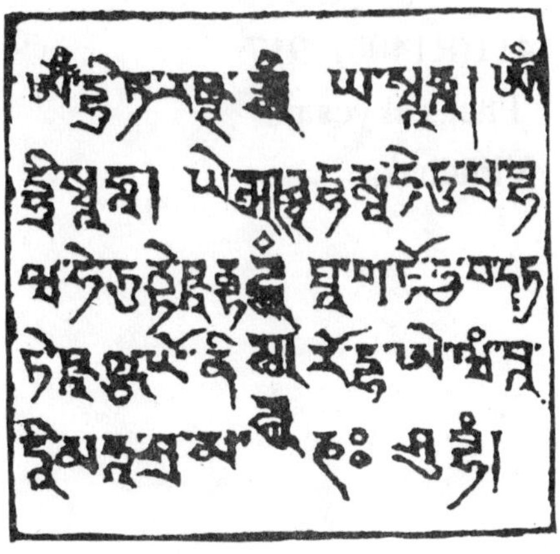

འཕགས་སྐྱེས་པོ་

411(R140b) 917
'Phags skyes po
Virūḍhaka

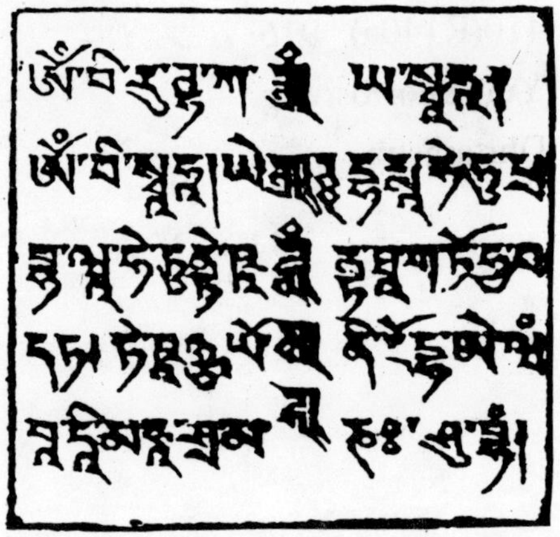

412(R140c) 918
sPyan mi bzang
Virūpākṣa

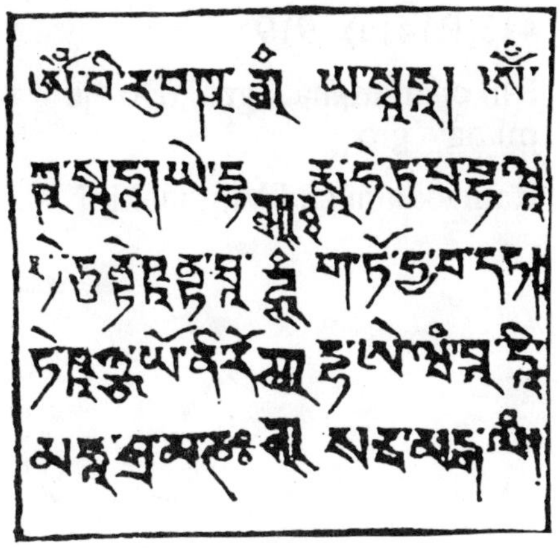

413(R141a) 919

Rin chen mkha' 'gro, rDo rje mkha' 'gro

Ratnaḍākinī and Vajraḍākinī

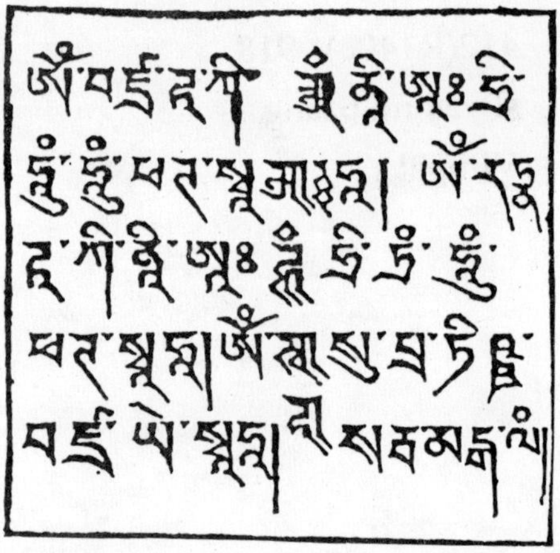
ཨོཾ་བཛྲ་ཌཱ་ཀི ཧྲཱིཾ་ཧྲཱི་ཨཱཿ་ཧེ་
ཧཱུཾ་ཧཱུཾ་ཕཊ་སྭཱཧཱ། ཨོཾ་རཏྣ
ཌཱ་ཀི་ཧྲཱི་ཨཱཿ་ཧྲཱིཾ་ཧེ་ཧཾ་ཧཱུཾ་
ཕཊ་སྭཱཧཱ། ཨོཾ་སྭཱ་ཧཱུ་སྭ་ཧི་ཛྙ་
བཛྲ་ཡེ་སྭཱཧཱ། གྱི་སྔགས་མཆན་ལོ།

414(R141b) 920

Sangs rgyas mkha' 'gro

Buddhaḍākinī

ཨོཾ་བུདྡྷ་ཌཱ་ཀི་ནྱཻ་ཧྲཱིཾ། ཛཿཧེ་ཨོཾ་
ཧཱུཾ་ཕཊ་སྭཱ་ཧཱ། ཡེ་དྷརྨཱ་ཧེ་ཏུ་པྲ་
བྷ་ཝཱ་ཧེ་ཏུ་ནྟེ་ཥཱཾ་ཏ་ཐཱ་ག་ཏོ་ཧྱ་
བ་ད་ཏ། ཏེ་ཥཱཉྩ་ཡོ་ནི་རོ་དྷ་ཨེ་
ཝཾ་བཱ་དཱི་མ་ཧཱ་ཤྲ་མ་ཎཿ་སྭཱ་ཧཱ

415(R141c) 921

Padma mkha' 'gro, Las kyi mkha' 'gro

Padmaḍākinī and Karmaḍākinī

ཨོཾ་པདྨ་ཌཱ་ཀི་ནཱིཾ ཧྲཱི་ཨཱཿཧཱུ
ཧྲཱིཿཧཱུཾ་ཕ་ཊ་ཨཱཿ སྭཱ་ཧཱ། ཨོཾ་
ཀ་རྨ་ཌཱ་ཀི་ནཱི་ཧྲཱིཾ ཨཱཿཧཱུ་ཨ
ཧཱུཾ་ཕ་ཊ་སྭཱ་ཧཱ།སྭཱ ཨོཾ་སུ་པྲ
ཏི་ཥྛ་བཛྲ་ཡེ་ནཱི་སྭཱ་ཧཱ།ཤུ་ཧྲཱུཾ

416(R142a) 922

Mi g'yo glang bzang ma, mThing gi zhal bzang ma

ཨོཾ་བཛྲ་ཌཱ་ཀི་ནཱི། སུ་ར་ཧྲཱིཾ་ཧྲོཿ
ཛཿ། ཨོཾ་བཛྲ་ཨཱ་ཡུ་ཥ་དྲ་སིང་སིང་
ཧྲཱིཾ་ཧྲོཿ་ཛཿ། ཧྲཱིཾ། ཨོཾ་སུ་སྭ་
ཧེ་ཕྱ་བཛྲ་ཨཱ་ཡེ་སྭཱ་ཧཱ།
ལ་ཆ་མཆོད་ཀྱི་ཡིཾ། ཛ་ཕཊ།

417(R142b) 923

bKra shis tshe ring ma

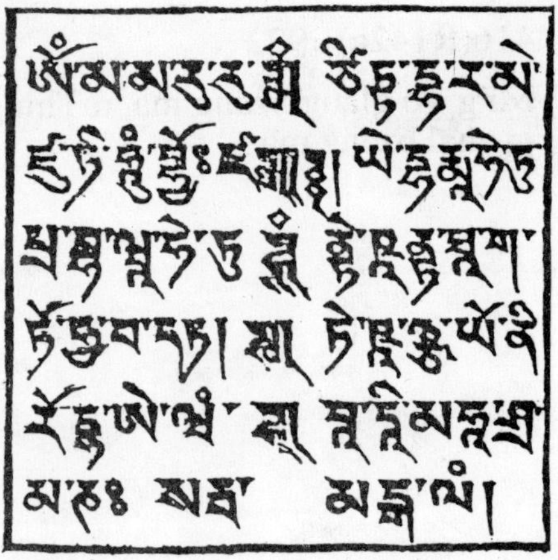

གཏད་དཀར་འགྲོ་བཟང་མ་ ཅོད་པན་མགྲིན་བཟང་མོ་

418(R142c) 924

gTad dkar 'gro bzang ma, Cod paṇ mgrin bzang ma

ཨོཾ་ཨ་ཤི་ར་ ཀླཱིཾ་ ནི་ཧཱུཾ་ཧྲཱུཾཿ
ཛཿ། ཨོཾ་ས་རི་ཀྵཱ་ཏི་ར་ཏིང་
ཁ་ཏི་ཀླི་ན་ཧཱུཾ་ཀླཱིཾ་ཧྲཱུཾཿ ཛཿ།
ཨོཾ་སུ་པྲ་ཏི་ཥྛ་བཛྲ་
ཡེ་སྭཱ་ཧཱ། །ཞེ་ས་ཐམ་རྟགས་ལོཾ།

༄༅། །ཨོཾ་སྭ་སྟི། མཐོང་ཐོས་དྲན་བཙམ་མཁྱེན་མ་སྐྱིད་པ་དང་། །ཞི་བའི་
ཀྱད་པ་ཀུན་ལས་རབ་བསྒྲལ་ཏེ། །ཚིའི་དོན་དང་ཚོས་གྲུབ་བདེ་ལྷག་སྟོལ་ལ་མཛད་པའི། །སྒྲུབ་ཕག་ས་རིན་
འབྲུག་པ་བརྒྱ་ཚོགས་སྣང་བ་རྣམ་པའི། །བཞེངས་པའི་དགེ་བས་རྒྱུ་ལ་འདི་རང་ཞེ་རབ་གོ་བའི། །མཐུ་རྣམ་ཆེན་སྒྲུབ་
པའི་ཡོན་གྱི་བཀའ་བོ་དང་། །སྟོ་རབ་གཉིས་ལྡན་བརྒྱ་བོ་རབ་བཅས་པ་ཀུན། །ས་ལམ་རིམ་བགྲོད་
རྣམ་མཁྱེན་རྒྱུར་བསྔོ་བ་ཞོག །གནས་སྐབས་ཚེ་རིང་ནད་མེད་བདེ་སྐྱིད་ཞིང་། །ཞིང་གི་མཆོག་ལ་

མཆོད་ཅིང་གསོལ་བ་འདེབས་པའི། །བསོད་ནམས་མཐུ་ཡང་བས་བཙོན་མ་ཡུས་པ། །རབ་དཔལ་
མེད་པ་ཡུན་གྱིས་ཁྱབ་བྱུར་ཅིག །མངྒ་ལཾ། །

419(N1a-c) 925
Thub pa gnas bcus bskor ba
Aṣṭādaśasthaviraparivāra Muni

ཡེ་དྷརྨ་ཧེ་ཏུ་ ཨོཾ་ པྲ་བྷ་ཝ་ཧེ་
ཏུནྟེ་ཥཱནྟ་ཐཱ་ ཨཱཿ ག་ཏོ་ཧྱ་ཝ་དཏ།
ཏེ་ཥཱཉྩ་ཡོ་ནི་རོ་ ཧཱུྃ་ དྷ་ཨེ་ཝཾ་ཝཱ་དཱི་
མ་ཧཱ་ཤྲ་མ་ཎཿ ཡེ་དྷརྨཱ་ཧེ་ཏུ་པྲ
བྷ་ཝཱ་ཧེ་ཏུནྟེ་ཥཱན྄ ཀཱ་ ཏ་ཐཱ་ག་ཏོ་ཧྱ་ཝ་
དཏ། ཏེ་ཥཱཉྩ་ ཝཱ་ ཡོ་ནི་རོ་དྷ་ཨེ་ཝཾ་
ཝཱ་དཱི་མ་ཧཱ་ཤྲ་མ་ ཎཿ སྭཱཧཱ།།

419(N1a-c) 925

Thub pa gnas bcus bskor ba

Aṣṭādaśasthaviraparivāra Muni

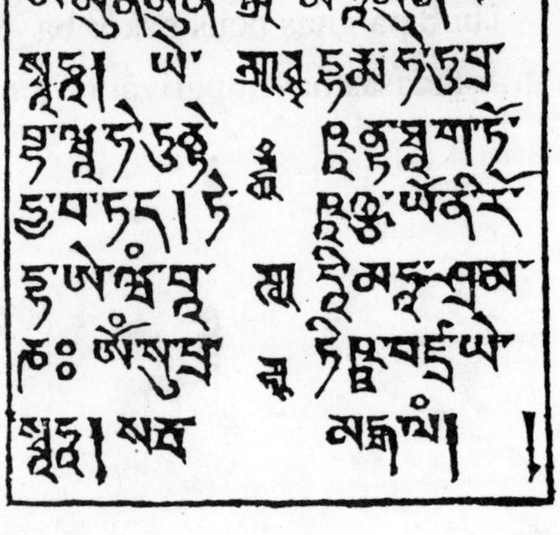

419(N1a-c) 925

Thub pa gnas bcus bskor ba

Aṣṭādaśasthaviraparivāra Muni

ཡེ་དྷརྨཱ་ཧེ་ཏུ་པྲ་ བྷྲཱུཾ་ ཝཱ་ཧེ་ཏུནྟེ་
ཥཱཾ་ཏ་ཐཱ་ག་ཏོ་ཧྱ་ ཝ་དཏ། ཏེ་ཥཱཾ་ཙ་
ཡོ་ནི་རོ་དྷ་ཨེ་ཝཾ་ བྷྲཱུཾ་ ཝཱ་དཱི་མ་ཧཱ་ཤྲ་
ཎཿ ཡེ་དྷརྨཱ་ཧེ་ བྷྲཱུཾ་ ཏུ་པྲ་ཝཱ་ཧེ་ཏུནྟེ་
ཥཱཾ་ཏ་ཐཱ་ག་ཏོ་ ཧྱ་ཝ་དཏ། ཏེ་
ཥཱཾ་ཙ་ཡོ་ནི་རོ་དྷ་ བྷྲཱུཾ་ ཨེ་ཝཾ་ཝཱ་དཱི་
མ་ཧཱ་ཤྲ་མ་ཎཿ སྭཱ་ཧཱ།

གཙུག་ཏོར་གདུགས་དཀར

420(N2a) 926

gTsug tor gdugs dkar

Uṣṇīṣasitātapatrā

ན་མཿ་སརྦ། ཨོཾ་ཨ་ཧཱུྃ། ཨ་ན་ལེ་ཨ་ན་ལེ་མེ་
ཤ་དེ་བི་ཤ་དེ་བི་ཏྲཱ་ཀྵ་བཻ་ར་བཛྲ་དྷ
རི་བ་ནྡྷེ་བནྡྷ་ནི་ ཧཱུྃ ཧཱུྃ་ཧཱུྃ་ཕ་ཊ་ཕ་ཊ་
སྭཱཧཱ། ཡེ་དྷརྨ ཧེ་ཏུ་པྲ་བྷ་ཝ་ཧེ
ཏུ་ཏེ་ཥཱན་ཏ་ཐཱ་ག་ཏོ ཧྱ་བ་དཏ྄།
ཏེ་ཥཱཉྩ་ཡོ་ནི་རོ་ དྷ ཨེ་ཝཾ་བཱ་དཱི་
མ་ཧཱ་ཤྲ་མ་ཎཿ མ་ཧཱ་ཡཾ།

421(N2b) 927
gTsug tor rnam rgyal lha dgu
9-deity Uṣṇīṣavijayā

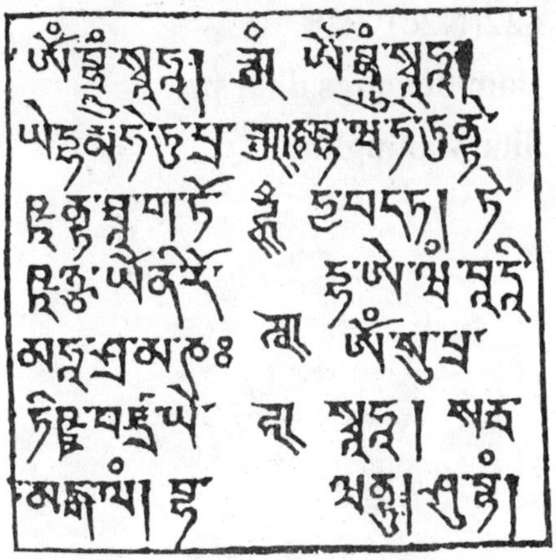

422(N2c) 928

’Jam dbyangs dkar po

Sita Mañjughoṣa

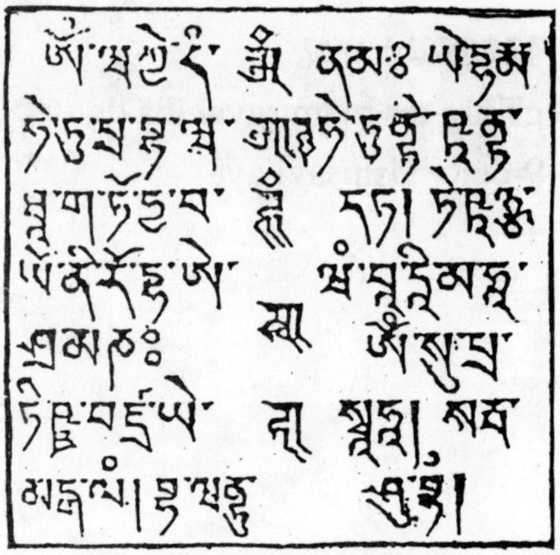

འཇམ་དབྱངས་ཨ་ར་པ་ཙ་ན

423(N3a) 929
’Jam dbyangs a ra pa tsa na
Arapacana Mañjughoṣa

ཨོཾ་ཨ་ར་པ་ཙ་ ཧཱུྃ་ ན་དྷཱིཿ ཡེ་དྷརྨཱ
ཧེ་ཏུ་པྲ་བྷ་ཝཱ་ཧེ་ ཨཱཿ ཏུནྟེ་ཥཱན་ཏ་ཐཱ་ག་
ཏོ་ཧྱ་བ་དཏ། ཏེ་ ཧྲཱིཾ་ ཥཱཉྩ་ཡོ་ནི་རོ་དྷ
ཨེ་ཝཾ་བཱ་དཱི་མ་ཧཱ་ ཤྲ་མ་ཎཿ ཡེ་
དྷརྨཱ་ཧེ་ཏུ་པྲ་བྷ་ ཀྵཱ ཝཱ་ཧེ་ཏུནྟེ་ཥཱན་ཏ་
ཐཱ་ག་ཏོ་ཧྱ་བ་དཏ། ཧྲཱ་ ཏེ་ཥཱཉྩ་ཡོ་ནི་རོ་
དྷ་ཨེ་ཝཾ་བཱ་དཱི་ མ་ཧཱ་ཤྲ་མ་ཎཿ

424(N3b) 930

'Jam dbyangs smra ba'i seng ge

Vādisiṃha Mañjughoṣa

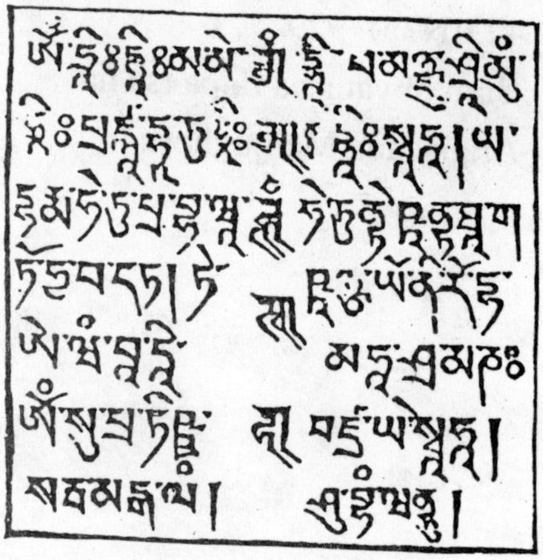

425(N3c) 931
So sor ’brang ma lha lnga
5-deity Pratisarā

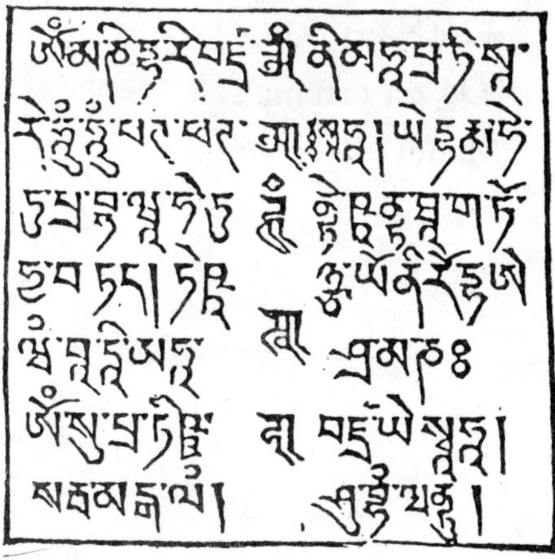

426(N4a) 932

'Od zer can ma

Mārīcī

ཨོཾ་མཱ་རཱི་ཙྱཻ་སྭཱ་ཧཱ། [illegible] ཨོཾ་མཱ་རཱི་ཙྱཻ་སྭཱ་ཧཱ།
ཡེ་དྷརྨཱ་ཧེ་ཏུ་པྲ་བྷཱ་ ཝཱ་ཧེ་ཏུན྄་ཏེ་ཥཱན྄་
ཏ་ཐཱ་ག་ཏོ་ཧྱ་ཝ་དཏ། ཏེ་ཥཱཉྩ་ཡོ་ནི་རོ་དྷ་
ཨེ་ཝཾ་ཝཱ་དཱི་མ་ཧཱ་ ཤྲ་མ་ཎཿ ཡེ་དྷརྨཱ་
ཧེ་ཏུ་པྲ་བྷ་ཝཱ་ ཧེ་ཏུན྄་ཏེ་ཥཱན྄་ཏ་ཐཱ་ག་ཏོ་
ཧྱ་ཝ་དཏ། ཏེ་ ཥཱཉྩ་ཡོ་ནི་རོ་དྷ་
ཨེ་ཝཾ་ཝཱ་དཱི་མ་ཧཱ་ ཤྲ་མ་ཎཿ མངྒ་ལཾ།

427(N4b) 933
rJe btsun byams pa
Bhaṭṭāraka Maitreya

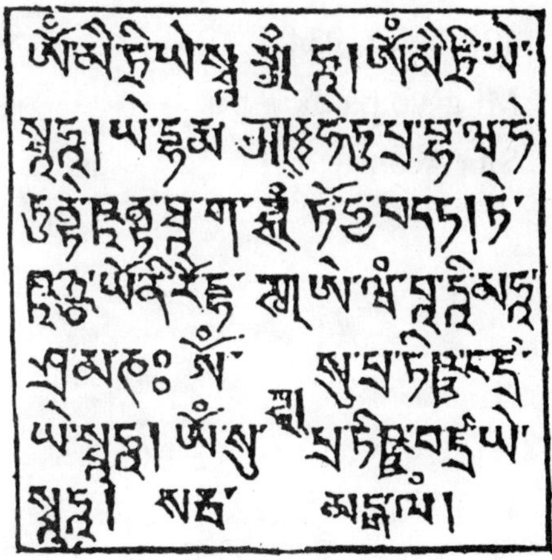

428(N4c) 934

Mi g'yo ba dkar po

Sita Acala

ཨོཾ་ཙཎྜ་མ་ཧཱ་ ཧཱ་ རོ་ཥ་ཎ་ཧཱུྃ་
ཕཊ། ཡེ་དྷརྨཱ་ཧེ་ཏུ་པྲ་བྷ་
ཝཱ་ཧེ་ཏུནྟེ་ཥཱན་ ཧཱུྃ་ ཏ་ཐཱ་ག་ཏོ་ཧྱ་ཝ་
དཏ། ཏེ་ཥཱཉྩ་ ཧཱ་ ཡོ་ནི་རོ་དྷ་ཨེ་
ཝཾ་ཝཱ་དཱི་མ་ཧཱ་ ཤྲ་མ་ཎཿ
ཨོཾ་སུ་པྲ་ཏིཥྛ་ ཧཱུྃ་ བཛྲ་ཡེ་སྭཱ་ཧཱ།
ལག་མཉྫ་ལི། ཤྲཱིཾ་ཥ་ཧཱ།

429(N5a) 935

Mi g'yo ba sngon po

Nīla Acala

ཨོཾ་ཙ་ཎྜ་མ་ཧཱ་ ཧྲཱི་ རོ་ཥ་ཎ་ཧཱུྃ་ཕཊ།
ཡེ་དྷརྨཱ་ཧེ་ཏུ་པྲ་བྷཱ་ཝ་ ཧེ་ཏུ་ནྟེ་ཥཱྀ
ཏ་ཐཱ་ག་ཏོ་ ཧྱ་ཝ་དཏ། ཏེ་
ཥཱཉྩ་ཡོ་ནི་རོ་ དྷ་ཨེ་ཝཾ་ཝཱ་དཱི་
མ་ཧཱ་ཤྲ་མ་ཎཿ སྭཱ། ཨོཾ་སུ་པྲ་ཏིཥྛ་
བཛྲ་ཡེ་སྭཱ་ཧཱ། སྭཱ་ ཨོཾ་སུ་པྲ་ཏིཥྛ་
བཛྲ་ཡེ་སྭཱ་ཧཱ། སརྦ་མངྒ་ལཾ།

430(N5b) 936
Thugs rje chen po bcu gcig zhal
Eleven-faced Mahākāruṇika

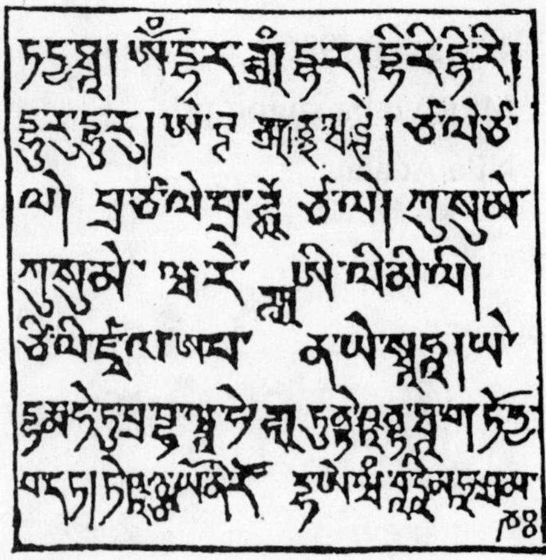

431(N5c) 937
sPyan ras gzigs phyag bzhi pa
Four-armed Avalokiteśvara

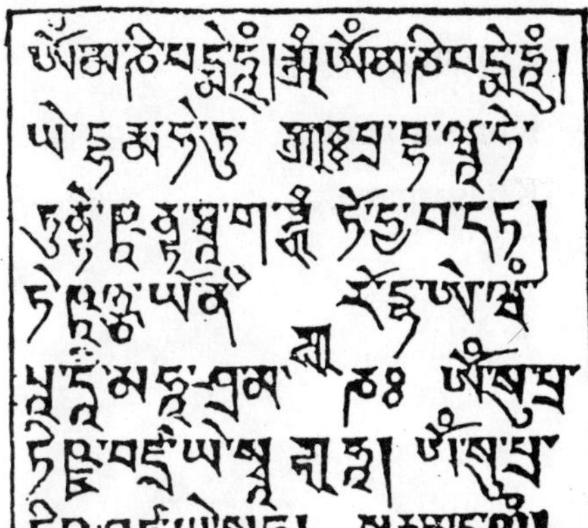

།ཁ་སར་པ་ཎི་

432(N6a) 938

Kha sarpa ṇi

Khasarpaṇa

ཨོཾ་ཨཱཿཧྲཱིཿཧཱུྃ་ ཤྲཱི་ཨོཾ་ཨཱཿཧྲཱིཿཧཱུྃ།
ཡེ་དྷརྨཱ་ཧེ་ཏུ་པྲ་བྷ་ཝཱ་ཧེ་ཏུན྄་ཏེ་ཥཱན྄་
ཏ་ཐཱ་ག་ཏོ་ཧྱ་ཝ་དཏ྄། ཏེ་
ཥཱཉྩ་ཡོ་ནི་རོ་དྷ་ཨེ་ཝཾ་ཝཱ་དཱི་
མ་ཧཱ་ཤྲ་མ་ཎཿ ཨོཾ་སུ་པྲ་ཏིཥྛ་
བཛྲ་ཡེ་སྭཱ་ཧཱ། [illegible]།

433(N6b) 939

Seng ge sgra

Siṃhanāda

ཨོཾ་ཨཱཿཧྲཱིཿ ཨཱཿ སིཾ་ཧ་ན་དཱ་ཧཱུྃ་
ཕཊ། ཡེ་དྷརྨཱ་ཧེ་ཏུ་པྲ་བྷ་ཝཱ་
ཧེ་ཏུནྟེ་ཥཱནྟ་ཐཱ་གཏོ་ཧྱ་ཝ་དཏ།
ཏེ་ཥཱཉྩ་ཡོ་ནི་རོ་དྷ་ཨེ་ཝཾ་བཱ་
དཱི་མ་ཧཱ་ཤྲ་མ་ ཎཿ ཨོཾ་སུ་པྲ་
ཏིཥྛ་བཛྲ་ཡེ་སྭཱ་ ཧཱ། མངྒ་ལཾ།

434(N6c) 940
sGrol dkar
Sita Tārā

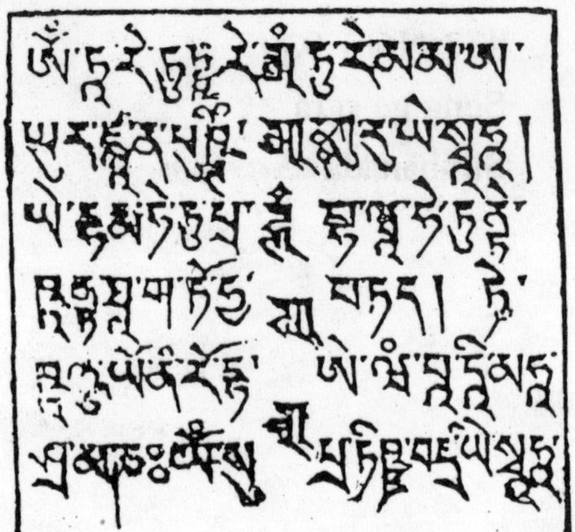

435(N7a) 941
sGrol ljang
Śyāma Tārā

ཨོཾ་ཏཱ་རེ་ཏུཏྟཱ་རེ་ཏྲཱཾ་ཏུ་རེ་སྭཱ་ཧཱ། ཡེ་
དྷརྨཱ་ཧེ་ཏུ་པྲ་བྷ་ཝཱ་ཧེ་ཏུན྄་ཏེ་ཥཱན྄་
ཏ་ཐཱ་ག་ཏོ་ཧྱ་ཝ་ད་ཏ྄། ཏེ་ཥཱཉྩ་
ཡོ་ནི་རོ་དྷ་ཨེ་ཝཾ་ཝཱ་དཱི་མ་ཧཱ་
ཤྲ་མ་ཎཿ ཨོཾ་ [illegible] སུ་པྲ་ཏིཥྛ་ཝཛྲེ་
ཡེ་སྭཱ་ཧཱ། སརྦ་མངྒ་ལཾ།

436(N7b) 942

rTa mgrin

Hayagrīva

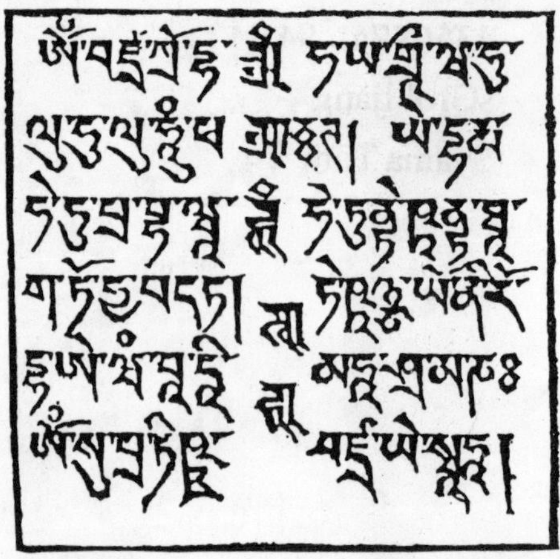

437(N7c) 943

Lo ma gyon ma

Parṇaśabarī

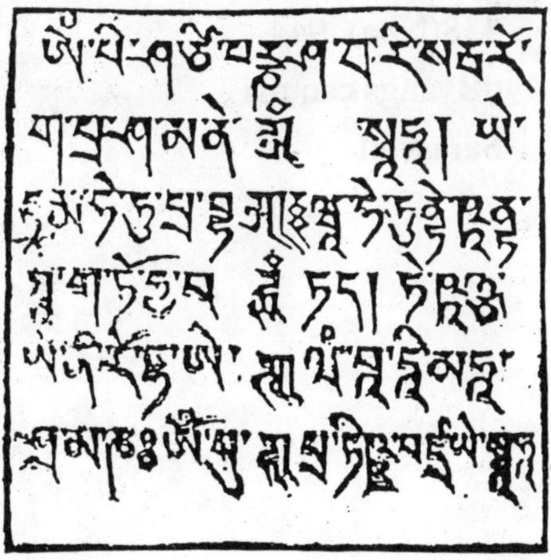

དབྱངས་ཅན་མ།

438(N8a) 944

dByangs can ma

Sarasvatī

ཨོཾ་པི་ཙུ་པི་ཙུ་ པྲཱ་ ཛྙཱ་བར་དྷ་ནི་
ཛྭ་ལ་ཛྭ་ལ་མེ་དྷཱ་བཱ་རྡྷ་ནི། དྷི་རི་
དྷི་རི། བུདྡྷི་བར་དྷི་ ཧྲ་ཎི་སྭཱ་ཧཱ། ཡེ་
དྷརྨཱ་ཧེ་ཏུ་པྲ་བྷ་ ཝཱ་ཧེ་ཏུན་ཏེ་ཥཱན་
ཏ་ཐཱ་ག་ཏོ་ཧྱ་ཝ་དཏ། ཏེ་ཥཱཉྩ་ཡོ་ནི་རོ་
དྷ་ཨེ་ཝཾ་ཝཱ་དཱི་ མ་ཧཱ་ཤྲ་མ་ཎཿ
ཨོཾ་སུ་པྲ་ཏིཥྛ་ བཛྲ་ཡེ་སྭཱ་ཧཱ།

439(N8b) 945
Mi 'khrugs pa
Akṣobhya

ན་མོ་རཏྣ་ཏྲ་ཡ་ཡ། ཨོཾ་ཀཾ་ཀ་ནི་
ཀཾ་ཀ་ནི། རོ་ཙ་ ཀྲཱ་ཧྲི་རོ་ཙ་ནི། ཏྲོ་ཊ་
ནི་ཏྲོ་ཊ་ནི། ཏྲ་ས་ནི་ཏྲ་ས་ནི། པྲ་ཏི་
ཧ་ན་པྲ་ཏི་ཧ་ན་ སརྦ་ཀརྨ་པ་རཾ་
པ་ར་ཎི་མེ་སརྦ་ སཏྭཱ་ནཉྩ་སྭཱ་ཧཱ།
ཡེ་དྷརྨཱ་ཧེ་ཏུ་པྲ་བྷ་ཝཱ་ཧེ་ཏུནྟེ་ཥཱནྟ་ཐཱ་ག་ཏོ་
ཧྱ་ཝ་དཏ྄་ཏེ་ཥཱཉྩ་ཡོ་ནི་རོ་དྷ་ ཨེ་ཝཾ་ཝཱ་དཱི་མ་ཧཱ་ཤྲ་མ་ཎཿ

440(N8c) 946

Phyag rdor mdo lugs

Sūtrakrama Vajrapāṇi

ཨོཾ་ཀྲི་ལི་བར་ ཧྲཱུཾ ཧ་ར་བཛྲ་པྲ་ཀོ
ར་ཏྲྀ་པ་ཡ་ཧི་ ཨཱཀྵ་སྭཱ་ཧཱ། ཡེ་དྷརྨཱ
ཧེ་ཏུ་པྲ་བྷ་ཝཱ་ ཧཱུཾ ཧེ་ཏུན་ཏེ་ཥཱན་ཏ་ཐཱ་
ག་ཏོ་ཧྱ་བ་དཏ། ཧྱ ཏེ་ཥཱཉྩ་ཡོ་ནི་རོ་
དྷ་ཨེ་ཝཾ་བཱ་དཱི་ མ་ཧཱ་ཤྲ་མ་ཎཿ
ཨོཾ་སུ་པྲ་ཏིཥྛ་ བཛྲ་ཡེ་སྭཱ་ཧཱ།
སརྦ་མནྟྲ་ཡཾ། ཤུ་ཧཾ་ཤཀྲ།

441(N9a) 947
Khro gnyer can ma
Bhṛkuṭī

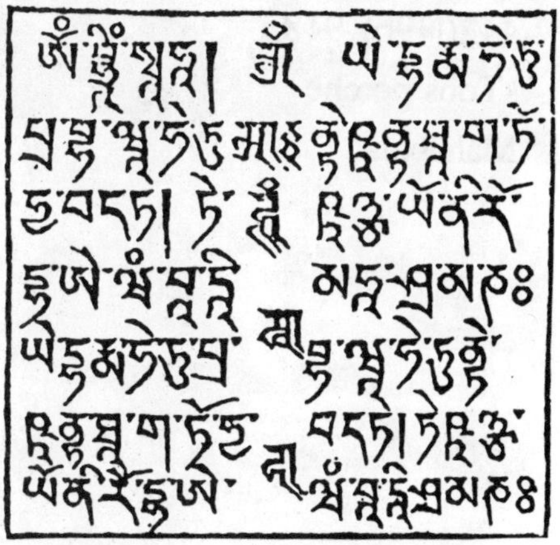

སྟོབས་པོ་ཆེ

442(N9b) 948
sTobs po che
Mahābala

ཨོཾ་མ་ཧཱ་བ་ལ་ཤྲཱི་སྭཱ་ཧཱ། ཡེ་དྷརྨཱ་
ཧེ་ཏུ་པྲ་བྷ་ཝཱ་ཧེ་ཏཱུན྄་ཏེ་ཥཱན྄་ཏ་ཐཱ་
ག་ཏོ་ཧྱ་ཝ་དཏ྄། ཏེ་ཥཱཉྩ་ཡོ་ནི་
རོ་དྷ་ཨེ་ཝཾ་ཝཱ་ དཱི་མ་ཧཱ་ཤྲ་མ་
ཎཿ ཨོཾ་སུ་པྲ་ ཏིཥྛ་བཛྲ་ཡེ་
སྭཱ་ཧཱ། ཨོཾ་སུ་པྲ་ ཏིཥྛ་བཛྲ་ཡེ་
སྭཱ་ཧཱ། སརྦ་ མངྒ་ལཾ།

ཁྲོ་བོ་སྨེ་བརྩེགས་

443(N9c) 949

Khro bo sme brtsegs

Krodha Sme brtsegs

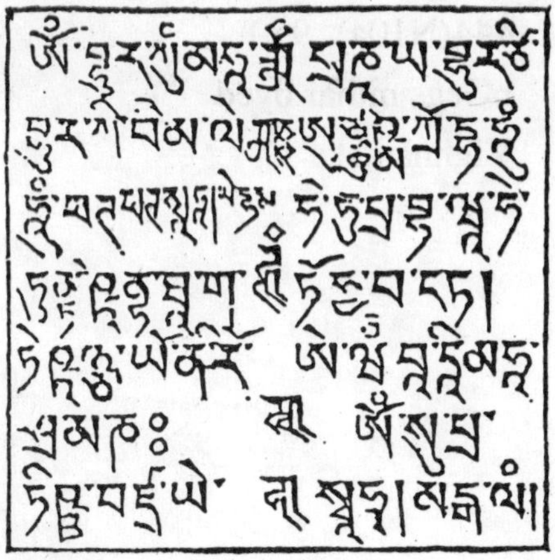

444(N10a) 950
bGegs mthar byed
Vighnāntaka

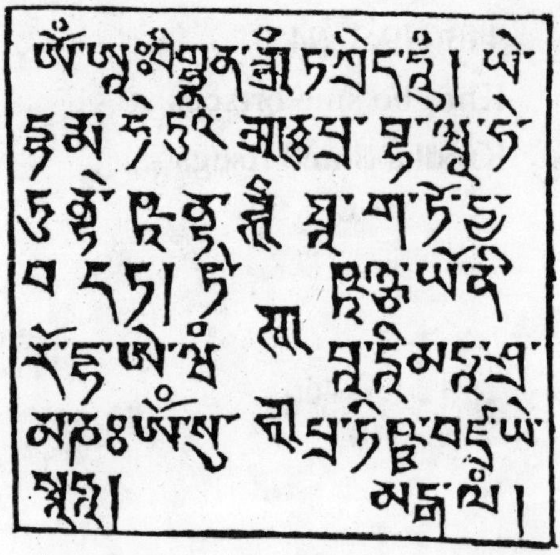

445(N10b) 951
rNam sras
Vaiśravaṇa

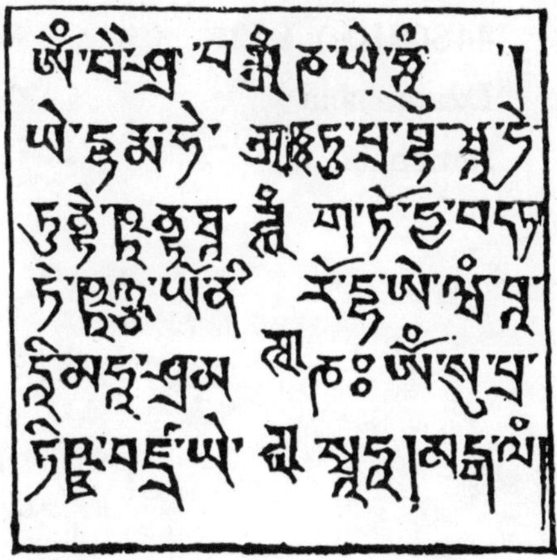

446(N10c) 952

Dzambha la

Jambhala

ཨོཾ་ཛམྦྷ་ལ་ ཛྲིཾ་ ཛ་ལེནྡྲ་ཡ་
སྭཱཧཱ། ཡེ་ དྷརྨཱ་ཧེ་ཏུ་
པྲ་བྷ་ཝཱ་ཧེ་ ཏུནྟེ་ཥཱན྄་ཏ་ཐཱ་
ག་ཏོ་ཧྱ་ཝ་དཏ྄། ཏེ་ཥཱཉྩ་ཡོ་ནི་རོ་
དྷ་ཨེ་ཝཾ་ཝཱ་དཱི་ མ་ཧཱ་ཤྲ་མ་ཎཿ
ཨོཾ་སུ་པྲ་ཏིཥྛ་ བཛྲ་ཡེ་སྭཱཧཱ།

447(N11a) 953
Nor rgyun ma
Vasudhārā

ཨོཾ་བསུ་དྷཱ་རེ་ཤྲཱི་རཏྣ་ནི་དྷཱ་ན་ཀ་
རེ་སྭཱ་ཧཱ། ཡེ་ དྷརྨཱ་ཧེ་ཏུ་པྲ་བྷ་
ཝཱ་ཧེ་ཏུནྟེ་ཥཱན་ཏ་ཐཱ་ག་ཏོ་ཧྱ་བ་
དཏ྄། ཏེ་ཥཱཉྩ་ཡོ་ནི་རོ་དྷ་ཨེ་
ཝཾ་ཝཱ་དཱི་མ་ཧཱ་ཤྲ་མ་ཎཿ ཨོཾ་
སུ་པྲ་ཏིཥྛ་བཛྲ་ཡེ་སྭཱ་ཧཱ།

448(N11b) 954
Sher phyin ma
Prajñāparamitā

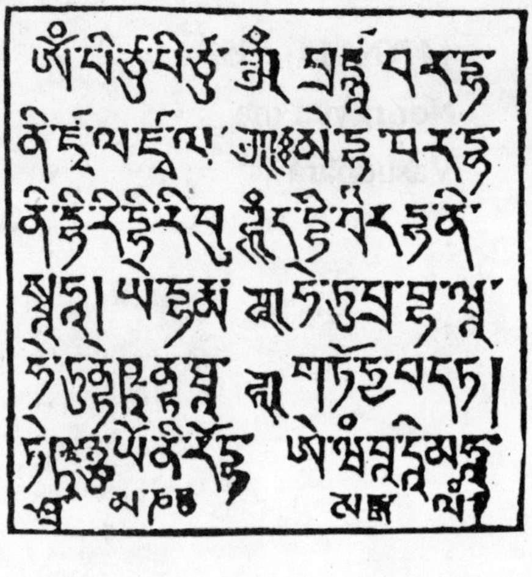

449(N11c) 955

Bla med phyag rdor 'byung po 'dul byed

Bhūtaḍāmara Anuttara Vajrapāṇi

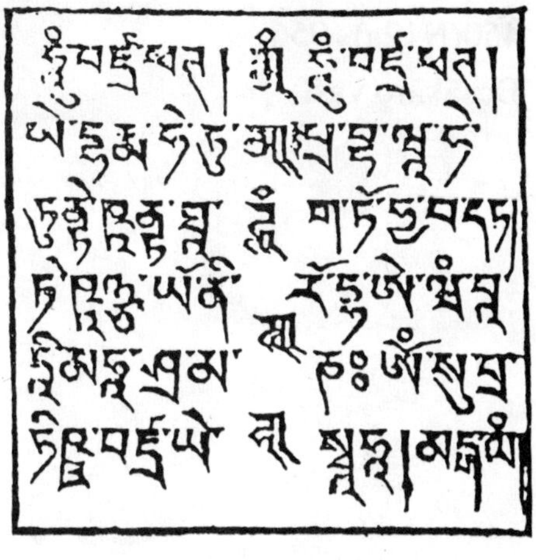

450(N12a) 956

Daśākāro vaśī

ཆོས་ཀྱི་རྒྱལ་པོ་ཙོང་ཁ་པའི། །
ཆོས་ཚུལ་རྣམ་པར་འཕེལ་བ་ལ། །
བགེགས་ཀྱི་མཚན་མ་ཞི་བ་དང་། །
མཐུན་རྐྱེན་མ་ལུས་ཚང་བར་ཤོག །
ཨོཾ་སརྦ་མངྒ་ལཾ་ཛ་ཡནྟུ་ཤུ་བྷཾ། །

451(N12b) 957

Gri gug mgon po

Kartarīdhara Mahākāla

ཨོཾ་མཧཱཀཱལ་ ཤྲཱིཾ ཧནཧནབཛྲ

ཀཧཱུཾཕཊ། ཡེ་དྷརྨཱཧེཏུཔྲབྷ་

ཝཱཧེཏུནྟེཥཱནྟཐཱ ཀྲྀ གཏོཧྱཝད

ཏེཥཱཉྩ་ཡོནིརོ ཀྑ དྷཨེཝཾཝཱ་

དཱིམཧཱཤྲམ་ ཎཿ

སཏ་མཧྭལཾ། ཛཱ

452(N12c) 958

Prajñākhaḍga

༔ཡང་དག་རྫོགས་ལ་བ་མི་རྟོགས་པའི།།
ཤེ།:པ་ཕྱིན་ཆོར་བུ་དབབ་བསམ་
ཤི་ང་། །སེམས་ཅན་རེ་བ་བསྐྱོད
མཛད་པའི། །བསམ་པ་འགྲུབ་
པའི་ཕྱག་ཤིས་ཕོག །མཎྜལཾ །

༄༅། །ཨོཾ་སྭསྟི། མཐོང་ཐོས་དྲན་པ་ཙམ་གྱིས་སྲིད་པ་དང་། །ཞི་བའི་རྒྱུད
བཀུན་ལས་རབ་བསྒྲལ་ཏེ། །ཚིར་དོན་པོ་ལས་གྲུབ་བདེ་སླག་སྟོབས་ཡེ་མཛད་པའི། །སྣ་ར་ཐང་བརྒྱ་ཅུའི་ལྷ་
ཚོགས་སྤྱན་དྲང་བརྟན་འདི། །བཞེངས་པའི་དགེ་བས་རྒྱལ་པ་འདི་རིང་རྒྱལ་ཡོ་བའི། །མཐུན་རྐྱེན་སྒྲུབ་པའི
ཡོན་གྱི་བདག་པོ་དང་། །སྤྱིར་རབ་བཅིངས་ལྡན་བཟོ་བོ་བཅས་པ་ཀུན། །ས་ལམ་རིམ་བགྲོད་རྣམ་
མཁྱེན་སྒྱུར་འཐོབ་པར་ཤོག །གནས་སྐབས་ཚེ་རིང་ནད་མེད་བདེ་སྐྱིད་ལྡན་ཞིང་། །ཞིང་གི་མཆོག་ལ་

མཆོད་ཅིང་གསོལ་བ་འདེབས་པའི། །བསོད་ནམས་མཐུ་ཡིས་བསམ་དོན་མ་ལུས་པ། །འབད་པ་
མེད་པར་ལྷུན་གྱིས་འགྲུབ་གྱུར་ཅིག །མངྒ་ལཾ། །

453(D1a) 959
gSang 'dus 'jam rdor
Guhyasamāja Mañjuvajra

ཨོཾ་ཨཱཿམཾ་ཧྲཱིཿཛྲཱིཿཨོཾ་ཨཱཿམཾ་ཧྲཱིཿ།
ཡེ་དྷརྨཱ་ཧེ་ཏུ་པྲ་བྷ་ཝཱ་ཧེ་
ཏུན་ཏེ་ཥཱན་ཏ་ཐཱ་ག་ཏོ་ཧྱ་ཝ་
དད། ཏེ་ཥཱཉྩ་ཡོ་ནི་རོ་
དྷ་ཨེ་ཝཾ་བཱ་དཱི་མ་ཧཱ་ཤྲ་མ་
ཎཿ ཨོཾ་སུ་པྲ་ཏིཥྛ་བཛྲ་ཡེ་སྭཱ་ཧཱ།

454(D1b) 960

rNam snang 'jam rdor

Vairocana Mañjuvajra

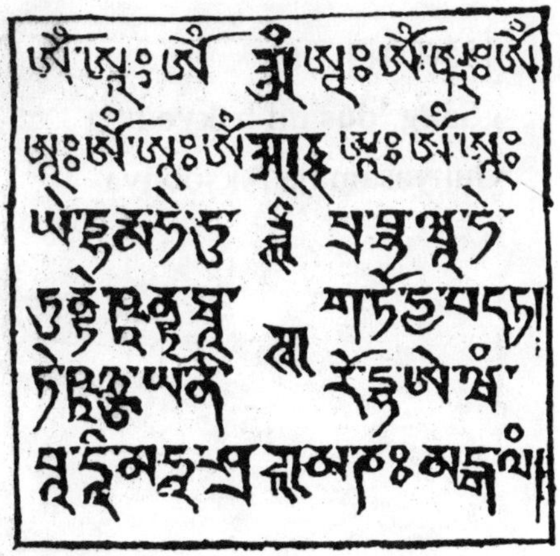

455(D1c) 961
gSang 'dus mi bskyod pa
Guhyasamāja Akṣobhya

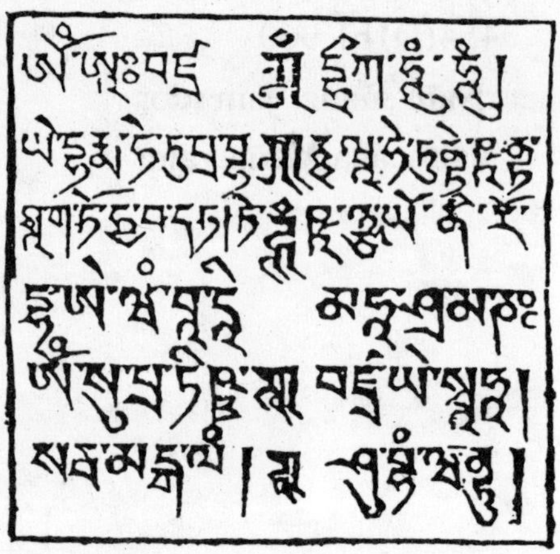

456(D2a) 962
dGra nag gshin rje gshed
Kṛṣṇāri Yamāntaka

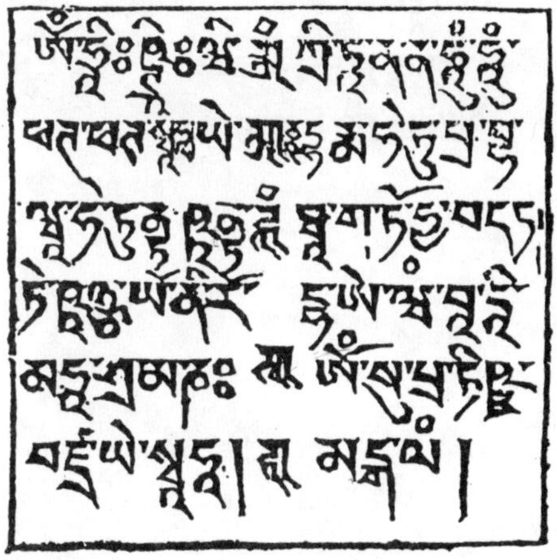

457(D2b) 963
sNying po kyai rdor
sNying po Hevajra

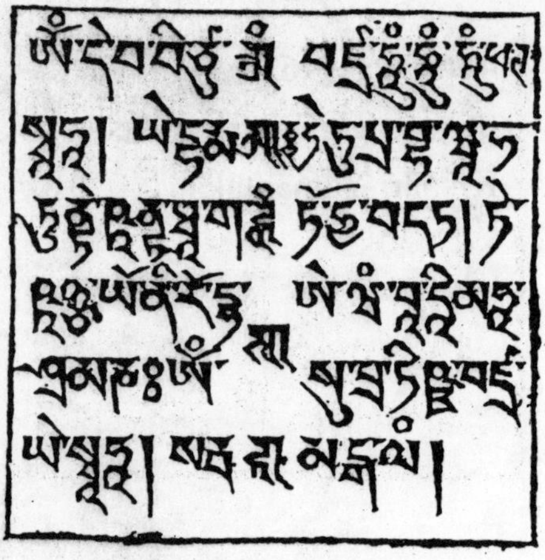

458(D2c) 964
Thugs kyai rdor
Citta Hevajra

ཨོཾ་ཤཱ་ཏེ་ཤཱ་ཏེ་བ་ཛྲཾ་ཧཱུྃ་ཧཱུྃ་ཧཱུྃ་ཕཊ་
སྭཱཧཱ། ཡེ་དྷརྨཱ་ཧེ་ཏུ་པྲ་བྷ་ཝཱ་ཧེ་
ཏུནྟེཥཱནྟ་ཐཱ་ག་ཏོ་ཧྱ་ཝ་དཏ྄། ཏེ་
ཥཱཉྩ་ཡོ་ནི་རོ་དྷ ཨེ་ཝཾ་ཝཱ་དཱི་མཧཱ་
ཤྲ་མ་ཎཿ ཨོཾ་སུ་པྲ་ཏིཥྛ་བཛྲེ་ཡེ་
སྭཱཧཱ། སརྦ་ཛཱ་ཡཾ། ཤུ་བྷཾ།

459(D3a) 965
gSung kyai rdor
Vāg Hevajra

ཨོཾ་རྡྷཱུ་ལ་རྡྷཱུ་ལ་ཨཱྀ་ཧྲཱུྃ་ཧཱུྃ་ཧྲཱུྃ་ཧཱུྃ་ཕཊ་
སྭཱཧཱ། ཡེ་དྷརྨཱ་ཧེ་ཏུ་པྲ་བྷ་ཝཱ་ཧེ་
ཏུནྟེ་ཥཱན་ཏ་ཐཱ་ག་ཏོ་ཧྱ་ཝ་དཏ྄། ཏེ་
ཥཱཉྩ་ཡོ་ནི་རོ་དྷ་ ཨེ་ཝཾ་ཝཱ་དཱི་མ་ཧཱ་
ཤྲ་མ་ཎཿ ཨོཾ་ སུ་པྲ་ཏིཥྛ་བཛྲ་
ཡེ་སྭཱཧཱ། སརྦ་ཝི་མངྒ་ལཾ །

460(D3b) 966
sKu kyai rdor
Kāya Hevajra

ཨོཾ་དེ་ཝ་པི་ཙུ་བཛྲ་ཧཱུྃ་ཧཱུྃ་ཧཱུྃ་ཕཊ
སྭཱ་ཧཱ། ཡེ་དྷརྨཱ་ཧེ་ཏུ་པྲ་བྷ་ཝཱ་ཧེ་
ཏུནྟེ་ཥཱན་ཏ་ཐཱ་ག་ཏོ་ཧྱ་ཝ་དཏ྄ ཏེ་ཥཱཉྩ་ཡོ་
ནི་རོ་དྷ་ཨེ་ཝཾ་ཝཱ་དཱི་མ་ཧཱ་ཤྲ་
མ་ཎཿ ཨོཾ་སུ་པྲ་ཏིཥྛ་བཛྲ་
ཡེ་སྭཱ་ཧཱ། སརྦ་མངྒ་ལཾ།

461(D3c) 967

rDo rje mkha' 'gro

Vajraḍāka

ཨོཾ་ཧ་ར་ཧ་ར། ཧྲཱི ཧ་ར་ཡ་ཧ་ར
ཡ།མ་ར་ཧ་མ་ར་ཀཱཿཧ། བཛྲ་ཌཱ་ཀ
ཕ་ཊ་སྭཱ་ཧཱ། ཡེ་དྷརྨཱ་ཧེ་ཏུ་པྲ་བྷ་ཝཱ
ཧེ་ཏུནྟེ་ཥཱནྟ་ཐཱ་ག་ཏོ་ཧྱ་ཝ་དཏ།
ཏེ་ཥཱཉྩ་ཡོ་ནི་རོ་དྷ་ཨེ་ཝཾ་བཱ
དཱི་མ་ཧཱ་ཤྲ་མ་ཎཿ ཡེ་ སྭཱ་ཧཱ།

462(D4a) 968

rDo rje bdag med ma

Vajranairātmā

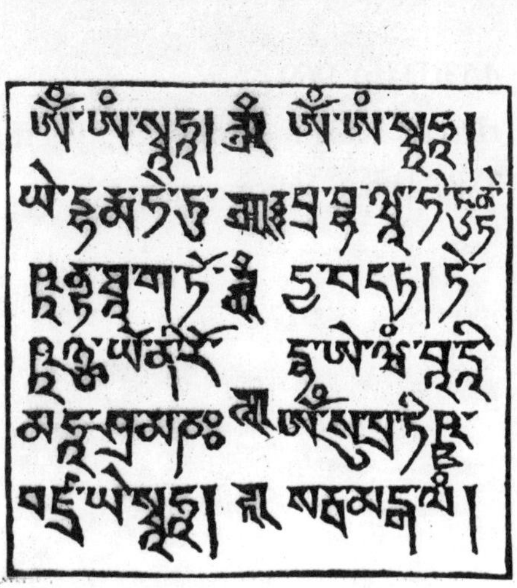

463(D4b) 969

rDo rje bdag med phyag gnyis ma

Two-armed Vajranairātmā

ཨོཾ་ཨ་ཨཱཿཧཱུཾ་ཧྲཱིཿ སྭཱ་ཧཱ། ཡེ་དྷརྨཱ
ཧེ་ཏུ་པྲ་བྷ་ཝཱ་ཧེ་ཏུནྟེ་ཥཱན་ཏ་ཐཱ
ག་ཏོ་ཧྱ་ཝ་དཏ། ཏེ་ཥཱཉྩ་ཡོ་ནི
རོ་དྷ་ཨེ་ཝཾ་ཝཱ་དཱི་ མ་ཧཱ་ཤྲ་མ་ཎཿ
ཨོཾ་སུ་པྲ་ཏིཥྛ་བཛྲ་ཡེ་སྭཱ་ཧཱ།
ས་ཪྦ་མངྒ་ལཾ། ཤྲཱི་ཛ་ཡནྟུ།

464(D4c) 970
Ku ru ku le
Kurukullā

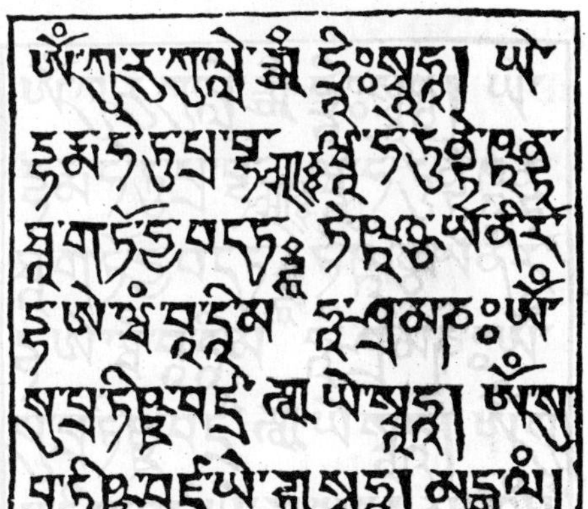

རྡོ་རྗེ་སྒྲོལ་མ

465(D5a) 971

rDo rje sgrol ma

Vajratārā

ཨོཾ་ཏཱ་རེ་ཏུཏྟཱ་རེ་ཏྲཱཾ་ ཏུ་རེ་སྭཱ་ཧཱ། ཨོཾ་
ཏཱ་རེ་ཏུཏྟཱ་རེ་ཏུ་ ཏྲཱཿ རེ་སྭཱ་ཧཱ། ཡེ་
དྷརྨཱ་ཧེ་ཏུ་པྲ་བྷ་ ཝཱ་ ཧེ་ཏུནྟེ་ཥཱཾ་ཏ་ཐཱ་
གཏོ་ཧྱ་ཝ་དཏ། ཏེ་ཥཱཉྩ་ཡོ་ནི་རོ་
དྷ་ཨེ་ཝཾ་ཝཱ་དཱི་ མ་ཧཱ་ཤྲ་མ་ཎཿ
ཨོཾ་སུ་པྲ་ཏིཥྛ་ བཛྲ་ཡེ་སྭཱ་ཧཱ།

466(D5b) 972

Kyai rdor

Hevajra

ཨོཾ་དེ་ཝ་པི་ཙུ་ཝཱཾ་ བཛྲ་ཧཱུྃ་ཧཱུྃ་ཧཱུྃ་ཕཊ་

སྭཱ་ཧཱ། ཡེ་དྷརྨཱ་ཧེ་ཏུ་པྲ་བྷ་ཝཱ

ཧེ་ཏུན་ཏེ་ཥཱན་ཏ་ཐཱ་ག་ཏོ་ཧྱ་བདད།

ཏེ་ཥཱཉྩ་ཡོ་ནི་རོ་ ཀྱཻ དྷ་ཨེ་ཝཾ་བཱ་དཱི

མ་ཧཱ་ཤྲ་མ་ཎཿ ཨོཾ་སུ་པྲ་ཏིཥྛ

བཛྲ་ཡེ་སྭཱ་ཧཱ། ཀྱཻ། ལབ་མཆན་ཡིན།

467(D5c) 973
Thugs kyai rdor
Citta Hevajra

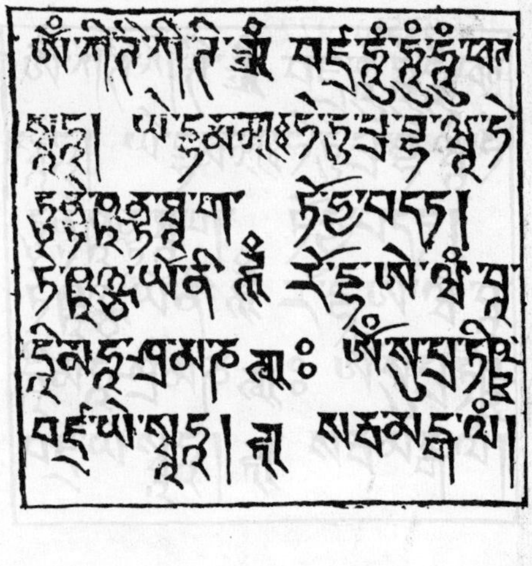

468*(D6a) 974
gSung kyai rdor
Vāg Hevajra

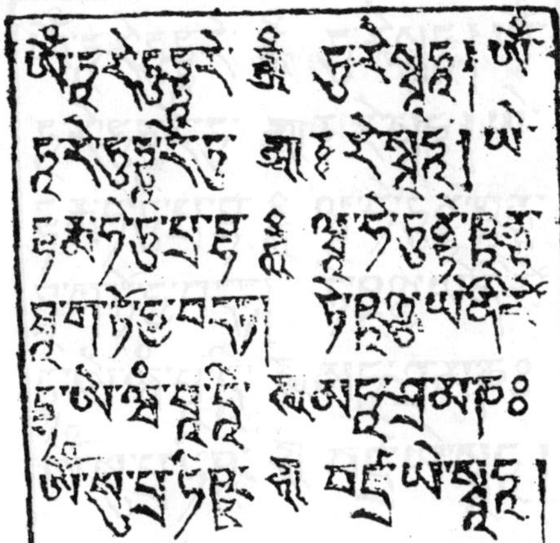

469*(D6b) 975
sKu kyai rdor
Kāya Hevajra

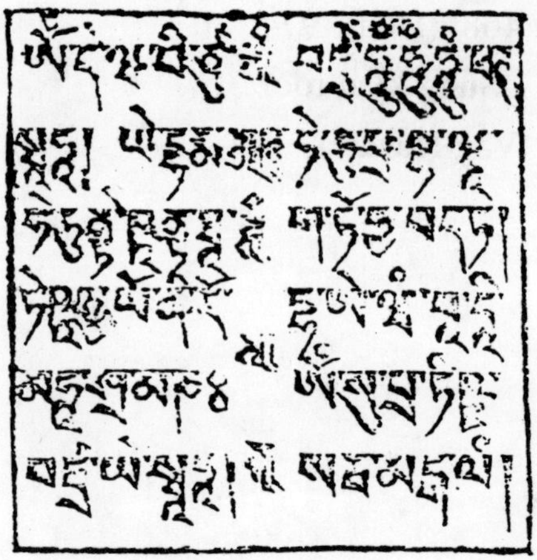

470*(D6c) 976
bDe mchog rdo rje sems dpa'
Vajrasattva Saṃvara

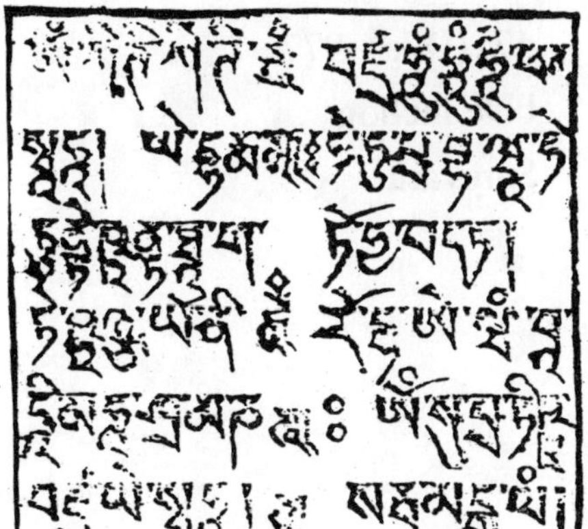

བདེ་མཆོག

471(D7a) 977
bDe mchog
Saṃvara

ཨོཾ་ཤྲཱི་བཛྲ་ཧེ་ཧེ་རུ་རུ་ཀཾ་ཧཱུྃ་ཧཱུྃ་ཕཊ།
ཌཱ་ཀི་ནཱི་ཛྭ་ལ་ཤཾ་བ་རཾ་སྭཱ་ཧཱ། ཡེ་
དྷརྨཱ་ཧེ་ཏུ་པྲ་བྷ་ཝཱ་ ཧེ་ཏུཾ་ ཏེ་ཥཱཾ་ཏ་ཐཱ་ག་ཏོ་
ཧྱ་བ་དཏ྄་བདད། ཏེ་ཥཱཾ་ཙ་ཡོ་ནི་རོ་
དྷ་ཨེ་ཝཾ་བཱ་དཱི་ ཙྭཱ་མ་ཧཱ་ཤྲ་མ་ཎཿ
ཨོཾ་སུ་པྲ་ཏིཥྛ་བ་ཛྲ་ཡེ་སྭཱ་ཧཱ།

472(D7b) 978
bDe mchog phyag gnyis
Two-armed Saṃvara

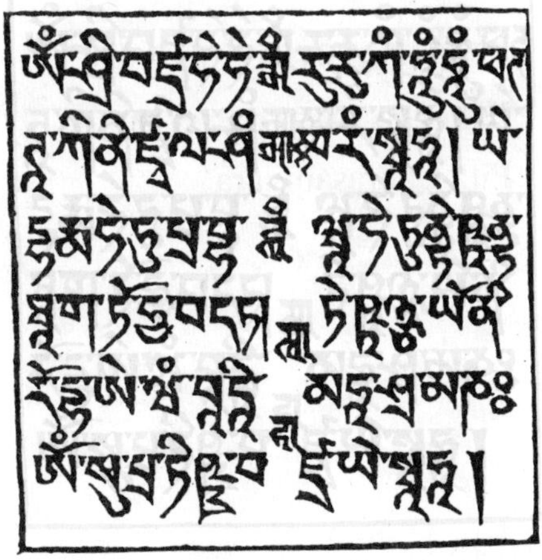

473(D7c) 979

’Khor lo sdom pa ser po

Pīta Cakrasaṃvara

ཨོཾ་ཤྲཱི་བཛྲ་ཧེ་ཧེ་རུ་རུ་ཀཾ་ཧཱུྃ་ཧཱུྃ་
ཕཊ། ཌཱ་ཀི་ནཱི་ཛྭ་ལ་ཤཾ་བ་རཾ་
སྭཱ་ཧཱ། ཡེ་དྷརྨཱ་ཧེ་ཏུ་པྲ་བྷ་ཝཱ་ཧེ་
ཏུནྟེ་ཥཱནྟ་ཐཱ་ག་ཏོ་ ཧྱ་ཝ་དཏ།
ཏེ་ཥཱཉྩ་ཡོ་ནི་རོ་དྷ་ ཨེ་ཝཾ་ཝཱ་དཱི་
མ་ཧཱ་ཤྲ་མ་ཎཿ ཧཱ། སརྦ་མངྒ་ལཾ།

474(D8a) 980
Phag mo dmar mo
Rakta Vārāhī

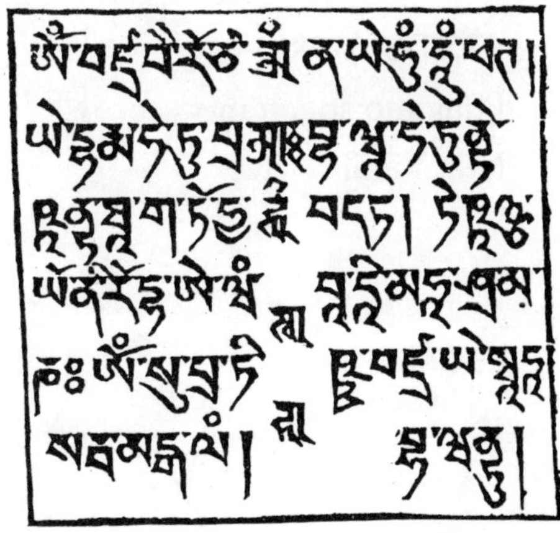

475(D8b) 981
Phag mo sngon mo
Nīla Vārāhī

ཨོཾ་བཛྲ་བཻ་རོ་ཙ་ནཱི་ཡེ་ཧཱུྃ་ཧཱུྃ་
ཕཊ། ཡེ་དྷརྨཱ་ཧེ་ཏུ་པྲ་
བྷ་ཝཱ་ཧེ་ཏུནྟེ་ཥཱཾ་ ཏ་ཐཱ་ག་ཏོ་
ཧྱ་བ་དཏ། ཏེ་ཥཱཉྩ་ཡོ་ནི་
རོ་དྷ་ཨེ་ཝཾ་བཱ་དཱི་མ་ཧཱ་ཤྲ་མ
ཎཿ ཨོཾ་སུ་པྲ་ཏིཥྛ་བཛྲ་ཡེ་སྭཱ་ཧཱ།

476(D8c) 982
Phag mo ser mo
Pīta Vārāhī

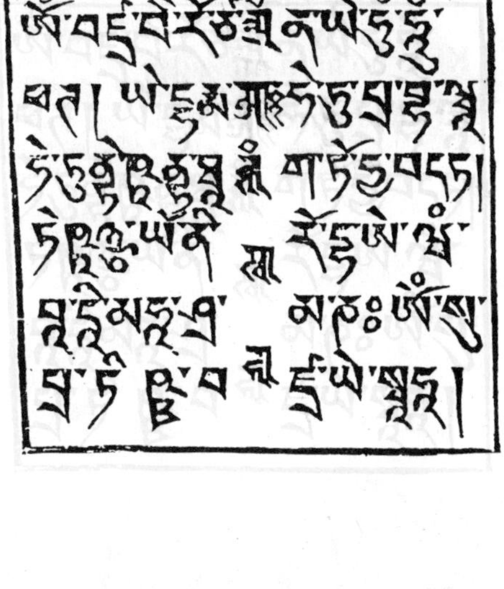

477(D9a) 983

Khro bo hūṃ mdzad

Krodhahūṃkāra

ཨོཾ་ཁ་བཛྲ་ཀྲོ་ཀ [illegible] བཛྲ་ཧཱུྃ་ཀཱ་ར
བཛྲ་ཧཱུྃ་ཕཊ། [illegible] ཡེ་དྷརྨཱ་ཧེ་ཏུ
པྲ་བྷ་ཝཱ་ཧེ་ཏུན་ཏེ་ཥཱན་ [illegible] ཏ་ཐཱ་ག་ཏོ་
ཧྱ་ཝ་དཏ། ཏེ [illegible] ཥཱཉྩ་ཡོ་ནི་རོ་དྷ
ཨེ་ཝཾ་བཱ་དཱི [illegible] མ་ཧཱ་ཤྲ་མ་ཎཿ
[illegible]། [illegible] ཧཱུྃ།

478(D9b) 984
rDo rje sems dpa'
Vajrasattva

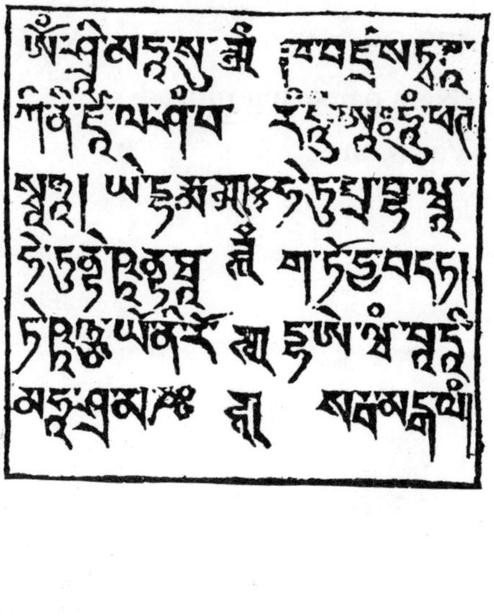

479(D9c) 985
rNam par snang mdzad
Vairocana

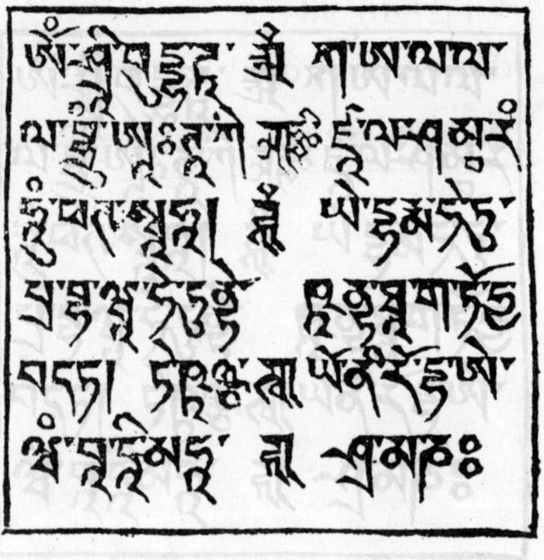

480(D10a) 986
Rin 'byung
Ratnasambhava

ཨོཾ་ཤྲཱི་རཏྣ་ཧེ་ཀ་ སྭཱ ཧཱུཾ་ཨཱཿཧཱུཾ་ཧྲཱིཿ ཀི་
ཏྲཱཾ་ཧྲཱི་ཡ་ཤཾ་ཧྲ་ ཏྲཱཿ རཾ་ཧྲཱུཾ་ཕཊ་སྭཱཧཱ།
ཡེ་དྷརྨཱ་ཧེ་ཏུ་པྲ་བྷ་ཝཱ་ ཧེ་ཏུནྟེ་
ཥཱན྄་ཏ་ཐཱ་ག་ཏོ་ཧྱ་ བདད། ཏེ་ཥཱཉྩ་
ཡོ་ནི་རོ་དྷ་ཨེ་ཝཾ་ ཝཱ་དཱི་མ་ཧཱ་ཤྲ་མ་
ཎཿ ཨོཾ་སུ་པྲ་ཏིཥྛ་བཛྲ་ཡེ་སྭཱཧཱ།

481(D10b) 947
sNang mtha'
Amitābha

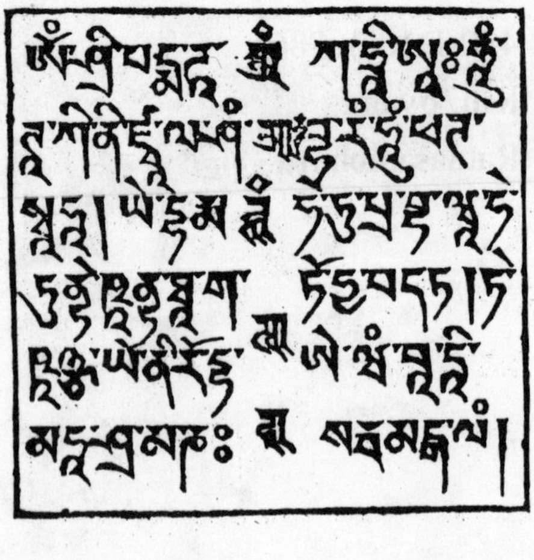

482(D10c) 988

Mi bskyod pa

Akṣobhya

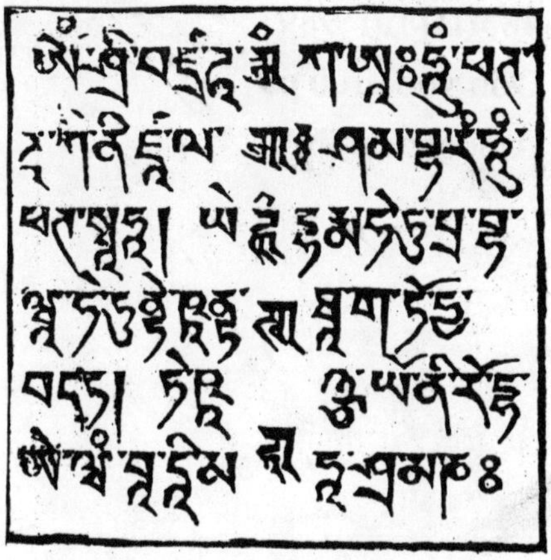

483(D11a) 989
Don yod grub pa
Amoghasiddhi

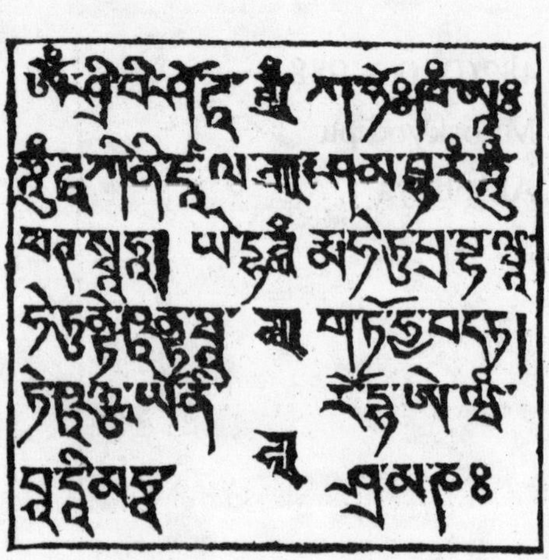

484(D11b) 990

rDo rje bdud rtsi

Vajrāmṛta

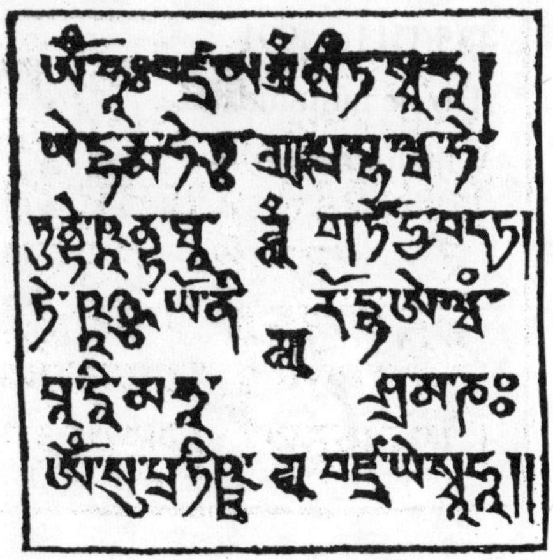

རྡོ་རྗེ་ཧཱུྃ་མཛད

485(D11c) 991
rDo rje hūṃ mdzad
Vajrahūṃkāra

ཨོཾ་བཛྲ་ཧཱུྃ་ཧྲཱི༔ ཀུར་བཛྲ་ཧཱུྃ་
ཕཊ། ཡེ་དྷརྨཱ་ཧེ་ཏུ་པྲ་བྷ་ཝཱ
ཧེ་ཏུན་ཏེ་ཥཱན྄ ཏ་ཐཱ་ག་ཏོ་ཧྱ
བདད། ཏེ་ཥཱཉྩ་ ཡོ་ནི་རོ་དྷ་ཨེ་
ཝཾ་ཝཱ་དཱི་མ་ཧཱ་ཤྲ་མ་ཎཿ ཨ་སྭཱ་ཧཱ
ཏེ་ཛཿ་བཛྲ་ཡ་སྭཱ་ཧཱ། མཉྫུ་ཤྲཱིཾ།

ཁྲག་འཐུང

486(D12a) 992
Khrag 'thung
Heruka

ཨོཾ་ཧྲཱི་ཡ་ཧྲཱི་ཡ་ ཀྲོཾ་ ཧཱུཾ་ཕཊ་ བྷྲཱུཾ་སྭཱཧཱ།
ཡེ་ཧྲྀ་མ་ཧེ་ཙུ་བྲ་ ཧཱུཾ་ཝཱ་ཧེ་ཙུ་རྗེ་
ཧཱུཾ་སྭཱ་བྷཱ་ཝ་ག་རྡེ་བྷྲུ་ཨཱཿབྷ་དྷྲཿ། ཏཏ་ཏཱ་ཙཾ་
ཡེ་ཏྲཱི་ཧྲེ་ཨེ་ཕཾ་ཀྲོཾ་ ཧཱུཾ་ཧྲཱི་མ་ཧཱ་ཤྲཱ་མ་
ཙཿ ཨོཾ་ཤུ་ཕྲ་ ཀྲ་ ཧྲཱི་ཀྵ་བ་རྡྷཱ་ཡེ་
སྭཱ་ཧཱ། ཕཊ་ ཀྲྀ་ མཎྜལ།

487(D12b) 993
bDud rtsi 'khyil ba
Amṛtakuṇḍalin

ཨོཾ་ཨ་མྲྀ་ཏ་ ཧྲཱིཾ་ ཀུ་ཎྜ་ལི་ཧཱུཾ་
ཨཾ་སྭཱ་ཧཱ། ཡེ་ དྷརྨཱ་ཧེ་ཏུ་པྲ་བྷ་
ཝཱ་ཧེ་ཏུནྟེ་ཥཱཾ་ཏ་ཐཱ་ག་ཏོ་ཧྱ་ཝ་ད་ཏ
ཏེ་ཥཱཉྩ་ཡོ་ནི་རོ་དྷ་ ཨེ་ཝཾ་ཝཱ་དཱི
མ་ཧཱ་ཤྲ་མ་ཎཿ ཡེ་ ཨོཾ་སུ་པྲ་ཏིཥྛ
བཛྲ་ཡེ་སྭཱཧཱ། ཧྲཱིཿ ས་བ་མ་ཉ་ཡ།

488(D12c) 994

Sangs rgyas thod pa

Buddhakapāla

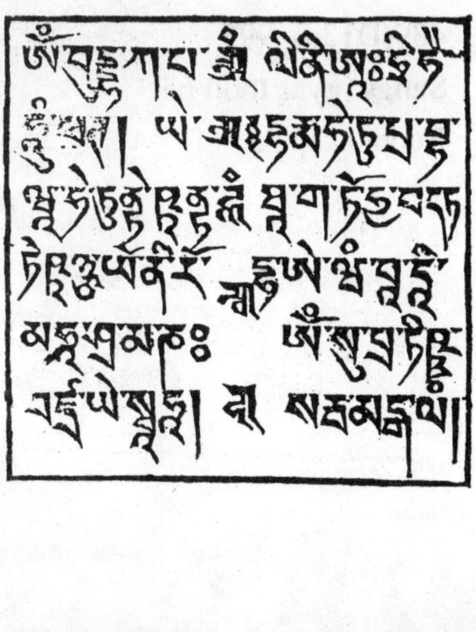

489(D13a) 995
Sangs rgyas thod pa
Buddhakapāla

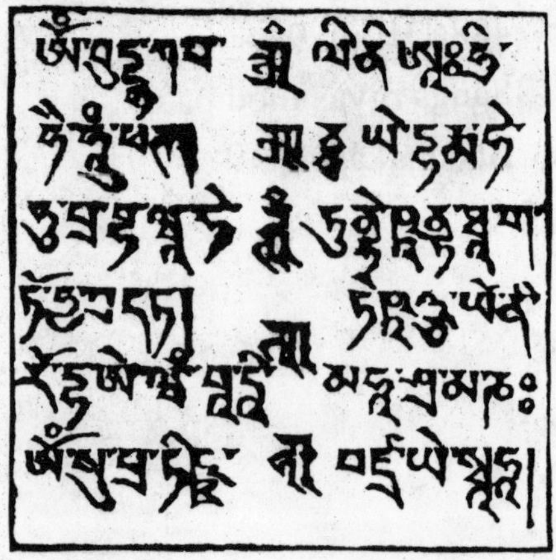

490(D13b) 996

Ma hā ma ya

Mahāmāyā

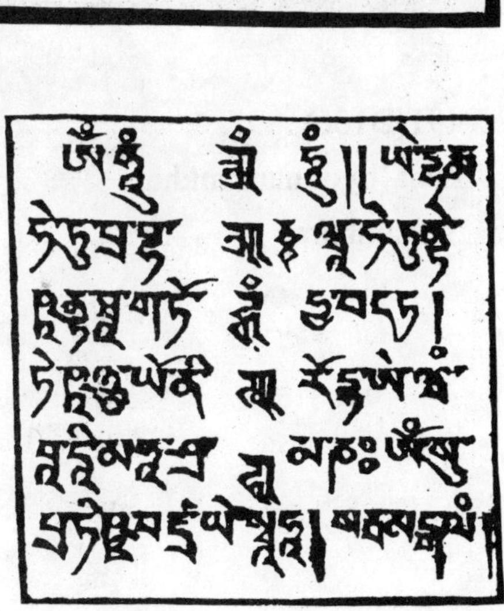

491(D13c) 997
rNal 'byor nam mkha'
Yogāmbara

ཨོཾ་ཧཱུཾ་ཧ་ ཀྲཱིཾ་ སྭཱ་ཧཱ།།
ཡེ་དྷརྨཱ་ཧེ་ཏུ་ ཨཱཿ པྲ་བྷ་བཱ་ཧེ
ཏུན་ཏེ་ཥཱན་ ཧཱུཾ་ ཏ་ཐཱ་ག་ཏོ
ཧྱ་བ་ད་ཏ་ཏེ་ཥཱཉྩ་ཡོ་ནི་རོ་དྷ་ ཧྲཱིཿ ཨེ་ཝཾ་བཱ་དཱི
མ་ཧཱ་ཤྲ་མ་ཎཿ ཏྲཱཾ ཨོཾ་ས་པྲ་ཏི་ཥྛ་
བཛྲ་ཡེ་སྭཱ་ཧཱ། ཀྲུ། མན་ཡཾ།

492(D14a) 998
Ye shes mkha' 'gro
Jñānaḍākinī

ཨོཾ་ཧྲཱིཿ ཧཱུྃ་ སྭཱཧཱ།
ཡེ་དྷརྨཱ་ཧེ་ཏུ་ པྲ་བྷ་ཝཱ་ ཧེ་ཏུན་ཏེ
ཥཱནྟ་ཐཱ་ག་ཏོ་ ཧྱ་ཝ་དཏ་ ཏེ་ཥཱཉྩ་
ཡོ་ནི་རོ་དྷ་ ཨེ་ཝཾ་ཝཱ་དཱི་
མ་ཧཱ་ཤྲ་མ་ཎཿ སྭཱཧཱ། ཨོཾ་སུ་པྲ་
ཏིཥྛ་བཛྲ་ཡེ་སྭཱཧཱ། མངྒ་ལཾ།

493(D14b) 999
Dus 'khor
Kālacakra

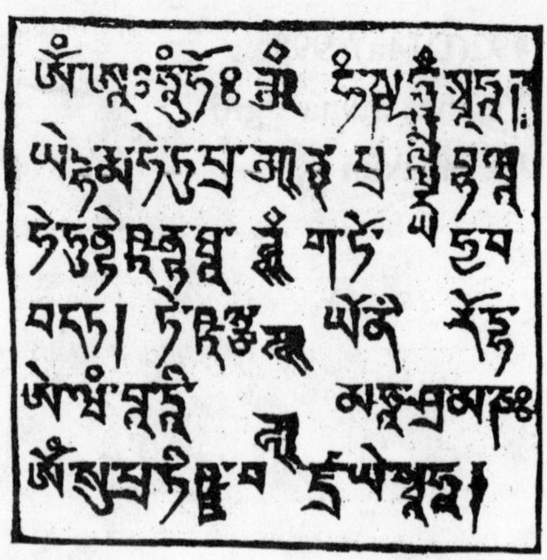

494(D14c) 1000
sNang mdzad rdor dbyings
Vajradhātu Vairocana

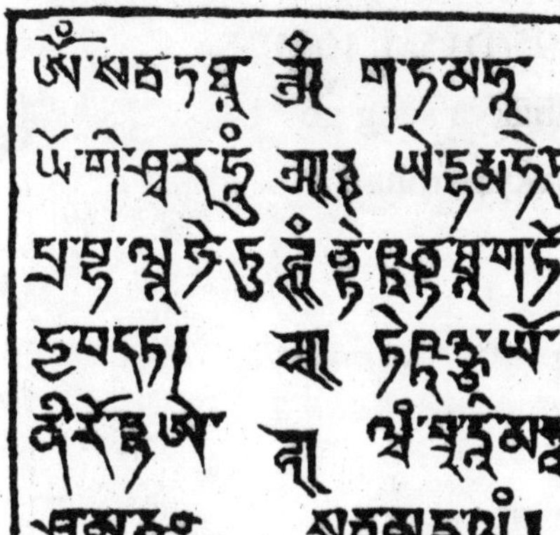

495(D15a) 1001
Shākya seng ge
Śākyasiṃha

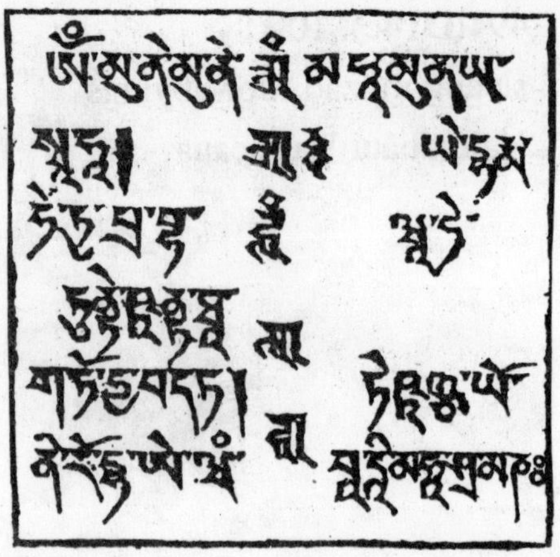

496(D15b) 1002
Chos dbyings gsung dbang
Dharmadhātuvāgīśvara

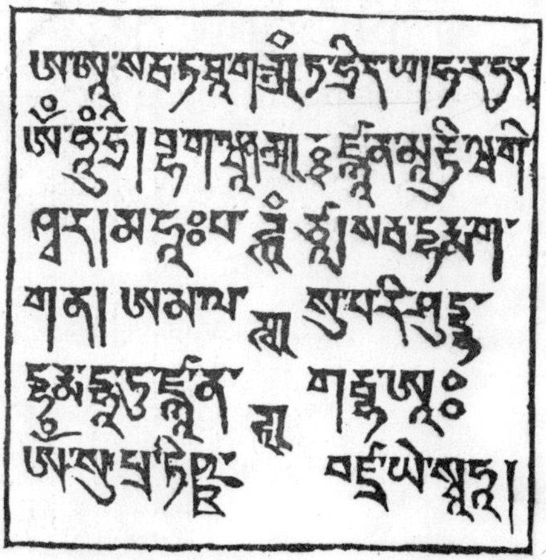

497(D15c) 1003
'Byung po 'dul byed
Bhūtaḍāmara

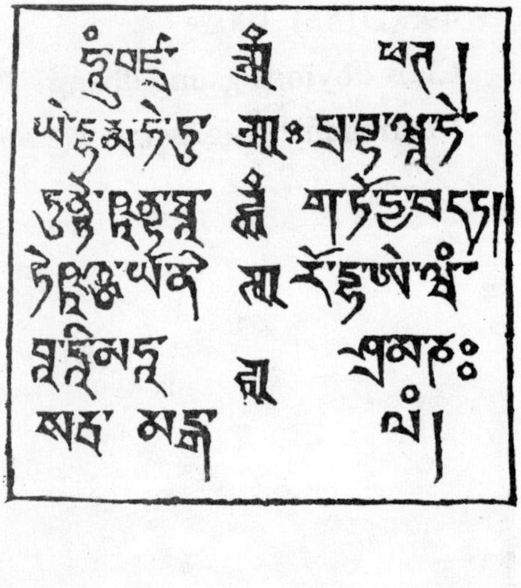

འོད་ཟེར་ཅན་མ

498(D16a) 1004
’Od zer can ma
Mārīcī

ཨོཾ་མ་རཱི་ཙྱེ་ མྃ་ སྭཱ་ཧཱ།
ཡེ་དྷརྨཱ་ཧེ་ཏུ་ པྲ་བྷ་ཝཱ་ཧེ་
ཏུནྟེ་ཥཱནྟ་ཐཱ་ག་ཏོ་ཧྱ་ཝ་དཏ། ཏེ་
ཥཱཉྩ་ཡོ་ནི་རོ་དྷ་ ཨེ་ཝཾ་ཝཱ་དཱི་
མ་ཧཱ་ཤྲ་མ་ཎཿ སྭཱ། ཨོཾ་སུ་པྲ་
ཏིཥྛ་བཛྲ་ཡེ་ སྭཱ་ ཧཱ།

499(D16b) 1005

So sor 'brang ma

Pratisarā

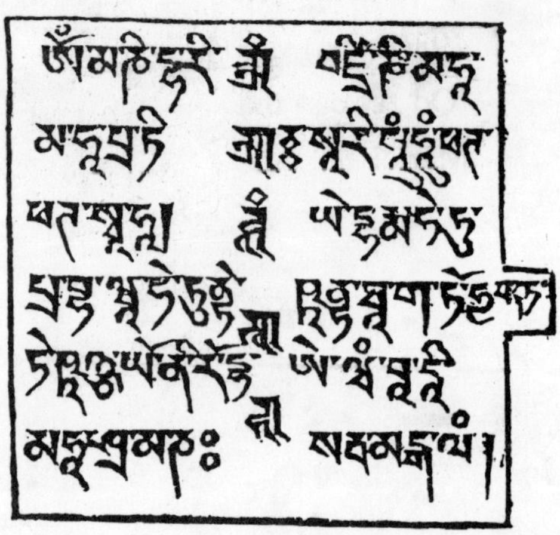

500(D16c) 1006

Nor rgyun ma

Vasudhārā

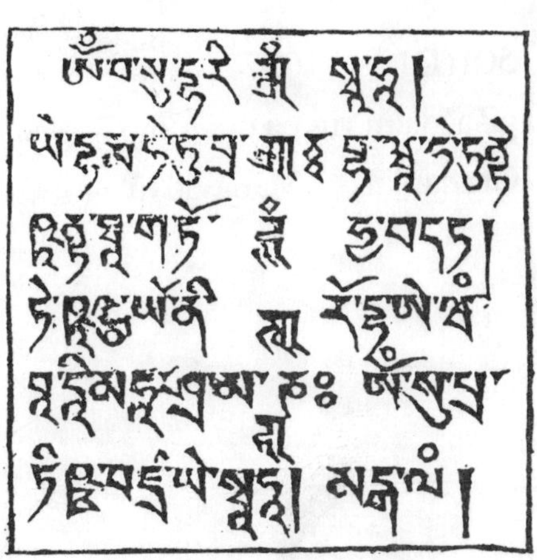

501(D17a) 1007

gZa' yum rig pa chen mo

Grahamātṛkā Mahāvidyā

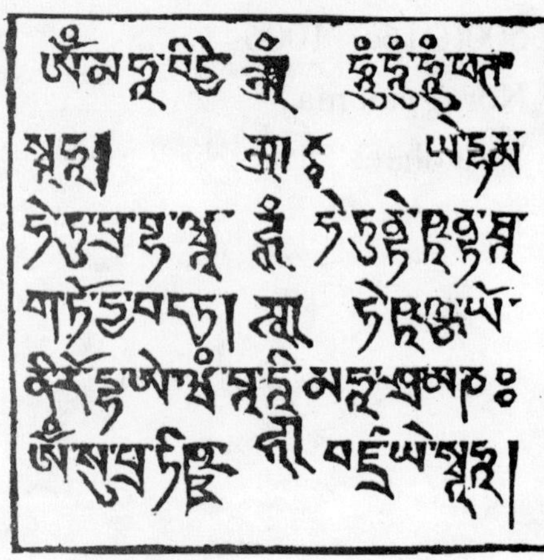

502(D17b) 1008
rNam rgyal ma
Vijayā

ཨོཾ་བྷྲཱུཾ་སྭཱ་ཧཱ། ཏྲཱཾ ཨོཾ་ཨ་མྲྀ་ཏ་ཨ
ཡུ་རྡ་དེ་སྭཱ་ཧཱ། ཨཱཿ ཡེ་དྷརྨཱ་ཧེ་ཏུ
པྲ་བྷ་ཝཱ་ཧེ་ཏུ ཧཱུྃ ཏེ་ཥཱན་ཏ་ཐཱ་ག་ཏོ
ཧྱ་ཝ་དཏ྄། ཧཱ ཏེ་ཥཱཉྩ་ཡོ་ནི
རོ་དྷ་ཨེ་ཝཾ་ཝཱ་དཱི མ་ཧཱ་ཤྲ་མ་ཎཿ
ཨོཾ་སུ་པྲ་ཏིཥྛ་ ཧྲཱ བཛྲ་ཡེ་སྭཱ་ཧཱ།

503(D17c) 1009

rGyan drug phyag mtshan

Ṣaḍābharaṇa

མི་འགྱུར་ལྷུན་པོ་སྐུ་ཡི་བཀྲ་ཤིས་
ཤོག །ཡན་ལག་དྲུག་བཅུ་གསུང་
གི་བཀྲ་ཤིས་ཤོག །མཐའ་བྲལ
ཏིང་འཛིན་ཐུགས་ཀྱི་བཀྲ་ཤིས་
ཤོག །རྒྱལ་བའི་སྐྱུག་སྤུང་ཕྱོགས
ཀྱི་བཀྲ་ཤིས་ཤོག །སརྦམངྒལཾ།།

༄༅། །ཨོཾ་སྭསྟི། ཐུབ་པའི་ལེགས་བཤད་ཀུན་གྱི་མཆོག་གྱུར་པ། །རྒྱུད་སྡེ་རྒྱ་
མཚོའི་སྙིང་ལེགས་རྫོགས་ནས། །ཐུབ་བསྟན་གསལ་བ་མཛད་པ་འཇིགས་མེད་འབྱུང་གནས་ཀྱི། །བཞེད་སྲོལ་
རིན་འཕྲེང་ཕྱི་ལ་གཏོར་སྤུང་བརྒྱན་འདི། །བཞེངས་པའི་དགེ་བས་རྒྱལ་བ་འདིར་ཞེར་མཁའ་བའི། །མཐུན་རྐྱེན་སྒྲུབ་
པའི་ཡོན་གྱི་བདག་པོ་དང་། །སྤྲོ་རབ་གཉིས་ལྡན་བཟོ་བོ་རབ་ཚོགས་བཅས་ཀུན། །ས་ལམ་རིམ་བགྲོད་ནས་
མཁྱེན་གསུམ་ར་ཏ་ཐོབ་ཤོག །ཀ་ནས་སྐྱབས་ཚེ་རིང་ནད་མེད་བདེ་ལྡན་ཞིང་། །ཞིང་གི་མཆོག་ལ་

མཆོད་ཅིང་གསོལ་བ་བཏབ་པའི། །བསོད་ནམས་མ་ལུས་ལས་བསམ་དོན་མ་ལུས་པ། །འཕེལ་
པ་མེད་པ་ལྷུན་གྱིས་འགྲུབ་གྱུར་ཅིག །མངྒ་ལཾ། ཅེས་པ་འདི་ནི་བསྟན་གྱི་ཁྲི་རབ་བཞུགས་
བཅོ་ལྔ་པར། །གང་གི་མཛོད་འཛིན་བློ་བཟང་དགོན་མཆོག་དང་། །ཆེ་འཕྲང་ཁྱུང་ཚོགས་རྡོ་རྗེ་ཕུས་ཀྲོན་
བཅས༔ ངོར་ཡོན་སྤྲུལ་སྐུ་ར་ཏྣ་བཛྲ་ཡིས། །སྤྱོད་འཚང་ནག་པོའི་སྐུ་འཕྲུལ་ཕུང་རྩོམ་འདིར། །ཕྲེན་
པའི་སྐྲ་འཕྲེང་བཞི་པ་རྩ་ཤེལ་བ་བཏབ་པས། །དང་པོའི་སངས་རྒྱས་དགྱེལ་ཡབ་བོར་ཆེན་པོའི་ནང་། །སྐལ་ལྡན་

ཁ་བྱང་།

༄༅། །འགྲོ་ནམས་ལས་བསྟན་སྐྱེ་བ་མེད་ཀྱིས་བསྟུས། །འཛམ་གླིང་བའི་དགའ་ལྡན་བོ་ཆེ་མ་ཡོད་ཆེན་མཁྱི། །དགའ་ལྡན་
སློབ་དཔོན་ཆེན་པོའི་དབང་། །རྒྱལ་བ་རྣམ་ཀོ་ལ་ཡལ་ཡ་སྐྱེ་ཡབ་ཀ་ཞུམས་ཀྱིས་མཆོད། །མཁན་ཆེན་ཤིལ་གོ་མ་ཡང་
ནི་མིན་དགེ། །ལྕི་ཤ་ཀུན་གོ་ལ་རྒྱུ་ཀེ་ལ་སྐྱོ་ཡི་བ། །དབུ་མཛད་ལ་སོགས་ལས་ཚན་ནི་བ་ཉམས་ཕ། །
བདག་ཅག་དགེ་འདུན་རྣམས་གཞི་ཡི་བསྟུས། །བྱོན་པོ་ལ་སོགས་ཚོ་ས་སྒྲ་བརྒྱ་ལྔ་ཡལ། །ཕབ་བཞི་སྤྲུལ་པ་ཡབས་འགྲོ་བའི
འདྲེན་པ་མཆོག །ཀྱིལ་བར་ཡ་ཡབ་སྐྱབས་མཛེང་ཆུ་དགེ་ལ་བ་སོགས། །རྒྱུན་པའི་རྟེན་སྤྱི་ཡ་ཡུ་ཡ་ཞབས་བརྟན།

ཨོཾ་༔ ༈ འགྲོ་ཀུན་རྟོགས་ས་བྱང་ཆུབ་ཕྱིར་བའི་འཛུད་དང་། །སྔར་ཐང་བརྒྱ་རྩ་རྟེར་འཕྲེང་ཀྱིས་འཁོར་གྱི། །བར་
བགོད་ཕྱིར་རྟ་གསོལ་བ་བདག་ཅག་པའི་ཚེ། །གསུང་གི་གཞན་བ་ཐོབ་ནས་དོ་དམ་པ། །ཆོས་རྗེ་མཁས་གྲུབ་དགེ་སློང་ཚེ་རིང་
དང་། །མ་དཔེ་འདྲི་མི་བློ་བཟང་སྨྲིན་པ་དང་། །སློབ་བཟང་བཀྲ་ཤིས་དཀག་དཔང་ལེགས་རབ་དང་། །བློ་བཟང་ཚོས་དར་སློབ་ཆེ
ཚེ་དཔལ་དང་། །པར་བགོད་བྱེད་མི་ཨེ་ར་རྗེ་དཔོན་ཚེ་རིང་། །བཀྲ་ཤིས་དགེ་སློང་ཚོམ་རབ་ཚོས་དཔོན་རོགས། །སྦྱིན་བདག
འབྲི་པོ་སོགས་ཀྱིས་ཡས་གྲུབ་ཚེ། །ཀ་རྟོགས་ཀ་ཞུག་ཀ་ལས་ལེགས་ཤི་བཞི་བཟང་། །ཐུ་རྫ་ལི་ཐུ་ག་ཡུ་རྡུ་རྡོ་རྗེ

རྗེ་འབྲེར། ཀྱེ་ཤྲཱི། བཞི་ལ།

༄༅། །ཧཱུྃ། །མཁན་ཆེན་བྱང་ཆུབ་རྡོ་རྗེ་ནོ་མིན་ཧན། །ཨེ་རྟེ་ནི་སེ་ཚེང་ཧྭ་ལས་ཕྱག་མཛོད་པ། །
མགོན་པོ་སྐྱབས་ཀ་ཤུང་རྐ་ཧྭ་ཉམ། །སོགས་ནས་བསྟན་འགྲོར་ཕན་པ་རྒྱ་ཆེན་པོ། །འབྱུང་ཆེད་པར་བྱང་སྐྱོན་ཚིག་འདི་ཀྲུ་
བྲུ༔ ༔སོགས་ཞེས་བསྐུལ་བ་དོར་གྲོ་བ་བཟང་དཔལ་ལ་ལྡན་པའི། །བསྟན་པའི་ཉི་མ་ཕྱོགས་ལས་རྣམ་རྒྱལ་གྱིས། །བཀོད་པའི་
པོ་བས་ཞུ་སེ་རི་ཏེ་ལུགས་ཆེ། །ཕྱོགས་དུས་ཀུན་ཏུ་དར་ཞིང་རྒྱས་གྱུར་ཅིག། ། །

Index